RELIGION
AND
CHALLENGES OF SCIENCE

RELIGION AND CHALLENGES OF SCIENCE

Dr Rajeev Prasad

MD PUBLICATIONS PVT LTD
NEW DELHI
www.mdppl.com

Published by :

MD Publications Pvt Ltd
"MD House", 11, Darya Ganj,
New Delhi - 110 002
Phone : +91-11-41563325 (Customer Service)
+91-11-41562846 (Editorial)
E-mail (orders): order@mdppl.com
Website: www.mdppl.com

ISBN: 978-81-7533-236-2

Published and Printed by Mr. Pranav Gupta on behalf of MD Publications Pvt Ltd at Mohit Enterprises, New Delhi.

Preface

Science and technology have become the most ubiquitous of human creations, changing how we perceive our world and shaping the way we live. We live in a home built with materials fabricated by technology. The food we eat was likely grown and processed using the tools of technology. Wherever we travel, technology provides the mode of transportation. Much of our entertainment comes to us through the medium of technology. When we seek medical care, science and technology usually provide the instruments for diagnosis and treatment, and give us the means and the information to care for our health.

Religion and science stand together, and faculty and other members of the College community believe that a dialogue about important issues from the perspective of science, theology, and religious studies is needed to strengthen and integrate the relationship of these significant components of intellectual life on the campus.

Science coexists and competes for influence with religion, which once dominated intellectual life and explained the world. Religion no longer has the pre-eminence it once had in the field of learning. Science gains influence each year as it brings forth discoveries, embraces new knowledge, and abandons old inadequate concepts.

Science and religion have their respective reasons. Each stand alone as independent human endeavors, having their own culture, body of knowledge, processes and procedures for verifying truth, and ways of serving humanity. They do not have the same viewpoints about the nature of the world or agree about how truth is perceived or confirmed.

Traditional religion endeavors to give life meaning and reason for existence in terms of its conceptions about God's actions and His authority as the guide for human behavior. A number of religions explain the existence of the world and the universe as due to a creative act of God. Science seeks to know the world and acquire understanding in terms of the laws of nature, gaining information by observing natural phenomena, testing and experimenting, and using reason in interpreting data.

Science earns acceptance by pragmatic demonstration of results. Most religions do not gain believers by demonstrating through evidence, as science does, the efficacy and validity of their claims. They rely, in large measure, on the cultural identification people have with traditions as they adopt the religion of their parents or community. Religions further have promotion techniques to convince uncommitted people, and those outside their cultural domain, to bring them into their fold.

I am very grateful to Mr. Pranav Gupta, Director of MD Publications Pvt Ltd, New Delhi for his kind cooperation and support for this book.

Dr Rajeev Prasad

Contents

1

Religion and Challenges of Science

An Introduction

Everything that the human race has done and thought is concerned with the satisfaction of deeply felt needs and the assuagement of pain. One has to keep this constantly in mind if one wishes to understand spiritual movements and their development. Feeling and longing are the motive force behind all human endeavor and human creation, in however exalted a guise the latter may present themselves to us. Now what are the feelings and needs that have led men to religious thought and belief in the widest sense of the words? A little consideration will suffice to show us that the most varying emotions preside over the birth of religious thought and experience.

With primitive man it is above all fear that evokes religious notions - fear of hunger, wild beasts, sickness, and death. Since at this stage of existence understanding of causal connections is usually poorly developed, the human mind creates illusory beings more or less analogous to itself on whose wills and actions these fearful happenings depend. Thus one tries to secure the favour of these beings by carrying out actions and offering sacrifices which, according to the tradition handed down from generation to generation, propitiate them or make them well disposed toward a mortal. In this sense I am speaking of a religion of fear. This, though not created, is in an important degree stabilized by the formation of a special priestly caste which sets itself up as a mediator between the people and the beings they fear, and erects hegemony on this basis.

In many cases a leader or ruler or a privileged class whose position rests on other factors combines priestly functions with its secular authority in order to make the latter more secure; or the political rulers and the priestly caste make common cause in their own interests. The social impulses are another source of the crystallization of religion. Fathers and mothers and the leaders of larger human communities are mortal and fallible. The desire for guidance, love, and support prompts men to form the social or moral conception of God. This is the God of Providence, who protects, disposes, rewards, and punishes; the God who, according to the limits of the believer's outlook, loves and cherishes the life of the tribe or of the human race, or even or life itself; the comforter in sorrow and unsatisfied longing; he who preserves the souls of the dead.

This is the social or moral conception of God. The Jewish scriptures admirably illustrate the development from the religion of fear to moral religion, a development continued in the New Testament.

The religions of all civilized peoples, especially the peoples of the Orient, are primarily moral religions. The development from a religion of fear to moral religion is a great step in peoples' lives. And yet, that primitive religions are based entirely on fear and the religions of civilized peoples purely on morality is a prejudice against which we must be on our guard. The truth is that all religions are a varying blend of both types, with this differentiation: that on the higher levels of social life the religion of morality predominates. Common to all these types is the anthropomorphic character of their conception of God.

In general, only individuals of exceptional endowments, and exceptionally high-minded communities, rise to any considerable extent above this level. But there is a third stage of religious experience which belongs to all of them, even though it is rarely found in a pure form: I shall call it cosmic religious feeling.

It is very difficult to elucidate this feeling to anyone who is entirely without it, especially as there is no anthropomorphic conception of God corresponding to it. The individual feels the futility of human desires and aims and the sublimity and marvelous order which reveal them both in nature and in the world of thought. Individual existence impresses him as a sort of prison and he wants to experience the universe as a single significant whole.

The beginnings of cosmic religious feeling already appear at an early stage of development, e.g., in many of the Psalms of David and in some of the Prophets. Buddhism, as we have learned especially from the wonderful writings of Schopenhauer, contains a much stronger element of this. The religious geniuses of all ages have been distinguished by this kind of religious feeling, which knows no dogma and no God conceived in man's image; so that there can be no church whose central teachings are based on it.

Hence it is precisely among the heretics of every age that we find men who were filled with this highest kind of religious feeling and were in many cases regarded by their contemporaries as atheists, sometimes also as saints. Looked at in this light, men like Democritus, Francis of Assisi, and Spinoza are closely akin to one another. How can cosmic religious feeling be communicated from one person to another, if it can give rise to no definite notion of a God and no theology?

In my view, it is the most important function of art and science to awaken this feeling and keep it alive in those who are receptive to it. We thus arrive at a conception of the relation of science to religion very different from the usual one. When one views the matter historically, one is inclined to look upon science and religion as irreconcilable antagonists, and for a very obvious reason. The man who is thoroughly convinced of the universal operation of the law of causation cannot for a moment entertain the idea of a being who interferes in the course of events - provided, of course, that he takes the hypothesis of causality really seriously. He has no use for the religion of fear and equally little for social or moral religion.

A God who rewards and punishes is inconceivable to him for the simple reason that a man's actions are determined by necessity, external and internal, so that in God's eyes he cannot be responsible, any more than an inanimate object is responsible for the motions it undergoes. Science has therefore been charged with undermining morality, but the charge is unjust. A man's ethical behavior should be based effectually on sympathy, education, and social ties and needs; no religious basis is necessary. Man would indeed be in a poor way if he had to be restrained by fear of punishment and hopes of reward after death. It is therefore easy to see why the churches have always fought science and persecuted its devotees.

On the other hand, I maintain that the cosmic religious feeling is the strongest and noblest motive for scientific research. Only those who realize the immense efforts and, above all, the devotion without which pioneer work in theoretical science cannot be achieved are able to grasp the strength of the emotion out of which alone such work, remote as it is from the immediate realities of life, can issue. What a deep conviction of the rationality of the universe and what a yearning to understand, were it but a feeble reflection of the mind revealed in this world, Kepler and Newton must have had to enable them to spend years of solitary labor in disentangling the principles of celestial mechanics!

Those whose acquaintance with scientific research is derived chiefly from its practical results easily develop a completely false notion of the mentality of the men who, surrounded by a skeptical world, have shown the way to kindred spirits scattered wide through the world and through the centuries. Only one who has devoted his life to similar ends can have a vivid realization of what has inspired these men and given them the strength to remain true to their purpose in spite of countless failures. It is cosmic religious feeling that gives a man such strength. A contemporary has said, not unjustly, that in this materialistic age of ours the serious scientific workers are the only profoundly religious people. During the last century, and part of the one before, it was widely held that there was an unreconcilable conflict between knowledge and belief.

The opinion prevailed among advanced minds that it was time that belief should be replaced increasingly by knowledge; belief that did not itself rest on knowledge was superstition, and as such had to be opposed. According to this conception, the sole function of education was to open the way to thinking and knowing, and the school, as the outstanding organ for the people's education, must serve that end exclusively. One will probably find but rarely, if at all, the rationalistic standpoint expressed in such crass form; for any sensible man would see at once how one-sided is such a statement of the position. But it is just as well to state a thesis starkly and nakedly, if one wants to clear up one's mind as to its nature. It is true that convictions can best be supported with experience and clear thinking. On this point one must agree unreservedly with the extreme rationalist. The weak point of his conception is, however, this, that those convictions which are necessary and determinant for our conduct and judgments cannot be found solely along this solid scientific way. For the scientific method can teach us nothing else beyond how facts are related to, and conditioned by, each other.

The aspiration toward such objective knowledge belongs to the highest of which man is capable, and you will certainly not suspect me of wishing to belittle the achievements and the heroic efforts of man in this sphere. Yet it is equally clear that knowledge of what is does not open the door directly to what should be. One can have the clearest and most complete knowledge of what is, and yet not be able to deduct from that what should be the goal of our human aspirations.

Objective knowledge provides us with powerful instruments for the achievements of certain ends, but the ultimate goal itself and the longing to reach it must come from another source. And it is hardly necessary to argue for the view that our existence and our activity acquire meaning only by the setting up of such a goal and of corresponding values. The knowledge of truth as such is wonderful, but it is so little capable of acting as a guide that it cannot prove even the justification and the value of the aspiration toward that very knowledge of truth. Here we face, therefore, the limits of the purely rational conception of our existence.

But it must not be assumed that intelligent thinking can play no part in the formation of the goal and of ethical judgments. When someone realizes that for the achievement of an end certain means would be useful, the means itself becomes thereby an end. Intelligence makes clear to us the interrelation of means and ends. But mere thinking cannot give us a sense of the ultimate and fundamental ends.

To make clear these fundamental ends and valuations, and to set them fast in the emotional life of the individual, seems to me precisely the most important function which religion has to perform in the social life of man. And if one asks whence derives the authority of such fundamental ends, since they cannot be stated and justified merely by reason, one can only answer: they exist in a healthy society as powerful traditions, which act upon the conduct and aspirations and judgments of the individuals; they are there, that is, as something living, without its being necessary to find justification for their existence. They come into being not through demonstration but through revelation, through the medium of powerful personalities.

One must not attempt to justify them, but rather to sense their nature simply and clearly. The highest principles for our aspirations and judgments are given to us in the Jewish-Christian religious tradition. It is a very high goal which, with our weak powers, we can reach only very inadequately, but which gives a sure foundation to our aspirations and valuations. If one were to take that goal out of its religious form and look merely at its purely human side, one might state it perhaps thus: free and responsible development of the individual, so that he may place his powers freely and gladly in the service of all mankind. There is no room in this for the divinization of a nation, of a class, let alone of an individual. Are we not all children of one father, as it is said in religious language? Indeed, even the divinization of humanity, as an abstract totality, would not be in the spirit of that ideal. It is only to the individual that a soul is given.

And the high destiny of the individual is to serve rather than to rule, or to impose himself in any other way. If one looks at the substance rather than at the form, then one can take these words as expressing also the fundamental democratic position. The true democrat can worship his nation as little as can the man who is religious, in our sense of the term. What, then, in all this, is the function of education and of the school?

They should help the young person to grow up in such a spirit that these fundamental principles should be to him as the air which he breathes. Teaching alone cannot do that. If one holds these high principles clearly before one's eyes, and compares them with the life and spirit of our times, then it appears glaringly that civilized mankind finds itself at present in grave danger, In the totalitarian states it is the rulers themselves who strive actually to destroy that spirit of humanity.

In less threatened parts it is nationalism and intolerance, as well as the oppression of the individuals by economic means, which threaten to choke these most precious traditions. A realization of how great is the danger is spreading, however, among thinking people, and there is much search for means with which to meet the danger—means in the field of national and international politics, of legislation, or organization in general. Such efforts are, no doubt, greatly needed. Yet the ancients knew something-which we seem to have forgotten. All means prove but a blunt instrument, if they have not behind them a living spirit. But if the longing for the achievement of the goal is powerfully alive within us, then shall we not lack the strength to find the means for reaching the goal and for translating it into deeds.

It would not be difficult to come to an agreement as to what we understand by science. Science is the century-old endeavor to bring together by means of systematic thought the perceptible phenomena of this world into as thoroughgoing an association as possible. To put it boldly, it is the attempt at the posterior reconstruction of existence by the process of conceptualization. But when asking myself what religion is I cannot think of the answer so easily. And even after finding an answer which may satisfy me at this particular moment, I still remain convinced that I can never under any circumstances bring together, even to a slight extent, the thoughts of all those who have given this question serious consideration.

At first, then, instead of asking what religion is I should prefer to ask what characterizes the aspirations of a person who gives me the impression of being religious: a person who is religiously enlightened appears to me to be one who has, to the best of his ability, liberated himself from the fetters of his selfish desires and is preoccupied with thoughts, feelings, and aspirations to which he clings because of their superpersonal value. It seems to me that what is important is the force of this superpersonal content and the depth of the conviction concerning its overpowering meaningfulness, regardless of whether any attempt is made to unite this content with a divine Being, for otherwise it would not be possible to count Buddha and Spinoza as religious personalities.

Accordingly, a religious person is devout in the sense that he has no doubt of the significance and loftiness of those superpersonal objects and goals which neither require nor are capable of rational foundation. They exist with the same necessity and matter-of-factness as he himself. In this sense religion is the age-old endeavor of mankind to become clearly and completely conscious of these values and goals and constantly to strengthen and extend their effect. If one conceives of religion and science according to these definitions then a conflict between them appears impossible. For science can only ascertain what is, but not what should be, and outside of its domain value judgments of all kinds remain necessary. Religion, on the other hand, deals only with evaluations of human thought and action: it cannot justifiably speak of facts and relationships between facts.

According to this interpretation the well-known conflicts between religion and science in the past must all be ascribed to a misapprehension of the situation which has been described. For example, a conflict arises when a religious community insists on the absolute truthfulness of all statements recorded in the Bible. This means an intervention on the part of religion into the sphere of science; this is where the struggle of the Church against the doctrines of Galileo and Darwin belongs. On the other hand, representatives of science have often made an attempt to arrive at fundamental judgments with respect to values and ends on the basis of scientific method, and in this way have set themselves in opposition to religion. These conflicts have all sprung from fatal errors. Now, even though the realms of religion and science in themselves are clearly marked off from each other, nevertheless there exist between the two strong reciprocal relationships and dependencies.

Though religion may be that which determines the goal, it has, nevertheless, learned from science, in the broadest sense, what means will contribute to the attainment of the goals it has set up. But science can only be created by those who are thoroughly imbued with the aspiration toward truth and understanding. This source of feeling, however, springs from the sphere of religion. To this there also belongs the faith in the possibility that the regulations valid for the world of existence are rational, that is, comprehensible to reason. I cannot conceive of a genuine scientist without that profound faith. The situation may be expressed by an image: science without religion is lame, religion without science is blind. Though I have asserted above that in truth a legitimate conflict between religion and science cannot exist, I must nevertheless qualify this assertion once again on an essential point, with reference to the actual content of historical religions.

This qualification has to do with the concept of God. During the youthful period of mankind's spiritual evolution human fantasy created gods in man's own image, who, by the operations of their will were supposed to determine, or at any rate to influence, the phenomenal world. Man sought to alter the disposition of these gods in his own favor by means of magic and prayer. The idea of God in the religions taught at present is a sublimation of that old concept of the gods. Its anthropomorphic character is shown, for instance, by the fact that men appeal to the Divine Being in prayers and plead for the fulfillment of their wishes. Nobody, certainly, will deny that the idea of the existence of an omnipotent, just, and omnibeneficent personal God is able to accord man solace, help, and guidance; also, by virtue of its simplicity it is accessible to the most undeveloped mind. But, on the other hand, there are decisive weaknesses attached to this idea in it, which have been painfully felt since the beginning of history.

That is, if this being is omnipotent, then every

occurrence, including every human action, every human thought, and every human feeling and aspiration is also His work; how is it possible to think of holding men responsible for their deeds and thoughts before such an almighty Being? In giving out punishment and rewards He would to a certain extent be passing judgment on Himself. How can this be combined with the goodness and righteousness ascribed to Him? The main source of the present-day conflicts between the spheres of religion and of science lies in this concept of a personal God. It is the aim of science to establish general rules which determine the reciprocal connection of objects and events in time and space. For these rules, or laws of nature, absolutely general validity is required--not proven.

It is mainly a program, and faith in the possibility of its accomplishment in principle is only founded on partial successes. But hardly anyone could be found who would deny these partial successes and ascribe them to human self-deception. The fact that on the basis of such laws we are able to predict the temporal behavior of phenomena in certain domains with great precision and certainty is deeply embedded in the consciousness of the modern man, even though he may have grasped very little of the contents of those laws. He need only consider that planetary courses within the solar system may be calculated in advance with great exactitude on the basis of a limited number of simple laws. In a similar way, though not with the same precision, it is possible to calculate in advance the mode of operation of an electric motor, a transmission system, or of a wireless apparatus, even when dealing with a novel development.

To be sure, when the number of factors coming into play in a phenomenological complex is too large, scientific method in most cases fails us. One need only think of the weather, in which case prediction even for a few days ahead is impossible. Nevertheless no one doubts that we are confronted with a causal connection whose causal components are in the main known to us. Occurrences in this domain are beyond the reach of exact prediction because of the variety of factors in operation, not because of any lack of order in nature. We have penetrated far less deeply into the regularities obtaining within the realm of living things, but deeply enough nevertheless to sense at least the rule of fixed necessity. One need only think of the systematic order in heredity, and in the effect of poisons, as for instance alcohol, on the behavior of organic beings. What is still lacking here is a grasp of connections of profound generality, but not knowledge of order in itself.

The more a man is imbued with the ordered regularity of all events the firmer becomes his conviction that there is no room left by the side of this ordered regularity for causes of a different nature. For him neither the rule of human nor the rule of divine will exists as an independent cause of natural events. To be sure, the doctrine of a personal God interfering with natural events could never be refuted, in the real sense, by science, for this doctrine can always take refuge in those domains in which scientific knowledge has not yet been able to set foot. But I am persuaded that such behavior on the part of the representatives of religion would not only be unworthy but also fatal. For a doctrine which is able to maintain itself not in clear light but only in the dark, will of necessity lose its effect on mankind, with incalculable harm to human progress. In their struggle for the ethical good, teachers of religion must have the stature to give up the doctrine of a personal God, that is, give up that source of fear and hope which in the past placed such vast power in the hands of priests.

In their labors they will have to avail themselves of those forces which are capable of cultivating the Good, the True, and the Beautiful in humanity itself. This is, to be sure, a more difficult but an incomparably more worthy task. After religious teachers accomplish the refining process indicated they will surely recognize with joy that true religion has been ennobled and made more profound by scientific knowledge. If it is one of the goals of religion to liberate mankind as far as possible from the bondage of egocentric cravings, desires, and fears, scientific reasoning can aid religion in yet another sense. Although it is true that it is the goal of science to discover rules which permit the association and foretelling of facts, this is not its only aim. It also seeks to reduce the connections discovered to the smallest possible number of mutually independent conceptual elements. It is in this striving after the rational unification of the manifold that it encounters its greatest successes, even though it is precisely this attempt which causes it to run the greatest risk of falling a prey to illusions.

But whoever has undergone the intense experience of successful advances made in this domain is moved by profound reverence for the rationality made manifest in existence. By way of the understanding he achieves a far-reaching emancipation from the shackles of personal hopes and desires, and thereby attains that humble attitude of mind toward the grandeur of reason incarnate in existence, and which, in its profoundest depths, is inaccessible to man. This attitude, however, appears to me to be religious, in the highest sense of the word.

And so it seems to me that science not only purifies the religious impulse of the dross of its anthropomorphism but also contributes to a religious spiritualization of our understanding of life. The further the spiritual evolution of mankind advances, the more certain it seems to me that the path to genuine religiosity does not lie through the fear of life, and the fear of death, and blind faith, but through striving after rational knowledge. In this sense I believe that the priest must become a teacher if he wishes to do justice to his lofty educational mission.

Religion and Science

Does there truly exist an insuperable contradiction between religion and science? Can religion be superseded by science? The answers to these questions have, for centuries, given rise to considerable dispute and, indeed, bitter fighting. Yet, in my own mind there can be no doubt that in both cases a dispassionate consideration can only lead to a negative answer. What complicates the solution, however, is the facts that while most people readily agree on what is meant by "science," they are likely to differ on the meaning of "religion." As to science, we may well define it for our purpose as "methodical thinking directed toward finding regulative connections between our sensual experiences." Science, in the immediate, produces knowledge and, indirectly, means of action. It leads to methodical action if definite goals are set up in advance. For the function of setting up goals and passing statements of value transcends its domain.

While it is true that science, to the extent of its grasp of causative connections, may reach important conclusions as to the compatibility and incompatibility of goals and evaluations, the independent and fundamental definitions regarding goals and values remain beyond science's reach. As regards religion, on the other hand, one is generally agreed that it deals with goals and evaluations and, in general, with the emotional foundation of human thinking and acting, as far as these are not predetermined by the inalterable hereditary disposition of the human species. Religion is concerned with man's attitude toward nature at large, with the establishing of ideals for the individual and communal life, and with mutual human relationship. These ideals religion attempts to attain by exerting an educational influence on tradition and through the development and promulgation of certain easily accessible thoughts and narratives (epics and myths) which are apt to influence evaluation and action along the lines of the accepted ideals.

It is this mythical, or rather this symbolic, content of the religious traditions which is likely to come into conflict with science. This occurs whenever this religious stock of ideas contains dogmatically fixed statements on subjects which belong in the domain of science. Thus, it is of vital importance for the preservation of true religion that such conflicts be avoided when they arise from subjects which, in fact, are not really essential for the pursuance of the religious aims.

When we consider the various existing religions as to their essential substance, that is, divested of their myths, they do not seem to me to differ as basically from each other as the proponents of the "relativistic" or conventional theory wish us to believe. And this is by no means surprising. For the moral attitudes of a people that is supported by religion need always aim at preserving and promoting the sanity and vitality of the community and its individuals, since otherwise this community is bound to perish. A people that were to honor falsehood, defamation, fraud, and murder would be unable, indeed, to subsist for very long.

When confronted with a specific case, however, it is no easy task to determine clearly what is desirable and what should be eschewed, just as we find it difficult to decide what exactly it is that makes good painting or good music. It is something that may be felt intuitively more easily than rationally comprehended. Likewise, the great moral teachers of humanity were, in a way, artistic geniuses in the art of living. In addition to the most elementary precepts directly motivated by the preservation of life and the sparing of unnecessary suffering, there are others to which, although they are apparently not quite commensurable to the basic precepts, we nevertheless attach considerable importance. Should truth, for instance, be sought unconditionally even where its attainment and its accessibility to all would entail heavy sacrifices in toil and happiness? There are many such questions which, from a rational vantage point, cannot easily be answered or cannot be answered at all. Yet, I do not think that the so-called "relativistic" viewpoint is correct, not even when dealing with the more subtle moral decisions.

When considering the actual living conditions of present day civilized humanity from the standpoint of even the most elementary religious commands, one is bound to experience a feeling of deep and painful disappointment at what one sees. For while religion prescribes brotherly love in the relations among the individuals and groups, the actual spectacle more resembles a battlefield than an orchestra. Everywhere, in economic as well as in political life, the guiding principle is one of ruthless striving for success at the expense of one's fellow men. This competitive spirit prevails even in school and, destroying all feelings of human fraternity and cooperation, conceives of achievement not as derived from the love for productive and thoughtful work, but as springing from personal ambition and fear of rejection. There are pessimists who hold that such a state of affairs is necessarily inherent in human nature; it is those who propound such views that are the enemies of true religion, for they imply thereby that religious teachings are utopian ideals and unsuited to afford guidance in human affairs.

The study of the social patterns in certain so-called primitive cultures, however, seems to have made it sufficiently evident that such a defeatist view is wholly unwarranted. Whoever is concerned with this problem, a crucial one in the study of religion as such, is advised to read the description of the Pueblo Indians in Ruth Benedict's book, Patterns of Culture. Under the hardest living conditions, this tribe has apparently accomplished the difficult task of delivering its people from the scourge of competitive spirit and of fostering in it a temperate, cooperative conduct of life, free of external pressure and without any curtailment of happiness. The interpretation of religion, as here advanced, implies a dependence of science on the religious attitude, a relation which, in our predominantly materialistic age, is only too easily overlooked.

While it is true that scientific results are entirely

independent from religious or moral considerations, those individuals to whom we owe the great creative achievements of science were all of them imbued with the truly religious conviction that this universe of ours is something perfect and susceptible to the rational striving for knowledge. If this conviction had not been a strongly emotional one and if those searching for knowledge had not been inspired by Spinoza's Amor Dei Intellectualist, they would hardly have been capable of that untiring devotion which alone enables man to attain his greatest achievements.

Science regards as "scientific" any fact established through empirical methods. Therefore, assertions not established through observation and experiments are only theories or hypotheses. As science cannot be sure about the future, it does not make definite predictions. Doubt is the basis of scientific investigation. However Prophet Muhammad, upon him is peace and blessings, who was taught by All-Knowing, made many decisive predictions.

Most have come true already; the rest are waiting for their time to come true. Many Qur'anic verses point to recently discovered and established scientific facts. As pointed out in the previous section, the Qur'an mentions many important issues of creation and natural phenomena that even the most intelligent person living fourteen centuries ago could not have known. Furthermore, it uses the Prophets' miracles to allude to the farthest reaches of science, which originated in the Knowledge of the All-Knowing One.

The Qur'an describes everything about humanity and the universe. It declares:

With Him are the keys of the Unseen. None but He knows them. And He knows what is in the land and the sea. Not a leaf falls but with His Knowledge, not a grain amid the darkness of the earth, nothing of wet or dry but (it is noted) in a Manifest Book.

Ibn Mas'ud says that the Qur'an provides information on everything, but that we may not be able to see everything in it. Ibn 'Abbas, the "Interpreter of the Qur'an" and "Scholar of the Umma," asserts that if he loses the rein of his camel, he can find it by means of the Qur'an. Jalal al-Din al-Suyuti, a major scholar who lived in Egypt in the 15th century CE, explains that all sciences or branches of knowledge can be found in the Qur'an. Before explaining this important matter, we should point out that to benefit from the Qur'an, which transcends time and location and is not bound by its audience's intellectual level; we have to prepare ourselves to do so. First, we should have firm belief in it and do our best to implement its principles in our daily life. Second, we must refrain from sin as much as possible. Third, the Qur'an declares we only get what we strive for (53:39), so we should, like a deep-sea explorer, dive into its "ocean" and, without becoming tired or bored, continue studying it until we die.

Fourth, we need a good command of Arabic and sufficient knowledge of all branches of the natural and religious sciences. Therefore, a good interpretation necessitates cooperation among scientists from all natural and social sciences, and religious scholars who are experts in Qur'anic commentary, Hadith, fiqh (Islamic jurisprudence), theology, and spiritual sciences. Fifth, while reciting and studying the Qur'an, we should regard it as being its first addressee, consciously aware that each verse addresses us directly. If we consider, for example, its historical accounts of the Prophets and their peoples as unrelated to us, we will derive no benefit. The Qur'an contains everything, but not to the same degree. It pursues four purposes: to prove the existence and Unity of God, Prophethood, bodily resurrection, and worship of God and justice. To realize its purposes, the Qur'an draws our attention to God's acts in the universe, His matchless art displayed through creation, the manifestations of His

Names and Attributes, and the perfect order and harmony seen in existence.

It mentions certain historical events, and establishes the rules of personal and social good conduct and morality, as well as the principles of a happy, harmonious social life. In addition, it explains how to worship and please our Creator, gives us some information about the next life, and tells us how to gain eternal happiness and be saved from eternal punishment. Is everything really found in the Qur'an? Yes everything is there, but at different levels. Therefore, not everything is readily apparent. As the Qur'an's main duty is to teach about God's perfection, essential qualities, and acts, as well as our duties, status, and how to serve Him, it contains them as seeds or nuclei, summaries, principles, or signs that are explicit or implicit, allusive or vague, or suggestive. Each occasion has its own form, and is presented in the best way for making each Qur'anic purpose known according to the existing requirements and context. For example:

Human progress in science and industry has brought about such scientific and technological wonders as airplanes, electricity, motorized transport, and radio and telecommunication, all of which have become basic and essential for our modern, materialistic civilization. The Qur'an has not ignored them and points to them in two ways:

- As will be explained below, by way of the Prophets' miracles;
- By way of certain historical events. In other words, the wonders of human civilization only merit a passing reference, an implicit reference, or an allusion in the Qur'an.

For example, if an aircraft told the Qur'an: "Give me the right to speak and a place in your verses," the aircrafts of the sphere of Divine Lordship—the planets, the Earth, the moon—would reply on the Qur'an's behalf: "You may take a place here in proportion to your size." If a submarine asked for a place, the submarines belonging to that sphere—the heavenly bodies "swimming" in the atmosphere vast "ocean" would say: "Compared to us, you are invisible." If shining, star-like electric lights demanded the right to be included, the electric lights of that sphere—lightning, shooting stars, and stars adorning the sky's face—would reply: "Your right to be mentioned and spoken about is proportional to your light."

If the wonders of human civilization demanded a place based on the fineness of their art, a single fly would reply: "O be quiet! Even my wing has more of a right than you. If all of humanity's fine arts and delicate instruments were banded together, the delicate members of my tiny body would still be more wonderful and exquisite. The verse: Surely those upon whom you call, apart from God, shall never create (even) a fly, though they banded together to do it (22:73), will silence you." The Qur'an's viewpoint of life and the world is completely different from the modern one. It sees the world as a guest-house, and people as temporary guests preparing themselves for eternal life by undertaking their most urgent and important duties. As that which is designed and used mostly for worldly purposes only has a tiny share in servanthood to and worship of God, which is founded upon love of truth and otherworldliness, it therefore has a place in the Qur'an according to its merit.

The Qur'an does not explicitly mention everything necessary for our happiness in this world and the next for another reason: Religion is a divine test to distinguish elevated and base spirits from each other. Just as raw materials are refined to separate diamonds from coal and gold from soil, religion tests conscious beings to separate precious "ore" in the "mine" of human potential from dross. Since the Qur'an was sent to perfect us, it only alludes to those future events pertaining to the world, which everyone will see at the appropriate time and only opens the door to reason to the degree necessary to prove its argument. If everything was explicit, the test would be meaningless, for the truth of the Divine obligations would be readily apparent. Given that we would then be unable to deny or ignore them, the competition behind our testing and trials would be unnecessary, for we would have to confirm their truth. "Coal" spirits would remain with and appear to be no different from "diamond" spirits.

As the great majority of people are always "average", the Qur'an uses a style and language that everyone can understand. An ordinary person and a great scientist can benefit from the Qur'an, regardless of his or her specialization. A most suitable way to do this is through symbols, metaphors and allegories, comparisons and parables. Those well-versed in knowledge (3:7) know how to approach and benefit from the Qur'an, and conclude that it is the Word of God. Earlier civilizations would neither have benefited from nor understood Qur'anic accounts of modern scientific and technological discoveries, so why mention them? Also, scientific "truths" change constantly and therefore are not eternal. God Almighty gave us intelligence, and the Qur'an urges us to use it to study ourselves, nature, and surrounding events.

If it mentioned modern scientific and technological discoveries or everything pertaining to life, nature, history, and humanity, creating us in our present form would have been pointless. God created us as the best pattern of creation, and gave us many intellectual faculties. But if everything were clear, we would not need these, for we would already know everything. Finally, if the Qur'an contained explicit references to everything we want to know, it would be so large that its complete recitation would be impossible. We would be unable to benefit from its spiritual enlightenment, and get really bored while reciting it. Such results contradict the reasons for the Qur'an's revelation and its purposes.

Despite the disasters caused by science and technology, their mistaken approach to the truth, and their failure to bring human happiness, we cannot condemn them outright and become pure idealists. Science and technology do not bear the full responsibility for humanity being devalued, human feelings being diminished, and certain human virtues along with health and the ability to think being seriously weakened. Rather, the fault lies with scientists who avoid their responsibilities, who cause science to develop in a materialistic and almost purely scientific atmosphere, and then let it be exploited by an irresponsible minority. Many worrying conditions probably would not exist if scientists had remained aware of their social responsibility, and if the Church had not forced it to develop in opposition to religion. Flowing to the future like a rapid flood full of energy and vitality, and sometimes resembling a dazzling garden, the natural world is like a book for us to study, an exhibition to behold, and a trust from which we can benefit.

We are responsible for studying the meaning and content of this trust so that we and future generations may benefit from it. If we wish, we can call this relationship "science." Science also can be described as comprehending what things and events tell us, what the Divine laws reveal to us, and striving to understand the Creator's purpose. Created to rule creation, we need to observe and read, to discern and learn about our surroundings so that we can find the best way to exert our influence and control. When we reach this level, by the decree of the Exalted Creator, everything will submit to us and we will submit to God. There is no reason to fear science. The danger does not lie with science and the founding of the new world it will usher in, but rather with ignorance and irresponsible scientists and others who exploit it for their own selfish interests.

If true science directs human intelligence toward eternity without expecting any material gain, undertakes a tireless and detailed study of existence to discover absolute truth, and follows the methods required to reach this aim, what can we say about modern science other than it cannot fulfil our expectations. Although usually presented as a conflict between Christianity and science, the conflicts during the Renaissance were mainly between scientists (not science per se) and the Church. Copernicus, Galileo, and Bacon were not anti-religious; in fact, we could say that their religious commitment drove them toward scientific truth. Before Christianity it was Islam, the religious thought springing from eternality, and the resulting love and zeal accompanied by feelings of poverty and impotence before the Eternal, All-Powerful and All-Wealthy Creator of the cosmos, that enabled the Muslim world's great five-century scientific advance until the close of the twelfth century CE.

Its driving concept of science as based on Divine Revelation was represented almost perfectly by illustrious figures who, imbued with eternality, tirelessly studied existence to attain eternity. Their commitment to Divine Revelation caused. It to diffuse a light that engendered a new concept of science in human souls. If Islamic civilization had not been so badly damaged by the horrific Mongolian and numerous destructive Crusader invasions, the world today certainly would be very different. If the Islamic concept of science as being approved and appropriated by the community, as if it were part of the Divine Message and pursued as an act of worship, had continued to flourish, our world would surely be more enlightened, its intellectual life richer, its technology more wholesome, and its sciences more promising. All Islamic science sought, based on eternality, was to benefit humanity by helping us to aspire for the other world and to handle things responsibly for the sake and pleasure of God Almighty.

According to Islam, the universe resembles a book written by God, a palace built by Him to make Himself known to conscious beings, primarily us. The universe essentially exists in God's Knowledge in meaning. Creation means that through His Will, He specifies or gives a distinct character and form to that meaning as species, races, families or individuals; and then, through His Power, clothes each in matter so that it will be in this time-and-space constrained material realm. After a thing ceases to exist, it continues to live in God's Knowledge, as well as in memories of those who saw it and through its offspring (if any). For example, a dead flower continues to exist in God's Knowledge, in the memories of those who saw it, and in its seeds. Everything has five stages or degrees of existence. First, and essentially, it exists in the Creator's Knowledge as meaning. Even if God Almighty did not create it (in the material realm), it would exist in His Knowledge as meaning, for meaning constitutes the essential existence of everything.

Then, it exists in the Divine Will as a form or a plan; as a material object in the material realm; as a memory and through its offspring (if any); and, finally, its eternal existence in the other world. God Almighty will use the debris of this world to construct the other one. There, animals will continue their existence, each species through a representative of its own species, while each human being will find the eternal life designed for him or her according to how he or she lived while in this world. The universe, which science studies, manifests God's Names and therefore has some sort of sanctity. Everything in it is a letter from God Almighty inviting us to study it and acquire knowledge of Him. Thus, the universe is the collection of those letters or, as Muslim sages calls it, the Divine Book of Creation issuing primarily from the Divine Attributes of Will and Power. The Qur'an, which issues from the Divine Will of Speech, is the universe's counterpart in written form. Just as there can be no conflict between a palace and the paper describing it, there can be no conflict between the universe and the Qur'an, for they are two expressions of the same truth. Similarly, humanity is a Divine book corresponding to the Qur'an and the universe. This is why the term used to signify a Qur'anic verse—ayah—also means events occurring within human souls and phenomena occurring in nature. Only the love of truth gives true direction to scientific studies. What we mean by "the love of truth" is approaching existence not to receive material advantage or worldly gain, but to observe and recognize it as it really is.

Those with such love will achieve their goal; those led by worldly passion, material aspiration, ideological prejudice and fanaticism, and who are devoid of such love, either will fail or, worse, make science into a deadly weapon to be used against what is best for humanity. Intellectuals, educational institutions, and the mass media must strive to deliver modern scientific studies from the current lethal atmosphere of materialism and ideological fanaticism by directing scientists toward human values. To do this successfully, minds must be freed from ideological superstition and fanaticism, and souls purified of desire for worldly gain and advantage. If this can be done, scientists will secure true freedom of thought and perform good science. Their centuries-long battle against the clergy and corrupt concepts formed in the name of religion, and their subsequent denunciation of religious people as backward, narrow-minded, and fanatic, should serve as a warning to scientists not to fall into the same trap.

Whether scientists or clerics allow intellectual and scientific despotism to arise from their own self-interest and power-seeking, ideology and fanaticism. Furthermore, they restrict their reasoning to their corrupt and distorted religious conceptions and domination. But despotism is despotism. Islam continually urges humanity to study nature, the exhibition of Divine works, to reflect on creation and what has been created, and to approach it responsibly in order to benefit humanity. When studied without prejudice and preconception, the Qur'an shows that it promotes the love of science and humanity, justice and order. Islam, as can be clearly seen in numerous verses of the Qur'an, urges the study of nature, which it sees as a place of exhibition of Divine works; it urges reflection upon creation and the created, and approaching it responsibly, without making mischief and causing corruption in the world.

Founded on the Qur'an, Islam has founded knowledge and the quest for it on the intention of discovering the meaning of existence in order to reach the Creator and to be beneficial to all human beings, indeed to all the creation, and combined it with belief, love and altruism. Humanity has seen such an ideal in practice: the exemplary life of Prophet Muhammad, upon him is peace and blessings, and the conduct of many of its representatives who perfected their thoughts and deeds.

So what is there to fear from science? Planned acts based on knowledge sometimes cause bad results, but certainly ignorance and disorganization always cause bad results. Instead of opposing the products of science and technology, we must use them to bring happiness to humanity. Herein lies the essence of our greatest problem, for we cannot take measures against the Space Age or erase atomic or hydrogen bomb-making knowledge from human knowledge.

Although science might be a deadly weapon in the hands of an irresponsible minority, we should not hesitate to adopt both it and its products and then use them to establish a civilization in which we can secure our happiness in this world and the next. It is pointless to curse machines and factories, because machines will continue to run and factories to operate. Science and its products will begin to benefit us only when people of truth and belief begin to direct our affairs. We have never suffered harm from a weapon in the hands of angels. Whatever we have suffered has come from those who still believe that only might is right. This situation will continue until we build a world on a foundation of faith and science.

2

Religion and Science

The Unity

A major source of conflict and disunity in the world today is the widespread opinion that there is some basic opposition between science and religion, that scientific truth contradicts religion on some points, and that one must choose between being a religious person, a believer in God, or a scientist, a follower of reason. The Bahá'í teachings stress the fundamental harmony of science and religion. This view derives from the belief that truth (or reality) is one. For if truth is indeed one, it is not possible for something to be scientifically false and religiously true. 'Abdu'l-Baha expressed forcefully this idea in the following passage:

If religious beliefs and opinions are found contrary to the standards of science, they are mere superstitions and imaginations; for the antithesis of knowledge is ignorance, and the child of ignorance is superstition. Unquestionably there must be agreement between true religion and science. If a question be found contrary to reason, faith and belief in it are impossible, and there is no outcome but wavering and vacillation.

Bahá'u'lláh affirmed that man's intelligence and reasoning powers are a gift from God: "*This gift giveth man the power to discern the truth in all things, leaded him to that which is right, and helpeth him to discover the secrets of creation."* Science results from our systematic use of these God-given powers. The truths of science are thus discovered truths. The truths of prophetic religion are revealed truths, i.e., truths which God has shown to us without our having to discover them for ourselves. Bahá'ís consider that it is the same unique God who is both the Author of revelation and the Creator of the reality which science investigates, and hence there can be no contradiction between the two. Contradictions between science and traditional religious beliefs are attributed to human fallibility and arrogance.

Over the centuries, distortions have gradually infiltrated the doctrines of many religious systems and diluted the pure teachings originally given by the Manifestation who was their Founder. With time these distortions become increasingly difficult to distinguish from the original message. Similarly, unsupported speculations of various schools of scientific thought have at times become more popular and influential than the results of rigorous scientific research, and have further blurred the picture.

'Abdu'l-Baha affirmed that religion and science are, in fact, complementary:

Religion and science are the two wings upon which man's intelligence can soar into the heights, with which the human soul can progress. It is not possible to fly with one wing alone! Should a man try to fly with the wing of religion alone he would quickly fall into the quagmire of superstition, whilst on the other hand, with the wing of science alone he would also make no progress, but fall into the despairing slough of materialism.

In another passage from the same work, He affirmed that the result of the practice of the unity of science and religion will be a strengthening of religion rather than its weakening as is feared by many religious apologists:

When religion, shorn of its superstitions, traditions, and unintelligent dogmas, shows its conformity with science, then will there be a great unifying, cleansing force in the world which will sweep before it all wars, disagreements, discords and struggles—and then will mankind be united in the power of the Love of God.

Relationship between Religion and Science

The relationship between religion and science has been a focus of the Demarcation problem. Statements about the world made by science and religion rely on different methodologies. Religions rely on revelation while science relies on observable, repeatable experiences. Some scholars say the two are separate, as in John William Draper's conflict thesis and Stephen Jay Gould's non-overlapping magisteria, while others propose an interconnection. The Pew Forum has published data on attitudes to religion and science.

Perspectives on the Relationship

The kinds of interactions that might arise between science and religion have been classified using the following typology:

1. Conflict when either discipline threatens to take over the legitimate concerns of the other
   - For example, John William Draper and Andrew Dickson White's conflict thesis
2. Independence treating each as quite separate realms of enquiry.
   - For example, Steven Jay Gould's NOMA
3. Dialogue suggesting that each field has things to say to each other about phenomena in which their interests overlap.
   - For example, William G. Pollard's studies in Physicist and Christian: A dialogue between the communities
4. Integration aiming to unify both fields into a single discourse.

- For example, Pierre Teilhard de Chardin's Omega point and Ian Barbour's sympathy towards process philosophy/process theology

This typology is similar to ones found in Ian Barbour and John Haught. More typologies that categorize this relationship can be found among the works of other science and religion scholars such as Arthur Peacocke.

Conflict Thesis

The conflict thesis view was popularized in the 19th century by John William Draper and Andrew Dickson White. Most contemporary historians of science now reject it, considering that the conflict thesis has been superseded by subsequent historical research. Today, much of the scholarship in which the conflict thesis was based is considered to be inaccurate. For instance, the claim that people of the Middle Ages widely believed that the Earth was flat was first propagated in the same period that originated the conflict thesis and is still very common in popular culture. This claim is mistaken, as the contemporary historians of science David C. Lindberg and Ronald L. Numbers write: "there was scarcely a Christian scholar of the Middle Ages who did not acknowledge [Earth's] sphericity and even know its approximate circumference."

Other misconceptions such as: "the Church prohibited autopsies and dissections during the Middle Ages", "the rise of Christianity killed off ancient science", and "the medieval Christian church suppressed the growth of the natural sciences", are all reported by Numbers as examples of widely popular myths that still pass as historical truth, even though they are not supported by current historical research. They help maintain the popular image of "the warfare of science and religion". While H. Floris Cohen states that most scholars reject crude articulations of the conflict thesis, such as Andrew D. White's, he also states that milder versions of this thesis still hold some sway. This is because "it remains an incontrovertible fact of history that, to say the least, the new science was accorded a less than enthusiastic acclaim by many religious authorities at the time."

Cohen therefore considers it paradoxical "that the rise of early modern science was due at least in part to developments in Christian thought — in particular, to certain aspects of Protestantism" (a thesis first developed as what is now known as the Merton thesis). A tight review of alternatives to the White/Draper conflict thesis has been composed by Ian G. Barbour, "Ways of relating science and theology" in Physics, philosophy, and theology: a common quest for understanding.

Independence

A modern view, described by Stephen Jay Gould as "non-overlapping magisteria" (NOMA), is that science and religion deal with fundamentally separate aspects of human experience and so, when each stays within its own domain, they co-exist peacefully. Gould's view can also be seen as an attitude of neglect towards religion. It has been compared with a similar attitude of neglect towards evolutionary science, which has been seen in the works of theologians Karl Barth, Emil Brunner, and Hans Kung (who's Theology for the Third Millennium (1988) has a chapter on the relationship between religion and science yet never mentions evolution).

Two Takes on Experience

Both science and religion represent distinct ways of approaching experience and these differences are sources of debate. Science is closely tied to mathematics—a very abstract experience, while religion is more closely tied to the ordinary experience of life. As interpretations of experience, science is descriptive and religion is prescriptive.

For science and mathematics to concentrate on what the world ought to be like in the way that religion does can be inappropriate and may lead to improperly ascribing properties to the natural world as happened among the followers of Pythagoras in the sixth century B.C. The reverse situation where religion attempts to be descriptive can also lead to inappropriately assigning properties to the natural world. A notable example is the now defunct belief in the Ptolemy planetary model that held sway until changes in scientific and religious thinking were brought about by Galileo and proponents of his views.

Parallels in Method

Many language philosophers (e.g., Ludwig Wittgenstein) and religious existentialists (e.g., those who ascribe to neo-orthodoxy) accepted Ian Barbour and John Polkinghorne's type II categorization of Independence. On the other hand, many philosophers of science have thought otherwise. Thomas S. Kuhn asserted that science is made up of paradigms that arise from cultural traditions, which is similar to the secular perspective on religion. Michael Polanyi asserted that it is merely a commitment to universality that protects against subjectivity and has nothing at all to do with personal detachment as found in many conceptions of the scientific method. Polayni further asserted that all knowledge is personal and therefore the scientist must be performing a very personal if not necessarily subjective role when doing science.

Polanyi added that the scientist often merely follows intuitions of "intellectual beauty, symmetry, and 'empirical agreement'". Polayni held that science requires moral commitments similar to those found in religion. Two physicists Charles A. Coulson and Harold K. Schilling both claimed that "the methods of science and religion have much in common." Schilling asserted that both fields—science and religion—have "a threefold structure—of experience, theoretical interpretation, and practical application." Coulson asserted that science like religion "advances by creative imagination" and not by "mere collecting of facts," while stating that religion should and does "involve critical reflection on experience not unlike that which goes on in science." Religious language and scientific language also show parallels.

Dialogue

A degree of concord between science and religion can be seen in religious belief and empirical science. The belief that God created the world and therefore humans, can lead to the view that he arranged for humans to know the world. This is underwritten by the doctrine of imago dei. In the words of Thomas Aquinas, "Since human beings are said to be in the image of God in virtue of their having a nature that includes an intellect, such a nature is most in the image of God in virtue of being most able to imitate God". Many well-known historical figures who influenced Western science considered themselves Christian such as Copernicus, Galileo, Kepler, and Boyle.

Concerns over the Nature of Reality

Science in the Enlightenment and Colonial eras was conceived as ontological investigation which uncovered 'facts' about physical nature. This was often explicitly opposed to Christian Theology and the latter's assertions of truth based on doctrine. This particular perspective on science faded in the early 20th century with the decline of Logical Empiricism and the rise of linguistic and sociological understandings of science. Modern scientists are less concerned with establishing universal or ontological truth (which is seen, and dismissed, as the pursuit of philosophy), and more inclined towards the creation of pragmatic, functional models of physical systems.

Christian Theology - excluding those fundamentalist

churches whose aim is to reassert doctrinal truths - has likewise softened many of its ontological claims, due to increased exposure to both scientific insights and the contrasting theological claims of other faiths. Scientific and theological perspectives often coexist peacefully.

Non-Christian faiths have historically integrated well with scientific ideas, as in the ancient Egyptian technological mastery applied to monotheistic ends, the flourishing of logic and mathematics under Hinduism and Buddhism, and the scientific advances made by Muslim scholars during the Ottoman Empire. Even many 19th century Christian communities welcomed scientists who claimed that science was not at all concerned with discovering the ultimate nature of reality.

Integration

Christianity and Science

The reconciliation of Christianity with science has had at least three attempted solutions that have proven themselves quite problematic. These three problematic solutions are biblical literalism, religious experience, and the evolving consensus of scientific truth. Each of these methods of reconciliation have various historical and present-day examples.

Respective examples include creationism, liberal Christianity, and scientific imperialism. Earlier attempts at reconciliation of Christianity with Newtonian mechanics appear quite different from later attempts at reconciliation with the newer scientific ideas of evolution or relativity. Many early interpretations of evolution polarized themselves around a struggle for existence. These ideas were significantly countered by later findings of universal patterns of biological cooperation.

According to John Habgood, all man really knows here is that the universe seems to be a mix of good and evil, beauty and pain, and that suffering may somehow be part of the process of creation. Habgood holds that Christians should not be surprised that suffering may be used creatively by God, given their faith in the symbol of the Cross. Habgood states that Christians have for two millennia believed in the love of God because he revealed "Himself as Love in Jesus Christ," not because the physical universe does or does not point to the value of love.

Reconciliation in the Early 20th Century

In Reconciling Science and Religion: The Debate in Early-twentieth-century Britain, historian of biology Peter J. Bowler argues that in contrast to the conflicts between science and religion in the U.S. in the 1920s (most famously the Scopes Trial), during this period Great Britain experienced a concerted effort at reconciliation, championed by intellectually conservative scientists, supported by liberal theologians but opposed by younger scientists and secularists and conservative Christians.

These attempts at reconciliation fell apart in the 1930s due to increased social tensions, moves towards Neo-orthodox Theology and the acceptance of the modern evolutionary synthesis.

Buddhism

In Buddhism, the Kalama Sutta precludes the use of numerous non-systematic methods and sources, including authority, common sense, opinions, tradition, and scripture.

Bahá'í View

A fundamental principle of the Bahá'í Faith is the harmony of religion and science.

Bahá'í scripture asserts that true science and true religion can never be in conflict. 'Abdu'l-Bahá, the son of the founder of the religion, stated that religion without science is superstition and that science without religion is materialism. He also admonished that true religion must conform to the conclusions of science.

Current Scholarship

The modern dialogue between religion and science is rooted in Ian Barbour's 1966 book Issues in Science and Religion. Since that time it has grown into a serious academic field, with academic chairs in the subject area, and two dedicated academic journals, Zygon: Journal of Religion & Science and Theology and Science. Articles are also sometimes found in mainstream science journals such as American Journal of Physics and Science.

Influence of a Biblical World View on Early Modern Science

In The Scientific Revolution: A Historiographical Inquiry historian of science H. Floris Cohen presents scholarship arguing for a Biblical influence on the early development of modern science. Cohen presents Dutch historian R. Hooykaas' argument that a Biblical world-view holds all the necessary antidotes for the hubris of Greek rationalism: a respect for manual labour, leading to experimentation and a greater level of empiricism and a supreme God that left nature "de-deified" and open to emulation and manipulation.

This argument gives support to the idea that the rise of early modern science was due to a unique combination of Greek and biblical thought. Cohen summarises Hooykaas' conclusion as attributing the rise of modern science to the combination of the "Greek powers of abstract reasoning and of thinking up idealized constructions" in combination with "the biblical humility toward accepting the facts of nature as they are, combined with a view of man as fitted out by God with the power to take nature on".

Historian and professor of religion Eugene M Klaaren holds that "a belief in divine creation" was central to an emergence of science in seventeenth-century England. The philosopher Michael Foster has published influential analytical philosophy connecting Christian doctrines of creation with empiricism.

Historian William B. Ashworth has argued against the historical notion of distinctive mind-sets and the idea of Catholic and Protestant sciences in "Catholicism and early modern science." Historians James R. Jacob and Margaret C. Jacob have published the paper "The Anglican Origins of Modern Science," which endeavors to show a linkage between seventeenth century Anglican intellectual transformations and influential English scientists. Two well-respected theological surveys, which also cover additional interactions occurring in the 18th, 19th, and 20th centuries, are John Dillenberger's Protestant Thought and Natural Science and Christopher B. Kaiser's Creation and the History of Science.

Religious Community's Perspective

Historical Judeo-Christian-Islamic View

In the Medieval era, some leading thinkers in Judaism, Christianity and Islam, undertook a project of synthesis between religion, philosophy, and natural sciences. For example, the Islamic philosopher Averroes, the Jewish philosopher Maimonides, and the Christian philosopher Augustine of Hippo, held that if religious teachings were found to contradict certain direct observations about the natural world, then it would be obligatory to re-evaluate either the interpretation of the scientific facts or the understanding of the scriptures. The best knowledge of the cosmos was seen as an important part of arriving at a better understanding of the Bible, but not yet equal with the authority of the Bible. This approach has continued down to the present day; Henry Drummond, for example, was a 19th century Scot who wrote many articles, some of which drew on scientific knowledge to tease out and illustrate Christian ideas.

From the 11th century, however, scientific methods were being applied by both Muslim scientists and Christian scientists to domains such as optics and planetary orbits, with results which threatened some of the Church's doctrines. Christianity asserted religious certainty at the expense of scientific knowledge, by giving more explicit sanction to officially correct views of nature and scripture. Similar developments occurred in other religions. This approach, while it tended to temporarily stabilize doctrine, was also inclined toward making philosophical and scientific orthodoxy less open to correction, as accepted philosophy became the religiously sanctioned science. Observation and theory became subordinate to dogma. In Europe, scientists and scholars of the Enlightenment responded to such restrictions with increasing skepticism.

Non-fundamentalist Religious Views

In between these positions lies that of non-fundamentalist religious believers. A great many Christians and Jews still accept some or many traditional religious beliefs taught in their respective faith communities, but they no longer accept their tradition's teachings as unquestionable and infallible (indeed this is a basic tenet of mainstream Protestant Christian thought and of other faith perspectives open to dialogue with science). Liberal religious believers do believe in god, and believe that in some way their god revealed their will to humanity. They differ from religious fundamentalists in that they accept that even if their religious texts were divinely inspired, they are also human documents which reflect the cultural and historic limitations and biases of their authors.

Many support allegorical interpretations of Genesis. Such believers are often comfortable with the findings of archaeological and linguistic research and historical-critical study. They will often make use of literary and historical analysis of religious texts to understand how they developed, and to see how they might be applied in our own day. This approach developed among Protestant scholars in the 18th and 19th centuries, and is now found among other Christians, Liberal Jewish communities and others. Some religious approaches acknowledge the historical relationship between modern science and ancient doctrines. For example, John Paul II, leader of the Roman Catholic Church, in 1981 spoke of the relationship this way: "The Bible itself speaks to us of the origin of the universe and its make-up, not in order to provide us with a scientific treatise, but in order to state the correct relationships of man with God and with the universe.

Sacred Scripture wishes simply to declare that the world was created by God, and in order to teach this truth it expresses itself in the terms of the cosmology in use at the time of the writer". This statement would reflect the views of many non-Catholic Christians as well. An example of this kind of thinking is Theistic evolution. This understanding of the role of scripture in relation to science is captured by the phrase: "The intention of the Holy Spirit is to teach us how to go to heaven, not how the heavens go." Thomas Jay Oord said: "The Bible tells us how to find abundant life, not the details of how life became abundant."

The Scientific Community's Perspective

The Attitudes of Scientists towards Religion

In the 17th century, founders of the Royal Society largely held conventional and orthodox religious views, and a number of them were prominent Churchmen. While theological issues that had the potential to be divisive were typically excluded from formal discussions of the early Society, many of its fellows nonetheless believed that their scientific activities provided support for traditional religious belief. Clerical involvement in the Royal Society remained high until the mid-nineteenth century, when science became more professionalised. Among contemporary scientists—physicists and biologists—about 40% hold strong religious beliefs, which closely matched those of a similar 1916 poll.

Prominent scientists advocating disbelief in religion include evolutionary biologist Richard Dawkins and Nobel prize winning physicist Stephen Weinberg. Prominent scientists advocating belief include Nobel Prize winning physicist Charles Townes and climatologist John T. Houghton. According to a 1996 survey, belief in a god that is "in intellectual and affective communication with humankind" and belief in "personal immortality" are most popular among mathematicians and least popular among biologists. In total, about 60% of scientists in the United States expressed disbelief or doubt in such a god.

This compared with 58% in 1914 and 67% in 1933. Among leading scientists defined as members of the National Academy of Sciences, 72.2% expressed disbelief and 93% expressed disbelief or doubt in the existence of a personal god in 1998. A survey conducted between 2005 and 2007 by Elaine Ecklund of University at Buffalo, The State University of New York and funded by the Templeton Foundation found that over 60% of natural and social science professors are atheists or agnostics. When asked whether they believed in God, nearly 34% answered "I do not believe in God" and about 30% answering "I do not know if there is a God and there is no way to find out," According to the same survey, "many scientists see themselves as having a spirituality not attached to a particular religious tradition."

In further analysis, published in 2007, Ecklund and Christopher Scheitle conclude that "the assumption that becoming a scientist necessarily leads to loss of religion is untenable" and that "it appears that those from non-religious backgrounds disproportionately self-select into scientific professions. This may reflect the fact that there is tension between the religious tenets of some groups and the theories and methods of particular sciences and it contributes to the large number of non-religious scientists." A explanation has been offered by Farr Curlin, a University of Chicago Instructor in Medicine and a member of the MacLean Center for Clinical Medical Ethics, that science-minded religious people instead elect to study medicine.

He helped author a study that "found that 76 percent of doctors believe in God and 59 percent believe in some sort of afterlife." and "90 percent of doctors in the United States attend religious services at least occasionally, compared to 81 percent of all adults." He reasoned, "The responsibility to care for those who are suffering and the rewards of helping those in need resonate throughout most religious traditions."

Scientific Study of Religion

Scientific studies have been done on religiosity as a social or psychological phenomenon. These include studies on the correlation between religiosity and intelligence (often IQ, but also other factors). A recent study on serotonin receptors and religiosity suggests a correlation between low density of serotonin receptors and intense religious experiences. Also of popular interest are the studies regarding prayer and medicine, in particular whether there is any causal or correlative link between spiritual supplication and improvement of health. Surveys by Gallup, the National Opinion Research Centre and the Pew Organisation conclude that spiritually committed people are twice as likely to report being "very happy" than the least religiously committed people.

An analysis of over 200 social studies that "high religiousness predicts a rather lower risk of depression and drug abuse and fewer suicide attempts, and more reports of satisfaction with life and a sense of well-being" and a review of 498 studies published in peer-reviewed journals concluded that a large majority of these studies showed a positive correlation between religious commitment and higher levels of perceived well-being and self-esteem, and lower levels of hypertension, depression and clinical delinquency, Surveys suggest a strong link between faith and altruism. Studies by Keith Ward show that overall religion is a positive contributor to mental health. Michael Argyle and others claim that there is little or no evidence that religion ever causes mental disorders. Other studies have showed that certain mental disorders, such as schizophrenia and obsessive-compulsive disorder, are also associated with high levels of religiosity.

In addition, anti-psychotic medication, which is mainly aimed to block dopamine receptors, typically reduces religious behaviour and religious delusions. Some historians, philosophers and scientists hope that the theory of memetics, reminiscent of the theory of genetics, will allow the modeling of the evolution of human culture, including the evolutionary origin of religions. Daniel Dennett's book breaking the Spell attempts to begin such an analysis of modern religions. The idea that evolutionary processes are involved in the development of human culture and religion is not particularly controversial among natural scientists, however other approaches based on social sciences such as anthropology, psychology, sociology and economics are more prevalent in academic use.

Religion and Science Community

The religion and science community consists of those scholars who involve themselves with what has been called the "religion-and-science dialogue" or the "religion-and-science field." The community belongs to neither the scientific nor the religious community, but is said to be a third overlapping community of interested and involved scientists, priests, clergymen, and theologians. Institutions interested in the intersection between science and religions include the Center for Theology and the Natural Sciences, the Institute on Religion in an Age of Science, and the Faraday Institute.

3

Religion and Science
The Future

Why is there conflict between science and western religions, that is Christianity, Judaism and Islam, but there is little conflict between science and eastern religions such as Hinduism and Buddhism? In order to answer that question, we must understand what the early church was like, and here will be addressing primarily the relationship between Christianity and Science.

The primitive church under Jesus and His disciples taught a message of love, personal piety and self-denial. There was little in the way of formal philosophy and theology, just a very simple message of love and personal transformation. However, the Church developed, and as it became stronger, especially after it became a State Church — the official religion of the Roman Empire — it was necessary to develop a structure of philosophy and theology to give it a base of intellectual support. And in some ways you can say that the church fathers that did this did a very successful job.

For a thousand years the system that they developed was dominant in the western world, and even today it exercises great influence, not only among Catholics but among Protestant Christians as well. One of these early church fathers was St. Augustine, perhaps the best known and in many ways the most influential. His teachings were influenced by two sources. First was the Platonic philosophy, particularly Plato's dualistic idea about the nature of being and ontology. While Plato was looking around for reality in the natural world, he saw nothing but flux and change, and things seemed to be very confusing. He reasoned that somewhere there must be pure forms of the reality that we see in this world. In other words, our world must be copies of objects in a world that exists beyond our sensory perception.

In Plato's viewpoint, there is a physical world in which exists real reality, the reality in the nature of form, which is an imperfect copy of the pure form of the metaphysical world. Plato also had a dualistic view of human beings. We have a human body which is developed by conception and birth, but we also have an immortal soul which, according to Plato, existed for eternity and will continue to exist. Of course this was not the only view of the physical world, but it is the one that was adopted and converted by St. Augustine. St. Augustine saw the soul as being brought forth at birth by God. Now here is an example of the use of revelation. A very important principle of Christian thought is that theology predominates over philosophy; revelation predominates over natural law or natural philosophy, and church dogma is dominant over human thought.

St. Augustine believed in revelation; he believed that God has revealed his thoughts to men primarily through the incarnation of His Son Jesus Christ, and the records of the incarnate, the Holy Scriptures, were given to the Church, and the Scriptures were to be interpreted by the Church. Of course, when the Church became a state religion, it guaranteed the power of the state to enforce these beliefs. Therefore, after it became a state religion, the "old" universities, including the one founded by Plato, were considered pagan institutions that were no longer needed. The church was the custodian of all truths, and any error that could be eradicated was to be eradicated through the power of the state. Some have called this time the Age of Belief, but some have also called it the Dark Ages. Now the system that had been so powerful in the western world remains powerful in the western world, although it has lost a great deal of its power and authority, which is why there has been this schism between religion and science.

According to the traditional viewpoints, and a view that is still very strong among religious conservatives and traditional Catholics, the final arbiter of all truth is the Bible — or the church's interpretation of the Bible. However, cracks had begun to develop, and slowly other ideas began to creep in and challenge the traditional views. First there was the ongoing Jewish influence; a great deal of medieval thought was really a reflection of the philosophies and thinking of Jewish scholars, although in those days they were not given credit for them, at least amongst gentiles. The second influence was felt primarily in the Iberian Peninsula, after it had been conquered by the Moors. Remember that the Moors were powerful in the Iberian Peninsula for about 900 years, from the late sixth century until the sixteenth century, when the Spanish Inquisition forced the Moors to leave and also forced the Jews to either convert or leave. But for those 900 years, Christians, Jews and those of Islamic faith existed side by side, and there was considerable exchange of ideas among them.

The Crusades were intended to free Jerusalem from the Turks and other Islamic invaders, but they led to further contacts with Islamic society, and the Islamic people knew something about science and about philosophy. They had some ideas that were foreign to Christians but which had a positive influence on later developments in the West. The Crusades also led to trade with the Far East in goods such as spices and silk and other things that enhanced the quality of life in the West. It was during this time that the writings of the Romans and Greeks were rediscovered. Now let's move on to something that began to bring light to the Dark Ages — the Renaissance. The Renaissance, which started in Italy, began to focus not primarily on the creator, although there were Christian humanists in those days, but on creation and on man. This was reflected first in architecture, and began to influence western man, not so much as a change in ways of thinking but as a change in the emphasis of thinking.

This was the time of the Reformation that split and weakened the Church. I want to quickly point out that the early Protestant theologians — primarily Luther and Calvin — were just as supportive, and maybe even more supportive, of the power of revelation and of the power of the Scriptures over science and any other intellectual endeavors as the Catholic Church were. But the Enlightenment Period did weaken the Church, even with the persecution of Galileo and Bruno, as was mentioned in earlier lectures. During the Renaissance there was another great Christian theologian, Saint Thomas Aquinas, who was influenced by Aristotle, somewhat in the way St. Augustine had been influenced by Plato. St. Thomas Aquinas re-interpreted Aristotle through the theology of his faith. For example, the argument of first cause that Aristotle advanced was used by St. Thomas Aquinas as the argument for the existence of God; of course, that was a great leap forward to jump from Aristotle's first cause to the Christian God of St. Thomas Aquinas. As has been pointed out in one of the earlier lectures, St. Thomas Aquinas also adopted Aristotle's static view of the universe, which held that the universe has remained unchanged since the beginning of creation.

St. Thomas Aquinas did, however, reject Aristotle's view of body and soul; otherwise Christianity would have taken a very different path. But again, it was a case of theology dominating over philosophy. Then in the early 17th Century the mathematician and philosopher Renee Descartes appeared. Descartes was of course a Christian, a

Catholic and a dualist, who said the world, was split into the physical and the metaphysical, which was to be the domain of the Church; the Church has authority over the metaphysical and the spiritual. As Galileo said then, "let the Church tell us how to get to heaven and let man, the scientist and natural philosopher, study the physical world." Even though this sounded good, there were problems with it. One of the problems was that it was never fully adopted by anyone, and another problem was the idea of mind-body split.

That is, Descartes gave the domain of man's mind to the Church; science can study the body but not the mind. This is very important as we look into the future, because this mind-body concept has been around for a very long time. Now, with the research being done on the brain, there is going to be a new challenge in the relationship between religion and science in the next few years, in the mind-body question. If you want to look at this from a scientific viewpoint, you may want to read a book written in 1944 by Francis Crick titled The Scientific Search for the Soul, which can be read by the layman. I want to jump ahead now and look at the work of another great writer, Adam Smith. His book, The Wealth of Nations, published in 1776, had something to say about the Church. He gave us a model to look at how churches had changed, and how the church might change and continue to change. Smith said the churches that were supported by contributions of the membership were more responsive to the membership.

He pointed out that the churches that attracted more affluent and educated membership usually had educated ministers, and the uneducated ministers went to churches of the common men. It was among the common men that churches had grown most rapidly. But the common men wanted simple answers to hard questions, and they wanted ministers who were exciting. What happened was that the Church continued to be split within itself. The churches of the common men split off, getting common men as their ministers. Now I think this has pretty much happened, first with the Methodist then the Anglican Church. The early leaders were educated men, including John Wesley, but many pastors of the new Methodist churches that were formed at the time of the Great Awakening were uneducated men who were able to excite the crowd and who supplied simple answers to tough questions; they had a literal interpretation of the Bible, and they were more radical than the mainstream ministers.

This led us to another very important movement in the 1900s, the fundamentalist-liberal split. But first let me back up a little. My hypothesis here, and it has been well demonstrated, is that those churches and their ministers who are well educated will generally be supportive of science; those relatively common churches with relatively less-educated ministers will tend to be more antagonistic to science. The 19th Century was linked to great progress in science: in physics, biology, psychology, and psychiatry. But in religion there had not been great advances, except that some theologians, particularly in the United States, said we need to study the Bible critically and to use scientific techniques to research the Bible. What they found caused a great disturbance in the Church, because it raised questions about the authorship of the Bible: Did Moses write Genesis? No. Did Moses even exist? Possibly not. There were all kinds of questions, not only about the Old Testament but also about the New Testament.

There seems to be great contradictions in the stories about Christ, even stories about His birth and about His death. So the Bible itself was called into question, and the literal interpretation of the Bible was questioned. Christians reacted in two ways. One group said we must re-interpret the Bible; we must look at the Bible not as a literal history or literal truth but as a record of man's experience of God. It's a mythological, symbolic characterization. After all, Jesus talked in symbolic language. There is much about the Christian faith that endears, despite changing times, and the greatest thing about the Christian faith is its teaching of love, which is the teaching of the early church. Therefore, this group says we should teach man to love and to show that love by service to humankind. This has led to the so-called social gospel movement that has gained cognizance among liberal Christians. The conservatives took a different view. They radically defended the Bible as being inspired by God. In fact, a group of conservative Christian theologians met in the 1890s and drew up the fundamentals that must be defended at all cost, and that's where the word fundamentalist came from.

In this view, every word of the Bible is inspired by God and with the authority of God, even though it was written by human authors, so it must be without errors. They believe in the virgin birth of Jesus, in victorious resurrection, and the visible return of Jesus — these are the things the conservatives say must be defended at all cost. The conservative theologians say, "We must defend the faith." Therein lays the fundamentalist-modernist controversy that has lasted for the last forty-five years in mainstream American churches. And it has been a very viciously-fought battle. The New York Times criticized both by saying that the liberals lack clarity and the fundamentalists lack charity. In mainstream denominations, the liberals prevailed, but not without tremendous cost, because the fundamentalists split off to form their own churches which outgrew the mainstream churches.

For example, the Westminister Theological Seminary was split off from the Princeton Theological Seminary. Now, many of these are really bible schools instead of theological seminaries, where they just teach the Bible. One exception was the Southern Baptist Convention, the second-largest denomination in the United States after Roman Catholic, which was not greatly affected by the first wave of the fundamentalist movement which ended in about 1930. Jay Frank Norris, the pastor of the First Baptist of Fort Worth, Texas, was a real fire-brand; he split off from the Texas Baptist Convention and formed his own seminaries, one in Fort Worth and one in Springfield, Missouri. One of the graduates of the Springfield, Missouri seminary is Jerry Falwell. I said the first phase of the fundamentalist-liberal debate ended in 1930, but it was revived in the late 1970s.

This time it was revived primarily among Southern Baptists, and it is still going on. But the fundamentalists are winning this time around. They have taken over many of the state Baptist conventions, including the six Baptist seminaries, and a formal split will eventually occur. However, the fundamentalists have not won totally, and they have suffered some losses, including institutions such as Baylor University, which remain outside the control of the fundamentalists. Today, the fundamentalists don't like to call themselves fundamentalists but instead call themselves conservatives, and they call the moderates the liberals. And this brings us up to the current time. I want to point out one important difference between the modern-day fundamentalists and the fundamentalists of the early days, and it is that the modern fundamentalists are more politically active, and that is largely due to the efforts of Jerry Falwell, who established the Moral Majority in the 1980s, which was replaced in the 1990s by the Christian Coalition.

Let's look at the future debate between Christianity and science. There will not be one Christian or religious response to science, but several. I want to summarize these responses into the following categories: For the fundamentalists, the teaching of science must be subservient to the teaching of the authority of the word of God — the Bible. They will not compromise; they believe they have the word of God in their interpretation of the Bible, and there is no way they will compromise. For them, there will always be confrontations between the fundamentalists and science. However, as powerful as the fundamentalists are, their views are still in the minority. They will attempt to use political power to gain public acceptance, and one area they are working on is public support of private schools. Now why should we be opposed to that? Besides weakening the public schools by taking money from public education to fund private schools, it will give legitimacy to the teaching of creation science.

There will also be many other areas where the fundamentalists will attempt to pass laws or amend the Constitution to give political acceptance and support to beliefs derived from their interpretations of the Bible. So this will be an area of confrontation that will continue indefinitely. The second category is what we might call the moderate conservative Christians. Again, there are a large number of subgroups within this group, with people ranging all the way from the followers of Billy Graham to Paul Baylor, the leader who is trying to rescue the Texas Baptist Convention from the control of the fundamentalists. This group is less hostile to science. The third group might be called the liberal Christians, who practice the essence of Christianity, and service to mankind is one way to express that practice. They tend to interpret the Bible symbolically. They will point out that even Jesus spoke in parables and used analogy to teach spiritual ideas. They look at the Bible in that regard.

Among them will be some who would like to reconstruct the Bible altogether, such as taking out the supernatural elements. Many women in this group would like to see a greater role for women in the Church. They see women already doing a great deal of work but until recently not being given any official capacity. Even the Roman Catholic Church is now beginning to look at this group of Protestant churches to see how it might better serve women. This group will tend to be supportive and accommodating to science. Another thing I want to do tonight is talk about some ways that scientists and religious individuals can work together. The first way that religious individuals and scientists can work together is to look at some of the ethical issues that grow out of scientific research such as genetic engineering.

The second way is to address scientific illiteracy of the American people, to eliminate some of the misunderstandings about science. I will close by talking about the good life for a moment. Bertrand Russell gave a good definition of a good life. He said a good life is a life inspired by love and guided by knowledge. All the great religions of the world teach the message that the way to a good life is inspired by love. So we can look to Christianity and other religions to make us more loving of our fellow men, and to science for knowledge to serve humankind.

Religion in an Age of Science

What is the place of religion in an age of science? How can one believe in God today? What view of God is consistent with the scientific understanding of the world? In what ways should our ideas about human nature be affected by the findings of contemporary science? How can the search for meaning and purpose in life be fulfilled in the kind of world disclosed by science? A religious tradition is not just a set of intellectual beliefs or abstract ideas. It is a way of life for its members. Every religious community has its distinctive forms of individual experience, communal ritual, and ethical concerns. Above all, religion aims at the transformation of personal life, particularly by liberation from self-centeredness through commitment to a more inclusive center of devotion.

Yet each of these patterns of life and practice presupposes a structure of shared beliefs. When the credibility of central religious beliefs is questioned, other aspects of religion are also challenged. For many centuries in the West, the Christian story of creation and salvation provided a cosmic setting in which individual life had significance. It allowed people to come to terms with guilt, finitude, and death. It provided a total way of life, and it encouraged personal transformation and reorientation. Since the Enlightenment, the Christian story has had diminishing effectiveness for many people, partly because it has seemed inconsistent with the understanding of the world in modern science.

Similar changes have been occurring in other cultures. Much of humanity has turned to science-based technology as a source of fulfillment and hope. Technology has offered power, control, and the prospect of overcoming our helplessness and dependency. However, for all its benefits, technology has not brought the personal fulfillment or social well-being it promised. Indeed, it often seems to be a power beyond our control, threatening nuclear holocaust and environmental destruction on a scale previously unimaginable.

The Success of the Methods of Science

The impressive achievements of science are widely known. Scientific research has yielded knowledge of many previously inaccessible domains of nature. The validity of such discoveries receives additional confirmation from the fact that they have led to powerful new technologies. For some people, science seems to be the only reliable path to knowledge. For them, the credibility of religious beliefs has been undermined by the methods as well as by the particular discoveries of science. Other people assert that religion has its own distinctive ways of knowing, quite different from those of science. Yet even they are asked to show how religious understanding can be reliable if it differs from scientific knowledge. Science as a method constitutes the first challenge to religion in a scientific age.

A New View of Nature

Many of the sciences show us domains of nature with characteristics radically different from those assumed in previous centuries. What are the implications of the novel features of quantum physics and relativity, such as the indeterminancy of subatomic events and the involvement of the observer in the process of observation? What is the theological significance of the "Big Bang," the initial explosion that started the expansion of the universe 15 billion years ago, according to current theories in astrophysics? How are the scientific accounts of cosmic beginnings and biological evolution related to the doctrine of creation in Christianity?

Darwin portrayed the long, slow development of new species, including the human species, from the operation of random variations and natural selection. More recently, molecular biologists have made spectacular discoveries concerning the role of DNA in evolution and in the development and functioning of organisms today. What do these discoveries tell us about the nature of life and mind?

A New Context for Theology

The main sources of religious beliefs, as systematized in theology, are the religious experience and the stories and rituals of a religious community. However, two particular areas of theological reflection must take into account the findings of contemporary science: the doctrine of human nature and the doctrine of creation.

Instead of reductionism, which holds that all phenomena are determined by the behavior of molecular components, I will develop a relational and multileveled view of reality. In this view, interdependent systems and larger wholes influence the behavior of lowerlevel parts. Such an interpretation provides an alternative to both the classical dualism of spirit and matter (or mind and body) and the materialism that often replaced it. I will suggest that process theology offers a distinctive answer to the question: How can God act in the world as understood by science today?

Religious Pluralism in a Global Age

The technologies of communication, travel, and today's global interdependence have brought adherents of differing world religions into increasing contact with each other. In the past, absolutist religious claims have led to repression, crusades, and religious wars, and they continue to contribute to hostilities in the Middle East, Northern Ireland, and elsewhere. In a world where some future conflict could escalate into nuclear war, we must take seriously the problem of religious pluralism.

There is also a great diversity of ideas within each tradition. For example, feminist authors have criticized the dominance of patriarchal assumptions in the history of Christian thought, and Third World liberation theologians have pointed to the influence of economic interests in theological interpretation. Religious pluralism calls into question exclusive claims for any one religious tradition or theological viewpoint.

The Ambiguous Power of Technology

Public support of science derives largely from a desire for the technological applications of science. But today there is widespread evidence, not only of the new scale of technological power, but also of the mixed character of its impact on humanity and nature. A nuclear holocaust would wipe out modern civilization and produce climate changes and famines that could conceivably jeopardize human life itself. Toxic chemicals, deforestation, soil erosion, and multiple pollutants, together with continued population growth, are severely damaging the environment. Ours is a planet in crisis. Computers, automation, and artificial intelligence will have powerful impacts on work, social organization, and our image of ourselves. Genetic engineering offers the prospect of altering the structure and behavior of living forms, including those of human beings. Large-scale technologies contribute to the concentration of economic and political power, increasing the gaps between rich and poor within nations and the gaps between rich and poor nations.

The control and direction of technology involves ethical values such as justice, freedom, and environmental stewardship. Respect for persons and for nature is not a scientific conclusion; wisdom in applying knowledge toward humane goals is not a product of the laboratory. Such ethical issues will be the topic of the second volume in this series, Ethics in an Age of Technology. But implications for ethics and technology will be evident already at many points in this first volume. Our view of nature will influence the way we treat nature, and our view of human nature will affect our understanding of human responsibility. The two volumes together will offer a unified treatment of science and technology on the one hand and religion and ethics on the other. In looking at these five challenges — science as a method, a new view of nature, a new context for theology, religious pluralism, and the ambiguous power of technology — my goals are to explore the place of religion in an age of science and to present an interpretation of Christianity that is responsive to both the historical tradition and contemporary science.

The Strategy for Global Development

The tasks entailed in the development of a global society call for levels of capacity far beyond anything the human race has so far been able to muster. Reaching these levels will require an enormous expansion in access to knowledge, on the part of individuals and social organizations alike. Universal education will be an indispensable contributor to this process of capacity building, but the effort will succeed only as human affairs are so reorganized as to enable both individuals and groups in every sector of society to acquire knowledge and apply it to the shaping of human affairs. Throughout history, human consciousness has depended upon two basic knowledge systems through which its potentialities have progressively been expressed: science and religion.

Through these two agencies, the race's experience has been organized, its environment interpreted, its latent powers explored, and its moral and intellectual life disciplined. They have acted as the real progenitors of civilization. Given the almost universal respect in which science is currently held, its credentials need no elaboration. In the context of a strategy of social and economic development, the issue rather is how scientific and technological activity is to be organized. If the work involved is viewed chiefly as the preserve of established elites living in a small number of nations, it is obvious that the enormous gap which such an arrangement has already created between the world's rich and poor will only continue to widen, with disastrous consequences for the world's economy. Indeed, if most of humankind continue to be regarded mainly as users of products of science and technology created elsewhere, then programs ostensibly designed to serve their needs cannot properly be termed "development."

A central challenge, therefore — and an enormous one — is the expansion of scientific and technological activity. Instruments of social and economic change so powerful must cease to be the patrimony of advantaged segments of society, and must be so organized as to permit people everywhere to participate in such activity on the basis of capacity. Apart from the creation of programs that make the required education available to all who are able to benefit from it, such reorganization will require the establishment of viable centers of learning throughout the world, institutions that will enhance the capability of the world's peoples to participate in the generation and application of knowledge.

Development strategy, while acknowledging the wide differences of individual capacity, must take as a major goal the task of making it possible for all of the earth's inhabitants to approach on an equal basis the processes of science and technology which are their common birthright. The challenges facing humanity in its religious life, if different in character, are equally daunting. For the vast majority of the world's population, the idea that human nature has a spiritual dimension — indeed that its fundamental identity is spiritual — is a truth requiring no demonstration. It is a perception of reality that can be discovered in the earliest records of civilization and that has been cultivated for several millennia by every one of the great religious traditions of humanity's past.

Its enduring achievements in law, the fine arts, and the civilizing of human intercourse are what give substance and meaning to history. In one form or another its promptings are a daily influence in the lives of most people on earth and, as events around the world today dramatically show, the longings it awakens are both inextinguishable and incalculably potent. It would seem obvious, therefore, that efforts of any kind to promote human progress must seek to tap capacities so universal and so immensely creative. Why, then, have spiritual issues facing humanity not been central to the development discourse? Why have most of the priorities — indeed most of the underlying assumptions — of the international development agenda been determined so far by materialistic world views to which only small minorities of the earth's population subscribe?

It may be argued that, since spiritual and moral issues have historically been bound up with contending theological doctrines which are not susceptible of objective proof, these issues lie outside the framework of the international community's development concerns. And that to accord them any significant role would be to open the door to precisely those dogmatic influences that have nurtured social conflict and blocked human progress. There is doubtless a measure of truth in such an argument. Exponents of the world's various theological systems bear a heavy responsibility not only for the disrepute into which faith itself has fallen among many progressive thinkers, but for the inhibitions and distortions produced in humanity's continuing discourse on spiritual meaning.

To conclude, however, that the answer lies in discouraging the investigation of spiritual reality and ignoring the deepest roots of human motivation is a self-evident delusion. The sole effect, to the degree that such censorship has been achieved in recent history, has been to deliver the shaping of humanity's future into the hands of a new orthodoxy, one which argues that truth is amoral and facts are independent of values.

So far as earthly existence is concerned, many of the greatest achievements of religion have been moral in character. Through its teachings and through the examples of human lives illumined by these teachings, masses of people in all ages and lands have developed the capacity to love. They have learned to discipline the animal side of their natures, to make great sacrifices for the common good, to practice forgiveness, generosity, and trust, to use wealth and other resources in ways that serve the advancement of civilization.

Institutional systems have been devised to translate these moral advances into the norms of social life on a vast scale. However obscured by dogmatic accretions and diverted by sectarian conflict, the spiritual impulses set in motion by such transcendent figures as Krishna, Moses, Buddha, Zoroaster, Jesus, and Muhammad have been the chief influence in the civilizing of human character. Since the challenge before humanity today is the empowerment of humankind through a vast increase in access to knowledge, the strategy that can make this possible must be constructed around an ongoing and intensifying dialogue between science and religion. It is — or by now should be — a truism that, in every sphere of human activity and at every level, the insights and skills that represent scientific accomplishment must look to the force of spiritual commitment and moral principle to ensure their appropriate application.

The Present Relations of Science and Religion

Fifty or sixty years ago anyone fluttering the pages of one of the many magazines which then catered for the cultivated and intelligent English reader would have been fairly certain to come upon an article bearing somewhat the same title as that of the present paper. The author would probably be an eminent scientist, such as Huxley or Clifford; a distinguished scholar, such as Frederic Harrison or Edmund Gurney; or a politician of cabinet rank, such as Gladstone or Morley. Whichever side he might take, he would write with the moral fervour of which Englishmen at that time had an inexhaustible supply. Nowadays the so-called 'conflict between Religion and Science', which was then appetizingly hot from the oven, has acquired something of the repulsiveness of half-cold mutton in half-congealed gravy.

There seems to be a widespread opinion that Sir Arthur Eddington and Sir James Jeans, with some highly technical and not readily intelligible assistance from Professor Whitehead, have enabled the lion to lie down with the lamb. Well, I have no wish to pipe a discordant note in this scene of Messianic harmony. But I cannot help reflecting that psychology, anthropology, and psychical research have made considerable advances as well as mathematical physics; and that they seem prima facie much more likely to be relevant to religion. Even the ordinary common sense of the lawyer and the historian may still have something useful to say on such topics. So, at the risk of being thought a profane disturber of the peace, I propose to raise once more the old questions, and to ask what bearing, if any, recent scientific developments have on the validity of religious beliefs.

In considering such beliefs I shall devote my attention mainly to Christianity, since this is the religion in which most of us were brought up, and is the only one with which most of us have any first-hand acquaintance. I fear that there may be some degree of unfairness in this. For there are certain peculiarities about Christianity which make it vulnerable to attacks that might be harmless to some of the other great religions, such as Buddhism, or to religion in general. I will therefore begin by mentioning the most striking of these peculiarities. The first and most important peculiarity of Christianity is that it is, to an unique degree, a doctrine about its own Founder. Some religions, e.g. Brahminism, do not claim to have any definite historical founder.

Others, such as Buddhism in its original form and Confucianism, which trace their origin to a certain ostensibly historical person, claim no more for their founder than that he was an exceptionally wise and good man who first discovered and promulgated certain important moral and philosophical truths, and illustrated his doctrine by the special sanctity of his life.

Others, again, such as Judaism and Mahometanism, would claim more than this for their founders. Moses and Mahomet are supposed to have been the recipients of special revelations from God. This, it is alleged, enabled them to know facts about God's nature and His commands to humanity which no amount of reflexion on the data of ordinary experience would have disclosed to even the wisest and the best of men. But Judaism and Mahometanism would claim no more than this for Moses and for Mahomet respectively.

These prophets are regarded as ordinary men who were extraordinarily favoured by God, not as supernatural beings occupying a uniquely important position in the universe. Now it is an essential part of Christian doctrine that, whilst it claims for the man Jesus all that Judaism claims for Moses or Mahometanism for Mahomet, it also claims something else which is different in kind and not in degree. I have not been so fortunate as to meet with any account of the details of this doctrine about Jesus which I could fully understand. But, for the present purpose, a rough outline will be enough; and it may be given in the following propositions:

i. There is a single eternal and supernatural existent on which everything else that exists depends one-sidedly both for its origin and its continuance. This may be called 'the Godhead'.
ii. Within the unity of the Godhead there are three and only three most intimately interrelated 'factors' or 'moments', each of which can properly be called God.
iii. A certain two of these factors in the Godhead stand in a peculiar kind of asymmetrical dyadic relationship, which is least imperfectly adumbrated by the analogy of fatherhood and sonship. In respect of this, one of them is called 'God the Father' and the other is called 'God the Son'. The third factor in the Godhead is related to both the others by another kind of asymmetrical dyadic relation. This is denoted by the phrase 'proceeding from', and the factor in question is called 'God the Holy Ghost'.
iv. There is some uniquely intimate relation between that eternal factor in the Godhead called 'God the Son' and a certain man Jesus who was born at the village of Bethlehem during the reign of Augustus. This relation is such that it is appropriate to say of Jesus (and of no other man) that He was divine as well as human, and to say of God the Son (and of no other factor in the Godhead) that He is eternally human as well as divine. (I must confess that I can think of no interpretation of these statements which would enable me to attach a meaning to them.)
v. The birth of Jesus was miraculous, in so far as He had no human father. His mother was caused to conceive Him through the direct agency of the third factor in the Godhead, viz. the Holy Ghost.

vi. After preaching, and collecting a body of disciples, Jesus was eventually crucified at the instigation of the Jewish ecclesiastical authorities at Jerusalem. He died on the cross and was buried, but His body never suffered decay. On the contrary, at some period during His burial it underwent a miraculous change in consequence of which it ceased to be subject to the physical and physiological limitations of the ordinary human organism. He emerged from His tomb, which was found empty and open, although it had been carefully guarded; and for a period of forty days He appeared from time to time, visibly, tangibly, and audibly, to certain groups of His disciples. The circumstances of some of these manifestations were such that no ordinary living man could have appeared and disappeared in the way in which Jesus is alleged to have done.

vii. After the expiry of a certain time these manifestations ceased, and Jesus is said to have ascended to His Father in heaven. Since this statement can hardly be admitted to be intelligible if taken in a literal spatial sense, it may perhaps be interpreted as follows. At the end of this period God the Son resumed a relationship with God the Father which had been suspended during the earthly life of Jesus, and He suspended or modified a relationship to the material world which He had entered into at the conception of Jesus. (I do not pretend to understand what could be meant by changes in the relationship of an eternal being either to another eternal being or to the temporal order of nature.)

viii. Henceforth Jesus guides and influences individual Christians and Christian communities by insensible means. He will continue to do this until the Day of Judgment, when He will reappear physically and sensibly, will allot fitting rewards and punishments to the whole human race, and bring the present order of nature for ever to an end.

The second peculiarity of Christianity is that it took over without question the Jewish sacred scriptures; that Jesus Himself appears to have accepted them; and that apostles, such as St. Paul, whose writings are held to be inspired by the Holy Ghost, used certain statements in them as premisses for the exposition and development of Christian doctrines. Now these scriptures contain an elaborate cosmogonical scheme purporting to describe the creation of the world, of animals, and of man. They profess to account for the origin and propagation of moral and physical evil by the dis-obedience of our first parents to God's commands at the instigation of an evil supernatural created being.

It is an essential part of the Christian doctrine that mankind was thus alienated from God, rendered incapable of amending themselves proprio motu, and justly liable to be eternally punished. It is also an essential part of that religion that the incarnation of the Son of God in the man Jesus, and the life, death, and resurrection of the latter, rendered it possible (though not inevitable) for men to reconcile themselves with God, to amend their lives, and to attain eternal happiness.

I think it is fair to say that there is no general agreement among Christians as to the precise way in which this cause renders this effect possible; and that there are profound differences of opinion about the part played by the voluntary co-operation of men, which is admitted to be, in some sense, a necessary condition of their salvation. There is a third peculiarity of Christianity which is closely connected with the first. The Christian scriptures and traditions, like those of most religions, contain accounts of ostensibly supernormal events.

Now these reported miracles fall into two very different classes, viz. those which are part of the content of Christianity, and those which are, at most, part of the evidence for Christianity. It is an essential part of Christian doctrine that Jesus survived the crucifixion, and in some sense emerged from the tomb with a transformed body. Any ground for doubting or denying this is ipso facto a ground for doubting or denying a part of Christian doctrine. But it is no part of Christian doctrine that Jesus raised Lazarus from the dead or walked on the water without sinking. If every one of the latter miracles were rejected, this would not directly involve the rejection of a single Christian doctrine; though it might weaken the force of one line of argument for accepting Christian doctrines. Now the miracles of most religions fall entirely into the second class; i.e. they are, at most, evidential and not constitutive. I hope that I have now indicated adequately and fairly the main peculiarities of Christianity.

We can now ask ourselves how far, if at all, the various sciences are relevant to the truth of that religion. I must begin by mentioning an elementary logical distinction which is often overlooked. It is one thing to say of a fact that it conflicts with a certain theory. It is quite another thing to say the same fact that it undermines the grounds on which people hold that theory. It is quite possible that the former statement should be false and the latter true. If that were so, the theory would not have been refuted and would not even have been shown to be intrinsically improbable; but we should have shown that those who accept it have no valid reason for doing so. Thus our question divides into two:

1. Do the generally accepted methods and results of the various sciences conflict with Christian doctrines, i.e. are they either logically incompatible with those doctrines or such as to render them extremely unlikely to be true?
2. Do they undermine the only grounds which people have ever had for believing Christian doctrines?

We will now take these two questions in turn.

The doctrines peculiar to Christianity may be divided into two classes, viz. those which are about Christ, and those which, though taught by Him or inferrible from His teachings, are not about Him. I have already enumerated the former doctrines. As examples of the latter we may take the ethical doctrines enunciated in the Sermon on the Mount.

Now it is quite clear that none of the empirical sciences has or could have any logical bearing on a great deal of the Christian doctrine about Jesus. It is absurd to suppose that empirical science could prove or disprove, make probable or improbable, the doctrine of the existence and triune structure of the Godhead and of the uniquely intimate connexion between one of its differentiations and the man Jesus. The fundamental question is whether any part of this doctrine is intelligible, or whether it is nothing but meaningless verbiage masquerading in the grammatical form of intelligible sentences. Obviously that question cannot be answered by appealing to the methods or results of natural science. If any part of the doctrine be intelligible, the second question is whether it is true or false, antecedently probable or improbable.

Now natural science is concerned with the interconnexions between things or events in space and time; and it is specially concerned to discover uniformities of co-existence and sequence among classes of phenomena, and to collect these, so far as may be, into a deductive system with a minimum of first principles. Therefore the question whether nature as a whole system depends on a timeless non-natural existent, and whether a certain one man once in the whole course of history was related in an absolutely unique way to the latter, evidently falls altogether outside the sphere of natural science. Either these questions are meaningless or they are not; and it is for philosophers, not scientists, to settle this preliminary question. If they are meaningless, conflict between science and Christian theology is impossible for the reason which prevents a lion from fighting with a hippogriff. If they are significant, such conflict is impossible for the reason which prevents a lion from fighting with a whale. And similar remarks apply to co-operation.

It would seem, however, that natural science might have a considerable bearing on the miraculous element which forms, as we have seen, an essential part of the content of Christian doctrine. This includes, undoubtedly, the resurrection of Jesus and His subsequent supernormal physical manifestations to His disciples. Whether it also includes the story of His supernormal conception is a doubtful matter which we may leave to experts. I think that here we are at once faced with the general question: 'Do the results of science make the occurrence of supernormal events impossible or highly improbable?' This question concerns other religions as well as Christianity, and it concerns alleged Christian miracles which are cited only as evidence for Christianity as well as those which are part of the content of Christian doctrine. Unless science has something to say against the possibility or probability of miracles as such, it can have nothing special to say against the possibility of those miracles whose occurrence is part of the content of Christianity. So it will be best to defer this question.

The sciences of geology, biology, archaeology, and anthropology have collected evidence which, in the opinion of everyone competent to judge, conclusively refutes the cosmogonical, biological, and anthropological doctrines of the Jewish scriptures. Though these doctrines are not in themselves essential parts of Christian theology, they are almost inextricably intertwined with others which are, e.g. with the doctrine that mankind is tainted and alienated from God, and that the incarnation, death, and resurrection of Jesus were necessary conditions without which no man could be saved.

Moreover, the fact that these false propositions were, to all appearance, accepted literally by Jesus and made the basis of certain parts of His teaching would seem prima facie to throw some doubt on the Christian doctrine of His divine nature. The only other point to be noticed under the present heading is that Christianity plainly presupposes that human beings survive the death of their present bodies and are, in fact, immortal. Since this doctrine is common to many religions, and is perhaps a necessary condition of any religion, we will defer the fundamental question whether science has anything relevant to say for or against it.

For the present it will suffice to remark that, unless science renders the doctrine of an after-life, as such, impossible or highly improbable, it will hardly affect the probability or improbability of the specifically Christian form of that doctrine. It is true that there are no empirical facts or scientific theories which would suggest that the present order of nature will be suddenly, radically, and permanently transformed at some date in the future. But it is no part of the Christian doctrine to assert that such a transformation will be due to the automatic development of natural processes. On the contrary, the Christian alleges that it will be due to the miraculous intervention of the Godhead. Therefore, unless science invalidates the other parts of Christian theology or renders survival and miraculous interventions unlikely or impossible, it has no relevant objection to make against specifically Christian eschatology. It remains to consider whether science could render those parts of Christian doctrine which are not about Jesus and the Godhead improbable or impossible.

For this purpose we may confine our attention to the ethical teachings of Jesus. Some people would hold that science makes complete determinism certain or extremely probable; and that, if men's actions be completely determined, the notions of moral good and evil and moral obligation can have no application. Some people would hold that anthropological and psychological investigations show that sentences in which ethical words and phrases occur merely express non-moral desires and emotions, repressed in the infancy of the individual or inherited from the prehistory of the race.

We might describe either of these views as a form of 'ethical nihilism' based on science. Now the question whether science proves or strongly supports ethical nihilism is absolutely fundamental, and goes far beyond the relation of science to Christianity. We will therefore defer it for the present and content ourselves with the following conditional statement. If we have any moral obligations, then natural science can throw no light whatever on those of them which are fundamental.

At most it might support or refute certain derivative and secondary moral rules which profess to tell us how to carry out our fundamental obligations in certain specified kinds of situation. No conceivable development of any of the natural sciences could be relevant to the question whether a person ought or ought not to love his neighbour as himself. At most it might show that some secondary rule, such as 'You ought to pour oil and wine into the wounds of persons whom you find lying injured by the wayside', should be rejected because it is not an efficient means of doing good to your neighbour in the circumstances supposed. Now most of the ethical teachings of Jesus express primary or fundamental obligations. Either science shows that all talk of moral obligation is meaningless or inapplicable to men; or, if not, it is completely irrelevant to this part of Christian doctrine.

It should now be fairly clear that there are not many points at which the results of science and the doctrines peculiar to Christianity come into close enough contact for either conflict or cooperation between them to be possible. I think that similar reasoning would lead to a similar conclusion about the doctrines peculiar to any of the other great religions. If there is conflict, it will be over doctrines like the occurrence of miracles, the immortality of the soul, the freedom of the will, and the question whether moral predicates are significant and applicable to men and their actions. These doctrines are common to all, or nearly all, religions, and they are peculiar to none. We can now pass to our second question. Do the methods or results of the natural or the historical sciences undermine the grounds on which men have believed the doctrines of Christianity?

It seems to me that there is a fundamental logical difficulty, which is prior to any special objections that might be made to the evidences for Christianity on the score of literary and historical criticism or the comparative study of religions. It is this. I think it would be admitted by most Christians that an essential part of their reason for believing specifically Christian doctrines is that these were directly taught by Jesus or are necessary or probable consequences of other statements which He made. But this at once raises the question: 'On what grounds do you accept Jesus as an authority on these matters?' I suppose that the answer would be: 'Because He was a being of superhuman wisdom and goodness, who was in a position to know the facts and whose mission on earth was to reveal them to men.' But this is itself the most central and fundamental of Christian doctrines; and, if Christians accept it on the ground that Jesus asserted it or other things which imply it, their whole position is logically circular.

Are there any independent grounds for accepting it? So far as I am aware, the only grounds that have been suggested are the following. Jesus wrought miracles in His lifetime, and was Himself the subject of the stupendous miracle of the resurrection after His death. He produced on those who knew Him so strong an impression of His divine nature and mission that many of them were ready to devote their lives and to meet a painful death in preaching His doctrines. St. Paul, who had never met Jesus and was bitterly and actively hostile to Christianity, underwent an experience which he took to be a manifestation of the risen Christ; he was converted thereby and confirmed in his new beliefs by subsequent supernormal experiences; and he spent the rest of his life in developing Christian doctrine and disseminating it throughout the Roman empire.

Lastly, throughout history many people have found that certain Christian doctrines harmonize with their own deepest convictions, they have been willing to live and die for them, and they have had experiences which seemed to them to be evidence for the continued existence of Jesus and for His personal intercourse with them.

Let us begin by giving the fullest weight to this evidence and raising no questions as to whether there is adequate ground for believing that the alleged miracles really happened. At the very utmost it would show only that Jesus was an extremely remarkable and impressive personality; that a whole cluster of noteworthy supernormal phenomena, both psychical and physical, were initiated by His death and continued for some time afterwards in the regions in which He had preached; that certain parts of His teaching harmonized with certain deep-seated feelings and aspirations which the existing philosophies and religions of the Roman Empire failed to stir or to satisfy; and that subsequently, when Christian institutions had been established and children were brought up in Christian tradition and doctrine, these teachings (developed, interpreted, supplemented, and modified almost out of recognition) continued to express the aspirations and to evoke the devoted loyalty of many good men. I can see nothing in all this to justify the doctrine that Jesus occupied that uniquely exalted position in the universe which Christians assign to Him.

Therefore it seems to me (as it has seemed to almost everyone not brought up in the Christian tradition) unreasonable to allege the mere ipse dixit of Jesus as an adequate ground for accepting otherwise unverifiable propositions about the Godhead, about His own relations to it, and about the supernatural origin and post-mundane continuance of the human race. I should hold, then, that the only reasons which have been alleged for accepting the doctrines peculiar to Christianity are invalidated by these general objections, prior to all appeal to the methods and results of natural or historical science. Similar remarks would apply, mutatis mutandis, to any other religion which grounds its specific doctrines on the authority of its founder or its prophets. No doubt it is true to say that the development of Christianity was a unique phenomenon; but, in the only sense in which this is true, it is also true of any other great historical process, taken as a whole.

No single historical event, such as the growth of communism or of National Socialism since 1918, is precisely analogous to the growth of the Christian Church. But we can find a number of different partial analogies which, taken together, suffice to bring it into line with the rest of history. Again, it is true that the survival of Christianity in its infancy and its subsequent immense development depended on certain unpredictable and antecedently most improbable events, such as the conversion of St. Paul. It is natural for Christians, afterwards, to point to these events as 'providential'. But a moment's reflexion shows that there have been, and indeed must be, such events in the early stages of any historical movement which starts from very small beginnings, is faced with strong opposition and has to compete with many rivals, and does nevertheless survive and become dominant. The innumerable germs of possible religions and polities which have perished and left no trace in history were just those in connexion with which no such unlikely event happened.

That is why such an event is called 'providential' when it does happen and is viewed in retrospect. Before leaving this part of the subject, I must very briefly consider the following contention, which is sometimes made by Christians. 'If and only if', it is said, 'you will consent to act as if Christianity were true and will take part uncritically in the corporate life of a Christian church, you will eventually have certain experiences which are in fact evidence for the truth of Christianity, and you will be in the right state of mind to appreciate their cogency.' Now it is just conceivable that this contention might be true. But it is evident that there would be other, and considerably more plausible, psychological explanations of the apparent facts.

Moreover, a precisely similar claim might be made by the adherents of any other religion, and it is in fact made by the practitioners of the Indian systems of Yoga. Lastly, it is obviously impracticable to carry out this recommendation in connexion with all the important rival religions, and it is unreasonable to pick out one of them and to perform the experiment with that one only.

So far we have supposed, for the sake of argument, that there is good evidence for the miracles recorded in the Christian scriptures. We must now examine this supposition. Here again we can go a long way with the help of ordinary logic and common sense without needing to appeal to the special methods and results of the sciences. Let us grant for the present that miracles are not impossible, and that it is not inconceivable that there should be evidence available of such strength that it would be unreasonable to doubt that a certain alleged event did happen and was miraculous.

Then I assert, without the slightest fear of contradiction from anyone who has studied the records, that there is no direct evidence for any of the New Testament miracles which is comparable in weight to the evidence for some of the alleged miracles of modern mediumship. For the levitation and other supernormal physical phenomena of D. D. Home we have the contemporary autographic testimony of Sir William Crookes, one of the ablest experimental scientists of the nineteenth century, who was deliberately investigating the phenomena in his own laboratory under controlled conditions. It would be merely impudent to suggest that the direct evidence for the resurrection or the ascension, available to us here and now, is comparable with this. Now either a Christian apologist accepts these alleged mediumistic miracles or he rejects them. If he accepts them, he acts consistently, and moreover he can use them to show that the New Testament miracles are not altogether without parallel and therefore not antecedently so improbable as sceptics allege.

But, if he does so, he must give up the contention that the New Testament miracles testify by their uniqueness to the umque status of Christ and the complete reliability of His metaphysical and ethical teachings. If he rejects them, he can continue to hold that the New Testament miracles are unique. But now he must justify himself in accepting, on very weak direct evidence, antecedently improbable stories similar to those which he rejects where the direct evidence is extremely strong. So far as I can see, there are two and only two moves open to him at this point. The first is to allege that it is antecedently very improbable that miracles should happen in connexion with a decidedly second-rate human being, like D. D. Home, whilst it is antecedently quite likely that they should happen in connexion with a divine being such as Jesus was. So weaker evidence will prove in the latter case what even the strongest evidence cannot prove in the former.

To this contention the simple and sufficient answer is that anyone who uses it cannot, without logical circularity, adduce the New Testament miracles as evidence for the divine nature and mission of Jesus; since he assumes the latter as part of his ground for accepting the former on the evidence available. The other possible move is as follows. It might be said that, although the direct evidence available to us for the resurrection and the subsequent appearances of Jesus is incomparably weaker than the direct evidence for certain mediumistic miracles, yet the indirect evidence is overwhelming. The indirect evidence would be such facts as the change in the attitude of the apostles from despair to an active and lifelong conviction of Christ's survival, the conversion of St. Paul, and so on. I am certainly not inclined to underrate the force of this contention, for these changes seem well attested and very remarkable, and they do demand some kind of explanation.

But the utmost that can be inferred is that something very queer must have happened soon after the crucifixion, which led certain of the disciples and St. Paul to believe that Jesus had survived in some supernatural way; and that they were able to transfer this conviction to many others. The following remarks may be made about this.

The careful work of the Society for Psychical Research has made it almost certain that there is a residuum of truth in the many accounts of phantasms of the living at crises in their lives, of the dying, and of the recently dead, being 'seen' by educated Englishmen who were awake and in normal bodily and mental health at the time. I assume that such experiences are initiated by some kind of telepathic 'impact' received from the person whose phantasm is 'seen'; that this sets up a subconscious process in the mind of the recipient, analogous perhaps to that which takes place in post-hypnotic suggestion; and that eventually this ends by producing a sensory hallucination relevant in its details to the circumstances of the person from whom the telepathic impulse originated. Now I should think it quite likely that Jesus, who was plainly a very remarkable personality, might be strongly gifted with the power to send out such telepathic impulses at the great crises of his life and perhaps at other times too. But this would not be anv good ground for attaching implicit belief to all His ethical and metaphysical teachings. I should not be at all surprised, e.g., to find that Herr Hitler had this power. But, if he had, I should not ipso facto accept without question all those racial and political theories which he preached with such intense conviction and applied for a time with such conspicuous success.

However this may be, it is plain that a telepathic impact, once received, would be much more likely to develop into a full-blown sensory hallucination in the minds of men like the disciples than in a contemporary educated Englishman. With the latter any such development has to overcome extremely strong inhibitions, since the final product would be utterly alien to the whole 'climate' of scientific materialism in which he has always lived and thought. Therefore I should expect that telepathically initiated sensory hallucinations, such as the S.P.R. have studied, would be far commoner and far more detailed and impressive among persons like the disciples than among contemporary educated Europeans.

A 'tough-minded' scientist, who rejects without question all the alleged evidence for contemporary supernormal phenomena, might find it difficult to deal with the indirect evidence for the resurrection and the subsequent appearances of Jesus, if he ever fairly faced it. Actually, of course, he adopts the attitude of the ostrich and faces neither problem. But even he could claim with justice that there might well have been some quite simple and honest mistake, or some deliberate malpractice or deception on the part of some interested person or group, in connexion with the body of Jesus; and that no direct evidence for it remains. Any particular theory of this kind will, no doubt, seem highly gratuitous and unlikely. But, after all, none of them can be so improbable antecedently as the theory that Jesus really rose from the dead, unless we assume what we have to prove, viz. that He was a divine being.

And we must remember that, whilst each one of a number of alternative theories may be antecedently very improbable, it may be highly probable that one or other of them is true in view of the facts to be explained. It is also safe to say that we could have used similar arguments to show that there are no grounds for accepting the specific doctrines of any rival religion which relies on the authority of its founder or its prophets as the evidence for its teachings. Has science anything to say for or against the possibility or the probability of miracles? Before we can answer this we must try to explain the term 'miracle' or 'supernormal event'. This is not easy to do, but I think that the following method of treatment is fairly satisfactory. There are certain very general principles, mostly of a negative or restrictive kind, about mind and matter and their mutual relations, which we all commonly assume without question.

These form the rigid framework within which all our everyday practice, our scientific theories, and even our ordinary fictions and speculations are confined. The following are some of the most important of these principles.

i. A body cannot enter or leave a closed vessel so long as the walls are intact.
ii. The weight of an object at the earth's surface cannot be altered except by immersing it in fluids of various densities.
iii. A human mind cannot directly initiate or modify the motion of any material thing except certain parts of its own organism, such as its arms and legs.
iv. It is impossible for a person to perceive any thing or event at a given moment unless this object has set up a physical process which affects the percipient's organism at that moment and produces characteristic sensations in his mind.
v. It is impossible for a person to have knowledge of a past event, except by inference or report, unless one or other of the following conditions is fulfilled.
    a. The past event initiated a physical process which was transmitted with a finite velocity through space and has now reached the observer's organism and produced a characteristic sensation in his mind. Or
    b. The past event was either an experience had by this person, or was the object of such an experience.

The first condition is fulfilled in the case of a man

perceiving an event which happened long ago in a remote star. The second condition is fulfilled in ordinary memory of past events.

vi. It is impossible for a person to have non-inferential knowledge of an event which has not yet happened. If he knows beforehand that such and such an event will happen, he must do so either by inferring this himself from his knowledge of general laws and particular facts about the past and the present, or by accepting the results of such an inference made and recorded by another person. Examples are provided by the two cases of an astronomer, and a student of the Nautical Almanac, knowing that a total eclipse of the sun will happen at a certain future date.

vii. It is impossible for one man A to know what experiences another man B is having, or what propositions B knows or believes unless one or other of the following conditions is fulfilled.

   a. B makes a statement in speech or writing or some other form of conventional symbolism, and A perceives the record and is able to understand and interpret it. Or

   b. A perceives B's gestures, facial expressions, interjections, etc., and draws inferences from them and from his knowledge of the general laws of human behaviour as to what is happening in B's mind.

viii. After a person has died, his mind either ceases to exist or, at any rate, ceases to be capable of affecting inanimate matter or the bodies or minds of living men and animals.

Phenomena which appear to conflict with well-established laws of nature, or which cannot be explained in terms of them, but which do not apparently conflict with any of these restrictive principles, may be called 'abnormal'; but they will not be even ostensibly supernormal or miraculous. Evidently there are always two questions to be asked about any account of an ostensible miracle.

i. Did such an event as is reported really happen, and is the description of it which the witnesses give completely accurate so far as it goes?
ii. If so, is it really miraculous? Does it really conflict with any of the restrictive principles which mark off the realm of normal and abnormal phenomena from that of supernormal phenomena? Could it not be accounted for without going outside these limits?

About the first question, two of the sciences, both of fairly recent origin, have something very important to say. These are Abnormal Psychology and Psychical Research. It had always been known that human testimony is somewhat unreliable, and that human observation is somewhat defective as regards the details of perceived things and events. But no one had suspected how extremely unreliable they are, even under quite favourable conditions, until the S.P.R. investigated the matter experimentally.

The extent to which intelligent and educated persons, who were under no emotional stress, erred, both by omission and by supplementation, in their reports of what they had seen, is almost incredible; but Mr. Davey's results have been fully confirmed by later experiments.

The contribution of abnormal psychology and psycho-analysis is to show that the real causes of much human action are hidden from the agent's introspection, and are concealed rather than revealed by his overt speech and action. We know that these causes often produce an inability to perceive or to remember or to report certain facts which were physically and physiologically well within the witness's field of observation. In regard to the second question the most important points to be made are the following.

i. We may dismiss at once, with the contempt which it deserves, the statement that 'Science proves miracles to be impossible'. This is just ignorant bluff and bluster, which a moment's reflexion on our definition of 'miracle' and the nature of inductive evidence suffices to deflate.

ii. The development of physical science has shown that many events which were ostensibly miraculous are capable of a normal explanation. The growth of our knowledge of hypnotism, of multiple and alternating personality, and of the extreme sensory hyperaesthesia which characterizes certain hypnotic and hysterical states, tends in the same direction.

iii. The facts and theories of psycho-analysis, already mentioned above, very much weaken the force of such familiar arguments as the following. 'This act must have been miraculous unless the agent was deliberately cheating. But it is incredible that a man of his high character, with absolutely nothing to gain by cheating, and much to lose if detected in fraud, should have practised deliberate deception. Therefore it must be miraculous.'

iv. In spite of all this, I must express my conviction that psychical research has made it far more probable than not that certain kinds of phenomena which are miraculous, in the sense defined above, do in fact occur. I include under this heading telepathy (both experimental and sporadic), certain of the mental phenomena of mediumship, and precognition. I should not, as at present advised, include with confidence any of the ostensibly supernormal physical phenomena of mediumship. It remains to note that, if these supernormal phenomena should ever become familiar and be found to fall under general laws, we should eventually reject the restrictive principles with which they conflict and should then cease to call them 'miraculous' or 'supernormal'.

This naturally leads to our next question. Has science

anything to say for or against the possibility or the probability of a person's mind in some sense surviving the death of his body? I will begin by remarking that, in my opinion, it is almost a sine qua non of any religious view of the world that some men at least should survive bodily death. I take it that one minimal demand of religion is that what we count to be the highest spiritual values shall not be merely ephemeral by-products of complicated material conditions which are fulfilled only occasionally in odd holes and corners of the universe, and are unstable and transitory when fulfilled. Another minimal demand is that there shall be at least rough justice, e.g. that evil deeds shall in the long run bring evil consequences on the doer of them, and not wholly or mainly on others.

For, if this be so, not only does all the value which depends on the character and dispositions and the personal relationships of an individual vanish at his death; but also human society must eventually come to an end, and with it must perish all the values stored up in social institutions, works of art, and scientific treatises. Moreover, it is a commonplace that wicked men often die before they have brought on themselves either bodily suffering or remorse, or the disintegration of their characters or intellects, whilst wise and good men are often stricken down at the height of their powers, or survive into an old age of disease and dotage. Therefore, if science does make human survival impossible or very improbable, it does, in my opinion, deliver a fatal blow to all religion. Now, with the doubtful exception of psychical research, none of the sciences tells us anything which lends the least probability to human survival.

On the contrary, all that biology teaches of the detailed affinity of ourselves with the other animals, and all that physiology and anatomy tell us of the intimate connexion between lesions of the brain and nervous system and aberrations or obliterations of consciousness, produce an overwhelming impression of the one-sided dependence of mental life on certain very specialized and delicate material structures and processes.

As a professional philosopher, perfectly well aware that these scientific facts do not constitute a 'knock-down' disproof of survival. If there were any positive grounds for believing in survival, it would be easy enough to devise hypotheses to reconcile it with the biological and physiological facts which seem to make it so unlikely. There is literally nothing but a few pinches of philosophical fluff to be put in the opposite scale to this vast coherent mass of ascertained facts, unless empirical evidence from psychical research should be available. Do the findings of psychical research up to date do anything serious to redress the balance? Here we must distinguish between direct evidence for survival, and evidence which tends in the first instance only to throw doubt on the epiphenomenalist view of the relation of mind and body.

As regards the direct evidence, there certainly exists a considerable amount of mediumistic communication which undoubtedly involves supernormal knowledge, and is in some respects strongly suggestive of the posthumous intelligent action of certain definite human beings, such as Edmund Gurney, Dr. Verrall, and others. Yet even this is so incoherent and repetitive, and so full of surprising ignorance and error, that one feels driven to seek some other supernormal explanation of it. Moreover, the contents of the communications give us no help in the frightfully difficult task of forming any plausible positive conception of life after the death of the present body.

This brings us to the second kind of evidence. If the occurrence of telepathy, clairvoyance, and precognition were established, this would have no direct bearing on the question of human survival. But it would have the following indirect relevance.

It would tend to throw doubt on the adequacy of the theory (which all other known facts seem to support so strongly) that the human mind is one-sidedly and completely dependent on the brain and nervous system both for its existence and for every detail of its actions. Now it is this apparently well-established fact which makes the hypothesis of human survival antecedently so incredible. On the other hand, the establishment of telepathy, etc., would also work, for a different reason, in the opposite direction. For, if we grant these powers to ordinary men during their lifetime, we may be able to explain by means of them the mediumistic communications which constitute the only direct evidence for survival.

For this essential doctrine of religion, psychical research is the only possible gift-horse in the field of the sciences, and that even it is quite likely to prove to be a Trojan horse. In spite of the ambiguous character of the animal, I should hesitate, if I were a religious man, to look it quite so superciliously in the mouth as the leaders of religion commonly do. Before leaving the subject of human survival I must touch very briefly on the following point. Christians often allege that the resurrection of Jesus constitutes evidence for human survival; that, without this evidence, the doctrine would be a mere pious aspiration; but that, with it, human survival becomes an established fact. This is a favourite theme of Easter Day sermons. Now, this seems to me to be one of the world's worst arguments. Let us grant, what is at best questionable, that the resurrection really happened as described.

Even so, the case of Jesus would differ from that of any ordinary man in at least two quite fundamental respects. In the first place, if Christianity be true, though Jesus was human, He was also divine. No other human being resembles Him in this respect. Secondly, the body of Jesus did not decay in the tomb, but was transformed; whilst the body of every ordinary man rots and disintegrates soon after his death. Therefore, if men do survive the death of their bodies, the process must be utterly unlike that which took place when Jesus survived His death on the cross. Thus the analogy breaks down in every relevant respect, and so an argument from the resurrection of Jesus to the survival of bodily death by ordinary men is utterly worthless.

i. The influence of a scientific discovery or theory on a religion can hardly ever be put in the form of a definite argument which can be tested by the criteria of formal logic or probability-theory. It may not refute the religion, but it may make one's whole intellectual and emotional background so utterly different from that in which the religion originated and flourished that it becomes psychologically impossible for one to take the religion seriously. The religious beliefs of the ancient Greeks have never been refuted, and I do not see how they possibly could be. But no one would think it worth while nowadays even to raise the question whether there are beings answering to the description of Zeus or of Hera given in classical writings.

ii. In the case of any religion which is still alive, such as Christianity in contemporary England, the effect of such influences as I have been describing varies enormously from person to person even among those of much the same level of intelligence and culture. Moreover, those who are differently influenced now will, for that reason, be liable to make very different estimates as to the influence which the sciences are likely to exercise on religion in the future. Where this element of subjectivity is greatest I intend to make it quite explicit by talking in the first person and stating how I am affected and what I should anticipate. Such statements need not be of merely biographical interest, for they might happen to make explicit what many of my contemporaries are vaguely feeling. If and only if this is so, they are not wholly impertinent.

For our present purpose we may divide the sciences into three groups, viz.

i. The sciences of ostensibly non-living matter,

ii. The biological sciences, and
iii. The sciences which deal with specifically human topics.

This classification is hierarchical, in the sense that the second group presupposes the first, and that the third presupposes the second. In the first group the most important for our purposes are astronomy and physics. In the third group the most important are history and archaeology and anthropology; psychology, normal and abnormal; and psychical research. Any religion which can be taken seriously by intelligent men must be cosmic and not merely parochial.

As men we shall necessarily be most concerned with that part of the divine system which immediately affects our race and our planet; and, if we believe that a religion has been revealed to men, we may reasonably expect that the revelation will be most explicit about that part of the system which most concerns ourselves, and which we could not have discovered by our own unaided efforts. Nevertheless, it is essential to any religion on the grand scale that what immediately concerns us should not be something isolated and self-contained, but should be an integral part of a wider system which covers the whole universe.

Now Christianity, like all the great religions, claims to be cosmic in range. But it is also to a very marked extent geocentric and anthropocentric. Christ came to earth, He became a man, and eventually He went back and ascended to His Father in heaven. Now, as it seems to me, Christianity contrived to be at once geocentric and cosmic only because it originated and evolved against a background of astronomical theory in which the earth was the centre of the universe. This would naturally be assumed without question as a popular belief by the apostles and all the early Christians; and, in the detailed scientific form of the Ptolemaic system, it is explicitly taken by the great medieval theologians as the material setting of the divine drama. It seems to me to be assumed by Christ Himself; and some of

His statements, which are perfectly sensible on that assumption, seem to be pointless on any other hypothesis.

Now, since the eighteenth century we have known that the earth is one of a number of planets at various stages of development circulating about one of a number of suns. Naturally I am not so silly as to suppose that this constitutes a refutation of Christianity. All I can do is to record the fact that for me personally the Christian story and the Christian theology in a Copernican universe wither like a plant taken from a hothouse and bedded out in the Siberian desert. I know well that many of the greatest astronomers have found no difficulty in remaining simple and earnest Christians. If there is anything at all in the difficulty that I feel at this point, no progress in astronomy which has been made since Galileo and Newton and no progress that may conceivably be made in the future can make any difference. The revolution in astronomy need have that detrimental effect on religion in general, or on most of the other great religions which, in my opinion, it has on Christianity. It has been said that an atheistic astronomer must be mad.

We may now leave astronomy and pass to physics. In my opinion the logical bearing of mathematical physics, whether of the classical or the relativistic and quantic kind, on any form of religion is quite trivial. I am inclined to think that the only real logical connexion is the following. The fact that all the immense variety of inorganic natural phenomena fall under a few very general laws, and that these laws are of a comparatively simple mathematical form, seems not to be logically necessary. It looks like a kind of uncovenanted mercy, and it constitutes a certain resemblance between inorganic nature and certain products of intelligent human action, such as games of skill, puzzles, musical compositions, etc. Again, the fact that human beings have been able to discover these fundamental laws of inorganic matter, and to acquire thereby a considerable degree of practical control over it, exalts our estimate of the human mind and enlarges the gap between it and any animal mind.

These two facts and their interrelation do, so far as they go, lend some support to a view of man and nature which may fairly be called 'religious'. A distinction has been drawn between two kinds of physical law, viz. 'deterministic' and 'statistical'. Until quite recently the fundamental laws of physics were held to be of the deterministic kind, and the statistical laws were held to be derivative. Nowadays, in the opinion of many eminent physicists, the situation has been reversed, and henceforth we must hold that the fundamental laws of physics are of the statistical kind. Now it has been alleged that, if the fundamental laws of physics are deterministic, all human volitions must be completely ineffective, i.e. that nothing in the material world would have been different if there had been no volitions, or if human beings had made different decisions. It is also alleged that, if the fundamental laws of physics are statistical, it is at least possible that some human volitions do make a difference to the course of events in the material world.

Now it is plain that the ethical content of religion is closely bound up with the common-sense opinion that some human violations are effective. Therefore, if the allegation which I have stated were correct, it would be true to say that the classical physics was incompatible with an essential presupposition of religion. And it would be true to say that recent developments of mathematical physics had eased, if they had not completely removed, this conflict.

If the principles of classical physics do entail that all human volitions are ineffective, they conflict with the presuppositions of natural science just as much as with those of religion. For every scientist who ever devises and carries out an experiment assumes that his thoughts and volitions are making a characteristic modification in the course of events in the material world. It remains for me to mention a certain psychological connexion which probably does exist in the minds of many people between their religious beliefs and what they have heard about recent developments in theoretical physics. The conceptions of classical physics were perfectly straightforward and easy for anyone to grasp and to picture.

Mathematical knowledge was needed only for working out their detailed consequences. The concepts of relativistic and quantum physics cannot be grasped except by a person of considerable mathematical training who sees them as factors in a whole complicated context of theory. And they cannot be pictured at all. When attempts are made to express these concepts and laws in familiar language to uninstructed persons who interpret it literally, a mass of paradoxical and apparently self-contradictory verbiage results. Now in the good old days those who attacked Christianity from the standpoint of science could make great play by contrasting the plain common sense of physics with the mind-destroying hocus-pocus of theology. It can now be retorted that the principles of modern physics look as nonsensical as the Athanasian Creed, and yet are vouched for by eminent scientists and validated by practical applications which we can all use and abuse. In consequence some people are inclined to think that there may be something in the mysterious and apparently nonsensical verbiage of Christian theology after all.

Well, it is not for me to say that there may not be. But I do say, without the slightest hesitation, that the psychological cause which I have just described is no rational ground for thinking that there is. There is nothing mysterious or paradoxical or self-contradictory in the physical concepts and laws so long as they are formulated in the symbolism which is appropriate to them and are viewed in their own proper context. The mystery and the paradox arise only when this symbolism is translated into ordinary words which have certain familiar associations, and when those words are heard or read by persons who lack the knowledge which would enable them to reject or correct the images and ideas which they naturally evoke. I do not think that any theologian would pretend that the paradoxes and apparent contradictions of Christian theology arise simply from this kind of distortion of something which can be quite clearly and intelligibly stated in an appropriate symbolism to experts who have mastered it. Be this as it may, the following reflexion is surely obvious.

The fact that contemporary physics has to enunciate its principles in the form of apparent paradox and nonsense may be a good reason for hesitating to reject off-hand any doctrine merely because it looks paradoxical and nonsensical when stated. But it cannot be a good reason for accepting any one form of apparent nonsense, e.g. the Athanasian Creed, in preference to any other form, e.g. the Kabbala or the Hegelian Dialectic. We can now leave the science of inorganic matter and pass to the biological sciences. We have considered its geocentric aspect in connexion with astronomy; it is the anthropocentric aspect of it to which biology is relevant. Christianity arose, and Christian theology developed, in a certain context of beliefs about the relation of man to other living beings on earth.

Man was created 'a little lower than the angels', and he occupies a unique status in a hierarchy of living beings at the dividing point between the angels, who are purely rational beings without material organisms, and the brutes, who are perceptive and sensitive but wholly non-rational animals. This seems to me to be still the best available description of the peculiarities of man as he now is and as he has been throughout the whole of his written history.

But contemporary biology makes it practically certain that, if we go back far enough into the pre-history of the human race, we find it developing by insensible steps from ancestors who were purely animal. Now, there need be any great difficulty in fitting religion in general, or certain of the great historical religions, such as Buddhism, into this changed biological framework. But, find it difficult to see how Christianity can be fitted into it without being so radically transformed as to be unrecognizable. Certainly no satisfactory attempt at such a reconstruction of Christian belief; and, unless it can be accomplished, Christianity will become less and less credible with each succeeding generation.

It may survive for a long time as a kind of religiously toned 'ethical uplift'; but cannot believe that this will persist indefinitely when cut off from its cosmological and biological roots. All that seems necessary about the bearing of abnormal psychology and psychical research on religious belief in general and on Christianity in particular. It only remains for me to add a few words about the influence of the other specifically human sciences. There is no doubt that, for many people, the results of the comparative study of religion, and the data supplied by anthropologists and archaeologists make religious belief impossible. It seems to them to be a pathetic survival of certain beliefs, emotions, and practices, which were natural enough in the childhood and ignorance and impotence of the human race, but have now lost all meaning and relevance.

It seems to me that science has equally humble and disreputable origins, that there has been a development in depth and insight in religion as well as in science, and that both must be judged ultimately by their fruits rather than by their roots. On the other hand, the facts of anthropology and comparative religion make any claim by any particular religion to an exclusive possession of the truth too utterly ridiculous to be worth a moment's consideration. To me the occurrence of mystical experience at all times and places, and the similarities between the statements of so many mystics the entire world over, seems to be a significant fact. Prima facie it suggests that there is an aspect of reality with which these persons come in contact in their mystical experiences, and which they afterwards strive and largely fail to describe in the language of daily life. This prima facie appearance of objectivity ought to be accepted at its face value unless and until some reasonably satisfactory alternative explanation of the agreement can be given.

Now certain psycho-analysts would give one explanation of it, and that certain Marxian theorists would give another. Such explanations do satisfy some people who have studied them, and they form the staple diet of a great many more that have not done so, but have swallowed them whole in order to be in the vanguard of culture. Now each of these two types of theory contains some interesting speculations which may turn out to be true, and may cover some of the facts. But each of them seems to me to suffer very obviously from two defects. The first is that they are plainly constructed by persons who have very little first-hand or even second-hand experience of religion, and are strongly antipathetic to it from one cause or another. The psycho-analytic and the Marxian theories of religion seem to me to wear too jaundiced a complexion to inspire complete confidence. The second defect is this.

Although the exponents of these theories make a tremendous parade of being 'scientific', it is perfectly plain to anyone who has studied any genuine science that they have no idea of the general difficulty of proving any far-reaching explanatory hypothesis, or of the special difficulties which exist in a field where experiment is impossible, and even the 'observations' consist largely of hearsay and tradition. The degree of their confidence is a measure of their scientific incompetence.

They seem to have no notion of the importance of confronting their theories with negative instances, or of considering whether half a dozen rival hypotheses would not explain the facts equally well. Whether Christianity be true or false, Christ's parable about the subsequent fate of the man who was left 'swept and garnished', after the expulsion of a demon that possessed him, seems to me to be profoundly true of humanity as a whole. Ordinary human nature abhors a vacuum, and it will not for long rest content without some system of emotionally toned and unverifiable apocalyptic beliefs for which it can live and die and persecute and endure.

4

Conflicts between Science and Religion

Science and religion are often not in conflict. Theologians don't care much about the tensile strength of steel when they have church buildings built. Scientists are generally not particularly interested in the functions of a soul. But sometimes science and religion overlap. Each then generally puts forth conflicting beliefs on the same topic.

Typical Conflicts

Two Current Examples are:

- Creation science and evolution: Many conservative Christians believe in the inerrancy of the Bible.

  Although they have are many competing theories over details, many conclude that a literal interpretation of Genesis in the Hebrew Scriptures indicates that God created the world during a six day, 144 hour period, between 4004 and 8000 BCE. Scientists have reached a near consensus that the universe is about 14 billion years old and that the Earth coalesced about 4.5 billion years ago.
- Homosexuality: Human sexuality researchers and therapists have reached a near consensus that homosexuality is a minority sexual orientation, one of three natural, normal orientations, mainly caused by genes;

it is unchosen and unchangeable. Many religious conservatives believe that it is an unnatural, abnormal lifestyle, mainly caused by inadequate parenting; it is chosen, and can be changed.

Disputes arise because science and religion are two very different disciplines. They are based on different foundations:

- Science is ultimately based on observation of nature. Scientists assume that things happen because of natural causes. Some scientists do not believe in the existence of one or more Gods or Goddesses. Others personally believe that one or more deities exist, but assume that he/it/they do not interfere with nature. In any given area, from astrophysics to medicine to zoology, a general consensus exists about most fundamental beliefs. Arguments among scientists exist at the frontiers of each area of science, where new discoveries are being interpreted and hotly debated. The debates are eventually settled by evidence, debates, dialogue, and consultation.
- Religion is largely based on faith. There are over one thousand religious organizations in the U.S. and Canada. By one account, there are 270 large religious groups in the world, and thousands of smaller ones. They hold diverse and often conflicting beliefs concerning deity, humanity and the rest of the universe. Many consider that their own faith is the only completely true one. They believe that the consensus of scientists and the beliefs of all other religions are at least partly false.

There is no simple way to resolve these conflicts:

- Religious beliefs are typically based on faith. Most religious folks believe that, through revelation, God has taught them absolute truth. Any compromise with the beliefs of scientists would require them to reject their own religious beliefs. Very few are willing to do that.
- Since different religions trace their beliefs back to different revelations from God, it is common for different faith

groups to conflict with each other concerning humanity, deity and the rest of the universe.

- Scientific beliefs are generally based on observation. Any compromise would require a scientist to reject hard evidence.

Reaching a consensus is generally impossible. Sometimes, debates are settled by a conscious decision to tolerate each other's beliefs. This is difficult to achieve between two groups who are certain of the validity of their own beliefs.

Science and Religion in the Modern World

In 13th century Europe, Christian theology was regarded as the queen of the sciences. "Science", in this Aristotelian sense, was a systematic exposition of an area of knowledge which was ideally founded on self-evident or certain first principles. The first principles of Christian theology, it was thought, provide the most certain of all principles, since they were revealed by God. Thus theology becomes the paradigm of science. Since that time, the word "science" has changed its meaning, so that now most people would regard a science as an experimental investigation into a physical phenomenon, where precise observations can be made and measurements taken, where experiments are repeatable and publicly testable, and where hypotheses need to be constantly tested and re-assessed. In such a context, theology is no longer seen as a science at all.

There are no precise measurements in religious faith, no repeatable experiments, no public testing, and no equations which might help one to predict events accurately. Since the 17th century, the way we see the history and character of the material universe has been revolutionized. In Europe at least, the Earth had been seen as the centre of the universe, which had existed for only a few thousand years. The human race had been directly created by God, and had fallen from a direct knowledge of God into lamentable ignorance. The whole universe was widely expected to be about to end at any time, and conditions of life on earth were not expected to change in any important way before then.

In the 20th century, most scientists see the universe as having existed for fifteen billion years or more, human beings as having evolved from simpler forms of organic molecules, and the Earth as a small planet on the edge of one galaxy out of billions in the universe. Moreover, technology has changed the way human beings live quite radically, so that instant communication, global travel, medical intervention, and increasing control of reproductive processes have transformed the conditions of life for millions of people. The impact of scientific method, scientific discovery, and technological change has been such that some have argued that religious faith has become wholly outdated. Instead of believing on authority, one has experimental proof, and instead of hope for a better afterlife, one has hope for progress through technological change. So one consequence of the scientific revolution has been the claim that religious belief belongs only to past history. Science replaces religion. That is the first main view of the relation between science and religion. Other responses, however, are possible.

A second view is to point out that religion and science are concerned with different areas of human life. They do not really conflict, because they talk different languages. Science is concerned with the physical, the measurable, and the repeatable, and there is plenty of that in the universe. Religion is concerned with the spiritual, the immeasurable, and the uniquely individual. It is concerned with an infinite spiritual reality, and with the sorts of conscious relationship human beings can have with it. These are more like personal relationships, where one is not concerned with measuring, analysing, and experimenting. In a personal relationship, one is concerned with understanding, responding, empathizing, and cooperating. It would be quite inappropriate to regard a person one loves as a subject for dispassionate experiments. One would be more concerned with their uniqueness, their personality, and their thoughts and feelings. So in religion one might be concerned with a spiritual dimension to the universe which is rather like a personal dimension. It would not be a proper subject for scientific experiment.

Poetry and art might be better vehicles for evoking the sense of such a Supreme Spirit. On such an understanding, science and religion are complementary activities. One could easily practise both, and there would be no conflict between them. Science and religion never meet. That is the second main view of the relation between science and religion. To many people, this is not wholly satisfactory. Christian faith does, for instance, make claims that God has a purpose in creating the universe, and that this purpose will be realized. God acts in history, in the history of Israel, in Jesus and in the Church. God does make a difference to how the universe is, and so conflict is possible between those who claim that science rules out divine action and those who affirm such action in the universe. In this case, one needs to distinguish carefully between the specific experimentally established data of the sciences and the very broad generalizations that are often extrapolated from them.

For example, it is established that the law of gravity operates, other things being equal, on any two material bodies. But it is a generalization from this to say that the law operates without exception everywhere in the universe. Indeed, such a generalization would be inaccurate, according to relativity theory, in the areas of the very small and the very large. In any case, as Isaac Newton thought, there might be many cases where the law does not operate, because the action of God modifies it—for instance, in causing miracles. There is a dispute between those who think that miracles occur, or that God acts in the universe providentially, and those who think there are no exceptions to the laws of nature, or that those laws—for example, the laws of mutational change in evolution—do not suggest or even allow any purposive "interference" from outside.

There are possible disputes about the facts. But these are not disputes which seem to be conclusively resolvable by any specific scientific experiment. They are disputes between a philosophical generalization from science, a "world-view" that everything is governed by seamless causal laws, and a different world-view, that there is an ultimate spiritual reality which directs the course of the universe, and which influences causal mechanisms in the universe in various ways, which are scientifically undetectable or at least usually undetected. Such disputes are very complex and wide-ranging.

Perhaps the most one can do is try to arrive at a balance of probabilities. So one person might think that the laws of physics are so well-established that it would be irrational to believe in exceptions to them. But another equally well-informed person might think that the elegance and intelligibility of the universe strongly suggests a wise creator, so that it would be irrational not to allow for the possibility of that creator causing particular and unique events in the universe, given a good enough reason.

The third main view of the relation between science and religion is that they can conflict, but it may be possible to revise one or the other so that they do not. Many religious believers might protest that it sounds odd to make religious belief a matter of balancing probabilities in this way. They may say that religion is founded on an experience of God which challenges them to turn away from greed and pride, and accept the grace, the love, of God.

One has to commit oneself in trust to the God who reveals himself in such ways. So God is not just a probable hypothesis, but a living, experienced reality. For the religious consciousness, that is probably correct. This is the strength of the second view, that religious faith is a matter of vision and commitment, not of speculative theories. Yet that vision needs to be consistent with our understanding of the nature of the universe. Such understanding has been largely built up by the sciences. For that reason, it is important to test one's vision against the scientific understanding, and to try to ensure that there are no insoluble conflicts.

This would move one towards the third view. One thing has become clear in the story of how religion and science have interacted over the past three hundred years. The experimental sciences give us the best grasp of the truth of how the material universe is. Ancient religions have to adapt to that. The crucial question religion poses is whether there is a spiritual dimension to the universe, which is not as such accessible to the methodologies of science, but which is compatible with what the sciences tell us. This question has not been resolved to the satisfaction of everyone, and perhaps it never will be. Some traditional believers would insist that it is modern, especially evolutionary, science that needs to be revised, where it conflicts with traditional religious claims. But religious views which take science seriously will have to place their beliefs in the context of an evolutionary world-view, for which human beings are one evolved species on a small planet in a tiny part of the universe.

They will probably need an account of evolution which sees it, not as a purely random process, but as compatible with some sort of cosmic purpose or goal—at the least, a propensity for evolving consciousness. That will have some impact on the way evolutionary theory is interpreted, and it will also change many traditional ways of putting things in religion. But it may be that religions testify to the existence of a transcendent value and reality, of which humans can become conscious through prayer and meditation, and which it may even be the goal of human life to know and love more fully.

Theology, the reflective aspect of religion, may no longer be the queen of the sciences. But it may keep alive intimations of transcendent meaning and value without which the sciences would limit human vision of what the universe really is. That is what religious believers will think. Scientists as such will not oppose them, though certain sorts of generalization from science undoubtedly pose problems for many sorts of religious belief. So these two basic human activities will unavoidably influence one another in many ways, and the exploration of the relationship between them remains one of the most fascinating and unresolved areas of human enquiry.

The Sciences

The problem of religion and science cuts much deeper than the (often superficial) debate about evolution. Indeed, the nature of this relationship has been one of the major intellectual problems of the modern world, and a vast literature of works by scientists, theologians, and philosophers addresses it—though the national science standards and science textbooks all but completely ignore it. Contrary to much of the conventional wisdom, this discussion has not become passé, but is, if anything, becoming livelier in light of recent developments in both science and theology.

We begin with a few historical generalizations about the impact of the scientific revolution on religion before discussing four ways of relating science and religion. We will take evolution as our major case study because it has generated the most heated battles in our curricular culture wars, but we will also consider several other areas in the science curriculum where religion is relevant, before drawing a number of educational implications.

The Scientific Revolution

Arthur Eddington's parable of the fisherman who, after a lifetime of fishing with a three-inch mesh net and never catching any fish shorter than three inches, concluded there were no fish in the ocean shorter than three inches.

Just as his fishing net determined what he caught, so our conceptual nets determine what we catch in the ocean of reality. Beginning with physics in the 17th century, then in chemistry in the 18th century and biology in the 19th century, scientists discarded older theological and philosophical nets for those of the modern scientific method—and worked a revolution in the process. All cultures other than modern Western culture have conceived of reality as having a spiritual dimension that could be known through religious experience.

In the Western religions, God was understood to be the creator of the world, and believers could understand nature only by seeing it as God's handiwork, designed to fulfill God's purposes. Because nature was the creation of God, it was good; indeed, it was infused by the spirit of God. Reality was understood to have the structure of a cosmic drama, and as actors in that drama, persons were responsible agents.

Not surprisingly, scientists find in reality only what the conceptual net of modern scientific method allows them to catch—what is measurable, what can be discerned through sense perception and scientific instruments, and what is replicable in scientific experiments. The physicists of the 17th century believed that the ultimate constituents of the world were (quantitatively distinguishable) atoms, and that change was the result of their (quantitatively distinguishable) rearrangement in accord with universal causal laws.

Matter was inert, dead. Qualitative colors and sounds were exiled from "objective" nature to the "subjective" minds of observers. The real world is matter in motion, a realm of pure factuality with no inherent moral structure; nature is not purposeful. Science is "value free." Although

20th century quantum mechanics discerns a level of indeterminacy in nature, classical science was deterministic. Indeed, much science continues to hold that our character and our actions are determined by our genes and biochemistry, our environment and various contingencies of reinforcement.

Science has radically extended our conception of the universe in terms of both time and space. Ours is not the cozy world of traditional religion, in which the earth was created to be our home a few thousand years ago. According to modern science, the earth came into being some 4.6 billion years ago, an incidental by-product of the cosmic evolution that began with the big bang some 10 or 20 billion years earlier.

And from the time Copernicus displaced our world from the center of a divinely created universe, the earth and its inhabitants have seemed increasingly insignificant in the overall scheme of things. As Carl Sagan once put it, and countless forms of life, some of them intelligent, are utterly destroyed. This is not the traditional benign universe of conventional religiosity in the West, constructed for the benefit of living and especially of human beings. Indeed, the very scale of the universe—more than a hundred billion galaxies, each containing more than a hundred billion stars—speaks to us of the inconsequentiality of human events in the cosmic context. Because science is willing to question the old "truths," we discover new truths and progress becomes possible—both in knowledge and, through technology, in our physical well-being. But if science makes progress possible in human affairs, it appears to deny progress in cosmic affairs. The forces of nature are indifferent to good and evil; science offers no assurance that all things work toward what is good.

Evolution, as biologists understand it, has no moral or spiritual purpose, and the second law of thermodynamics tells us that in the long run the universe will run out of energy and die in the cold darkness of space. One goal of traditional religion was to structure and sustain an understanding of reality as trustworthy; religions provided people with moral and spiritual guidance in living their lives. Science makes no such claims. Rather, its goal is to provide the kind of knowledge that gives us predictive power and, through technology, control over our environment. The philosopher E.M. Adams puts it this way: Before the scientific revolution, humankind faced reality asking, what is demanded of me? From within the modern scientific worldview, by contrast, we ask: How do I impose my will on the world? Arguably, this has been the most profound revolution in human history.

Of course, the great scientists of the scientific revolution were not atheists, and, as we shall see, there are ways of reconciling science and religion. As it is practiced, however, science assumes that God is irrelevant to understanding nature, for scientific method prohibits appeal to miracles, divine purposes, religious experience, or Scripture in its explanations. And, at least implicitly, science has become the arbiter of intellectual respectability; the modern scientific worldview pervades the curriculum. Yet, students might well wonder whether there is more to reality than scientific nets can catch. Indeed, might our understanding of nature be distorted if we rely on scientific method only? Of course, theologians, using different nets, claim to catch other dimensions of reality.

The Relationship of Science and Religion

Individuals often take one of four different positions on the relationship of science and religion.

1. *Conflict:* Religion Trumps Science. Science and religion sometimes make conflicting claims about reality; when there is conflict, only religion provides reliable knowledge. It is through inerrant Scripture or religious tradition that we come to know the ultimate truth about nature. No

doubt good science would always agree with Scripture or religious tradition; but, unhappily, not all science is good science. Religion trumps science.

Most "creation-scientists," for example, begin from the assumption that the truth about nature is to be found in Scripture, and they work to find scientific evidence to confirm what they already know to be true. To be a member of the Creation Research Society, a scientist must affirm the divine inspiration of the Bible, the creative acts of God during the Creation week, the historicity of the Great Flood, and Jesus Christ as savior.

2. *Conflict:* Science Trumps Religion. Science and religion sometimes make conflicting claims about reality, but only science provides reliable knowledge. It is through scientific method that we come to know the ultimate truth about nature. If the scientific net doesn't catch something, it's because it doesn't exist. Science trumps religion. Sometimes this position is called scientism or naturalism or scientific materialism—the "ism" suggesting that a philosophical claim about ultimate reality is being made. On this account, religion possesses no competence to make claims about nature, and scientists need not consider religious claims in constructing their picture of nature.
3. *Independence:* Science and religion cannot conflict because they are incommensurable, autonomous endeavors, each with its own methods, and each with its own domain. (This is sometimes called the "two-world" approach.) One common expression of this view is that science asks objective "how" questions, whereas religion asks personal "why" questions. Their conceptual nets capture aspects of reality so different that they stand in no logical relationship. Science and religion can each be true (or false) in their own terms; they are conceptual apples and oranges. While working in their own domains, neither scientists nor theologians need consider the conclusions of the other; religion and

science can be intellectually compartmentalized.

This position is widely held by both theologians and scientists. Adopting it was, at first, a defensive move made by 19th century theologians who believed that science was able to give a complete account of physical reality. As a result, religion must be about a different world, a different dimension of reality. For these liberals, religion was never meant to be a science textbook; its claims about nature simply reflected the fallible prescientific understanding of ancient cultures. What is central to Scripture is its account of the encounters of people with God. Religion is about our existential situation, not physical reality; it is about the meaning of life, not its chemical composition.

Many scientists have also adopted this view. For example, according to a 1981 resolution of the National Academy of Sciences, "religion and science are separate and mutually exclusive [emphasis added] realms of human thought whose presentation in the same context leads to a misunderstanding of both scientific theory and religious belief".

4. *Integration:* Science and religion are commensurable endeavors; they can conflict and they can reinforce each other, for they make claims about the same world. Neither can ignore the other, and neither automatically trumps the other; they provide, in effect, complementary methods for rationally pursuing truth. Because science and religion are each competent to illuminate aspects of the same reality, a fully adequate picture of reality must draw on—and integrate—both.

For integrationists, scriptural passages about nature should not be taken literally, but they must still be taken seriously. There is, of course, a theological risk in the integrationist position, for it leaves theological claims subject to revision, or even falsification, by modern science. Still, theological integrationists would hold with Arthur Peacocke, the distinguished biochemist and theologian that religion and science are "ultimately converging" in that the scientific and theological enterprises are interacting and mutually illuminating approaches to reality.

Roughly a third of Americans believe that the Bible is inerrant and would presumably adopt the view (if asked) that religion trumps science. Very few scientists take this position; it is, after all, utterly at odds with the normal practice of science. No doubt many scientists believe that science always trumps religion; some say so (often in response to creationists), though most scientists simply don't go on record about such things. Because many scientists believe in God yet make no effort to integrate science and religion, instead compartmentalizing them, we suspect that most religious scientists take the independence position. Most liberal theologians, influenced by the intellectual authority of modern science, have adopted some version of either the independence or integrationist positions.

Over the last several decades a shift from the independence to the integrationist position appears to have occurred among both theologians and scientists. Certainly a literature of dialogue has grown rapidly. Why? There are several reasons. First, some scholars argue that recent developments in science—particularly in quantum mechanics, cosmology, chaos theory, and ecology—have provided openings for religious analyses: the world of 20th century science appears to be more hospitable to religion than the classical scientific world of atoms and determinism. Second, recent work in the history, philosophy, and sociology of science has convinced a good number of scholars that science is culturally shaped rather than pristinely "objective." At the same time, many theologians have argued that (liberal) theology can be "rational" or "objective" in some sense; theological claims can be testable—though not in quite the same way as scientific claims. That is, theology and science are not nearly so different as has often been believed, and integration has become a possibility.

Religious and Scientific Modes of Knowledge

Generally speaking, religion and science use different methods in their effort to ascertain Truth. Religious methods are generally subjective, appealing to personal intuition or experience, or the authority of a perceived prophet or sacred text. Scientific methods are generally objective, appealing only to observation and interpretation of observable and verifiable phenomena.

Similarly, there are two types of questions which religion and science attempt to answer: questions of observable and verifiable phenomena (such as the laws of physics, or human moral codes), and questions of unobservable phenomena and value judgments (such as how the laws of physics came to be, and what is "good" and "bad"). People apply the two methods to the two categories of questions in a variety of ways.

- Some apply religious methods to all questions, both observable and unobservable; for example, Theravada Buddhists assert from the authority of the Buddha that the universe and the self are illusions and non-existent, despite scientific evidence to the contrary.
- Some apply religious methods to most questions, and apply scientific methods to a few; for example, up to the mid-16th Century most clergy and natural philosophers asserted, from purported Biblical authority, that the Earth was the center of the universe and subject to certain natural laws, despite physical evidence that the Earth was not the center of the universe, and subject to radically different laws.
- Some apply religious methods only to questions of the unobservable and values, and apply scientific methods only to questions of the observable and verifiable; for instance, those that note the empirical evidence of

evolution today but assert from a religious basis that a supernatural god created the Universe and all the laws and phenomena therein.

- Some apply scientific methods to most questions, and apply religious methods to a few; for example, many atheists assert that there are no gods for lack of empirical evidence, but still assert that there are fundamental moral laws and values that man ought to follow, a priori.
- Some apply scientific methods to all questions, both observable and unobservable.

The Attitudes of Religion towards Science

Hinduism, Buddhism, Confucianism, Taoism, Judaism and Christianity all developed millennia before the existence of the scientific method, followed by Islam about a thousand years prior to the modern era; their classical works show an appreciation of the natural world, but express little or no interest in any systematic investigation of it for its own sake. Nevertheless, historians of science owe a debt, particularly to Islam, for the collection and preservation of early scientific texts originating from China to Africa, and from Iberia to India. In the Medieval era some leading thinkers in Judaism, Christianity and Islam, undertook a project of synthesis between religion, philosophy, and natural sciences. For example, the Jewish philosopher Maimonides, like the Christian philosopher Augustine of Hippo, held that if religious teachings were found to contradict certain direct observations about the natural world, then it would be obligatory to reinterpret religious texts to match the known facts.

The best knowledge of the cosmos was seen as an important part of arriving at a better understanding of the Bible.

However, by the 1400s tension was keenly felt under the pressures of humanistic learning, as these methods were brought to bear on scripture and sacred tradition, more directly and critically. In Christianity, for instance, to bolster the authority of religion over philosophy and science, which had been eroded by the autonomy of the monasteries, and the rivalry of the universities, the Church reacted against the conflict between scholarship and religious certainty, by giving more explicit sanction to officially correct views of nature and scripture. Similar developments occurred in other religions. This approach, while it tended to temporarily stablize doctrine, was also inclined toward making philosophical and scientific orthodoxy less open to correction, when accepted philosophy became the religiously sanctioned science. Observation and theory became subordinate to dogma.

This was especially true for Islam, which canonized medieval science and effectively brought an end to further scientific advance in the Muslim world. Somewhat differently in the West, early modern science was forged in this environment, in the 16th and 17th centuries: a tumultuous era, prone to favor certainty over probability, and disinclined toward compromise.

In reaction to this religious rigidity, and rebelling against the interference of religious dogma, the skeptical left-wing of the Enlightenment increasingly gained the upper hand in the sciences, especially in Europe. The phenomenon of religious fundamentalism, especially Protestant, Christian fundamentalism which has arisen predominantly in the United States, has been characterized by some historians as originating in the reaction of the conservative Enlightenment against the liberal Enlightenment. In these terms, the scientific community is entirely committed to the skeptical Enlightenment, and has incorporated, into its understanding of the scientific method, an antipathy toward all interference of religion at any point of the scientific enterprise, and especially in the development of theory.

While many popularizers of science rely heavily on

religious allusions and metaphors in their books and articles, there is absolutely no orthodoxy in such matters, other than the literary value of eclecticism, and the dictates of the marketplace. But fundamentalism, in part because it is an undertaking primarily directed by scientific amateurs, tends to be inclined toward maximal interference of dogma with theory. Typically, fundamentalists are considerably less open to compromise and harmonization schemes than their forebears. They are far more inclined to make strict identification between religiously sanctioned science, and religious orthodoxy; and yet, they share with their early Enlightenment forebears the same optimism that religion is ultimately in harmony with "true" science. They typically favor a cautious empiricism over imaginative and probabilistic theories.

This is reflected also in their "grammatical-historical" approach to scripture and tradition, which is increasingly viewed as a source of scientific, as well as religious, certainty. Most significantly, they are openly hostile to the scientific community as a whole, and to scientific materialism: that is, science undertaken without commitment to faith. The fundamentalist approach to modernity has also been adopted by the Islamist movement among Sunni and Shi'a Muslims across the world, and by some Orthodox Jews. For example, an Enlightenment view of the cosmos is accepted as fact, and read back into ancient texts and traditions, as though they were originally intended to be read this way. Fundamentalists often make claims that issues of modern interest, such as psychology, nutrition, genetics, physics and space travel, are spoken to directly by their ancient traditions, "foretold", in a sense, by their religion's sacred texts.

For example, some Muslim fundamentalists claim that quantum mechanics and relativity were predicted in the Qur'an, long before they were formulated by modern scientists; and some Jewish fundamentalists make the same claim in regards to the Torah.

In response to the free-thought encouraged by Enlightenment thinkers over the last two centuries, many people have left organized religion altogether. Many people became atheists or agnostics, with no formal affiliation with any religious organization. Many others joined Secular Humanism or the Ethical Culture Society: non-religious organizations that have a social role similar to that which religion often plays; others joined non-creedal religious organizations, such as Unitarian Universalism. People in these groups no longer accept any religious doctrine or perspective which rests solely on dogmatic authority. In between these positions lies that of non-fundamentalist religious believers.

A great many Christians and Jews still accept some or many traditional religious beliefs taught in their respective faith communities, but they no longer accept their tradition's teachings as unquestionable and infallible. Liberal religious believers do believe in gods, and believe that in some way their god(s) revealed their will to humanity. They differ with religious fundamentalists in that they accept that the Bible and other religious documents were written by people, and that these books reflect the cultural and historic limitations and biases of their authors.

Thus, liberal religious believers are often comfortable with the findings of archaeological and linguistic research and critical textual study. Some liberal religious believers, such as Conservative Jews, make use of literary and historical analysis of religious texts to understand how they developed, and to see how they might be applied in our own day. Liberal religious Jewish communities include Reform Judaism and Conservative Judaism.

The Attitudes of Science towards Religion

Scientists have many different views of religious belief.

- Some scientists consider science and religion mutually exclusive;

- others believe that scientific and religious belief are independent of one another;
- Others believe that science and religion can and should be united or "reunited".

It has been argued that conceptions of God by scientists are generally more abstract and less personal than the conceptions of deities in common religions, and sometimes approach pantheism (as in the case of Albert Einstein). While this is undoubtedly true in many cases, no individual polling of the entire scientific community exists to date. Atheism, agnosticism and logical positivism are especially popular among people who believe that the scientific method is the best way to approximate an objective description of observable reality, although the scientific method generally deals with different sets of questions than those addressed by theology.

The general question of how we acquire knowledge is addressed by the philosophical field of epistemology.

According to a recent survey, belief in a God which is "in intellectual and affective communication with humankind" and in "personal immortality" is most popular among mathematicians and least popular among biologists. In total, about 60% of scientists in the United States expressed disbelief or doubt in the existence of deities in 1996. This percentage has been fairly stable over the last 100 years. Among "leading" scientists, 93% expressed disbelief or doubt in the existence of a personal God in 1998. The phrasing of the question can be criticized as presenting an overly narrow definition of God. The survey among NAS scientists was conducted via mail and had a low and perhaps statistically biased return rate of 50%.

Moving From Antagonism to Mutual Respect

Three reasons are offered for why religion should be embraced by the scientific community as a potentially legitimate source of truth.

1. Science, being limited in scope to that which is constrained within the bounds of time and space (the natural realm), cannot directly address that which might lie beyond those boundaries. There is no scientific methodology that can test the existence or non-existence of a God who is not confined within the boundaries of the natural realm. Rejection of religion is not a logical result of scientific inquiry, but is based on faith that only that which is scientifically testable can be true.
2. Religion is often viewed as a hindrance to scientific advancement. Misapplied religion has certainly had such an effect, but the advance of scientific discovery has also been hindered by the rejection of traditional religious beliefs. A classic example can be found in the early days of modern cosmology and Einstein's mathematical model of the universe. Einstein's original model implied expansion, which in turn implied a beginning and, in the view of some, a Creator. Insertion of the famed cosmological constant to achieve a static universe was not based on scientific evidence, but on a philosophical rejection of a religious concept of creation. Two decades of rigorous analysis and debate were required to purge the error from scientific thought.
3. Science offers no rational substitute for religion in the governing of society. In a purely naturalistic universe, any sense of morality is merely a chemically induced response to an environmental stimulus, and exists only because those in the population with this chemical response tend to build communities resulting in higher reproduction rates. Any individual in this population, once becoming enlightened to the randomness of its existence and the purely chemical nature of what is "moral", has no abiding reason to perpetuate the species or to behave in any altruistic fashion.

The Genome Revolution

The history of science is marked by periodic revolutions

– major paradigm shifts that, either quickly or slowly, change the way science is performed, expands the range and immediacy of its applications, and deepen its impact on society at large. The most profound revolutions have a transforming quality; they change not only science and society, but also how we view our place in the world. Science has brought us Copernicus, Newton, the Curies, the nuclear age, the space age, the agricultural revolution and even the sexual revolution. (OK, the last one wasn't all science, but it was a revolution nonetheless...) Each of these has effected pervasive social change, but also raised a host of new concerns and problems to be confronted and pondered.

In considering the implications of the human genome project and Duke's particular response to its scientific opportunities and social challenges, we have come to use the term "Genome Revolution". It's worth considering what we mean by this phrase, viewed through the lens of previous scientific revolutions. In my view, the Industrial Revolution offers the most potent and salient lessons to those of us experiencing the Genome Revolution for at least two reasons. First, the Industrial Revolution signaled a profound change for society. Over a 200-year period beginning around 1700, industrialization spawned urban life where before it had been agrarian. The Industrial Revolution was ubiquitous. One need only tick off a partial list of inventions and discoveries to begin to get a sense of the seismic changes that arrived in that period, from the steam engine and its progeny (the steam locomotive and steamboat), to the cotton gin,

Fox Talbot's photographs, Morse Code, the sewing machine, fermentation, the telephone, Edison's phonograph and incandescent lamp, the Brooklyn Bridge, radio and aspirin. What is most remarkable, even from this abbreviated list, is the breadth of innovation that took place. Similarly, we have little doubt that the Genome Revolution's impact will span just about every facet of human activity.

Second, the Industrial Revolution gave rise to a myriad of new concerns for society: overcrowding, inhumane working conditions, child labor, poor hygiene, urban poverty. Innovation always has the potential for abuse, and even what most people might perceive to be good—or at least benign—uses of technology can arouse resentment, anger and mistrust. Had we thought our families' welfare depended on it, we might have had no compunction about smashing a few machines as the Luddites did in 1811.

People's perceptions of technology vary widely, and their feelings can run deep. Today's parallels? Gene therapy, cloning, playing God, stem cells, genetically modified foods – all have raised (and continue to rise) the ire of at least a few and often many. Will the Genome Revolution represent a true paradigm shift for society on the scale of the Industrial Revolution? We can't pretend to know definitively, but it is clear that the proliferation of genomic data and technology, though just beginning, is already being felt. Already, forensic DNA analysis has transformed the criminal justice system; defense lawyers have championed the tool as a means for finding their clients innocent while prosecutors see it as a way to put away the bad guys. Civil libertarians are up in arms at the prospect of government-controlled DNA banks.

Elsewhere, we know that gene profiling in cancer can affect treatment decisions, while relative success in containing the SARS virus owes a lot to genome sciences. DNA technology has also made inroads into agriculture, business, religion, politics, philosophy, even the arts and popular culture. And yet, as scientific revolutions go, the Genome Revolution is just warming up. When did it begin? The discovery of Mendel's laws (1900)? The first use of the term "gene"(1909)? Watson and Crick (1953)? Collins and Venter (2001)? Take your pick. My own sense is that we can trace the roots of this revolution to Charles Darwin in 1859. Our view of the universe and our place in it surely changed as profoundly at that moment in time as at any time before or since. And some are still wrestling with the implications of his theory of evolution for theology and education. How long will this revolution take? Probably a long time.

Thirty years ago many thought we would have colonized the moon and Mars by now, and, despite recent attention, it seems unlikely that that will have happened even thirty years from today. True scientific revolutions require generations before their effects can be universally felt or measured. But unlike those who lived at the dawn of the Copernican or Industrial Revolutions, we have the advantage of knowing that we are standing on the precipice of something enormous. That enormity – the ability to understand and manipulate every organism's genetic material – has the potential to fundamentally alter our view of the world and our place in it. It is an exciting and exhilarating time, fraught with peril and potential.

The Human Genome Project

The publication of the rough draft of the completed sequence of the human genome on June 26 was an outstanding scientific achievement, the outcome of an international collaboration spanning a decade and involving hundreds of scientists. The researchers used the most advanced sequencing machines and analysed the resulting data with the aid of powerful computers.

Yet the official announcement of this scientific breakthrough became the occasion for the US chief of state and the head of the publicly funded National Human Genome Research Institute to invoke the almighty. At a White House news conference held by President Bill Clinton, Dr. Francis Collins of the Research Institute and Craig Venter of the privately owned Celera Genomics Company, Clinton declared, "Today, we are learning the language in which God created life." He went on to add that "we are gaining ever more awe for the complexity, the beauty, the wonder of God's most divine and sacred gift."

Collins seconded Clinton's religious take on the event, saying, "We have caught the first glimpse of our own instruction book, previously known only to God." Summed up in the press conference was a contradiction of modern life whose import can hardly be exaggerated—immense progress in the fields of science and technology existing side by side with the most backward forms of social consciousness. The elaboration of the human genome sequence is a major step in demystifying the evolution of the human species and the workings of the human body. Aided by technology, such scientific discoveries puncture the clouds of superstition that surround human existence and weaken the grip of religion over the minds of men and women. But Clinton and Collins were at pains to present this achievement of science as a vindication of religion.

Any serious reflection on the genome project reveals the absurdity of invoking it to reinforce religion. If, indeed, the human genome is God's "instruction book," it is not very well written. A rational designer would hardly have written his instructions in such a complex and even confused way, causing frequent "mistakes" in the way the instructions are "read." One result of such mistakes is the emergence of genetic disorders. Scientists have revealed that DNA has a very complex structure that is largely made up of "junk" DNA. Most of the genome does not code for any proteins at all, and so has no apparent function. Genes for proteins have other genes, located on other chromosomes, to turn them on and off. Such a complex situation can only be understood as a product of humanity's long evolutionary history.

Life started four billion years ago from unicellular organisms that went through innumerable transformations, producing many organisms along the way. Of these, many are long extinct and only known to us through the fossil record or in the form of our developing embryos. Are we to believe that some supernatural power devised such a tortuous and laborious path of development? Are we, moreover, to attribute to God all the parasites and diseases which plague the human species? In fact, the path which has led to the human genome sequence did not pass through heaven. Rather, it can be established through the work of particular scientists.

There were milestones along the way: In 1838 Matthias Jakob Schleiden and Theodor Schwann discovered the cell as the fundamental unit of life. In 1859 Charles Darwin published *On the Origin of Species*, which elaborated a mechanism of evolution and set a coherent framework for all the biological sciences. In 1865 the Austrian monk Gregor Mendel developed the foundations of modern genetics. T.H. Morgan in 1910 determined that genes are organised along chromosomes. In 1942 researchers established that genes are made of DNA, a chemical found in the cell nucleus. In 1953, James Watson and Francis Crick elaborated the structure of DNA. In 1973 Stanley Cohen and Herbert Brown invented genetic engineering by transplanting a gene between bacteria, and in 1990 the Human Genome Project began.

To attribute all this to God belittles mankind's struggle to understand nature, which has been achieved with enormous sacrifice. The mystification represented by the remarks by scientists such as Collins does not speak for the whole of the scientific community. At a reception where he was presented the Philadelphia Liberty Medal on July 4, James Watson argued that scientific investigation and knowledge were essential for democracy. In his speech he opposed religious conceptions, declaring that "as a product of the eighteenth century intellectual enlightenment, Jefferson saw truth arising from observations and experiments. So he wanted his state of Virginia to select, for special educational enrichment, youths of inherent genius who were sprinkled as liberally among the poor as the rich. He saw the knowledge so learned as the ultimate safeguard of liberty."

Watson continued: "Today, 224 years after Jefferson so eloquently expressed these ideas in the Declaration of Independence; biology is witnessing the completion of an intellectual renaissance that Charles Darwin began in the nineteenth century. Through his Theory of Evolution through Natural Selection, Darwin forever changed our view of human life. He saw us as the products not of creation by a God as revealed in Genesis, but as arising through a series of evolutionary events going back to a common ancestor of many eons ago. "Much more recently we have learned that the variation upon which natural selection acts reflects mutational changes in DNA, the molecule of heredity."

How is one to explain the persistence of religious superstition alongside science and technology? The development of religious ideas occurred as an attempt by primitive man to explain phenomena which had a profound influence on his life, such as astronomical events, fire, the weather, the seasons and the migration of herd animals, in a period when a scientific understanding of the world was impossible. Karl Marx's co-thinker Fredrick Engels explained in his pamphlet *Ludwig Feuerbach and the End of Classical German Philosophy* that religion had its roots "in the narrow-minded and ignorant notions of savagery." This primitive stage of human development was superseded millennia ago, and mankind has not only elaborated a scientific explanation for his own origins, but also for how the universe itself was formed. Yet religious ideas stubbornly remain.

The most basic reason is that mankind has yet to consciously master his own social organisation. So long as the masses of people have not grasped the law-governed workings of society, and on that basis reconstructed society on more rational, humane and egalitarian foundations, superstition and religion will persist. The great twentieth century Marxist Leon Trotsky wrote in *Literature and Revolution* that "so long as man will not have mastered his social organisation, the latter will hang over him as his fate. Whether at the same time society casts a religious shadow or not is a secondary matter and depends upon the degree of man's helplessness." Karl Marx revealed the underlying laws of capitalist society and the ultimate source in the modern world of the contradiction between scientific and technological advance and social backwardness.

The forms of capitalist society by their very nature obscure the real, objective relations within that society. Marx showed that under capitalism relations between people appear as relations between things, thereby masking a fundamentally exploitative relation between labour and capital. The conflict between the progressive potential of science as expressed in the genome mapping and the existing social and political order is not only expressed in the attempt to wrap this development in a religious framework. It is also reflected in the way this advance is subordinated to the drive for profit. Craig Venter's Celera Genomics is only one of numerous companies positioning themselves to exploit the genome. There is a scramble—a modern gold rush—to patent as much of the genome as possible.

This will not only complicate research, it will place enormous obstacles in its way. Companies have already taken out hundreds of patents for genes in a bid to head off competitors. Researchers who wish to investigate a gene will have to pay substantial royalties for the privilege. As important and potentially beneficial as this development is, it would be naïve to assume that it will automatically work to the advantage of the world's people. So long as science and technology are subordinated to the narrow and private interests of corporate owners, and the capitalist governments that serve them, the achievements of human intellect and industry can be, and usually are, perverted to produce tragic consequences. Last century the discovery of nuclear power had the potential to resolve the energy problems of society once and for all. Instead it was used to develop new weapons of mass destruction. Do we face a future which includes the deployment of "gene bombs," capable of killing off certain genetic types while leaving property intact?

The scientific goal was to map the genes and sequence human DNA. Mapping would eventually reveal the position and spacing of the then predicted one hundred thousand genes in each of the human body's cells; sequencing would determine the order of the four base pairs—the A (adenine), T (thymine), G (guanine), and C (cytosine) nucleotides—that compose the DNA molecule. The primary motive was that which drives all basic science, namely, the need to know. The secondary motive was perhaps even more important, namely, to identify the four thousand or so genes that were suspected to be responsible for inherited diseases and prepare the way for treatment through genetic therapy. This would benefit society, HGP architects thought, because a library of DNA knowledge would jump start medical research on many fronts. Many early prophecies found their fulfillment. Some did not.

What was not anticipated was the competition between the private sector and the public sector. J. Craig Venter (b. 1946) led the private sector effort. While on a grant from NIH, Venter applied for nearly three thousand patents on Expressed Sequence Tags (ESTs). The ESTs located genes but stopped short of identifying gene function. A furor developed when researchers working with government money applied for patents on data that merely reports knowledge of what already exists in nature—knowledge of existing DNA sequences—and this led to the 1992 resignation of James Watson (b. 1928) from the directorship of NIH's National Center for Human Genome Research (NCHGR). Watson, who along with Francis Crick (b. 1916) is famed for his discovery of the double helix structure of DNA, was the first to head the NCHGR.

Venter then established The Institute for Genomic Research (TIGR) and began using Applied Biosystems automatic sequencers twenty-four hours per day to speed up nucleotide sequencing and the locating of ESTs. By 1998 Venter had established Celera Genomics with sequencing capacity fifty times greater than TIGR, and by June 17, 2000, he concluded a ninety percent complete account of the human genome. It was published in the February 16, 2001, issue of Science. Francis Collins (b. 1950) took over NCHGR leadership from Watson and found himself driving the public sector effort, racing with Venter toward the mapping finish line. Collins drew twenty laboratories worldwide with hundreds of researchers into the International Human Genome Sequencing Consortium, which he directed from his Washington office.

Collins repudiated patenting of raw genomic data and sought to place DNA data into the public domain as rapidly as possible so as to prevent private patenting. His philosophy was that the human genome is the common property of the whole human race. The public project finished almost simultaneously with the private, and the ninety percent complete Collins map appeared one day prior to Venter's on February 15, 2001, in Nature. Human DNA, as it turns out, is largely junk—that is, 98.6 percent does not code for proteins. Half of the junk DNA consists of repeated sequences of various types, most of which are parasitic elements inherited from our distant evolutionary past. Only 1.1 percent to 1.4 percent constitutes sequences that code for proteins that function as genes. Of dramatic interest is the number of genes in the human genome.

At the time of the announcement, Collins estimated there are 31,000 protein-encoding genes; he could actually list 22,000. Venter could provide a list of 26,000, to which he added an estimate of 10,000 additional possibilities. For round numbers, the estimate in 2001 stood at 30,000 human genes. This is philosophically significant, because when the project began in 1987 the anticipated number of genes was 100,000. It was further assumed that human complexity was lodged in the number of genes: the greater the number of genes, the greater the complexity. So, confusion appeared when, nearing the completion of HGP, scientists could find only a third of the anticipated number. Confusion was enhanced when the human genome was compared to a yeast cell with 6,000 genes, a fly with 13,000 genes, a worm with 26,000 genes, and a rice cell with 50,000 genes.

On the basis of the previous assumption, a grain of rice should be more complex than Albert Einstein. With the near completion of HGP, no longer could human uniqueness, complexity, or even distinctiveness be lodged in the number of genes. Collins began to speculate that perhaps what is distinctively human could be found not in the genes themselves but in the multiple proteins and the complexity of protein production. Culturally, DNA began to lose some of its magic, some of its association with human essence.

The Theology and Ethics of HGP

At the outset, HGP scientists anticipated ethical and public policy concerns; they were acutely aware that their research would have an impact on society and were willing to share responsibility for it. When in 1987 James Watson counseled the U.S. Department of Health and Human Services to appropriate the funds for what would become HGP, he recommended that three percent of the budget be allotted to study the ethical, legal, and social implications of genome research. Watson insisted that society learn to use genetic information only in beneficial ways; if necessary, the government should pass laws at both the federal and state levels to prevent invasions of privacy and discrimination on genetic grounds. Moral controversy broke out repeatedly during the near decade and a half of research.

Religious responses to the advancing frontier of genetic knowledge emerge mainly from people's concern to relieve human suffering and employ science to improve human health and wellbeing. A statement prepared by the National Council of Churches under the leadership of Union Seminary ethicist Roger L. Shinn affirms that churches in the United States must be involved with genetic research and therapy. "The Christian churches understand themselves as communities dedicated to obeying the will of God through service to others. The churches have a particular concern for those who are hurt or whose faith has been shaken, as demonstrated by the long history of the churches in providing medical care. Moreover, the churches have a mission to prevent suffering as well as to alleviate it."

In 1990 the Center for Theology and the Natural Sciences (CTNS) at the Graduate Theological Union (GTU) in Berkeley, California, obtained one of the first grants offered by the Ethical, Legal, and Social Issues (ELSI) division of NCHGR. A team of molecular biologists, behavioral geneticists, theologians, and bioethicists monitored the first years of HGP research to articulate theological and ethical implications of the new knowledge. Many religious and ethical issues eventually became public policy concerns. These are adumbrated below.

Genetic Discrimination

When Watson recommended the establishment of ELSI, the first public policy concern was what he called privacy, here called genetic discrimination. An anticipated and feared scenario took the following steps. As researchers identify and locate most if not all genes in the human genome that either condition or, in some cases, cause disease, the foreknowledge of an individual's genetic predisposition to expensive diseases could lead to loss of medical insurance and perhaps loss of employment opportunities. As HGP progressed, the gene for cystic fibrosis was found on chromosome seven and Huntington's chorea on chromosome four.

Alzheimer's disease was sought on chromosome twenty-one, and colon cancer on chromosome two. Disposition to muscular dystrophy, sickle-cell anemia, Tay Sachs disease, certain cancers, and numerous other diseases turned out to have locatable genetic origins. More knowledge is yet to come. When it comes, it may be accompanied by an inexpensive method for testing the genome of each individual to see if he or she has any genes for any diseases. Screening for all genetic diseases may become routine for newborns just as testing for phenylketonuria (PKU) has been since the 1960s. A person's individual genome might become part of a data bank to which each person, as well as health care providers, would have future access. The advantage is clear: Medical care from birth to grave could be carefully planned to delay onset, appropriately treat, and perhaps even prevent or cure genetically-based diseases.

Despite the promise for advances in preventative health care, fear arises due to practices of commercial insurance. Insurance works by sharing risk. When risk is uncertain to all, then all can be asked to contribute equally to the insurance pool. Premiums can be equalized. Once the genetic disorders of individuals become known, however, this could justify higher premiums for those demonstrating greater risk. The greater the risk, the higher the premium. Insurance may even be denied those whose genes predict extended or expensive medical treatment. Some ethicists are seeking protection from discrimination by invoking the principles of confidentiality and privacy. They argue that genetic testing should be voluntary and that the information contained in one's genome be controlled by the patient. This argument presumes that if information can be controlled, then the rights of the individual for employment, insurance, and medical care can be protected. There are grounds for thinking this approach will succeed.

Title VII of the 1964 Civil Rights Act restricts pre-employment questioning about work-related health conditions. Paragraph 102.b.4 of the Act potentially protects coverage for the employee's spouse and children. Legislative proposals during the 1990s and early 2000s seem to favor privacy. Other ethicists argue that privacy is a misguided cure for this problem. Privacy will fail, say its critics, because insurance carriers will press for legislation fairer to them, and eventually protection by privacy may slip. In addition, computer linkage makes it difficult to prevent the movement of data from hospital to insurance carrier and to anyone else bent on finding out. Most importantly, the privacy argument overlooks the principle that genome information should not finally be restricted. The more society knows, the better the health care planning can be. In the long run, what society needs is information without discrimination.

The only way to obtain this is to restructure the employment-insurance-health care relationship. The current structure makes it profitable for employers and insurance carriers to discriminate against individuals with certain genetic configurations—that is, it is in their best financial interest to limit or even deny health care. A restructuring is called for so that it becomes profitable to deliver, not withhold, health care. To accomplish this whole nation will have to become more egalitarian—that is, to think of the nation itself as a single community willing to care for its own constituents.

The Abortion Controversy

Given the divisiveness of the abortion controversy in the United States and certain other countries, fears arise over possible genetic discrimination in the womb or even prior to the womb in the petri dish. Techniques have been developed to examine in vitro fertilized (IVF) eggs as early as the fourth cell division in order to identify so-called defective genes, such as the chromosomal structure of Down syndrome. Prospective parents may soon routinely fertilize a dozen or so eggs in the laboratory, screen for the preferred genetic make up, implant the desired zygote or zygotes, and discard the rest. What will be the status of the discarded embryos? Might they be considered abortions? By what criteria does one define "defective" when considering the future of a human being? Should prospective parents limit themselves to eliminating "defective" children, or should they go on to screen for enhancing genetic traits such as blue eyes or higher intelligence? If so, might this lead to a new form of eugenics, to selective breeding based upon personal preference and prevailing social values? What will become of human dignity in all this?

Relevant here is that the legal precedent set by Roe v. Wade (1973) would not serve to legitimate discarding pre-implanted embryos. This Supreme Court case legalized the use of abortion to eliminate a fetus from a woman's body as an extension of a woman's right to determine what happens to her body. This would not apply to pre-implanted embryos, however, because they are life forms outside the woman's body.

The Roman Catholic tradition has set strong precedents regarding the practice of abortion. The Second Vatican Council document Gaudium ET spes (1965) states the position still held today: "... from the moment of its conception life must be guarded with the greatest care, while abortion and infanticide are unspeakable crimes." The challenge to ethicists in the Roman Catholic tradition in the near future will be to examine what transpires at the pre-implantation stage of the embryo to determine if the word abortion applies. If it does, this may lead to recommending that genetic screening be pushed back one step further, to the gamete stage prior to fertilization. The genetic make up of sperm and ovum separately could be screened, using acceptable gametes and discarding the unacceptable. The Catholic Health Association of the United States pushes back still further by recommending the development of techniques of gonadal cell therapy to make genetic corrections in the reproductive tissues of prospective parents long before conception takes place—that is, gametocyte therapy.

Genetic Determinism, Human Freedom, and the Gene Myth

Religious thinkers must deal not only with laboratory science but with the cultural interpretations of science, as well as public policy influenced by both. A cultural myth has grown up with media coverage of the Human Genome Project that assumes "it's all in the genes." DNA has emerged as a cultural icon, holding the "blueprint" for humanity or being thought of as the "essence" of what makes a person a person. Even though molecular biologists withdraw from such extreme forms of genetic determinism, a cultural myth has arisen. Some commentators refer to it as the strong genetic principle; others call it the gene myth.

Genes, Sin, Crime, and Racial Discrimination

The belief in determinism promulgated by the gene myth raises the question of moral and legal culpability. Does a genetic disposition to antisocial behavior make a person guilty or innocent before the law? Over the next decade legal systems will have to face a rethinking of the philosophical planks on which concepts such as free will, guilt, innocence, and mitigating factors have been constructed. There is no question that research into the connection between genetic determinism and human behavior will continue and new discoveries will become immediately relevant to the prosecution and defense of those accused of crimes. The focus will be on the concept of free will, because the assumption of the Western philosophy coming down from Augustine that underlies understanding of law is that guilt can only be assigned to a human agent acting freely.

The specter on the genetic horizon is that confirmable genetic dispositions to certain forms of behavior will constitute compulsion, and this will place a fork in the legal road: Either the courts declare the person with a genetic disposition to crime to be innocent and set him or her free, or the courts declare him or her so constitutionally impaired as to justify incarceration and isolation from the rest of society. The first fork would jeopardize the welfare of society; the second fork would violate individual rights.

That society needs to be protected from criminal behavior, and that such protection could be had by isolating individuals with certain genetic dispositions, leads to further questions regarding insanity and race. The issue of insanity arises because the genetic defense may rely upon precedents set by the insanity defense. The courts treat insanity with a focus on the insane person's inability to distinguish right from wrong when committing a crime.

When a defendant is judged innocent on these grounds, he or she is incarcerated in a mental hospital until the medical evaluators judge that the individual is cured. Once cured, the person may be released. In principle, such a person might never be judged "cured" and may spend more time in isolation than the prison penalty prescribed for the crime, maybe even the rest of his or her life. Should the genetic defense tie itself to the insanity defense, and if one's DNA is thought to last a lifetime, then the trip to the hospital may become the equivalent of a life sentence. In this way the genetic defense may backfire. With this prospect, we have returned to the specter of genetic discrimination.

The current discussion of possible genetic influence on antisocial behavior is riddled with fears of discrimination, especially its racial overtones. Because the percentage of black men among the population of incarcerated prisoners is growing, society could invoke the gene myth to associate genes with criminal predispositions and with race. A stigma against black people could arise, a presumption that they are genetically predisposed to crime. University of California sociologist Troy Duster fears that if we identify crime with genes and then genes with race, we may inadvertently provide a biological support for prejudice and discrimination.

The Gay Gene

Theological and ethical debate has arisen over the 1993 discovery of a possible genetic disposition to male homosexuality. Dean H. Hamer and his research team at the U.S. National Cancer Institute announced that they discovered evidence that male homosexuality—at least some male homosexuality—is genetic. Constructing family trees in instances where two or more brothers are gay combined with actual laboratory testing of homosexual DNA; Hamer located a region near the end of the long arm of the X chromosome that likely contains a gene influencing sexual orientation. Because men receive an X chromosome from their mother and a Y from their father (women receive two X's, one from each parent), this means that the possible gay gene is inherited maternally. Mothers can pass on the gay gene without themselves or their daughters being homosexual.

A parallel study of lesbian genetics is as yet incomplete; and the present study of gay men will certainly require replication and confirmation. Scientists do not yet have indisputable proof. The ethical implications, should a biological basis for homosexuality be confirmed, could point in more than one direction. The scientific fact does not itself determine the direction of the ethical interpretation of that fact. The central ethical question is this: Does the genetic disposition toward homosexuality make the bearer of that gene innocent or guilty? Two answers are logically possible. On the one hand, a homosexual man could claim that because he inherited the gay gene and did not choose a gay orientation by his own free will, he is innocent. The biological innocence position could be buttressed by an additional argument that homosexual activity is not itself sinful; it is simply one natural form of sexual expression among others.

One could go still further to say that because it is biologically inherited that it is God's will; that a person's homosexual predisposition is God's gift. On the other hand, one could follow the opposite road and identify the gay gene with a carnal disposition to sin.

Society could claim that the body inherited by each person belongs to who they are—people are determined at least in part by what their parents bequeathed them—and that an inherited disposition to homosexual behavior is just like other innate dispositions such as lust or greed, which are shared with the human race generally; all this constitutes the state of original sin into which we are born. Signposts point in both ethical directions. Beyond the question of guilt or innocence ethicists anticipate another issue, namely, the risk of stigma. Might the presence of the gay gene in an unborn fetus be considered a genetic defect and become grounds for abortion? Would routine genetic testing lead to a wholesale reduction of gay men in a manner parallel to that of children with Down syndrome? Would this count as class discrimination?

Somatic Therapy Versus Germ Line Enhancement

The debate over two distinctions—somatic versus germline intervention and therapy versus enhancement intervention—involves both secular and religious discussions. The term somatic therapy refers to the treatment of a disease in the body cells of a living individual by trying to repair an existing defect. The term germline therapy refers to intervention into the gametes, perhaps for the purpose of eliminating a gene such as that for cystic fibrosis so that it would not be passed along to future generations. Both somatic and germline therapies are conservative when compared to genetic enhancement. Enhancement goes beyond mere therapy for existing genes that may be a threat to health by selecting or adding genes to make an individual "superior" in some fashion. Enhancement might involve genetic engineering to increase bodily strength or intelligence or other socially desirable characteristics.

Ethical commentators almost universally agree that somatic therapy is morally desirable, and they look forward to the advances HGP will bring for expanding this important work. Yet they stop short of endorsing genetic selection and manipulation for the purposes of enhancing the quality of biological life for otherwise normal individuals or for the human race as a whole. New knowledge gained from HGP might locate genes that affect the brain's organization and structure so that careful engineering might lead to enhanced ability for abstract thinking or to other forms of physiological and mental improvement. Religious ethicists argue that somatic therapy should be pursued, but enhancement through germline engineering raises cautions about protecting human dignity. In a 1982 study, the World Council of Churches stated: "Somatic cell therapy may provide a good; however, other issues are raised if it also brings about a change in germline cells.

The introduction of genes into the germline is a permanent alteration. Nonetheless, changes in genes that avoid the occurrence of disease are not necessarily made illicit merely because those changes also alter the genetic inheritance of future generations. There is no absolute distinction between eliminating defects and improving heredity". The primary caution raised by the WCC here has to do with the lack of knowledge regarding the possible consequences of altering the human germline. The present generation lacks sufficient information regarding the long term consequences of a decision today that might turn out to be irreversible tomorrow. Thus, the WCC does not forbid forever germline therapy or even enhancement; rather, it cautions people to wait and see.

The Catholic Health Association is more positive: "Germline intervention is potentially the only means of treating genetic diseases that do their damage early in embryonic development, for which somatic cell therapy would be ineffective. Although still a long way off, developments in molecular genetics suggest that this is a goal toward which biomedicine could reasonably devote its efforts". Another reason for caution regarding germline enhancement, especially among the Protestants, is the specter of eugenics. The word eugenics connotes the ghastly racial policies of Nazism, and this accounts for much of today's mistrust of genetic science in Germany and elsewhere. No one expects a resurrection of the Nazi nightmare; yet some critics fear a subtle form of eugenics slipping in the cultural back door. The growing power to control the design of living tissue will foster the emergence of the image of the "perfect child," and a new social value of perfection will begin to oppress all those who fall short.

Gene Patenting

A controversy exploded in 1991 over gene patenting prompted by the filing for intellectual property rights by J. Craig Venter on nearly three thousand ESTs, expressed sequence tags. Each of these ESTs consisted of three hundred to five hundred base pairs made from cDNAs, copies of DNA sequences produced by polymerase chain reaction. ESTs are gene fragments, not whole genes; hence they mark the location of a gene but cannot identify gene function. Two issues became the focus of controversy. First, should the U.S. Patent and Trademark Office grant patents on genomic data?

Even though the patents applied for were on copies of DNA sequences, their only value was to report raw genomic information. It appeared to critics that these applications failed to meet the three patenting criteria: novelty, utility, and nonobviousness. Second, should the U.S. government apply for and receive such patents in competition with the private sector? Venter's first patent applications were filed while he was working on a government grant; later he moved to the private sector and continued filing for intellectual property rights on his discoveries. James Watson followed by Francis Collins at the NIH both opposed patenting raw genomic data.

Cloning

Technically known as "somatic cell nuclear transfer," cloning techniques were developed in 1996 by Ian Wilmut at the Roslin Institute near Edinburgh, Scotland. Wilmut announced the cloning of Dolly the sheep in February 1997. The scientific breakthrough consisted of returning an already differentiated DNA nucleus to its pre-differentiated state and then transferring it to an ennucleated oocyte to make an embryo. The new embryo thus contains the genome of the donor nucleus. In the worldwide controversy that broke out in 1997 and continues in bioethical discussion, the debate seems to bypass the science of nuclear transfer; rather, the focus is on producing multiple human beings with duplicate genomes.

Critics of reproductive cloning argue that children produced by cloning would suffer from loss of individuality, identity, and dignity. Roman Catholic critics along with Wilmut himself oppose human reproductive cloning on the grounds of safety—that is, the imperfect technology would lead to the destruction of many early embryos. Defenders of nuclear transfer research distinguish sharply between reproductive cloning, which they oppose, and therapeutic cloning, which is necessary for stem cell research.

Stem Cells

The isolation of human embryonic stem cells (hES cells) was accomplished in August 1997 by James Thomson at the University of Wisconsin on funds from the Geron Corporation. The hES cells are removed from the inner mass of the blastocyst, an embryo at four to six days old. When isolated and placed on a feeder tray, hES cells become immortal—that is, they divide indefinitely. In addition, they are pluripotent and able to differentiate into any and every tissue.

The research goal is to control gene expression so as to make designated tissue for rejuvenating human organs. Some progress in gene control has been achieved. The next hurdle to jump is histo-compatibility, namely, to avoid organ rejection by matching donor and recipient genetic codes. It is likely that experiments with somatic cell nuclear transfer will be required to attain histo-compatibility. Ethical objections to stem cell research from Roman Catholics center on destruction of blastocysts for research purposes. Ethical support for stem cell research stresses beneficence; it emphasizes the marvelous advances in human health and wellbeing that this medical science might offer the human race.

Theological Commitments to Human Dignity

Virtually all Roman Catholics and Protestants who take up the challenge of the new genetic knowledge seem to agree on a handful of theological axioms. First, they affirm that God is the creator of the world and, further, that God's creative work is ongoing. God continues to create in and through natural genetic selection and even through human intervention in the natural processes. Second, the human race is created in God's image. In this context, the divine image in humanity is tied to creativity. God creates; so do human beings. With increasing frequency, humans are described by theologians as co-creators with God, making their human contribution to the evolutionary process. In order to avoid the arrogance of thinking that humans are equal to the God who created them in the first place, people must add the term created to make the phrase created co-creators. This emphasizes human dependency on God while pointing to human opportunity and responsibility. Third, these religious documents place a high value on human dignity.

By dignity they mean what eighteenth-century German philosopher Immanuel Kant meant, namely, that each human being is treated as an end, not merely as a means to some further end. As church leaders respond responsibly to new developments in HGP, one thing can be confidently forecast: This affirmation of dignity will become decisive for thinking through the ethical implications of genetic engineering. Promoting dignity is a way of drawing an ethical implication from what the theologian can safely say, namely, that God loves each human being regardless of his or her genetic makeup and, therefore, people should love one another according to this model.

To commemorate the 50th anniversary of the discovery of DNA's structure, the human genome sequence and the Human Genome Project were declared complete on April 14, 2003. Using the "working draft" announced on February 12, 2001, scientists from around the world (the International Human Genome Sequencing Consortium) put draft fragments in order so that researchers could use the data "out of the box" without additional sequencing. "If you are looking for a disease gene, you can be confident that it exists in one continuous stretch of highly accurate sequence," said Dr. Francis Collins, director of the genome center at the U.S. National Institutes of Health.

The current vision for using the completed sequence flows along three themes, and includes "grand challenges" such as developing a catalog of genetic variation. Online resources such as Nature magazine's OmicsGateway (which includes A User's Guide to the Human Genome), the U.S. Department of Energy's DOEgenomes.org, and the U.S. National Human Genome Research Institute's genome.gov help scientists and the general public alike to track the status of these challenges. The ultimate success of the Human Genome Project resides in its celebration of the complexity of biology. "It is a rare and wonderful moment when success teaches us humility indeed, of all the benefits that genomics has bequeathed on us, this humility may ultimately prove to have been its greatest contribution."

Scientists throughout the world have embarked upon a long-term biological investigation that promises to revolutionize the decisions people make about their lives and lifestyles, the way doctors practice medicine, how scientists study biology, and the way we think of ourselves as individuals and as a species. It is called the Human Genome Project, and its ultimate goal is to map and determine the chemical sequence of the three billion nucleotide base pairs that comprise the human genome. These three billion base pairs include an estimated 50,000 to 100,000 genes. The rest of the genome - perhaps 95 percent of it - is nongenic sequences with unknown function, sometimes called "junk." Determining the order and organization of all this material has been likened to tearing six volumes of the Encyclopaedia Brittanica into pieces, then trying to put it all back together to read the information.

The effort could be well worth it, many scientists say, because it is expected to yield major insights into many common and complex diseases, including cancer, cardiovascular disease, and Alzheimer's disease. The Human Genome Project is not without controversy, however. Many scientists fear that funding for it will be diverted from other areas of research, rather than obtained from new funding sources. This has enlivened the debate about the relative value of "big" versus "small" science.

Also, the value of undertaking a complete sequencing of the genome has been questioned, especially given the high proportion of nongenic sequences. Advocates of the effort converted many critics by making two alterations in the original plan.

Plans were included to simultaneously determine the nucleotide sequence of the genomes of other organisms; this provides comparisons and points of reference for the human sequence. Second, in response to concerns about the high cost of developing technology to sequence the whole genome, the focus moved from large-scale sequencing to mapping the genome, which would hasten the search for disease genes. The ideal map would be both *genetic,* locating DNA markers and signposts, at closely spaced intervals along the chromosomes, and *physical,* indicating the exact distance between these markers, for descriptions and access points for genome mapping databases).

The United States Effort

The first serious discussions about sequencing the entire human genome occurred at a workshop at the University of California at Santa Cruz in 1985. A second workshop, organized by the U.S. Department of Energy (DOE) and held in March 1986, addressed the feasibility of an organized program. Shortly thereafter, DOE instituted its own genome project. Reports in early 1988 from the National Research Council (NRC) of the National Academy of Sciences (NAS) and Congress' Office of Technology Assessment, (OTA) served as catalysts, and in fiscal year 1988, the U.S. Congress officially launched the Human Genome Project by appropriating funds to both the Department of Energy and the National Institutes of Health (NIH).

To avoid potential congressional "meddling", NIH and DOE drafted a memorandum of understanding for interagency coordination in October 1988. The agencies then created both separate and joint committees, and working groups to administer the project. NIH established the Office of Human Genome Research in 1988 (directed by James D. Watson) to plan and coordinate NIH genome activities. That office evolved first into the National Center for Human Genome Research (NCHGR), an independent funding unit with authority to award grants and contracts, and subsequently into the National Human Genome Research Institute (NHGRI)). Institute status at the National Institutes of Health is necessary for NHGRI's director to coordinate genome research with other projects at NIH.

International Involvement

International involvement has increased steadily over the life of the project. The programs of the countries involved vary, depending on their particular concerns, capabilities and funding. The European Community also has played a role in the Human Genome Project. In 1988, the EC introduced a proposal entitled the "Predictive Medicine Programme." A few EC countries, notably Germany and Denmark, claimed the proposal lacked ethical sensitivity; objections to the possible eugenic implications of the program were especially strong in Germany. The initial proposal was dropped but later modified and adopted in 1990 as the "Human Genome Analysis Programme". This program committed substantial resources to the study of ethical issues.

The need for an organization to coordinate these multiple international efforts quickly became apparent. Thus the Human Genome Organization (HUGO), which has been called the "U.N. for the human genome," was born in the spring of 1988. Composed of a founding council of scientists from seventeen countries, HUGO's goal is to encourage international collaboration through coordination of research, exchange of data and research techniques, training, and debates on the implications of the projects. It has been suggested that the Human Genome Project will benefit not only industrialized countries but developing nations as well. In an effort to include these countries in the project and discussions about it, UNESCO assembled an advisory committee in 1988, to examine UNESCO's role in facilitating international dialogue and cooperation.

Ethical, Legal and Social Aspects

The Human Genome Project has generated widespread interest in a large spectrum of questions regarding the ethical, legal, and social implications of the existence and use of human genetic sequences. Many groups concur that sequencing the human genome does not raise ethical questions in and of itself. Questions center on how the information is used and its implications for individuals, society and the human species.

It is generally accepted that the questions rose by the accessibility of and increase in information generated by the Human Genome Project are not new. Rather, the volume, variety, and the ease with which such information can be obtained, and the vast number of people affected, make it imperative that the possible use or misuse of the project's findings be anticipated and addressed.

The ability to generate any individual's genetic profile raises important questions of privacy, confidentiality, ownership and autonomy. How should information be protected? Who should have access to the information and under what circumstances? What rights, if any, do employers, insurers, and family members have to an individual's genetic information?

Diagnosis of many genetic disorders will be possible before treatment becomes available. How will we resolve dilemmas raised by such a gap? In addition, the potential trend towards understanding diseases or traits in genetic terms may raise questions about human nature and our fundamental beliefs about us and our species. Will we view an individual as merely a product of interacting genes? How will we define normalcy, abnormalcy, or disability?

The recognition of the importance of such questions, and the increased dialogue surrounding them has resulted in an international commitment to and interest in addressing issues of ethical, legal, and social import. Many nations and organizations participating in the Human Genome Project have allocated funding and/or assembled committees to address such concerns. It is likely that these initial efforts will increase as national programs and the number of countries involved expands.

5

Full Genome Sequencing

Full genome sequencing (FGS), also known as whole genome sequencing, complete genome sequencing, or entire genome sequencing, is a laboratory process that determines the complete DNA sequence of an organism's genome at a single time. This entails sequencing all of an organism's chromosomal DNA as well as DNA contained in the mitochondria or chloroplast, depending respectively on whether the organism is an animal or plant. Almost any biological sample—evens a very small amount of DNA or ancient DNA—can provide the genetic material necessary for full genome sequencing. Such samples may include saliva, epithelial cells, bone marrow, hair (as long as the hair contains a hair follicle), seeds, plant leaves, or anything else that has DNA-containing cells. Because the sequence data that is produced can be quite large (for example, there are approximately three billion base pairs in each human genome), genomic data is stored electronically and requires a large amount of computing power and storage capacity. Full genome sequencing would have been nearly impossible before the advent of the microprocessor, computers, and the Information Age.

Full genome sequencing only refers to the laboratory process of deducing a person's entire genetic code and, on its own, may not contain any clinical assessment or useful clinical information. However, this may change over time as a large number of scientific studies continue to be published detailing clear associations between specific genetic variants and disease.

The first full genome sequenced was J. Craig Venter's. Although it was not known during the race to sequence the first entire human genome during the 1990s, it was later revealed that Celera Genomics' sequence was that of Venter, the company's chief executive officer. Since that time, many other full genomes have been sequenced, such as James Watson's, although as of March 2009 true commercialization of full genome sequencing has yet to be achieved.

New Techniques

One possible way to accomplish the cost-effective high-throughput sequencing necessary to accomplish full genome sequencing is by using Nanopore technology, which is a patented technology held by Harvard University and Oxford Nanopore and licensed to biotechnology companies. To facilitate their full genome sequencing initiatives, Illumina licensed nanopore sequencing technology from Oxford Nanopore and Sequenom licensed the technology from Harvard University. Another possible way to accomplish cost-effective high-throughput sequencing is by utilizing fluorophore technology.

Pacific Biosciences is currently using this approach in their SMRT (single molecule real time) DNA sequencing technology. Complete Genomics is developing DNA Nanoball (DNB) technology that is arranged on self-assembling arrays. Pyrosequencing is a method of DNA sequencing based on the sequencing by synthesis principle. The technique was developed by Pål Nyrén and his student Mostafa Ronaghi at the Royal Institute of Technology in Stockholm in 1996, and is currently being used by 454 Life Sciences in their effort to deliver an affordable, fast and highly accurate full genome sequencing platform.

Older Techniques

Full genome sequencing of the entire human genome was first accomplished in 2000 partly through the use of shotgun sequencing technology. While full genome shotgun sequencing for small (4000–7000 base pair) genomes was already in use in 1979, broader application benefited from pairwise end sequencing, known colloquially as double-barrel shotgun sequencing. As sequencing projects began to take on longer and more complicated genomes, multiple groups began to realize that useful information could be obtained by sequencing both ends of a fragment of DNA.

Although sequencing both ends of the same fragment and keeping track of the paired data was more cumbersome than sequencing a single end of two distinct fragments, the knowledge that the two sequences were oriented in opposite directions and were about the length of a fragment apart from each other was valuable in reconstructing the sequence of the original target fragment.

The first published description of the use of paired ends was in 1990 as part of the sequencing of the human HPRT locus, although the use of paired ends was limited to closing gaps after the application of a traditional shotgun sequencing approach. The first theoretical description of a pure pairwise end sequencing strategy, assuming fragments of constant length, was in 1991. In 1995 Roach et al introduced the innovation of using fragments of varying sizes, and demonstrated that a pure pairwise end-sequencing strategy would be possible on large targets. The strategy was subsequently adopted by The Institute for Genomic Research (TIGR) to sequence the entire genome of the bacterium Haemophilus influenzae in 1995, and then by Celera Genomics to sequence the entire fruit fly genome in 2000, and subsequently the entire human genome.

Applied Biosystems, now called Life Technologies, manufactured the shotgun sequencers utilized by both

Celera Genomics and The Human Genome Project. While shotgun sequencing was one of the first approaches utilized to successfully sequence the full genome of a human, it is too expensive and requires too long of a turn-around-time to be utilized for commercial purposes. Because of this, shotgun sequencing technology, even though it is still relatively 'new', is being displaced by technologies like pyrosequencing, SMRT sequencing, and nanopore technology.

Disruptive Technology

Full genome sequencing provides information on a genome that is orders of magnitude larger than that provided by the current leader in sequencing technology, DNA arrays. For humans, DNA arrays currently provides genotypic information on up to one million genetic variants, while full genome sequencing will provide information on all three billion base pairs in the human genome, or 3,000 times more data. Because of this, full genome sequencing will be disruptive to the DNA array markets once the accuracy (> 99.998%), precision (> 99.998%), and consistent reproducibility of extremely high-quality results (> 99.998%) is demonstrated and its cost becomes competitive with DNA arrays (less than $500 per sample)

It is unknown whether Agilent, another established DNA array manufacturer, is also working on full genome sequencing technologies or services. It is thought that Affymetrix, the pioneer of array technology in the 1990s, has fallen behind due to significant corporate and stock turbulence and is currently not working on any known full genome sequencing approach.

It is unknown what will happen to the DNA array market once full genome sequencing becomes commercially viable, especially when companies and laboratories providing this disruptive technology starts to realize economies of scale. It is postulated, however, that this new technology may significantly diminish the total market size for arrays and any other sequencing technology once it becomes commonplace for individuals and newborns to have their full genomes sequenced.

Societal Impact

Inexpensive, time-efficient full genome sequencing will be a major accomplishment not only for the field of Genomics, but for the entire human civilization because, for the first time, individuals will be able to have their entire genome sequenced. Utilizing this information, health care professionals, such as physicians and genetic counselors, will be greatly empowered by this information and be able to use it to predict what diseases a person may get in the future and attempt to either minimize the impact of that disease or avoid it altogether through the implementation of personalized, preventive medicine. Full genome sequencing will allow health care professionals to analyze the entire human genome of an individual and therefore detect all disease-related genetic variants, regardless of the genetic variant's prevalence or frequency.

This will enable the rapidly emerging medical fields of Predictive Medicine and Personalized Medicine and will mark a significant leap forward for the clinical genetic revolution. Illumina's CEO, Jay Flatley, stated in February 2009 that "A complete DNA read-out for every newborn will be technically feasible and affordable in less than five years, promising a revolution in healthcare" and that "by 2019 it will have become routine to map infants' genes when they are born."

Human Genome

The human genome is the genome of Homo sapiens, which is stored on 23 chromosome pairs. Twenty-two of these are autosomal chromosome pairs, while the remaining pair is sex-determining. The haploid human genome occupies a total of just over 3 billion DNA base pairs. The Human Genome Project produced a reference sequence of the euchromatic human genome, which is used worldwide in biomedical sciences. The haploid human genome contains an estimated 20,000–25,000 protein-coding genes, far fewer than had been expected before its sequencing.[1] In fact, only about 1.5% of the genome codes for proteins, while the rest consists of RNA genes, regulatory sequences, introns and (controversially) "junk" DNA.

Features

Chromosomes

There are 24 distinct human chromosomes: 22 autosomal chromosomes, plus the sex-determining X and Y chromosomes. Chromosomes 1–22 are numbered roughly in order of decreasing size. Somatic cells usually have 23 chromosome pairs: one copy of chromosomes 1–22 from each parent, plus an X chromosome from the mother and either an X or Y chromosome from the father, for a total of 46.

Genes

There are estimated 20,000–25,000 human protein-coding genes.. The estimate of the number of human genes has been repeatedly revised down from initial predictions of 100,000 or more as genome sequence quality and gene finding methods have improved, and could continue to drop further. Surprisingly, the number of human genes seems to be less than a factor of two greater than that of many much simpler organisms, such as the roundworm and the fruit fly.

However, human cells make extensive use of alternative splicing to produce several different proteins from a single gene, and the human proteome is thought to be much larger than those of the aforementioned organisms. Besides, most human genes have multiple exons, and human introns are frequently much longer than the flanking exons. Human genes are distributed unevenly across the chromosomes. Each chromosome contains various gene-rich and gene-poor regions, which seem to be correlated with chromosome bands and GC-content. The significance of these nonrandom patterns of gene density is not well understood. In addition to protein coding genes, the human genome contains thousands of RNA genes, including tRNA, ribosomal RNA, microRNA, and other non-coding RNA genes.

Regulatory Sequences

The human genome has many different regulatory sequences which are crucial to controlling gene expression. These are typically short sequences that appear near or within genes. A systematic understanding of these regulatory sequences and how they together act as a gene regulatory network is only beginning to emerge from computational, high-throughput expression and comparative genomics studies. Identification of regulatory sequences relies in part on evolutionary conservation.

The evolutionary branch between the human and mouse, for example, occurred 70–90 million years ago. So computer comparisons of gene sequences that identify conserved non-coding sequences will be an indication of their importance in duties such as gene regulation. Another comparative genomic approach to locating regulatory sequences in humans is the gene sequencing of the puffer fish. These vertebrates have essentially the same genes and regulatory gene sequences as humans, but with only one-eighth the "junk" DNA. The compact DNA sequence of the puffer fish makes it much easier to locate the regulatory genes.

Genetic Disorders

Most aspects of human biology involve both genetic (inherited) and non-genetic (environmental) factors. Some inherited variation influences aspects of our biology that are not medical in nature (height, eye color, ability to taste or smell certain compounds, etc). Moreover, some genetic disorders only cause disease in combination with the appropriate environmental factors (such as diet). With these caveats, genetic disorders may be described as clinically defined diseases caused by genomic DNA sequence variation. In the most straightforward cases, the disorder can be associated with variation in a single gene.

For example, cystic fibrosis is caused by mutations in the CFTR gene, and is the most common recessive disorder in caucasian populations with over 1300 different mutations known. Disease-causing mutations in specific genes are usually severe in terms of gene function, and are fortunately rare, thus genetic disorders are similarly individually rare. However, since there are many genes that can vary to cause genetic disorders, in aggregate they comprise a significant component of known medical conditions, especially in pediatric medicine? Molecularly characterized genetic disorders are those for which the underlying causal gene has been identified, currently there are approximately 2200 such disorders annotated in the OMIM database.

Studies of genetic disorders are often performed by means of family-based studies. In some instances population based approaches are employed, particularly in the case of so-called founder populations such as those in Finland, French-Canada, Utah, Sardinia, etc. Diagnosis and treatment of genetic disorders are usually performed by a geneticist-physician trained in clinical/medical genetics. The results of the Human Genome Project are likely to provide increased availability of genetic testing for gene-related disorders, and eventually improved treatment. Parents can be screened for hereditary conditions and counselled on the consequences, the probability it will be inherited, and how to avoid or ameliorate it in their offspring.

As noted above, there are many different kinds of DNA sequence variation, ranging from complete extra or missing chromosomes down to single nucleotide changes. It is generally presumed that much naturally occurring genetic variation in human populations is phenotypically neutral, i.e. has little or no detectable effect on the physiology of the individual (although there may be fractional differences in fitness defined over evolutionary time frames). Genetic disorders can be caused by any or all known types of sequence variation. To molecularly characterize a new genetic disorder, it is necessary to establish a causal link between a particular genomic sequence variant and the clinical disease under investigation. Such studies constitute the realm of human molecular genetics.

With the advent of the Human Genome and International HapMap Project, it has become feasible to explore subtle genetic influences on many common disease conditions such as diabetes, asthma, migraine, schizophrenia, etc. Although some causal links have been made between genomic sequence variants in particular genes and some of these diseases, often with much publicity in the general media, these are usually not considered to be genetic disorders per se as their causes are complex, involving many different genetic and environmental factors. Thus there may be disagreement in particular cases whether a specific medical condition should be termed a genetic disorder.

The Diploid Genome Sequence of an Individual Human

Each of our genomes is typically composed of DNA packaged into two sets of 23 chromosomes; one set inherited from each parent whose own DNA is a mosaic of preceding ancestors. As such, the human genome functions as a diploid entity with phenotypes arising due to the sometimes complex interplay of alleles of genes and/or their noncoding functional regulatory elements. The diploid nature of the human genome was first observed as unbanded and banded chromosomes over 40 years ago, and karyotyping still predominates in clinical laboratories as the standard for global genome interrogation.

With the advent of molecular biology, other techniques such as chromosomal fluorescence in situ hybridization (FISH) and microarray-based genetic analysis provided incremental increases in the resolution of genome analysis. Notwithstanding these approaches, we suspect that only a small proportion of genetic variation is captured for any sample in any one set of experiments. Over the past decade, with the development of high-throughput DNA sequencing protocols and advanced computational analysis methods, it has been possible to generate assemblies of sequences encompassing the majority of the human genome. Two versions of the human genome currently available are products of the Human Genome Sequencing Consortium and Celera Genomics, derived from clone-based and random whole genome shotgun sequencing strategies, respectively.

The Human Genome Sequencing Consortium assembly is a composite derived from haploids of numerous donors, whereas the Celera version of the genome is a consensus sequence derived from five individuals. Both versions almost exclusively report DNA variation in the form of single nucleotide polymorphisms (SNPs). However smaller-scale (<100 bp) insertion/deletion sequences (indels) or large-scale structural variants also contribute to human biology and disease and warrant an extensive survey. The ongoing analyses of these DNA sequence resources have offered an unprecedented glimpse into the genetic contribution to human biology.

The simplification of our collective genetic ancestry to a linear sequence of nucleotide bases has permitted the identification of functional sequences to be made primarily through sequence-based searching alignment tools. This revealed an unexpected paucity of protein coding genes (20,000–25,000) residing in less than 2% of the DNA examined, suggesting that alternative transcription and splicing of genes are equally important in development and differentiation. The sequencing of DNA of various eukaryotic genomes, such as for murine and primate as well as many others, has enabled a comparative genomics strategy to refine the identification of orthologous genes. These genomic datasets have also enabled the identification of additional functional sequence such as *cis*-regulatory DNA as well as both noncoding and microRNA.

Building on the existing genome assemblies, numerous initiatives have explored variation at the population level, in particular to generate markers and maps as a means of understanding how sequence variation evolves and can contribute to phenotype. The initial drafts of the two human genomes provided an excess of 2.4 million SNPs providing a platform for the initial phase of the HapMap project. This ambitious project initially catalogued genetic variation at more than 1.2 million loci in 269 humans of four ethnicities, enabling a definition of common haplotypes and resulting in tag SNP sets for these populations. The use of these data has already allowed the mapping and identification of susceptibility genes and loci involved in complex diseases such as asthma, age related macular degeneration, and type II diabetes.

Notwithstanding, there are limitations with current SNP-based genome-wide association studies, because they rely on reconstructing haplotypes based on population data and can be uninformative or misleading in regions of low linkage disequilibrium (LD). Further, association studies have been designed to detect common disease variants and are not optimized to detect rare etiological variants. The ability to generate a diploid genome structure via haplotype phasing for the HapMap samples is limited by the SNPs that were genotyped and their spacing. By using LD measures, it was possible to identify diploid blocks of DNA averaging 16.3 kb for Caucasians (CEU), 7.3 kb for Yorubans (YRI), and 13.2 kb for grouped Han Chinese and Japanese (CHB+JPT). However, LD varies across the genome, and regions of low LD, i.e., high recombination, cannot be represented by haplotype blocks.

Furthermore, these diploid blocks are incomplete because there may be unknown variants between the SNP loci sampled. These results do not permit a comprehensive definition of the sequence present at each allele nor the information that produces the relevant allelic combinations, which are essential in identifying the differences of biological information encoded by the diploid state.

The ability to perform, in a practical manner, whole-genome sequencing in large disease populations would enable the construction of haplotypes from individuals' genomes, thus phasing all variant types throughout the genome without assumptions about population history. Clearly, to enable the forthcoming field of individualized genomic medicine, it is important to represent and understand the entire diploid genetic component of humans, including all forms of genetic variation in nucleotide sequences, as well as epigenetic effects.

To understand fully the nature of genetic variation in development and disease, indeed the ideal experiment would be to generate complete diploid genome sequences from numerous controls and cases. Here we report our endeavor to fully sequence a diploid human genome. We used an experimental design based on very high quality Sanger-based whole-genome shotgun sequencing, allowing us to maximize coverage of the genome and to catalogue the vast majority of variation within it.

We discovered some 4.1 million variants in this genome, 30% of which were not described previously, furthering our understanding of genetic individuality. These variants include SNPs, indels, inversions, segmental duplications, and more complex forms of DNA variation.

We used the variant set coupled with the sequence read information and mate pairs to build long-range haplotypes, the boundaries of which provide coverage of 11,250 genes (58% of all genes). In this manner we achieved our goal of the construction of a diploid genome, which we hope will serve as a basis for future comparison as more individual genomes are produced.

Donor Pedigree and Karyotype

The individual whose genome is described in this report is J. Craig Venter, who was born on 14 October 1946, a self-identified Caucasian male. The DNA donor gave full consent to provide his DNA for study via sequencing methods and to disclose publicly his genomic data in totality. The collection of DNA from blood with attendant personal, medical, and phenotypic trait data was performed on an ongoing basis. Ethical review of the study protocol was performed annually. Additionally, we provide here an initial foray into individualized genomics by correlating genotype with family history and phenotype; however, a more extensive analysis will be presented elsewhere.

The donor has three siblings and one biological son, his father died at age 59 of sudden cardiac arrest. There are documented cases of family members with chronic disease including hypertension and ovarian and skin cancer. According to the genealogical record, the donor's ancestors can be traced back to 1821 (paternal) and the 1700s (maternal) in England. Genotyping and cluster analysis of 750 unique SNP loci discovered through this project support that the donor is indeed 99.5% similar to individuals of European descent, consistent with self-reporting. This is further corroborated by an extensive five-generation family history provided by the donor (unpublished data). Cytogenetic analysis through G-banded karyotyping and spectral karyotypic chromosome imaging reveals no obvious chromosomal abnormalities that need to be considered in interpretation of genome assembly results or phenotypic association analyses.

Genome Sequencing and Assembly

The assembly, herein referred to as HuRef, was derived of approximately 32 million sequence reads generated by a random shotgun sequencing approach using the open-source Celera Assembler. The approach used is similar in many respects to the whole-genome shotgun assembly (WGSA) reported previously, but there are three major differences:

i. HuRef was assembled entirely from shotgun reads from a single individual, whereas WGSA was based on shotgun reads from five individuals, albeit the majority of reads were from the same individual as HuRef;
ii. The approximate depth of sequence coverage for HuRef was 7.5 versus 5.3 for WGSA, although the clone coverage was about the same for both; and
iii. The release of Celera Assembler as an open-source project has allowed us and others to continue to improve the assembly algorithms.

As a consequence, we made modifications for the specification of consensus sequence differences found at distinct alleles. The multiple sequence alignment methodology was improved and reads were grouped by allele, thus allowing the determination of alternate consensus sequences at variant sites.

HuRef is a high-quality draft genome sequence as evidenced from the contiguity statistics. Improving the assembly algorithms and increasing the sequencing depth of coverage (compared to WGSA) resulted in a 68% decrease in the number of gaps within scaffolds from 206,552 (WGSA) to 66,815 (HuRef) as previously predicted. We also observed a more than 4-fold increase in the N50 contig size (the length such that 50% of all base pairs are contained in contigs of the given length or larger) to 106 kb (HuRef) from 23 kb (WGSA). We used a fairly standard, but arbitrary, cutoff of 3,000 bp (similar to what was used for WGSA) to distinguish between scaffolds that were part of the HuRef assembly proper versus partially assembled and poorly incorporated sequence.

This resulted in 4,528 scaffolds (containing 2,810 Mb) of which 553 scaffolds were at least 100 kb in size (containing 2,780 Mb), whereas WGSA had 4,940 scaffolds (containing 2,696 Mb) of which 330 scaffolds were at least 100 kb (containing 2,669 Mb). The scaffold lengths for HuRef (N50 = 19.5 Mb) were somewhat shorter than WGSA (N50 = 29 Mb) primarily due to the difference in insert size for bacterial artificial chromosome (BAC) end mate pairs—HuRef 91 kb versus WGSA > 150 kb. We determined that 144 of the 553 large HuRef scaffolds could be joined by two or more of the WGSA BAC mate pairs, and 98 more by a single WGSA BAC mate pair, suggesting that use of large insert BAC libraries (>150 kb) would generate larger scaffolds.

Assembly-to-Assembly Mapping

Genomic variation was observed by two approaches. First, we identified heterozygous alleles within the HuRef sequence. This variation represents differences in the maternal and paternal chromosomes. In addition, a comparison between HuRef and the National Center for Biotechnology Information (NCBI) version 36 human genome reference assembly, herein referred to as a one-to-one mapping, also served as a source for the identification of genomic variation. These comparisons identified a large number of putative SNPs as well as small, medium, and large insertion/deletion events and some major rearrangements described below. For the most part, the one-to-one mapping showed that both sequences are highly congruent with very large regions of contiguous alignment of high fidelity thus enabling the facile detection of DNA variation.

The one-to-one mapping to NCBI version 36 (hereafter NCBI) was also used to organize HuRef scaffolds into chromosomes. HuRef scaffolds were only mapped to HuRef chromosomes if they had at least 3,000 bp that mapped and the scaffold was mostly not contained within a larger scaffold. With the exception of 12 chimeric joins, all scaffolds were placed in their entirety with no rearrangement onto HuRef chromosomes. The 12 chimeric regions represent the misjoining of a small number of chimeric scaffold/contigs by the Celera Assembly, as detected with mate pair patterns, and are also apparent by comparison to another assembly.

The 12 chimeric joins in the HuRef scaffolds were split when these scaffolds were assigned to build HuRef chromosomes. Inversions and translocations within the nonchimeric scaffolds relative to NCBI are thus maintained within the HuRef chromosomes. The final set of 24 HuRef chromosomes were thus assembled from 1,408 HuRef assembly scaffolds and contain 2,782 Mb of ordered and oriented sequence. The NCBI autosomes are on average 98.3% and 97.1% represented by runs and matches, respectively, in the one-to-one mapping to HuRef scaffolds. A match is a maximal high-identity local alignment, usually terminated by indels or sequence gaps in one of the assemblies. Runs may include indels and are monotonically increasing or decreasing sets of matches (linear segments of a match dot plot) with no intervening matches from other runs on either axis.

The Y chromosome is 59% covered by the one-to-one mapping due to difficulties when producing comparison between repeat rich chromosomes. In addition, the Y chromosome is more poorly covered because of the difficulties in assembling complex regions with sequencing depth of coverage only half that of the autosomal portion of the genome. The X chromosome coverage with HuRef scaffolds is at 95.2%, which is typical of the coverage level of autosomes (mean 98.3% using runs). However it is clear that the X chromosome has more gaps, as evidenced by the coverage with matches (89.4%) compared with the mean coverage of autosomes using matches (97.1%). The overall effects of lower sequence coverage on chromosomes X and Y are clearly evident as a sharp increase in number of gaps per unit length and shorter scaffolds compared to the autosomes. Similarity between the sex chromosomes is another source of assembly and mapping difficulties.

For example, there is a 1.5-Mb scaffold that maps equally well to identical regions of the X and Y chromosomes and therefore cannot be uniquely mapped to either. From our one-to-one mapping data, we are also able to detect the enrichment of large segmental duplications on Chromosomes 9, 16, and 22, resulting in reduced coverage based on difficulties in assembly and mapping. Since NCBI, WGSA, and HuRef are all incomplete assemblies with sequence anomalies, assembly-to-assembly mappings also reflect issues of completeness and correctness. We compared three sets of chromosome sequences to evaluate this issue NCBI with the exclusion of the small amount of unplaced sequences, HuRef, and WGSA were thus compared in a pairwise manner.

The comparison of WGSA and HuRef revealed 83 Mb more sequence in HuRef in matched segments of these genomes. This sequence is predominantly from HuRef that fills gaps in WGSA. Comparisons of HuRef and WGSA to NCBI showed the considerable improvement of HuRef over WGSA. Correspondingly, in HuRef there are approximately 120 Mb of additional aligned sequence, composed of 47 Mb of HuRef sequence that aligns to NCBI that was not aligned in WGSA and 73 Mb within aligned regions that fill gaps in WGSA. This comparison also showed an improvement factor of two in rearrangement differences (order and orientation) from WGSA to HuRef when mapped to the NCBI reference genome at small (<5 kb), medium (5–50 kb), and large (>50 kb) levels of resolution.

HuRef includes 9 Mb of unmatched sequences that fills gaps in NCBI or are identified as indel variants. An additional 14 Mb of HuRef chromosome sequence outside of aligned regions with NCBI represents previously unknown human genome sequence. The large regions of novel HuRef sequence are identified to be either:

a. Gap filling or insertions,
b. Unaligned NCBI chromosome regions, or
c. Large scaffolds not mapped to NCBI chromosomes. Some of these were investigated using FISH analysis and are discussed below. Although we were able to organize HuRef scaffolds into HuRef chromosome sequence, all of the subsequent analyses in this report were accomplished using HuRef scaffold sequences.

Identification of DNA Variants

Variant Identification Internal to the One-to-one Map

The HuRef assembly and the one-to-one mapping between the HuRef genome and the NCBI reference genome resulted in the identification of 5,061,599 putative SNPs, heterozygous indels, and a variety of multi-nucleotide variations events, of which 62% are in the database for DNA variants. A significant fraction of these putative variants resulted from sequence reads with variant base having reduced quality value (QV) scores, the presence of variants in homopolymer runs and erroneous base calls at the beginning and end of reads. The inclusion of these reads was important to the assembly process, and therefore we chose to perform post-assembly processing to filter these variants to reduce false positives while limiting false negatives.

The filters deemed most productive in creating a high-confidence variant set involved the application of a minimal QV threshold and testing for the location of a variant in sequence read. In addition, we applied the filter that a variant required supporting evidence from at least two reads and that the second allele had a minimum fraction of representative reads (20% reads with minor allele for heterozygous SNP and 25% for heterozygous indels. After applying the filters, 81% of heterozygous indels, 29% of heterozygous SNPs, 7% of homozygous SNPs, and 19% homozygous indels were removed from the initial set. The filtering mainly affects heterozygous variants by reducing the number of reads that can be used for support. The cumulative application of the filters generated a set of variants from which a subset of 95,733 could be combined further into clusters. The first case where variants were clustered was when two SNPs were within 2 bp of each other.

We clustered these, because there was more accuracy in classifying whether the variant caused a change in protein coding and not because they necessarily represent single mutational events. The second scenario for clustering involved non-SNP variants within 10 bp of other non-SNP variants, such as indels or complex variants. We decided to cluster these variants because extensive manual inspection showed that closely spaced indels were frequently better defined as one variant after realignment. Consequently, the clustering of variant positions was coupled with a localized realignment of sequence reads to define either two distinct alleles or haplotypes. Overall, the filtering and clustering refinements that were applied to the "raw" variant set resulted in a set of 3,325,530 variants within the one-to-one HuRef-to-NCBI mapping, of which 85% were found in dbSNP.

Variant Identification External to the One-to-one Map

The one-to-one mapping of HuRef to NCBI produced approximately 150 Mb of unaligned HuRef sequence inclusive of partially mapped and nonmapped HuRef scaffolds. Within this unaligned HuRef sequence, we identified 233,796 heterozygous variants including SNPs, indels, and complex variants after application of the same filters described above.

Other sources of variant external to the one-to-one mapping between the HuRef and NCBI human genome assemblies are putative homozygous insertions, deletions, and inversions, of which 693,941 were detected. This number of putative insertions and deletions was reduced by 19% by the application of a series of filters designed to eliminate the bulk of spurious variation.

Therefore, variants were not called at the read margins (thresholds were the same as previously used for SNP and indels internal to the HuRef-NCBI map), and any identified variants required the supporting evidence of at least two reads and one satisfied mate pair with no ambiguous bases constituting the sequence of the insertion or deletion. In addition to the aforementioned filtering approach, a small fraction (1%) of the 693,941 putative homozygous insertion/ deletion variants were subsequently characterized as heterozygous variants.

This was accomplished by finding exact matches of 100-bp sequence 52 and 32 of the insertion point sequence and the deletion sequence in both HuRef scaffolds and unassembled reads. This fraction of heterozygotes is likely to be a conservative estimate of the total number of true heterozygotes.

The alternate alleles of these heterozygous variants were primarily found (96% of the time) in scaffolds less than 5,000 bp long or in unassembled reads.

This highlights the value of small scaffolds and unassembled reads in defining the variant set in an assembled genome and suggests that these elements are a rich source of genomic variation.

The Human Genome Initiative and Theological Anthropology

The Human Genome Initiative and the Body

The Human Genome Initiative (or Project) represents an ambitious attempt to map the entire genetic structure of human beings. This effort is not concentrated in a single lab, but refers to work taking place all over the world. Begun in 1988, it is projected to span 15 years and cost $3 billion, of which $200 million will be spent at labs around the United States. The basic goal of the project is to increase knowledge of humanity, or in the words of co-founder, James Watson, "to find out what being human is." The project proposes to do this by mapping the human genome, which contains an estimated 100,000 genes.

To give some sense of how ambitious the project is, it has been called "biology's moon shot," and "the Holy Grail of genetics." Much of the technology needed to accomplish its goal will have to be invented as the project unfolds.

The Human Genome Initiative was funded, after several years of debate, largely because of the anticipated practical payoffs. It promises to enable physicians and scientists better to diagnose and treat what are considered to be genetic disorders. Already, at a cost less than anticipated and at a pace much quicker than expected, the project has begun to fulfill some of those promises. People working at several of the centers which make up the Human Genome Initiative have discovered genes which seem to predispose some people to certain inherited forms of breast and cervical cancer, as well as the loci for diseases such as cystic fibrosis, Fragile X Syndrome, myotonic dystrophy and others.

In all, some 50 diseases causing genes have been identified and tests developed for a dozen genetic disorders. In addition to the therapeutic gains expected from the project, another anticipated payoff to the Human Genome Initiative is increased understanding of genetic bases of behavior, such as alcoholism and homosexuality. It goes without saying that the Human Genome Initiative has generated a vast amount of literature thus far, and that more will be forthcoming as the project progresses. Much of the theological literature has concentrated on identifying and responding to ethical concerns about how the knowledge produced may impact on matters such as abortion, privacy and personal responsibility.

Missing in the literature, however, is any extended and explicit discussion of how the Human Genome Initiative will impact our philosophical and theological understandings of human embodiment. To be sure, the ethical and theological directions taken in the literature have stressed that human beings are deeply embedded in a biocultural world, but they have had little to say about how we are to understand, experience and understand our experiences of the human body. This gap is a bit surprising, since Michael Polanyi and, more recently, numerous feminist thinkers has suggested that human embodiment is vitally important to human existence and self-understanding. For Polanyi, the biological or physical body is the basic building block for all knowledge. It is the means by which we discover, explore and learn about the world around us.

As he puts it, "Our body is the ultimate instrument of all our external knowledge, whether intellectual or practical. In all our waking moments, we are relying on our awareness of contacts of our body with things outside for attending to these things." As Polanyi describes the process of knowing, the body provides the means of proximal or subsidiary awareness, an awareness to which we seldom pay attention, but by which we achieve distal or focal awareness of things which exist beyond ourselves. But that is not all Polanyi says about the body. He refuses to separate the biological and cultural, by insisting that both dimensions of human existence are thoroughly intertwined. The body, as the means by which we attend to other things, can be extended in numerous ways, such as through the use of tools and the development of language. Language development provides a clear example of how body and culture are connected.

The precise vocabulary and grammatical structure of language is specific to culture, but language builds on physical capacities for making and shaping sounds, extending them to create meaning.

In short, the physical body is best understood as part of a multilevel system which allows for the emergence of properties and skills that cannot woodenly be predicted from the properties of the physical body. In sum, one might conclude that for Polanyi the body is an important part of human existence, and as the basic instrument for human knowing, not one to be trifled with lightly. In a manner reminiscent of Polanyi, Beverly Wildung Harrison talks about the body as the means or instrument by which we engage, indwell and otherwise come to know the world around us.

Furthermore, she identifies embodiment as one of the base points of feminist theory, an emphasis designed to help overcome the mind/body dualism of our intellectual and cultural heritage. These perspectives have not won the day on this issue, nor have they brought this insight to bear on the topic of the Human Genome Initiative or genetics, so far as I can find. This is unfortunate, because such ideas might deepen the ethical and theological reflections on the Human Genome Initiative. Rather, it is to explore ways in which the Human Genome Initiative might impact our notions of embodiment and put those ways into conversation with some options in contemporary theological anthropologies, all the while bringing Polanyian insights to bear on the conversation.

Two possible points of impact immediately suggest themselves. First, the Human Genome Initiative's findings might contribute to a richer understanding of the human body. At the same time, the Human Genome Initiative might threaten a full understanding of embodiment by reinforcing both a reductionistic view of human being in which we are nothing but our genes and dominant construals of the body as an object to be manipulated and commodified. These dual concerns suggest a two-part agenda. First, I will set out ways in which genetic knowledge can illumine theological understandings of the body by putting the theological anthropologies of Karl Rahner, Wolfhart Pannenberg and Stanley Hauerwas into conversation with issues raised by the Human Genome Initiative.

The ambiguous potential of the Human Genome Initiative further suggests that we should explore potential constraints or checks which might minimize the negatives. Thus, drawing from the work of James William McClendon, I set out ways in which theological understandings of the body, especially as created, redeemed and resurrected, can generate a critical perspective on projects such as this. This chapter thus aspires to serve as a model for mutually-critical and open dialogue between the disciplines. Often, the dialogue is carried on in such a way that one partner gets the upper hand.

The Human Genome Initiative

Clearly, the kind of knowledge of what it means to be human sought by the Human Genome Initiative is knowledge of the body, of the corporeal, of the stuff which makes us up. The assumption is that such knowledge is available to us and valuable for us to hold. Such an assumption challenges many contemporary theological anthropologies; I shall briefly survey three of the more influential ones. Karl Rahner is the first of these theologians and is important because of his place among influential contemporary Roman Catholic thinkers. He is important also because he has addressed issues of genetics which touch on the promise and peril of the Human Genome Initiative in such a way as to converse with the sciences.

As Rahner sets out his theological anthropology, he emphasizes the capacities of human beings for self-transcendence, for self actualization and for freedom. Human existence is, in Rahner's words "open and in determined," i.e., open to the infinite horizon which ultimately is fulfilled by God. He thus counsels against simple condemnation of genetic research and its application, calling it "symptomatic of a cowardly and comfortable conservatism hiding behind misunderstood Christian ideals." He goes on to suggest that genetic self-manipulation, the form which human freedom takes in our time, is indeed required by that freedom, christianly understood. To be fair to Rahner, we must note that he does acknowledge, here and there, that this freedom is neither absolute nor abstract but is mediated and qualified by "materiality and history." Thus, Rahner finds built-in checks to what we can do, checks which take the form of biological, psychological and social laws, as well as the ultimate horizon which we call God.

More importantly, the limit to legitimate interventions comes when those interventions threaten humanity's transcendent nature. In short, he offers some qualifications to our freedoms to do what we wish with ourselves, which leaves us with an uneasy tension between two affirmations: material givenness and transcendental freedom.

In contrast to Rahner, Wolfhart Pannenberg explicitly sets out to integrate the work of the sciences, particularly biology, psychology cultural anthropology and sociology, into his theological anthropology. Here, I shall focus only on his appropriation of biology. In that realm, Pannenberg draws upon discussions of human uniqueness in order to establish that human instincts "exist in only singularly rudimentary and attenuated form" and therefore that human beings are uniquely "open to the world." Thus, he concludes that whatever innate dispositions to behavior exist in human beings, they are significant only for providing "the abiding point of departure for the human adventure of self transcendence and historicity." In the end, the general shape of Pannenberg's anthropology, although rooted in biological sciences, differs little from Rahner's.

For both, the essence of human existence is its openness to the future. Biological givens, the stuff which the Human Genome Initiative investigates, provide—at best— the launching pad which makes possible the exercise of our freedom and openness. Both Rahner and Pannenberg thus offer what we might call anthropology of transcendence. Stanley Hauerwas operates with a theological anthropology which contrasts nicely with those of Rahner and Pannenberg. Instead of their transcendental anthropologies, Hauerwas offers what we might call a socio-historical anthropology. The titles of two early essays capture the core of his anthropology: "The Self as Story" and "The Virtues and Our Communities: Human Nature as History." Too oversimplify his position, human life is constituted and oriented by the stories which we learn from the communities to which we belong.

Ian Burns summarizes Hauerwas's understanding of the self nicely, saying that for Hauerwas, "the self is neither a transcendental essence existing prior to human social action, nor describable in purely naturalistic terms but is constituted within the discursive space of moral meaning embodied in various social practices and narrative traditions."Not all that surprisingly given our previous sketches, we find little room for—or even mention of—the biological side of human existence in Hauerwas's work—with one surprising and suggestive exception. In an essay on medical ethics, Hauerwas talks about "the wisdom of the body." In this context, the body serves his argument in several ways. He describes the body as the source of its own healing. It stands outside both physician and patient as an authority to which both must defer. The body further teaches us our finitude and limitations. Finally, it forces us to face our need for one another and drives us into community.

In short, the body functions for Hauerwas, in the end, as the goad which reminds us of our creatureliness, and drives us into the community which trains us in the virtues which enable us to live truthfully as creatures. We have here then three examples of contemporary and widely-discussed theological anthropologies.

In spite of important differences between these various figures, all of them end up ignoring the biological rootedness of the human body. From the perspective of Human Genome Initiative supporters, this gap will be most distressing. If work in human genetics is correct and there are genetic links to diseases, as well as certain behaviors, such as alcoholism or sexual orientation, then notions of radical transcendental freedom, as well as radical social formation, will have to be qualified.

Such anthropologies will also be suspect from the perspective of those informed by Polanyi, since they fail to register two facts about the body. The first is how it is the foundation for all human knowledge. The second is that the body exists as part of a complex, hierarchically-ordered system. Again, from Polanyi's perspective, the body should neither be seen as the only word on human existence, nor as an insignificant facet. Rahner and Pannenberg's emphasis on transcendence focuses attention on the individual self, whereas Hauerwas's strict attention to community all obscure the complex relationship between body, society and human possibilities for growth and transformation which Polanyi nicely registers. Interestingly, other work in the natural sciences supports Polanyi's views.

The picture that begins to emerge is that our bodies, especially as constituted by its genes, serve as both the basis for our higher level activities and as our connection to the rest of the world around us. It is worth calling attention to the fact that higher level processes such as thought emerge out of and are dependent upon biological and chemical processes, knowledge of which does not fully explain the phenomenon of thought.

It is also worth noting that human beings share more than 99 percent of their genetic makeup with African chimpanzees and gorillas and that investigation into the molecular structure of proteins indicate close kinship between human beings and other living creatures. The Human Genome Initiative may teach another, even more sobering lesson to theologians. Rather than simply providing a launching pad for human powers, human biology and genetics may place some boundaries around human possibilities.

The Human Genome Initiative and its offshoots therefore take on theological importance in helping to qualify exaggerated or misplaced claims. Clearly, there must be more to the self than simply freedom or social formation at work in human existence. There is something there for that social formation to work on and with and to which it is responsive. James William McClendon is one theologian who would support such an observation.

His work is notable in this context because it contains important affinities to Polanyi's views in that he seeks to take the body seriously and to learn from the natural sciences. Additionally, McClendon does all this at the same time that he, like Hauerwas, is committed to maintaining vigorous Christian convictions and identity. The focal point of McClendon's discussion of the body lies in his discussion of ethics, which attends to the body primarily as created.

By way of background, we should note that McClendon insists that Christian ethics concerns itself with three different dimensions which he pictures as interrelated strands that together form a single rope: the bodily, the social and the anastatic. These strands correspond to three dimensions of human existence: we are simultaneously part of the natural or organic order, the social world and an eschatological realm, i.e., the kingdom of God. His commitment to linking the biological and social is strikingly reminiscent of Polanyi's (although there is no direct linkage between the two), while it extends Polanyi by introducing a third, explicitly theological dimension to the fabric of human existence.

Theological Anthropologies

Before proceeding, however, it is important to take stock. We have seen that the Human Genome Initiative raises some important questions for at least certain theological anthropologies. A genuine dialogue between disciplines will require that these questions be addressed. But a genuine dialogue will also require that the Human Genome Initiative be open to interrogation by theologians. Take one concern over what will be done with information provided by the Human Genome Initiative.

Already we can begin to "engineer" the human body to express certain traits and inhibit others. For example, patients have been successfully treated for ADA deficiency by gene replacement therapy. The knowledge and technology produced by the Human Genome Initiative promises to enhance those skills significantly, and thus raises worries of "the perfect child syndrome" or of eugenics, that deliberate intervention into the genetic code intended to produce offspring with what are deemed socially-desirable or ideal traits.

This worry is not unfounded, as many clinics which do simple ultrasound and other fetal testing often make it a policy to withhold information on gender from the parents until they confer with their physician. The reason is that many couples want to use abortion as a means to practice sex-selection of offspring, a crude form of eugenics. Already, a consensus is emerging in the literature that somatic therapy is warranted, but not germline therapy. What this means is that it would be allowable to alter the genetic structure of a single person who suffers from a disease like diabetes so that the person's body starts to produce insulin on its own (somatic therapy). On the other hand, it would not be allowable to do the same thing in a fertilized ovum where the changes will be passed on to future generations (germline therapy). Regardless of questions some may want to ask about this particular distinction, what is at stake in the larger discussion is whether the bodies of future generations should be treated as commodities to be designed according to individual whims or tastes. What ought theological anthropology to say to this scenario?

A good place to begin is with Hauerwas, who reminds us that biology is never simply biology, that the body is never simply the body. It is also the "lived body," the body as experienced, understood and interpreted by a community. That insight alone should raise questions about the meaning of what we are doing when we manipulate the body by tinkering with its genetic code, for to tinker with the biological body is also to tinker with some of a community's most cherished notions about who it thinks it is. But we should go further to explore what some robust Christian convictions might suggest in response to our concern.

McClendon reminds us that we are part of the organic world created by God, that we find ourselves endowed with certain open-ended instincts, built-in needs and what he calls our "natural moral equipment" (i.e., capacities for delight, horror, shame, blame, guilt, conscience and moral judgment). The claim that human beings are created with these capacities by God adds a certain weight to them. After all, if we are created this way, then these capacities indicate to us something of God's desires and purposes. This inference generates caution in interfering with the genetic material from which these capacities emerge. Any interventions which would diminish these capacities would thus be out of line from a Christian perspective.

But, for McClendon, the givenness of creation is not the last word on how things ought to be; there are at least two other words that need to be spoken about the body as created. First, we can look to his recent treatment of the doctrine of creation. There he characterizes creation, using his own words, as "work in progress." Secondly, that work in progress cannot be understood apart from "what lasts and what comes last" and "the new that comes in Christ." Put differently, creation is ongoing and cannot be understood apart from redemption and eschatology. While the doctrinal focus of his most recent work precludes an explicit treatment of the ethical implications of these beliefs, we can extrapolate from what he says to what his views might mean for understanding the body and therefore for interrogating the Human Genome Initiative.

The fact that creation is ongoing suggests that the way things currently are is not necessarily the way things ought to remain. McClendon clearly affirms a place for "the creature's own creativity," creativity apparently to be assessed with reference to God's intentions for creation, intentions which are disclosed as much in what is to come as in what is. And what is to come is already present via redemption, i.e., "what is new in Christ."

As McClendon reads creation in light of redemption and eschatology, redemption brings into creation signs (the biblical miracles which McClendon calls historic, remembering and providential signs) of the "point" of creation, i.e., the reign of God. Or, in McClendon's own words, "The ultimate end of creation and redemption alike is the fulfillment of God's great kingdom rule. This rule, when it is achieved, will mean God's glory fully shared, imparted to all, incorporating all."

The ultimate criterion, by which interventions in the created order should be judged, then, would appear to be God's glory. Such a claim is, however, abstract and formal. As such, its application to the Human Genome Initiative will likely be multi-faceted and contestable. Still, we can offer three suggestive, although far from definitive connections. First, honoring the body as created and thereby as the bearer of signals of God's intentions and purposes, establishes a presumption against intervention with the genetic code. This claim cannot be held absolutely, however, as it is qualified by the continuing nature of creation, which is expressed in the creativity of the creature and the fact of redemption.

Honoring the body as redeemed thus provides limited warrant for intervention in genetic materials for the sake of redeeming or healing what is injured or what is not correct.

Furthermore, honoring the body as resurrected means that interventions to genetic code must serve God's intended end for creation. Secondly, this anthropology raises questions about the assumptions behind the project. As noted earlier, Watson claims that the Human Genome Initiative will tell us what it means to be human. Implied in that remark, given the nature of the project, is a belief that knowledge of the body exhausts what it means to be human. McClendon's perspective warns against such reductionism by reminding us that human beings inhabit social and anastatic realms as well.

Put differently, he reminds us that there is more to being human than being a body. On this point, Polanyi would be an ally, since he perceives this reductionism as endemic to the natural sciences. He criticizes the natural sciences for assuming that the laws which govern inanimate objects are appropriately applied to the organic realm. More specifically, he argues that by failing to account for emergence, the laws of nature that are manifest in the inanimate domain fail... to account for the rise of living beings." Moreover, McClendon's perspective helps us to identify what may be a bit of hubris at work in the Human Genome Initiative. The project would appear to reflect the old Baconian drive to control a nature that is only raw material for manipulation to human benefit. The project may thus continue to underwrite and reinforce partial truths about human existence which ignore or underestimate the implications of our genetic indebtedness, our connections to all around us and the limits of our abilities.

Thirdly, McClendon's (and Polanyi's) reminder that we are social creatures points toward the realization that illnesses and diseases are social constructions as much as biological facts. Thus what counts as an illness and therefore worthy of treatment cannot simply be determined biologically. Socially-conditioned values impact those kinds of judgments and therefore vigorous social debate must be part of the process. What overall assessment of the Human Genome Initiative is warranted then by this particular theological anthropology? It must clearly be a nuanced assessment. On the one hand, McClendon's perspective leads us to affirm the project as a way of gaining more knowledge of the body as created. It further suggests that we affirm the therapeutic possibilities which are likely to arise from the project. Moreover, it suggests a way to limit the kinds of interventions into genetic material that are warranted. Finally, his perspective forces consideration and debate over what it means to be human and over what conditions constitute disease or illness and why.

6

A Theology of Evolution and Biology

The New Biology and Mormon Theology

Exegetes as willing and capable as early Mormon apostle and intellectual Orson Pratt, who combined empirical and theological insights in sermons and pamphlets, have all but disappeared from the Mormon scene. His successors have retained the enthusiastic optimism of early Mormonism, but they have not replaced the empirical beliefs of the nineteenth century with more correct information which is available to us now.

One can only wish that the discoveries of modern science had been available to Pratt and his contemporaries, for some of the discoveries open up new possibilities for theological discussion. The new biology has given us insights into the nature of life that bring into question many of the easy assumptions that were made about the nature of the soul (body and spirit). Recent developments raise interesting ethical and theological issues. Apostle Pratt believed that the spirits of human beings were created before the earth was formed, and that these spirits had the same dimensions and appearance as individual physical human bodies. It is now possible in laboratory experiments to remove cells from a human being and keep them alive indefinitely—long after the donor has died.

Organs can be transplanted into another human being, where they function as part of the new body. Finally it is possible to keep a human body "alive" long after the brain is dead. Conversely there are organisms which begin life as single, independent cells, which at a certain time crawl together and form a new organism with specialized body parts and a new form of behavior. One wonders where the spirit is in these examples.

Do new spirits inhabit the cultured cells? Does a "general" spirit quicken lower life forms? It is also possible to fuse two or more mouse embryos to produce a single mouse (a chimera) with three, four, or more parents. As pointless as such a creation sounds it has great practicality for the study of biological processes.

It is almost certainly possible to create human chimeras. If the spirit is present from the moment of conception or from very early embryonic development, how many spirits are housed in a chimera? Closely related to this question is the phenomenon of identical twinning. Identical twins begin as a single embryo which at some point in development splits into two. At what point are two spirits present? Identical twins are clones. Another type of clone can be formed by removing a nucleus from an individual and implanting it into an enucleated egg. After the egg has developed into a many-celled embryo, several of the nuclei from the embryo can again be transferred to other enucleated eggs. These eggs develop into adults which are genetically identical to the original nucleus donor. This procedure proved to be valuable to stock breeders.

If it can be applied to cattle, it can also be applied to humans. If human cloning is ever accomplished, what role will the spirit play—and at what stage of development? The test tube baby is a reality. Ripe eggs in the ovary of infertile women are removed surgically and then fertilized by the husband's sperm. One or more healthy embryos are reimplanted into the woman's uterus.

From this point on the pregnancy is not unusual. The unused embryos may be discarded or frozen. Are the discarded embryos human souls? What is the status of a frozen embryo? Mormons have a plethora of opinions but no clear doctrine on this point. External fertilization offers several other new possibilities. Women have borne children without being pregnant, surrogate mothers having nurtured the embryos. It is possible that two women could have a child, since it seems possible to use one egg to fertilize another egg to produce an apparently healthy embryo.

A woman who was totally incapable of producing eggs could bear children produced by external fertilization of a donated egg by her husband's sperm and the implantation of the embryo into her uterus. This last procedure is much like artificial insemination by a donor, a procedure accepted by the LDS church but not encouraged. Stock breeders are perfecting techniques to allow them to maintain sperm, eggs, and embryo banks. Thus a mating which produces superior stock could be repeated thousands of times, with the embryos being implanted into surrogate mothers. If perfected, these techniques would allow humans to "custom order" their children from human embryo banks.

For instance, a couple who wanted a superior athlete as their progeny could order an embryo produced from the sperm of a professional basketball player and the egg of a professional tennis player. The sex of the child could be controlled by discarding the embryos of the unwanted sex. There do not seem to be any great technical obstacles to these procedures. The LDS church does not seem to be inordinately concerned with biological parentage, judging from its encouragement of adoption and its tolerance of artificial insemination. Perhaps then the crucial question would revolve around the fate of unused embryos. The emotionally charged issue of abortion requires some comment. Spontaneous abortion is common in humans. Somewhere between 20 percent and well over half of all conceptions end in spontaneous abortion. Most of these happen in the first days or weeks of pregnancy, usually escaping the notice of physicians and even of the pregnant woman. When aborted fetuses are examined, high percentages are found to be genetically defective.

Thus abortion appears to be nature's way of eliminating most seriously defective fetuses. If one were to assume that every embryo is a human soul, the simplest conclusion would be that many (perhaps most) of our brothers and sisters never experience mortality in a meaningful way. There are more complicated assumptions—for instance, the nineteenth-century Mormon view that the spirit of the aborted fetus is reassigned to another body. The common belief that mothers will be allowed to raise a baby to adulthood after the resurrection should the child die early in this life is a variation on this theme. Scripture does not allow us to identify any of these assumptions as doctrine.

Amniocentesis is often (incorrectly) identified with abortion. This procedure, in which fluid and cells are removed from the amniotic sac for examination, can be used to determine whether or not a fetus is mature enough to survive outside the womb. It also allows the diagnosis and treatment in the womb of certain disorders such as methylmalonic acidemia and blood-type incompatibilities, conditions which are often lethal to the untreated fetus. Additionally it is possible to determine whether a high-risk fetus has a particular genetic disorder. These procedures allow couples who are known to carry defective genes or chromosomes and older women to have children without fear. These high-risk parents often forego having children altogether if such procedures are not available. Although there is still some risk of other birth defects, the overall risk is greatly reduced.

The ethical problem associated with clinical abortion of defective fetuses is fairly obvious. At one extreme are those who consider abortion synonymous with murder.

Perhaps at the other extreme are those who believe that all considerations of abortion are private matters which are not the legitimate concern of society. The position of the LDS church is less clear. Although abortions are clearly forbidden in most cases, they are permitted under exceptional circumstances when the health of the mother is threatened or following rape. Abortion of defective fetuses has not been explicitly approved or disapproved, and it can be argued that clinical abortion is an extension of spontaneous abortion when defective fetuses are involved.

Recent discoveries raise other questions about the spirit-body relationship. At least two mental illnesses—manic-depressive syndrome and schizophrenia—seem to be genetically controlled. The new science of sociobiology—which has shown to be at least as controversial as the ideas of Darwin and his successors—argues that altruistic behavior is also genetic. If it indeed is true that much of human behavior is genetically controlled and is responsive to chemical modification and perhaps genetic engineering, what role should be ascribed to the spirit in overcoming sin? Recombinant-DNA experiments (gene splicing) allow the transfer of genes from any organism into bacteria. It is very likely that soon we will be able to place genes from any source into any organism, including human beings.

This would allow the insertion of "good" genes in place of "bad" genes in some cases. Few people would argue that such gene therapy is unacceptable. However, if it should prove possible to alter behavior or some other socially sensitive trait, the impact on our ideas about the spirit-body relationship could be profound. Some people believe that the moment of death is divinely determined. If this is so, why is death routinely interfered with by the use of antibiotics, surgery, and prayer? If the hour of death is determined, is it sinful to intervene or is it commendable because it demonstrates our love? A related issue is the phenomenon of faith healing. Physicians who are not necessarily religious use the techniques of psychosomatic medicine to achieve "faith" healings which are at least outwardly similar to those we see in the church. What is the relationship between the spirit and the body in these situations?

Many of these discoveries and techniques have worked together to create a paradoxical attitude in many people. On the one hand there is awe and admiration for the feats of science. On the other hand there is suspicion and fear that science is tampering with things that ought not to be interfered with. The resulting anxiety is sometimes relieved by a general feeling that "God would not let that happen." Perhaps there is a Murphy's Law of history: anything that can be used for evil will be. However, it seems that the appropriate response to a potential for evil is to seek to do good rather than attempt to set limits on science. Although the new biology may alter the way in which Mormons think about some ethical problems, it will not fundamentally change the need to live by faith in a world not fully comprehendable.

The Lord may have placed very few constraints on us in our search for knowledge and understanding. Science moves inevitably toward synthesis of living things, as it has already achieved the ability to alter species. It is reassuring to know that Mormon theology offers the chance to eternal progression, not only in this life but in the life to come. As we discover more and more about the nature of God's universe, we are given the opportunity to use that knowledge to do good works.

Towards a Constructive Theology of Evolution

Before Evolution

In today's urban technological civilization, we are disconnected from the natural processes necessary for the sustenance of human life. Most today could not name a dozen indigenous plant or animal species, let alone a dozen invasive non-indigenous species. Most today cannot see the stars at night and do not know the phases of the moon. Most today have little understanding of agriculture and what it means to work in the soil and muck with domesticated plants and animals. If we think back a mere fifty or one hundred years ago, such concerns were of primary importance to the vast majority of humans on the planet. Understanding the natural world was necessary to humanity's physical survival. Interpreting the natural world was of primary importance to constructing human culture. It turns out that these concerns are no less important today, but we shall return to this radically different contemporary context of understanding nature in the 21st century at the end of the talk.

When we look attentively upon the natural kinds, we notice that plants and animals appear to be elegantly designed to inhabit different niches, different modes of being in the world. The nature of an owl, for instance, is vastly different than the nature of a tiger or a mouse, for that matter of a reptile, fish, or plant. Aristotle saw this diversity of species in their independent "natures" or "natural kinds". Aristotle saw these natural kinds as eternal and unchanging. The theistic religions of the Judaism, Christianity, and Islam interpreted Aristotle in the middle Ages with the doctrine of separate creation, which is to say that God created each species as a separate entity. In many ways, the theories of natural kinds and separate creation are much more intuitively self-apparent than the theory of evolution that would replace them in the 19th century. In this matter, evolution is no different than the uncommon vision of other sciences.

For instance, it is not self-apparent that the Earth rotates on its axis and revolves around the Sun as in the new 17th century heliocentric model of the solar system. We still talk of the Sun rising and setting, even though we know this not to be the case. The world of nature was significant also in the construct of human culture. In the Middle Ages, nature was understood to be hierarchically organized with plants and animals at the bottom, followed by humans in the middle, angels and archangels above the humans, and God at the top. The hierarchy of nature was then also mapped out onto political and ecclesiastical hierarchies in human culture. People knew where they stood in the orders of culture and who their natural superiors and inferiors were. All of this was rationalized through an understanding of natural orders and cosmic purpose. Our revealed texts were placed along side the Book of Nature, which nature could be read for its theological and moral significance, as well as its scientific and practical significance.

The Rise of Evolution

Why then would people abandon this intuitively pleasing and culturally sanctified worldview? In the 18th and 19th centuries, European naturalists began to travel the world on scientific expeditions. In trying to classify the great variety of natural kinds discovered in far off places, they paid closer attention to morphological similarities between species. For instance, Alfred Russell Wallace, credited with co-publishing the theory of natural selection with Charles Darwin in 1858, did extensive fieldwork in the Indonesian archipelago.

Biologists wondered about why the same bone structure repeats itself in the arms of mammals as different as dolphins, bats, chimpanzee, and humans? Why did the embryos of different species go through similar patterns of development (i.e., ontogeny recapitulates phylogeny)? Why are the internal structures of organs in animals similar (e.g., hearts, lungs, digestive tracks, nervous systems, and brains)? Geologists discovered the fossil remains of extinct species like dinosaurs. Fossils of sea creatures were found high on top of mountains.

A new geological time scale was postulated dating the history of the Earth in millions and later billions of years. Today we would add radiographic dating and shared genetic structures to the mounting evidence for some kind of evolution from common descent over a vast time scale. Biologists have come to accept that the Earth is approximately 4 billion years old, that life began as single cellular bacteria, which complexified approximately 2 billion years ago into Eukaryotic cells, which then gave rise to plants, fish, amphibians, reptiles, birds, mammals, and also humans. What troubled our 18th and 19th century forebears was not evolution per se but a mechanism that could describe how evolution occurred. The French biologist Jean Baptiste Lamarck (1744-1829) proposed a theory of evolution prior to Darwin's theory of natural selection. Lamarck argued that acquired characteristics could be passed on to future generations.

A giraffe, for instance, that acquired its food by browsing leaves and twigs from trees would always be stretching its neck to reach higher into the trees. The offspring of the giraffe would then be born with longer necks. Unfortunately, such evolutionary patterns cannot be observed in nature, though it did not prevent some, like Charles Darwin's father, from being attracted to this theory, largely on political grounds. Today, the term "Lamarckism "is used in Anglo-American biological circles as a term of derision, though as we shall see later, the process of passing on acquired characteristics to future generations is precisely the pattern that we observe in human cultural evolution. Charles Darwin (1809-1882) is widely credited with discovering the mechanism by which evolution from common origins occurs.

Darwin was trained in theology at Cambridge University. He was most interested in what was then still called Natural Theology or Natural Philosophy. One of Darwin's favorite books as a student at Cambridge was

William Paley's *Natural Theology: Evidences of the Existence and Attributes of the Deity, Collected from the Appearances of Nature* (1802). Paley employed the metaphor of a watch discovered on a beach. One would not know who made the watch, but one could infer that there was certainly a watchmaker. What might even come to understand the design and function of the watch? In such a way, human studying nature could also come to understand God as the creator and designer of nature. Darwin would come to reject this design metaphor and question the existence of God. Darwin circumnavigated the world as the naturalist on the HMS Beagle from 1831 to 1836. He published *The Origin of Species* in 1859. The impact of his new theory of natural selection was immediate and widespread. Darwin's long argument consists of a few simple premises.

First, there are among offspring not only similar hereditary characteristics resulting from having the same parents, but there are also variations among offspring from the same parents. Second, every species exhibits an exponential ratio of increase resulting from the number of offspring they are able to produce. Third, this exponential rate of increase results in a universal struggle for survival as individual members of a species compete for food, water, habitat, and mates. Fourth, those variations among offspring that increase the likelihood of survival and reproduction for individual members of a species will tend to persist over time, while those variations that do not increase the likelihood of survival and reproduction will tend to die off. Fifth, the accumulation of all of these "selections" over long periods of time, involving also changes in the environment and geographic isolation, will result in the transmutation of one species into others, hence the title of Darwin's revolutionary book, "The Origin of Species".

Darwin Wrote

Owing to this struggle for life, any variation, however slight and from whatever cause proceeding, if it be in any degree profitable to an individual of any species, in its infinitely complex relations to other organic beings and to external nature, will tend to the preservation of that individual, and will generally be inherited by its offspring. The offspring, also, will thus have a better chance of surviving, for, of the many individuals of any species which are periodically born, but a small number can survive. I have called this principle, by which each slight variation, if useful, is preserved, by the term of Natural Selection, in order to mark its relation to man's power of selection (i.e., in the breeding of domesticated plants and animals in agriculture). We have seen that man by selection can certainly produce great results, and can adapt organic beings to his own uses, through the accumulation of slight but useful variations, given to him by the hand of Nature. But Natural Selection, as we shall hereafter see, is a power incessantly ready for action, and is as immeasurably superior to man's feeble efforts, as the works of Nature are to those of Art.

The Challenges of Evolution to Religious Worldviews

In the *Origins*, Darwin did not discuss the place of humans in this evolutionary story, but others latched on to the theory and applied it to human affairs. In 1871, Darwin published *The Descent of Man*, in which he explicitly laid forth the argument that humans evolved from ancestors common to today's primates. Indeed, if we go back far enough in the genetic, evolutionary muck, we share a common ancestry with all life on the planet. This is perhaps the most significant insight gained from the recent mapping of the human genome – that we carry inside of us lengthy strings of base pairs in our DNA which we have in common to bacteria, chickens, dinosaur and just about any other species to be found on the planet. On the genetic level, we are kissing cousins with chimpanzees with a 98 percent overlap in our genetic structure.

Humans, as noted above, always seem to use nature as a metaphor and context for interpreting cosmic purpose and moral order. This is no less true of Darwinism, than the earlier Aristotelian view of natural kinds and separate creation. Darwinism seemed to support the view that the universe is governed not by a powerful and benevolent God, but by random genetic drift and natural selection. The process necessitated an inordinate amount of suffering, death, and waste. If God exists, then natural selection rendered God an incompetent or malevolent Creator. Of course, the challenge of theodicy existed prior to Darwinism, but this theory of evolution multiplied the doubts of God's goodness with the magnitude of the ages and the multitude of struggling species. So Darwin's theory of evolution contributed to undermining the earlier cosmological hierarchy and sense of moral purpose.

Some latched on to the new theory of evolution to argue for the natural superiority of the European races over other races of the world; so late 19th and 20th century racism shares an ugly legacy which often used Social Darwinism to lend it "scientific" legitimacy. Others latched on to the theory to promote predatory capitalism. Herbert Spencer coined the phrase "survival of the fittest," which Darwin incorporated into later editions of *The Origins.* The term "survival of the fittest" would quickly become the short-hand for natural selection cited by the baron-robber capitalists of the early 20th century to rationalize their extreme wealth. Karl Marx, however, also saw Darwin's theory as a validation of his theory of dialectical materialism and wanted to dedicate *Das Kapital* to Charles Darwin, though Darwin declined the offer.

Early twentieth century eugenics also drew on Darwin's theory, though the controlled breeding of humans was sometimes cast as moral response to the immoral implications of Social Darwinism and sometimes involved mixing races rather than preserving racial purity. Of course, both eugenics and Social Darwinism would provide ideological fuel to Stalinism and Nazism, which on sheer scale were perhaps the greatest tragedies in human history. Historians suggest that the real impetus for the conservative religious reaction against Darwinism arose not from concern about the origins of species, but from the perception that the theory of natural selection as applied to humans was inherently immoral.

The challenge of Darwinism was also that it undermined our early sense of cosmic purpose and made atheism intellectually plausible and contributed to scientism as the dominant ideology of the modern university. Richard Dawkins, the contemporary biologist, notorious atheist, and prolific writer, notes that "The [Darwinian] universe we observe has precisely the properties we should expect if there is, at bottom, no design, no purpose, no evil and no good, nothing but blind, pitiless indifference." Dawkins represents one of the theological responses to evolution, which is to say that evolution by natural selection proves that God does not exist or at least need not exist in order to account for the origins of life. This should be understood as a theological response, because like many atheists, Dawkins has very definite ideas about the kind of God that he believes does not exist.

Dawkins sees Darwinism as a revolutionary break from the past. All of the old attempts of theology and philosophy to answer the questions of how humans ought to live and act are no longer valid. "The point I want to make now," writes Dawkins, "is that all attempts to answer that question before 1859 are worthless and that we will be better off if we ignore them completely" (1989). Now there are many others we might quote here who would support this contention that Darwinism proves atheism, notably E.O. Wilson, Daniel Dennett, Michael Ruse, and Stephen Jay Gould. Suffice it to say, that if such thinkers did not exist, many religious thinkers would have had to invent them in order to carry on their feud with Darwinism. In the context of the warfare between evolution and creationism in the United States, the problem is less with believers who read the Bible as a literal account of Creation and more with believers who read Dawkins, et. al., as a literal account of evolution.

Anti-Evolutionary Responses

There is an array of religious positions in opposition to Darwinism. Christian fundamentalism originally saw evolution as evidence of God's greatness at the turn of the 20th century, but later adopted anti-evolution as a central tenant of their belief and began interpreting the Bible as a scientific text seeking evidence to undermine evolution and support specific Biblical interpretations. The most extreme version of this is called alternately Scientific Creationism, Young Earth Creationism, or simply Creationism. The term Creationism might better apply more broadly to any religious believer, including those that affirm evolution, but in popular usage today it refers specifically to those who deny evolution.

On both sides of this polarized conflict, there is a tendency to conflate the *observed pattern* with the *theorized process*. The long natural history of this planet with the gradual complexification of life forms and periodic mass extinctions of species is now well established.

The process by which this happens and the significance of this process are open to debate and interpretation, as we will soon see. Evolution is not the same as Darwinism, though the terms are often conflated. Evolution is the observed natural history of the planet. Darwinism, or more precisely natural selection, is a theory of how this evolution occurred. This demarcation between *what happened when* and *how and why* is critical in distinguishing competing religious responses to evolution. Always clarify what is the timeline account of natural history.

It is one thing to debate the meaning and significance of the Cambrian Explosion, or for that matter the French Revolution; it is another thing completely to deny that they ever happened. Young Earth Creationism is a misreading of science and, I would argue, also a misunderstanding of scripture. Scientific Creationism has a bad case of science envy by trying to flatten a richly complicated and challenging scriptural tradition into a one-dimensional "literal" interpretation. Unfortunately, the Christian fundamentalist rejection of evolution has found followers in the Muslim world and apparently these Christians also offer financial support to such efforts. Of particular significance in the Muslim world is the work of Harun Yahya (Adnan Oktar) in Turkey, who has latched on to this unfortunate logic — Evolution equals Darwinism equal Materialism equals Atheism equals Everything-that-is-wrong-in-the-world.

Other religious intellectuals have tried to latch scriptural apologetics onto scientific prestige by arguing that the Bible or the Koran anticipated specific scientific discoveries, for instance dinosaurs, quantum mechanics, or Big Bang cosmology. Contemporary science is then offered as evidence for the validity of the sacred scripture. Here we might wonder again about the hermeneutics of the "precursor-it is" that turns science into a proof-text for our holy scriptures. We might also wonder about what happens ten or a hundred years hence when the science turns out to be radically different.

In the last few years, the Intelligent Design movement has gotten a lot of press in the United States. While vague about which version of natural history they support, the young or old Earth variety, the Intelligent Design advocates argue that random genetic drift and natural selection alone cannot account for "irreducibly complexity" in certain natural phenomena. The classic example of this is the human eye, to which Darwin himself called attention. How could such a complex mechanism with so many independent parts have arisen by incremental changes, when the mechanism would not function without all of the parts working together? Intelligent Design advocates argue that some outside agency would be needed to specify such complexity. This can be seen as a new version of the God-of-the-Gaps argument and suffers from all of the earlier attempts to insert God as an explanatory fix in science's progressive history of accounting for the unknown. God is either everywhere present in Creation in all processes at all times or God is nowhere.

Beyond Darwinism

The theory of evolution has itself evolved in the last 150 years. Darwin, of course, knew nothing about modern genetics. He knew that there is a pattern of inheritance with variation among offspring, but not how this happens. It is not until the work of the Austrian monk Gregor Mendel (1822-1884) was rediscovered at the turn of the 20th century and synthesized with Darwin's theory that we get Neo-Darwinism, also known as the Modern Synthesis. Mendel discovered laws of inheritance based on dominant and recessive "genes".

Today, scientists have extended these insights to understanding the complex macromolecules of life and the biochemical reactions that structure protein synthesis, reproduction, and development. Genetics adds a structure of inheritable traits and rates of mutation or drift within species upon which natural selection operates through the necessities of survival and reproduction.

As paleontologists collected more evidence of the fossil record of the evolution of species, it was noted that the actual history of evolution is often abrupt with long periods of stases and relatively short periods of rapid change. When first presented by Stephen Jay Gould and Niles Eldridge, this theory of "punctuated equilibrium" was touted as a serious blow to the gradualism implied in Darwin's theory, but such concerns have largely evaporated. At this point we start moving into serious debates in biology about what might be called Post-Darwinism. For instance, biologists do not agree about the level upon which natural selection operates.

Some have argued that selection operates only at the level of the gene that genes are "selfish," noting for instance the capacity of "outlaw" genes to survive independently of the well-being of the host individual. Others argue that selection occurs at the level of groups of genes or with the individual as a whole, or how else would any gene be able to reproduce. Others argue that selection also occurs with groups, for instance in social species. Group selection theory provides a tentative answer to the riddle of altruism within a theory that would otherwise predict reproductively selfish maximizing behavior. Still others note that a kind of selection exists within and between ecosystems and between groups of species in symbiotic relations. Far from nature being at war, many species exhibit complex symbiosis.

Sometimes life appears to be the proverbial Darwinian Jungle in which survival and reproduction is paramount, while in other instance life seems more like a "White Elephant Sale" with a hodge-podge of eclectic knick-knacks thrown together by happenstance in the bazaar. Multi-level selection theory presents serious challenge the reductionistic, explanatory simplicity that makes Darwinism so appealing to some.

In the case of bacteria, which have the largest biomass on the planet and are still in some sense also the most foundational kind of biological entity, it may not even be appropriate to talk of clear lines of descent required by Darwin's theory. Among bacteria, genetic information is shared not only by cell division, but also via viral vectors and direct membrane transfers throughout the gene pool of like and unlike bacteria.

So it would seem that in addition to making room for symbiosis and multi-level selection in our Post-Darwinist view of evolution, we are going to allow for some context specific confusion within life itself about the genetic boundaries between what were previously thought to be distinct breeding populations. Other Post-Darwinian theories deal with saltation or non-gradual jumps between forms observed in the fossil records, but poorly understood. One clue might lie in the bureaucratic nature of the genome itself, which far from being a linear system of causation is inter-linked in complex mutually determinative relations and feedback loops. We might better think of the genome as a molecular bureaucracy that has its own emergent, collectivist agenda.

Another Post-Darwinian frontier deals with indirect Lamarckism, whereby rates of adaptation, for instance in the stress breeding of *ecoli* bacteria, exceed what would be expected from the background rate of genetic mutations. Again, contrary to the so-called Central Dogma of biology, we should actually expect to discover some kinds of indirect feedback loops from the phenotype to the genotype, which will probably emerge in the field of developmental genetics and embryology. Nor does natural selection per se illuminate anything about the mathematical patterns often manifested by natural entities. The field of mathematical biology lies wholly outside of the orthodox Neo-Darwinism, like a Platonist idea among radical materialists. This leads to the related fields of systems theory and complexity theory as applied to life.

Biologists have made a lot of progress on some levels by abstracting individuals from the webs of their relationships, even though the individual never really exists apart of these relational matrices. So whether we're talking about a single gene or a single individual or even an entire species separate from its ecosystem, these are abstractions from reality, and we risk committing what A.N. Whitehead referred to in science as "the fallacy of misplaced concreteness". Systemic analyses of natural phenomena will reveal different patterns, complex patterns, often not easily accounted for by the reigning Neo-Darwinian orthodoxy. Here we see the productive application of mathematical complexity theory to illuminating the workings of nature in nonlinear systems and fractal-like elegance.

Speaking of Neo-Darwinism, biologist Lynn Margulis says "It is totally wrong. It's wrong like infectious medicine was wrong before Pasteur. It's wrong like phrenology is wrong. Every major tenet of it is wrong." Those are fighting words for most biologists, but Margulis has in mind the symbiosis she observes in bacteria and other species and the vectors of genetic information sharing which cross-lines of descent. A more carefully argued case for rejecting Neo-Darwinism in favor of some kind of Post-Darwinism is made by David Depew and Bruce Weber in their book *Darwinism Evolving: Systems Dynamics and the Geneaology of Natural Selection* (1997). They conclude:

> Whatever else may happen, we are reasonably certain that evolutionary theory will remain incomplete as long as self-organizational and dissipative phenomena are kept at a distance. This still leaves open, of course, whether complex dynamical models and nonequilibrium thermodynamics will testify in favor of the developmentist or of the Darwinian tradition... Can self-organization and dissipative structures be brought into the present evolutionary synthesis or some expanded version of it? Alternately, will assimilation be so challenging that it will require a change of background assumptions in the Darwinian tradition comparable to that which produced the modern synthesis itself? Or, finally, are self-organization and dissipative structuring so foreign to Darwinism's core concept, natural selection, that giving them an important place in evolutionary theory will put an end to the Darwinian tradition itself? By framing the history of the Darwinian tradition in the way we have, we have in

effect been arguing for the second alternative. We concede that it is far too early to be entirely confident about this. Nonetheless.

Now in arguing for Post-Darwinism, we need only quote Darwin in our defense, who wrote in the Introduction to *The Origin of Species*: "I am fully convinced that species are not immutable; but that those belonging to what are called the same genera are lineal descendants of some other and generally extinct species..." Which is to say that the fact of evolution from common descent seemed to him to be incontrovertible, and has become even more so in the ensuing years of scientific advance. Darwin continues, however, to note that the process by which evolution occurs is open to debate. "Furthermore," writes Darwin, "I am convinced that Natural Selection has been the most important, but not the exclusive, means of modification." As an outsider and non-expert, I need only note that there are serious and heated debates within contemporary biology about the qualifiers "most important" and "exclusive." Perhaps we might formulate the problem as such, natural selection is necessary but not sufficient explanation for the evolution of the diversity of life forms. It does not help matters that evolutionists and their critics regularly equate evolution and Darwinism, the former being an observed pattern and the latter being a theory to account for the process which animates this pattern.

These debates in biology have important implications for religious thought, though the battles are more appropriately waged in the professional journals of biology. Certainly these Post-Darwinian accounts undermine a thorough-going reductionism and leave much more room for divine participation in the evolutionary epic than the standard model, but we should not pretend that it solves all of the religious questions. For instance, the challenge of theodicy remains before, during, and after the question of how evolution occurs.

Evolutionary Psychology

There is a new academic fad that seeks to apply evolutionary theory to understanding human nature, though with much greater sophistication and nuance than the early Social Darwinists. The term sociobiology has become stigmatized, so the scholars refer to this new paradigm as evolutionary psychology. The project seeks to apply evolutionary concepts to understanding human psychological and social phenomena. For instance, Richard Dawkins coined the term "memes" to refer an imagined mental equivalent of a gene, which replicates in human culture. The metaphor has inspired some to chase after mathematical models and empirical studies for the spread of memes in culture, whether they are an advertising jingo or a religious movement.

Evolutionary psychology tends to analyze human nature always with a view towards questions of survival and reproduction. Many books and articles have been penned and processed in this endeavor, which try to explain religion away as an elaborate fiction which promotes group cohesion and increased fitness for individual and group survival and reproduction.

For instance, Moses' Ten Commandments become a recipe for enhancing the group fitness of the Hebrews in competition with their neighbors, the Canaanites. While the claims of evolutionary psychology often lack humility and make far too much of very limited data, religionists need in principle not fear the attempts of the social scientists to account for the functionality of religion in promoting human well-being.

Authentic religion should also certainly welcome any help in trying to understand and reform the dysfunctionalities that manifest them in the name of religion. Nevertheless, by reducing all human thought and behavior to merely an expression of survival and reproduction, this new sociobiology misses the truly big story of human history as a rupture with previous biological processes.

Human culture evolves in a Lamarckian pattern in which the acquired, learned characteristics of one generation are passed on more or less directly to the next generation. Our children do not need to reinvent the wheel or the microprocessor; they do not need to recreate Shakespeare or the Bhagavad-Gita; nor need they be directly related to those who did so as they benefit by virtue of their education and common humanity.

Through our abilities to learn, humans have dramatically changed every bioregion in the world and the atmosphere as a whole, thus changing the selective environment for all future evolution. Humans are about to embark upon large-scale genetic engineering of other species and ourselves. So the human phenotype now directly edits the selective environment and the genotype through intentional processes. Humans are now the motive force for future evolution for better or ill. This innovation in the how-of-evolution is as profound and potentially catastrophic as the invention of photosynthesis some two billion years ago. Humans are a Lamarckian wildcard in the epic of evolution. In this respect it will not be science and technology so much as our religiously-derived moral and aesthetic sensibilities which determine the future of our planet and our humanity.

Constructive Theologies of Evolution

Let us turn now to a number of constructive theologies of evolution, in which Christian thinkers and others have sought to understand their traditions anew within an evolutionary framework. I draw here in broad brushstrokes on the works of Alfred North Whitehead and Pierre Teilhard de Charden and their contemporary interpreters. First, we must contextualize the evolutionary account of life on Earth within the larger cosmic adventure. Scientists now believe that the universe is approximately 12 to 15 billion years old, that it began in a singularity of infinite heat and infinite density, that the specific laws of physics coalesced in the early stages of the universe, and that there are a number of extremely specific values that needed to be just so in order for more complex entities like stars, galaxies, and heavy elements to evolve.

Push a hard-nose physicist and you're likely to find a soft-hearted Neo-Platonist. In the beginning, it seems God created mathematics. The material domain of the universe is generated from an immaterial informational domain. In the words of physicist John Archibald Wheeler, "It comes from Bit". Of course, religionists have long intuited the significance of this preexistent immaterial domain. The Gospel of John reads "In the beginning was the Word." On the other hand, the universe is so big and so old that we should all feel rather puny on this little planet with our rather parochial images of God and our own self-importance. Catholic theologian John Haught uses the following mnemonic to make the point. Imagine that the history of the universe is told in thirty volumes, each volume consisting of five hundred pages, each page lasting one million years.

The first twenty volumes is "lifeless, mindless matter." The Earth story begins in volume twenty-two. Life begins as simple bacteria in volume twenty-three and continues as mostly microbial life up until volume twenty-nine, when we witness the Cambrian Explosion. Dinosaurs go extinct on page 435 of volume thirty. All of human history is a brief footnote at the end of volume thirty. In the words of the philosopher Bertrand Russell, if the purpose of the universe is to create human intelligence, then why did it take so long to create so little. One could imagine a God who would be more like a Chairman Mao or a Comrade Stalin. This God would have designed a universe with photographs of himself hung everywhere in nature.

We would be compelled to believe in the existence of this God, because everywhere we turned with our microscopes and telescopes there would be both the evidence for his existence and the secret police to enforce our acquiescence. Everything in the universe would occur by divine order, micromanaged in five-year plans and designed in a command economy. Some people today actually choose to believe in such a vision of God and appoint themselves to be the secret police, though we might wonder whether such a dictator God would be worthy of our admiration and love. The God whom we encounter through the contemporary science of evolution and the God whom we encounter through our revealed scriptures is not such a dictator.

The philosopher-theologian Holmes Rolston notes in his book, *Genes, Genesis, and God: Values and Their Origins in Natural and Human History*, that:

> The word 'design' nowhere occurs in *Genesis*, though the concept of creativity pervades the opening chapters. There in divine fiat, divine doing, but the mode is an empowering permission that places productive autonomy in the creation. It is not that there is no 'watchmaker'; there is no 'watch.' Looking for one frames the problem the wrong way. There are species well adapted for problem solving, ever more informed in their self-actualizing. The watchmaker metaphor seems blind to the problem that here needs to be solved: that informationless matter-energy is a splendid information maker. Biologists cannot deny this creativity; indeed, better than anyone else biologists know that Earth has brought forth the natural kinds, prolifically, exuberantly over the millennia, and that enormous amounts of information are required to do this.

So while the God of Creation chooses to be or at least seems to be concealed from our direct perception, yet we can discern in the universe as understood today by science a kind of directionality. If not the telos of traditional Aristotelian cosmology, there is still an observable teleonomy in which the universe gives rise to greater complexity of form. With the increasing differentiation of form, there is also a greater integration of entities in a marvelous communion of beings. Take for instance our very bodies, a condominium for microorganisms. We have now come to recognize that our bodies are continually circulating material with the outside world. Every two weeks you practically become a brand new person as you exchange air, water, food, and excretions with the outside environment. Only the calcium in our bones stays with us for any duration. We are a complex manifestation of ocean water contained in a sack of epidermis talking about ourselves. Every atom in our bodies is literally recycled stardust and has been on a 15 billion year journey towards our particular consciousness.

The universe can appreciate its pathos and beauty through us, because we are part of the universe. The very energy with which we conduct these deliberations is brought to us courtesy of our sun through photosynthesis and the food chain. And the languages that we use to express these insights are themselves the accumulated wisdom of generations of human civilization, which language humans originally acquired in the semiotically and semantically rich schools of nature. Rather than seeing our minds and personalities as incidental to the universe, we may begin to see them as signs of a greater mind and greater personality that animates the universe. The beginning and end of our thirty-volume history of the universe, and everything in between, may be an expression not of materiality, but of a universal mind that we only dimly perceive. Our religious traditions can now be seen as profound intuitions about the deep structure of the universe.

This new view of the cosmos and ourselves allows us to recover some of the insights of our traditions that have been lost in the early Enlightenment synthesis of science and religion, when we turned God into a mechanical engineer of nature reduced to a wind-up watch. The Creator-Sustainer-Redeemer God of this Universe could not be an authoritarian, control freak, but a God of mercy and compassion, as the Koran so oft repeats. This is a God who manifests divine providence in humble, self-giving love and promise, as emphasized in the Christian tradition.

This universe as we now understand through science requires a God who values adventure, beauty, the interplay of order and open possibilities. God must surely value freedom, the self-creative, autopoeisis of other creatures and us. God understood in light of this evolutionary epic can lure the universe towards the future, the good, and the beautiful, through divine inspiration. Our trials, tribulations, failures, and deaths are resolved not through the dogmatic certainties of our beliefs, but through a warranted faith in an eschatological promise of redemption. Such a faith is fully consistent with the best of science, which can only intimate at this transcendence, and the best of our religions, which reveal to us this future promise.

Faith of Biology and the Biology of Faith

Science and the scientific method are grounded in facts, in objective data, in the realm of the rational. Science has as its goal the shrinking of the unknown. Theology and religion deal with revelation, the irrational and the Unknowable. Yet Robert Pollack ably demonstrates that science and theology not only share some aspect of the irrational, that is, scientific insights/ "Aha" moments, and religious revelation/prophetic visions, but that they need each other in order for twenty-first century humans to make crucial decisions about the use and meaning of scientific discoveries. For the scientific novice, Pollack details the basic scientific facts about Darwin's theory of evolution, the way in which DNA and the genes which comprise it work, and the challenges such scientific data pose for the religious believer.

Are we just the product of a neutrally random process of evolution? As Pollack points out, "In terms of evolution's mutation driven mechanism, every one of us is precisely a genetic experiment that can end only in death." Yet, he argues, this self-evident fact of our mortality is precisely where science and theology come together. Science answers the "How" and Theology answers the "Why." Science works at the boundary of the known and the unknown, while religion is lived out at the boundary of the known and the unknowable. Pollack helps the religious person, clergy or lay, understand the importance of accepting as valid both the rational facts of science and the irrational facts of religious insight. He defines free will as "the uniquely dangerous but powerful human capacity to choose a belief or an action on emotional grounds, rather than deciding it on the basis of rational argument."

Furthermore, he points out that the loss of free will produces passivity, dogma, and fundamentalism, in science as well as religion. Pollack clearly understands the Anglican via media. In this small volume, the reader will encounter a serious man of science who is also a faithful believer in the Unknowable. Pollack not only explains DNA-based medicine but grapples openly with the ethical and moral implications of that medicine. Using the Scriptures, the oral law of the Jewish faith, and his own background as a member of a limited genetic family with a risky gene (the Ashkenazim), Pollack demonstrates the ways in which religious insights can guide pastoral and personal applications of scientific discoveries. After reading Pollack's book, I heartily recommend tackling theologian John F. Haught's work God after Darwin. This book is clearly written and especially valuable because he proposes that the central and original content of Christian faith "provides us with an image of God that is not only logically consistent with, but also fruitfully illuminative of the Dar-winian picture of life."

In a series of thought-provoking chapters Haught demonstrates how religion and theology can acquire a "new vitality" while maintaining "intellectual honesty alongside of and in concert with the evolutionary discoveries of modern science." He argues that the ongoing controversy between evolutionists and Christian apologists is misdirected by their focus on an underlying design or order in the universe. Instead, Haught proposes a God of evolution as opposed to the more traditional God of Order and Design. What is needed, Haught declares, is a God who is "less Alpha and more Omegas." A God who beckons to us from the future, operating as Emmanuel, the "withusgod" who brings hope and vision into our lives.

This God of evolution is not a designer par excellence, but instead "an infinitely liberating source of new possibilities and of new life." Haught directly confronts original sin, the presence of evil and suffering in the universe, the kenosis of God, and the difficulty of reconciling the concept of the soul with the findings of genetic science. In carefully presented material Haught reviews the traditional understandings of these doctrines before engaging his theology of evolution in dialogue with the theology of Whitehead, Teilhard de Chardin, and Nasr, distinguished philosopher and Muslim religious thinker.

Biology Meets Theology

When conservative Christians take a stand against evolutionary theory, everyone notices. When biologists such as Richard Dawkins or E. O. Wilson claim that evolutionary biology excludes faith, disproves God or shows how much human beings are like other primates, the religious community becomes irate and newspapers spread the story across their front pages. But the real work on evolution and faith is being done by two sets of scholars whom the popular press would rather ignore. One group consists of Christians who are attempting to combine the idea of God's providential design with evolution. The other is made up of non-believing or agnostic biologists who eschew radical anti-religious claims in favor of sober assessments of genetic influence. The books by Holmes Rolston and Michael Ruse and the collection of essays edited by Robert Russell, William Stoeger and Francisco Ayala represent the best recent thought of both camps.

Rolston, whose mediating position is signaled by his book's subtitle, is one of the sober and intelligent Christian voices in the discussion. He cares deeply about preserving the non-biological aspects of culture, ethics and religion. He searches for the "brooding Spirit of God" in the world, and believes that religion is about "the finding, creating, saving, redeeming of... persisting sacred value in the world." Yet Rolston is willing to embrace the results of the scientific study of the biological world: "This has been Darwin's century, and we have more understanding than any people before us of the evolutionary natural history by which we arrived," he states.

Our genetic makeup results from an evolutionary process; we share most of our genetic structure with other animals, particularly with the higher primates; and this genetic code influences vast areas of human behavior, The strength of the influence results in the strong pull to "naturalize" and "socialize" the domains of culture, ethics and religion. Yet Rolston finds good reasons for rejecting a reduction of these domains to natural causes. Biological evolution, heproclaims, leaves room for religious truth. Is Rolston's apologetic successful? Consider his central arguments. One is that cultural history rises above genetic influences: "With the coming of humans there appears the genesis of ideas; encultured thereafter, ideas are perennially generated and regenerated." For him biology and culture are ultimately separate, parallel aspects of the human person: "The self is not simply biological and somatic but cultural and ideological," he argues.

"The self is expansive and finds an entwined destiny with many other persons. Cultural evolution renders genetic evolution relatively powerless. "One doesnot have to have Darwin's genes to be a Darwinian, or Jesus' to be a Christian." The notion that our biological equipment is "like a computer hardware, as a given to work with," is crucial for Rolston's case against genetic determinism. An extremely large number of software programs can be run on a given piece of hardware. You can use your home computer to write about shagging or Shakespeare, to play games or search the heavens, to buy stocks or solve differential equations. The same degree of freedom, Rolston contends, characterizes the whole realm of human culture and thought. Though some have argued that ethics and values have their roots in evolution, Rolston thinks that only religion puts them in an adequate context.

Ethics involves altruism, the placing of the interests of others above one'sown. Many biologists have found the animals sometimes behave altruistically. Indiscriminate altruism — acting for the good of all and not merely for those who carry our genes — contributes to a healthy society, and thus, indirectly, to biological fitness. But Rolston maintains that altruism and other forms of ethical behavior must be measured not only for their biological survival value but also for their contribution to the flourishing of culture. Morality is emergent: our species has risen from "is" to "ought."

In the end, Rolston insists, the "ought" that is basic to ethics cannot be derived from the descriptive "is" of biological research. To be a person is to be "moral, valuable, and evaluating." Only the language of transcendence can grasp the human mind, which is able "to reach truths about realms that it does not inhabit, extrapolating and reasoning from the realms it does."

In making his case for Christianity, Rolston's starting point is our ability to transcend ourselves, our social or historical context and even our biology.

This, he states, is strong evidence in support of religion and of a personal, transcendent God. Ralston argues not only that theism has a positive biological function for human culture and survival, but also that there is good reason to regard it as true. Tribal religions are "nonexportable" (and therefore false?); "only the universalist synoptic creeds have proven exportable, globally functional, because they speak to the common condition of humankind." The fertility of the idea of God and the fact that a biological species could produce such an idea need to be explained; for Rolston, the only adequate explanation is the actual existence of God.

The evolution of biology and culture demonstrate that "there is a Ground of Information or an Ambiance of Information otherwise known as God." God is a "countercurrent to entropy, a sort of biogravity that lures life upward.... God introduces new possibility spaces" into human existence. Rolston is cautious about presenting God as a miracle worker or regular causal force in the world, but he is optimistic about demonstrating a God who gives meaning to the world. Christians will of course want Rolston's project to succeed. A natural theology that makes God the best explanation of biological evolution wouldeliminate both atheistic naturalism and the antiscientism of creationism. But is Rolston's picture too easy, too good to be true? Consider how Rolston's arguments look from the standpoint of Ruse, a leading moderate theorist of evolution.

According to Ruse's view, Rolston bias failed to take Darwin seriously. Ruse argues convincingly that culture is not parallel to biology. It is not a relatively independent sphere built on top of its biological basis, like software running on hardware. Instead, researchhas shown that the biological constraints on culture are much more pervasiveand influential than Rolston's allows. The type of language we produce is determined by our mouth and throat structure; the mental categories we use are either responses to our environment or reflections of our own physiological structure (as in the case of color categories); and our interaction with our physical environment is our only means for establishing which of our beliefs are true. Truth and biological survival are, Ruse insists, the closest of allies. The strict "bottom up" model of determination by our genes — a model passionately advocated by Dawkins — may have been replaced by the more complex model, according to which nongenetic factors influence gene expression and thus behavior.

But, Ruse insists, though the circle may be broader than the "gene reductionists" believe, it still starts and ends with gene expression. Brains do not evolve and then function as a sort of tabula rasa, molded and formed by culture. Rather, humans are born with highly structured brains, hormonal and behavioral dispositions, and strong tendencies to think and behave in particular ways — all of which bear the mark of our evolutionary history. The same holds true for ethics. Though the specific ways we formulate our ethical principles are not totally determined by their genetic basis, we cannot load just any ethical software onto our biological hardware, to take an obvious example, if a given population accepted a moral injunction against sexual intercourse (and its substitutes), it would have no more than a one generation life span.

Ruse's string of examples fall into two categories: those that underscore biological constraints on ethical positions, and those that trace biological influences on ethical beliefs. Thus Ruse connects the universal taboos against sexual relations between siblings with the biologically based tendency for people raised in the same house to lose sexual interest in each other. In general, "epigenetic rules giving us a sense of obligation have been put in place by selection, because of their adaptive value." In the end, "morality is a function of (subjective) feelings"; we just think that morality must be something more because "we have (and must have) the illusion of objectivity."

Our brains and bodies — and the genetic coding that transmits these patterns to our offspring — are able to increase our chances of survival "by filling us full of thoughts about obligations and duties"; that is, we survive better "because we think morality is something lay upon us." But any sense that obligations are something more, something transcendent or "real," is an illusion. What is true of ethics applies with a vengeance to religion; first, the same constraints hold sway: when religious beliefs and practices conflict with biological survival, they and their holders will soon find themselves decisively selected against. Strong lines of influence run from our survival needs as a species to the sorts of religious beliefs we form.

Religious belief is not like the content we type into our word processors, which is presumably unaffected by whether we are using a Mac or a PC. Biological factors may not determine our doctrine of the Trinity or our particular theory of the Eucharist, but they do affect the sort of beliefs and practices that tend to be developed and preserved within successful religious communities. Think, for example, of the links between the physiological characteristics of bread and wine, the social role that these two foodstuffs have played, and the religious use to which Christianity has put them. In many ways Ruse remains a moderate. His most recent book, Mystery of Mysteries: Is Evolution a Social Construction?, challenges the claim made by radical evolutionists like Dawkins and Daniel Dennett that Darwinism counts against theism and makes religious practice absurd.

Ruse believes that biological evolution leaves open the question of the ultimate meaning or purpose of the universe. Religious beliefs just might be true. Still, his argument is the antipode to Rolston's theistic evolution. For Ruse, Darwinian evolution is sufficient unto itself; it doesn't need any support from God, and it certainly doesn't by itself provide the direct evidence for God's existence that Rolston hopes to find.

How can one mediate this dispute? Evolutionary and Molecular Biology: Scientific Perspectives on Divine Action provides a sober assessment of what can and cannot be discovered at the interface of biology and theology. These essays are part of a ten-year project cosponsored by the Vatican Observatory and the Center for Theology and the Natural Sciences in Berkeley, seeking to rediscover a place for divine action in a scientific age.

The book does not exhibit neither Rolston's optimistic exuberance nor has Ruse dogged insistence on the explanatory power of Darwinism. Its moderate stance, technical (occasionally highly technical) argument and cautious inferences are an effective response to Rolston and Ruse's sometimes overstated conclusions. Most of the essayists don't think that the emergence of order, design, culture or religion in the natural world can be the basis for an argument that there is a divine purpose to the universe. In "Evaluating the Teleological Argument for Divine Action," Wesley Wildman challenges all attempts to use evolutionary biology either to prove or to disprove theism. Wildman's analysis of the limitations of teleological (purpose-based) arguments, when combined with the careful summaries of the scientific data by Ayala, Cela-Conde and Chela-Flores, sound a powerful cautionary note to Rolston's apologetic project.

Though biology and theology don't occupy separate worlds, neither is they bosom buddies. Evil, as in the massive deaths of individuals and species within biological evolution, is a weighty negative counterbalance to Rolston's positive interpretation. The most helpful positive argument in this volume may be Paul Davies's "Teleology without Teleology: Purpose through Emergent Complexity." Davies notes that the laws of physics are responsible for the emergence of ever higher orders of organized complexity within the natural world.

Each of these orders represents the emergence of a genuinely new type of reality. Ruse is right that complexity appears gradually, and only through the evolutionary process. Still, what results is something new in the natural order: cells; organisms that strive to exist and to reproduce; ecosystems in which living things exist in complex interdependence; and, in the higher primates, complex modes of thought leading, eventually, to consciousness. With consciousness come moral beliefs, rational arguments and self awareness. Perhaps most surprising of all, consciousness is accompanied by the preoccupation with transcendence — with God, freedom and immortality — that characterizes our species.

Had he done justice to this pattern of emergence, Ruse would have been more hesitant about basing ethics and knowledge on Darwinian principles alone. Influence "from below" is undeniable; but emergence forces us also to acknowledge that rationality and ethics — and perhaps religion — depend on meta-biological factors as well. It's not a big step from this insight to the recognition of a basic "directionality" to the evolutionary process, as William Stoeger describes it. If there is "purposiveness without purpose" in natural history, then the Christian language of divine guidance and care may find at least a handhold within the biological sciences. The essays in this volume represent the real cutting edge in discussions between Christianity and biology. They provide a careful, sober assessment of the biological story in all its complexity.

Their story is more ambiguous than Rolston would have it — though it doesn't justify conclusions as strong as Ruse's. Certainly the essays provide an effective answer to antireligious biologists like Dawkins and Dennett, who argue that biological evolution rules out religious belief. Missing from all three volumes are the acerbic and extremist views that the press loves to trumpet from the street corners. Rolston does not claim that evolution shouldn't be taught in schools or that it stands opposed to the belief in a revealing and providential God. He considers it an ally — even if he sails ambitiously beyond the evidence at certain points.

Ruse does not claim that Christian beliefs have been falsified by evolution. Instead, he understands that the question of theism is left open by the evidence for evolution — even if he does go too far in reducing the explanations for religion to biological terms. One can only hope that church people will enter into the debate with the care and reasonableness these authors have shown.

7

Creation, Metaphysics, and Cosmology

Plane (Metaphysics)

In metaphysics and esoteric cosmology, a plane, other than the physical plane (actually a hyperplane, as are any larger ones,) is conceived as a subtle state of consciousness that transcends the known physical universe. The concept may be found in religious, metaphysical and esoteric teachings - e.g. Vedanta (Advaita Vedanta), shamanism, Neoplatonism, Gnosticism, Kashmir Shaivism, Sant Mat/ Surat Shabd Yoga, Sufism, Druze, Kabbalah, Theosophy, Anthroposophy, Rosicrucianism (Esoteric Christian), Eckankar, Ascended Master Teachings, etc. - which propound the idea of a whole series of subtle planes or worlds or dimensions which, from a center, interpenetrate themselves and the physical planet in which we live, the solar systems, and all the physical structures of the universe. This interpenetration of planes culminates in the universe itself as a physical structured, dynamic and evolutive expression emanated through a series of steadily denser stages, becoming progressively more material and embodied.

The emanation is conceived, according to esoteric teachings, to have been originated, at the dawn of the universe's manifestation, in The Supreme Being Who sent out - from the unmanifested Absolute beyond comprehension - the dynamic force of creative energy, as sound-vibration ("the Word"), into the abyss of space. On the other hand, it states that this dynamic force is being sent forth, through the ages, framing all things that constitute and inhabit the universe.

Origins of the Concept

The concept of planes of existence might be seen as deriving from shamanic and traditional mythological ideas of a vertical world-axis — for example a cosmic mountain, tree, or pole (such as Yggdrasil or Mount Meru) — or a philosophical conception of a Great Chain of Being, arranged metaphorically from God down to inanimate matter. However the original source of the word "plane" in this context is the late Neoplatonist Proclus, who refers to platos, "breadth", which was the equivalent of the 19th century theosophical use. An example is the phrase en to psuchiko platei.

Conceptions in Ancient Traditions

Directly equivalent concepts in Indian thought are lokas and bhuvanas. In Hindu cosmology, there are traditionally seven lokas or worlds, while Buddhist cosmology has a much larger number of "deva lokas", identified with both traditional cosmology and states of meditation. Planes of existence are sometimes referred to as "eggs". For example, the Sanskrit term Brahmanda translates to "the Egg of God". In this context, Brahmanda is thought to encompass the Anda (astral or subtle) and Pinda (physical or gross) eggs, in a way metaphorically analogous to a set of Russian dolls — the larger containing the next smaller, which contains the next smaller, and so on.

The ancient Norsemen and the Teutonic mythology called "Ginnungagap" to the primordial "Chaos," which was bounded upon the northern side by the cold and foggy "Niflheim"—the land of mist and fog—and upon the south side by the fire "Muspelheim." When heat and cold entered into space which was occupied by Chaos or Ginnungagap, they caused the crystallization of the visible universe. In the medieval West and Middle East, one finds reference to four worlds (olam) in Kabbalah, or five in Sufism (where they are also called tanazzulat; "descents"), and also in Lurianic Kabbalah. In Kabbalah, each of the four or five worlds are themselves divided into ten sefirot, or else divided in other ways.

Most cosmologies suggest that there are both positive and negative planes. They indicate that an Earth-departed soul is propelled towards the plane that corresponds to the level of its merits or demerits.

One example of this understanding can be found in the secular or popular Christianity, where in afterlife, a departed soul finds itself in either heaven or hell. Other traditions, including the inner or esoteric Christianity, suggest that there are finer differences between various positive and negative planes, and that each plane beyond Earth plane becomes more and more subtle. It is commonly believed that positive planes are inhabited by subtle bodies doing righteous deeds, whereas negative planes are inhabited by subtle bodies doing unrighteous deeds.

Cosmology

Cosmology is study of the Universe in its totality, and by extension, humanity's place in it. Though the word cosmology is recent (first used in 1730 in Christian Wolff's Cosmologia Generalis), study of the Universe has a long history involving science, philosophy, esotericism, and religion.

Disciplines

In recent times, physics and astrophysics have to play a central role in shaping the understanding of the universe through scientific observation and experiment; or what is known as physical cosmology shaped through both mathematics and observation in the analysis of the whole universe. In other words, in this discipline, which focuses on the universe as it exists on the largest scale and at the earliest moments, is generally understood to begin with the big bang (possibly combined with cosmic inflation) - an expansion of space from which the Universe itself is thought to have emerged ~$13.7 \pm 0.2 \times 10^9$ (13.7 billion) years ago.

From its violent beginnings and until its various speculative ends, cosmologists propose that the history of the Universe has been governed entirely by physical laws. Theories of an impersonal universe governed by physical laws were first proposed by Roger Bacon, a somewhat persecuted member of the Catholic Church. Between the domains of religion and science, stands the philosophical perspective of metaphysical cosmology. This ancient field of study seeks to draw intuitive conclusions about the nature of the universe, man, god and/or their relationships based on the extension of some set of presumed facts borrowed from spiritual experience and/or observation.

But metaphysical cosmology has also been observed as the placing of man in the universe in relationship to all other entities. This is demonstrated by the observation made by Marcus Aurelius of a man's place in that relationship: " He who does not know what the world is does not know where he is, and he who does not know for what purpose the world exists, does not know who he is, nor what the world is."

This is the purpose of the ancient metaphysical cosmology. However, Stoicism rejected Aristotle's theory of universals as being "in the things themselves," calling them "figments of the mind." Stanford Encyclopedia of Philosophy adopting the concept of universals as being "concepts," and therefore of the mind, and therefore controllable by free will. Thus, we get the analysis of Aurelius' that the nature of the universe is not from "intuition," but from a free-will, conceptual understanding of the nature of the universe. Cosmology is often an important aspect of the creation myths of religions that seek to explain the existence and nature of reality. In some cases, views about the creation (cosmogony) and destruction (eschatology) of the universe play a central role in shaping a framework of religious cosmology for understanding humanity's role in the universe.

A more contemporary distinction between religion and philosophy, esoteric cosmology is distinguished from religion in its less tradition-bound construction and reliance on modern "intellectual understanding" rather than faith, and from philosophy in its emphasis on spirituality as a formative concept. There are many historical cosmologies:

"...the universe itself acts on us as a random, inefficient, and yet in the long run effective, teaching machine. ...our way of looking at the universe has gradually evolved through a natural selection of ideas." —Steven Weinberg

Physical Cosmology

Physical cosmology is the branch of physics and astrophysics that deals with the study of the physical origins and evolution of the Universe. It also includes the study of the nature of the Universe on its very largest scales. In its earliest form it was what is now known as celestial mechanics, the study of the heavens. The Greek philosophers Aristarchus of Samos, Aristotle and Ptolemy proposed different cosmological theories. In particular, the geocentric Ptolemaic system was the accepted theory to explain the motion of the heavens until Nicolaus Copernicus, and subsequently Johannes Kepler and Galileo Galilei proposed a heliocentric system in the 16th century.

This is known as one of the most famous examples of epistemological rupture in physical cosmology. Wit Isaac Newton and the 1687 publication of Principia Mathematica, the problem of the motion of the heavens was finally solved. Newton provided a physical mechanism for Kepler's laws and his law of universal gravitation allowed the anomalies in previous systems, caused by gravitational interaction between the planets, to be resolved. A fundamental difference between Newton's cosmology and those preceding it was the Copernican principle that the bodies on earth obey the same physical laws as all the celestial bodies. This was a crucial philosophical advance in physical cosmology.

Modern scientific cosmology is usually considered to have begun in 1917 with Albert Einstein's publication of his final modification of general relativity in the paper "Cosmological Considerations of the General Theory of Relativity," (although this chapter was not widely available outside of Germany until the end of World War I).

General relativity prompted cosmogonists such as Willem de Sitter, Karl Schwarzschild and Arthur Eddington to explore the astronomical consequences of the theory, which enhanced the growing ability of astronomers to study very distant objects.

Prior to this (and for some time afterwards), physicists assumed that the Universe was static and unchanging. In parallel to this dynamic approach to cosmology, a debate was unfolding regarding the nature of the cosmos itself. On the one hand, Mount Wilson astronomer Harlow Shapley championed the model of a cosmos made up of the Milky Way star system only. Heber D. Curtis, on the other hand, suggested spiral nebulae were star systems in their own right, island universes.

This difference of ideas came to a climax with the organization of the Great Debate at the meeting of the (US) National Academy of Sciences in Washington on 26 April 1920. The resolution of the debate on the structure of the cosmos came with the detection of novae in the Andromeda galaxy by Edwin Hubble in 1923 and 1924. Their distance established spiral nebulae well beyond the edge of the Milky Way and as galaxies of their own. Subsequent modeling of the universe explored the possibility that the cosmological constant introduced by Einstein in his 1917 paper may result in an expanding universe, depending on its value.

Thus the big bang theory was proposed by the Belgian priest Georges Lemaître in 1927 which was subsequently corroborated by Edwin Hubble's discovery of the red shift in 1929 and later by the discovery of the cosmic microwave background radiation by Arno Penzias and Robert Woodrow Wilson in 1964.

These findings were a first step to rule out some of many alternative physical cosmologies. Recent observations made by the COBE and WMAP satellites observing this background radiation have effectively, in many scientists' eyes, transformed cosmology from a highly speculative science into a predictive science, as these observations matched predictions made by a theory called Cosmic inflation, which is a modification of the standard big bang theory. This has led many to refer to modern times as the "Golden age of cosmology".

Metaphysical Cosmology

In philosophy and metaphysics, cosmology deals with the world as the totality of space, time and all phenomena. Historically, it has had quite a broad scope, and in many cases was founded in religion. The ancient Greeks did not draw a distinction between this use and their model for the cosmos. However, in modern use it addresses questions about the Universe which are beyond the scope of science. It is distinguished from religious cosmology in that it approaches these questions using philosophical methods (e.g. dialectics). Modern metaphysical cosmology tries to address questions such as:

- What is the origin of the Universe? What is its first cause? Is its existence necessary?
- What are the ultimate material components of the Universe?
- What is the ultimate reason for the existence of the Universe? Does the cosmos have a purpose?

Religious Cosmology

Many world religions have creation myths that explain the beginnings of the Universe and life. Often these are derived from scriptural teachings and held to be part of the faith's dogma, but in some cases these are also extended through the use of philosophical and metaphysical arguments. In some creation myths, the universe was created by a direct act of a god or gods who are also responsible for the creation of humanity. In many cases, religious cosmologies also foretell the end of the Universe, either through another divine act or as part of the original design.

- Both Christianity and Judaism rely on the Genesis narrative as a scriptural account of cosmology.
- Islam relies on understanding from the Qur'an as its major source for explaining cosmology.
- Certain adherents of Buddhism, Hinduism and Jainism believe that the Universe passes through endless cycles of creation and destruction, each cycle lasting for trillions of years (e.g. 331 trillion years, or the life-span of Brahma, according to Hinduism), and each cycle with sub-cycles of local creation and destruction (e.g. 4.32 billion years, or a day of Brahma, according to Hinduism). The Vedic (Hindu) view of the world sees one true divine principle self-projecting as the divine word, 'birthing' the cosmos that we know from the monistic Hiranyagarbha or Golden Womb.
- A complex mixture of native Vedic gods, spirits, and demons, overlaid with imported Hindu and Buddhist deities, beliefs, and practices are the key to the Sri Lankan cosmology.
- The Australian Aboriginal concept of Dreaming explains the creation of the universe as an eternal continuum; everywhen. Through certain ceremonies, the past "opens up" and comes into the present. Each topographical feature is a manifestation of dormant creation spirits; each individual has personal Dreamings

and ceremonial responsibilities to look after the spirits/land, determined at birth, within this belief framework.

Many religions accept the findings of physical cosmology; in particular the Big Bang, and some, such as the Roman Catholic Church, has embraced it as suggesting a philosophical first cause. Others have tried to use the methodology of science to advocate for their own religious cosmology, as in intelligent design or creationist cosmologies.

Esoteric Cosmology

Many esoteric and occult teachings involve highly elaborate cosmologies. These constitute a "map" of the Universe and of states of existences and consciousness according to the worldview of that particular doctrine. Such cosmologies cover many of the same concerns also addressed by religious and philosophical cosmology, such as the origin, purpose, and destiny of the Universe and of consciousness and the nature of existence. For this reason it is difficult to distinguish where religion or philosophy end and esotericism and/or occultism begins. Common themes addressed in esoteric cosmology are emanation, involution, evolution, epigenesis, planes of existence, hierarchies of spiritual beings, cosmic cycles (e.g., cosmic year, Yuga), yogic or spiritual disciplines, and references to altered states of consciousness. Examples of esoteric cosmologies can be found in modern Theosophy, Gnosticism, Tantra (especially Kashmir Shaivism), Kabbalah, or Sufism.

Whitehead, God, and Relativity

Process Theism

Process theism typically refers to a family of theological ideas originating in, inspired by, or in agreement with the metaphysical orientation of the English philosopher-mathematician Alfred North Whitehead (1861-1947) and the American philosopher-ornithologist Charles Hartshorne

(1897-2000). For both Whitehead and Hartshorne, it is an essential attribute of God to be fully involved in and affected by temporal processes. This idea contrasts neatly with traditional forms of theism that hold God to be *in all respects* non-temporal (eternal), unchanging (immutable,) and unaffected by the world (impassible). Process theism does not deny that God is *in some respects* eternal, immutable, and impassible, but it contradicts the classical view by insisting that God is *in some respects* temporal, mutable, and passable.

The views of Whitehead and Hartshorne should also be distinguished from those that affirm that the divine being, by an act of self-limitation, opens itself to influence from the world. Some neo-Thomists hold this view and a group of Evangelical Christian philosophers, calling themselves "open theists," promote similar ideas. These forms of theism were influenced by process theism, but they deny its claim that God is *essentially* in a give-and-take relationship with the world. Moreover, process theism is a genuinely *philosophical* theology in the sense that it is not grounded in claims of special insight or revealed truth but in philosophical reflection. Specifically, process theism is a product of theorizing that takes the categories of becoming, change, and time as foundational for metaphysics.

The metaphysical underpinning of process theism is often called process philosophy, a label suggested by the title of Whitehead's magnum opus, *Process and Reality*. In order to bring out this philosophy's emphasis on relatedness, many scholars follow Bernard Loomer in calling it process-relational philosophy. Whitehead's preferred expression for his metaphysical viewpoint is "the philosophy of organism." This chapter concerns primarily the concept of God in process theism, although we shall conclude with a brief discussion of arguments for the existence of God in process thought and a note on the historical influences on process theism.

God and Creativity

The question of the metaphysical relation of God and creativity is a watershed between process theism and more traditional forms of theism. Process philosophy, modifying a statement from Plato's *Sophist* (247e), affirms that the most concrete real beings—in Whitehead's language, actual entities—are characterized by the power to act *and* to be acted upon (Plato says real beings act *or* are acted upon). In process metaphysics no actual entity is wholly determined by the activity of another; or phrased positively, every actual entity retains *some* power of self-determination, however minimal or slight it may be. According to this view, to have power in relation to others is to have power in relation to other entities with some degree of power. This is process philosophy's doctrine of universal creativity. Hartshorne says, "To be is to create". The logic of the matter does not change if God is included in the metaphysical scheme. For process theism, God is the supreme or eminent creative power, but not the only creative power. Thus, process theists speak of God and the creatures as co-creators.

Process theism's doctrine of creativity differs from that of classical theism according to which God alone is genuinely creative. Thomas Aquinas says that in the proper sense of the word, only God creates. Aquinas explains that to create is to bring something from nothing, and this is possible only for deity. This is the famous doctrine of *creatio ex nihilo*, or creation from no pre-existing material. This *ex nihilo* creation is logically distinct from the claim that the universe is temporally finite. Aquinas, for example, treats the questions whether God is the creator and whether the universe had a beginning under separate headings. Aquinas is clear that he accepts the temporal finitude of the universe as a matter of faith, from revelation, and not because of rational argument. On the other hand, like other traditional theists, Aquinas holds that God could have created a temporally infinite universe, but it too would have been created *ex nihilo*.

Process theists generally, though not unanimously, deny that the universe had a first temporal moment. Those wishing to demonstrate the compatibility between process theism and Jewish and Christian Scripture commonly follow David Griffin's arguments that the Bible neither requires nor implies an absolute beginning of the universe. There is still the objection, however, that by conceiving both God and the creatures as creative, process theists seem to destroy one of the most meaningful contrasts between God and the world: God as creator and the world as created. Indeed, Whitehead says, "It is as true to say that God creates the World, as that the World creates God".

One must, however, separate Whitehead's poetic expression from his philosophical meaning. In process theism, as in traditional theism, the *existence* of God is in no way precarious, in no way dependent upon the activity of other entities; likewise, process theism and traditional theism are in agreement that non-divine individuals are contingent (they can fail to exist)—in the case of non-angelic beings, they are born and they die. In process theism, God's existence is everlasting, but the existence of any particular creature is not. Nevertheless, the creatures, being lesser creators, create something in God, if only the knowledge of their own activity. For process theism, the activity of the creatures makes no difference to God's existence, only to God's experience of them.

Implicit in traditional theism's doctrine of creation are the ideas that God's creative act and God's knowledge of the world are non-temporal. Augustine, for example, in the *Confessions,* considers it nonsensical to ask what God was doing before the creation of the world; God, in creating the universe, brings time—and with it, relations of before and after—into existence; thus, it is no more meaningful to ask what came *before* the first moment of time than it is to ask what is north of the north pole. In traditional theism, the temporal world is spread out before God who can see it in its entirety from an eternal vantage point, like an observer on a hill viewing travelers in a caravan. As Boethius says in *The Consolation of Philosophy*, eternity is the complete, simultaneous and perfect possession of everlasting life.

Process theism takes a contrary view that *time is the process of creation*. In other words, the order of beings in time is the process whereby beings are created. For process metaphysics, there is no eternal act of divine creation that fixes the world in existence and there is no eternal perspective from which the universe can be considered a finished product. Furthermore, the "creative advance," as Whitehead calls the universe, is inherently open-ended and growing, like a line to which tiny segments are continually being added. Where Aquinas could liken God's prescience to a man viewing a caravan of travelers from a high tower, Hartshorne says, "There is not (either now or eternally) a fixed totality of travelers for God to survey, but a new totality each moment". Whitehead remarks that, "In all philosophic theory there is an ultimate which is actual in virtue of its accidents". In process thought, this ultimate is creativity. It would be misleading, however, to speak as though creativity were "the ultimate reality" according to process theism.

Creativity is not a metaphysical agency that produces anything; rather, it is the character of every concrete fact, from the humblest flicker of existence in non-divine actual entities to God. Whitehead's pithy summary of process philosophy is, "The many become one, and are increased by one". Creativity, then, is the ultimate metaphysical principle. A principle, however, is not a real being. Whitehead explained to his student A. H. Johnson that God is not a principle but an actuality. That which is best described, in process theism, as the ultimate reality, is God. For Whitehead and Hartshorne, God should not be treated as the exception to metaphysical principles; otherwise, there can be no reasoned discourse about the divine (that is, no theology). Ideally, God is to be the chief exemplification of metaphysical principles, and it is this ideal that Whitehead and Hartshorne strive to realize. In process theism, the divine or eminent form of creativity provides the basis for cosmic order and achieved value. In Whitehead's words, God is "the poet of the world," leading it with tender patience by the divine vision of truth, beauty, and goodness.

Process theism is critical of the traditional metaphysical question, "Why is there something rather than nothing?" In process thought, the proposition, "Something exists," is a necessary truth. Insofar as traditional theism maintains the doctrine of the necessary existence of God, it too accepts the necessity of something existing. Therefore, the difference between process theism and traditional theism is not in whether something necessarily exists, but in the *nature* of the necessarily existent. According to traditional theism, the *totality* of non-divine entities is a multiplicity in need of grounding in a primordial unifying activity—the "pure act" (*actus purus*) of existing that is God. Process theism refuses to give a privileged metaphysical status to the one over the many. In Whitehead's words, "The term 'many' presupposes the term 'one,' and the term 'one' presupposes the term 'many'".

Taking creativity as the category of the ultimate is an attempt to keep the one and the many on equal metaphysical footing by taking reality itself as necessarily social. God, considered as the ultimate reality in any version of process metaphysics, necessarily exists as a social being in dynamic interaction with all non-divine entities. Clearly, treating creativity as the ultimate metaphysical principle has far-reaching consequences for the concept of God and of God's relations to others. It is not possible, in process metaphysics, to conceive divine activity as a "supernatural" intervention into the "natural" order of events. Process theists usually regard the distinction between the supernatural and the natural as a by-product of the doctrine of creation *ex nihilo*.

In process thought, there is no such thing as a realm of the natural in contrast to that which is supernatural. On the other hand, if "the natural" is defined more neutrally as "what is in the nature of things," then process metaphysics characterizes the natural as the creative activity of actual entities. In Whitehead's words, "It lies in the nature of things that the many enter into complex unity". It is tempting to emphasize process theism's denial of the supernatural and thereby highlight what the process God cannot do in comparison to what the traditional God can do (that is, to bring something from nothing). In fairness, however, equal stress should be placed on process theism's denial of the natural (as traditionally conceived) so that one may highlight what the creatures cannot do, in traditional theism, in comparison to what they can do in process metaphysics (that is, to be part creators of the world with God).

Real Relations in God

Process theists generally regard the notion of creation *ex nihilo,* as explained above, as going hand-in-hand with the idea that the relations between God and the world are one-way relations. God creates, but the creatures lack all creative power, the one wholly uncreated, the other wholly uncreative. It is not within the ability of any creature, according to this view, to make a difference to God. Aquinas's way of expressing this asymmetry is to say that the relation from God to the creatures is real (for it makes a difference, all the difference, to them) whereas the relation from the creatures to God is rational, or in the mind only (for the existence of the creatures makes no difference to the being of God). Aquinas borrows, and places in a Christian context, Aristotle's terms of "pure act" and "unmoved mover" to apply to God. To say that God is pure act is to say that anything God could be, God already is—there is no potentiality in God for any type of change.

To say that God is the unmoved mover is to say that the divine moves others but is unmoved by another—this includes the idea that God is impassible, literally, without feeling or emotion. In the view of process theism, the denial of real relations in God renders classical theism paradoxical to the point of incoherence. According to classical theism, God has perfect knowledge of a contingent and changing world, yet nothing in God could be other than it is. The one condition, however, contradicts the other. If any event is contingent then it could be otherwise—for example, this bird at this place and time is singing rather than sleeping; but if the event could be otherwise, then God's knowledge of the event could be otherwise—knowing this bird at this place and time as singing rather than as sleeping.

The contingency implied for God's knowing is not that God might have been ignorant of something but that the thing that God knows might have been different. An infallible knower necessarily knows whatever exists; it does not follow, however, that what exists is necessary *unless* one adds the premise, taken from classical theism, that nothing in God could be other than it is. Process theism jettisons the premise that there is nothing contingent in God. The only other non-atheistic alternatives, say process theists, are to follow Aristotle and deny that God knows the world or to follow Spinoza and deny that nothing in God or in the world could be other than it is. What is impossible is a God with no contingent aspects knowing a contingent world. Classical theism's denial of real relations in God also has paradoxical consequences for the concept of divine goodness. If God is unaffected by the creatures, then God is impassible, not moved by their suffering. Anselm, in *Proslogion* chapter VIII, asks how God can be compassionate towards the creatures without feeling sympathy for them.

His answer—in effect a kind of theological behaviorism — is that the creatures feel the effects of divine compassion but that God feels nothing. This leaves unanswered how non-sympathetic compassion is possible. Aquinas provides a less obviously question begging reply. He says that to love another is to will the good of the other; God necessarily wills the good of the other, so God is love. Process theists do not deny that love requires willing the good of the other, but they maintain that it requires something more, or at very least that there are greater forms of love of which willing the good of the other is a necessary aspect. Divine love is more than beneficence; it includes sensitivity to the joys and sorrows of the beloved. This idea is expressed in Whitehead's depiction of God as "the great companion—the fellow-sufferer who understands". Hartshorne points out that Anselm's God can give us "everything except the right to believe that there is one who, with infinitely subtle and appropriate sensitivity, rejoices in all our joys and sorrows in all our sorrows".

Closely related to the problem of passionless love, for classical theism, is the question of the world's value. The denial of real relations in God, coupled with the concept that the world and its creatures have no value except as it is borrowed from God, implies that that total reality described by *God-and-the-world* contains no more value than that described by *God-without-the-world*. This view has two unhappy consequences. First, it implies that there is no value in God's creating the world—nothing is gained, or lost, in God's decision to create. Second, it implies that there is no value in God's interaction with the creatures. Process theists point out that these ideas do not square with analogies drawn from human experience.

There is value in giving one's love to another, as for instance, bringing children into the world and loving them; there is also value in one's love being received and returned, as when the children mature and cherish relations with their parents. Yet, one cannot love another unless the other exists, or once existed. Thus, if there is a value in love, it requires *the existence of the other*, not merely *the idea of the existence of the other*.

Process theism rejects the counter-intuitive claim that the world as actually existing has no more value than the world as possibly existing. By parity of reasoning, process theism rejects the view that it is no better for God to create the world than to contemplate the possibility of creating it. Perhaps the most disastrous consequences of the denial of real relations in God, as far as process theists are concerned, are the problems that it poses for free will and creaturely suffering. The creative or causal relation flows one way only, *from* God *to* the world. The world and its creatures are products of a unilateral divine decision that things should be one way rather than another.

Hartshorne poses a dilemma for this view. Either biological parents are part creators of their children or they are not. If they are then God alone is not the creator. On the other hand, if parents are not genuine creators of their children then the creatures never create anything and we don't know what "create" means, for parents having children would seem to be a paradigm of creation—note the word "procreative". Classical theists accept precisely the implication that Hartshorne finds absurd, namely, that the creatures never create anything. The Thomist, for example, holds that one's parents are not creative; they are the vehicles whereby matter-energy is rearranged so as to form (not to create) a new human being. Strictly speaking, for Aquinas, what God creates is *your-parents-having-you*. Your parents had no part in your creation. Aquinas's theory poses complications for human freedom. The reality described by *your-parents-having-you* includes the decisions they make in having you. God, in creating that reality, also creates those decisions. Aquinas says that God's will is perfectly efficacious—that is, what God wills comes to pass. Therefore, your parents' decisions in *your-parents-having-you* must occur. Would this view of decision making jeopardize human freedom?

Aquinas, representing classical theism, says no, but Hartshorne, representing process theism, says yes. In Aquinas's view, one's free decisions have *two* sufficient explanations, one's own will and God's will. In other words, God brings it about not only *that* one freely decides something, but *what* one freely decides. Process theists counter that multiple freedom (whether between God and the creatures or among the creatures) implies the possibility of wills coming into conflict or being in harmony. Hartshorne says, "Risk and opportunity go together, not because God chooses to have it so, but because opportunity without risk is meaningless or contradictory". If this is true, then it must be possible for the will of the creatures to be at cross purposes with the divine will. We have already seen that classical theists and process theists agree that God wills the good of the creatures. Human beings, however, do not always will their own good, or the good of other people. In those cases, on the classical view, God brings it about that people freely decide not to will the good of others.

Process theists argue that this makes God responsible for evil and suffering in a way that contradicts divine goodness. On the classical view, for example, the crimes that disfigure human history are the fault of human beings, but they are also God's doing. Classical theists are not without responses to these criticisms. One well-known reply, used by Augustine and Aquinas, is to invoke the distinction between divine permission and divine causation of human wickedness and suffering. On this view, the evil in the world is permitted by God in order to bring about a greater good. For example, the Exultet of the Easter Vigil, sometimes ascribed to Ambrose of Milan, speaks of the sin of Adam and Eve as a blessed fault that made possible the sacrificial death of Christ. Process theists argue that there can be no distinction between permitting and causing in a being that creates the universe *ex nihilo*. On the principles of classical theism, whatever is divinely "permitted" is also divinely created to be as it is —this is one of the few points on which process theism agrees with John Calvin.

On the process view, the idea that God allows human decisions to occur which conflict with the divine purpose is no more meaningful than saying that God allows the outcome of a game to be decided by chance, by a roll of the dice, but that God loads the dice. Albert Einstein is reported to have said that God does not play dice with the universe. Although he was not a classical theist, his view on this issue is in accord with that philosophy. Hartshorne replies, "Einstein's rejection of a 'dice-throwing God' was a great man's error. And human individuals are some of the dice ...".

Dual Transcendence in Whitehead and Hartshorne

The dominant theological position in the West, which we have been referring to as classical theism, denies all relativity to God. One might suppose that the Christian doctrines of the Trinity and the Incarnation of God in Christ would temper disbelief in divine relativity. The trend, however, was to argue that these doctrines do not conflict with the denial of real relations in God. Claims of revealed truth aside, the core doctrine has been that God, to be God, must be in all respects absolute and in no respects relative. As goes the contrast between absolute and relative, so go other metaphysical contrasts. Theists traditionally held that God is *in all respects* creator, active, infinite, eternal, necessary, independent, immutable, and impassible and *in no respects* created, passive, finite, temporal, contingent, dependent, mutable, or passable.

This view can be interpreted either as a doctrine about the nature of God or as a thesis about the parameters of responsible discourse about God (in the latter case it is called the *via negativa,* or negative path). Hartshorne complains that, on either interpretation, traditional theology is guilty of a "monopolar prejudice," placing God (or talk about God) on one side of polar contrasts and the world on the other. It is *monopolar* insofar as deity is characterized by only one side of each pair of contrasts; it is *prejudicial* insofar as it holds to the invidious nature of the contrasts. As Hartshorne notes, "One pole of each contrary is regarded as more excellent than the other, so that the supremely excellent being cannot be described by the other and inferior pole".

Hartshorne notes that ordinary language provides scanty support for and abundant evidence against the superiority of one pole over the other. We have already seen that process theism finds positive value in God's love being active as well as passive; it is as important that God wills the good of the creatures as that God is affected by their joy and suffering. Here is another of Hartshorne's many examples, expressed with some humor:

> The venerable dogma, 'agent is superior to patient', is not derived from the study of knowledge. Indeed, it is not derived from any careful examination of ordinary cases. To speak is to be agent, to listen is to be patient, and those who want to show their superiority by speaking without listening are not trustworthy authorities in the theory of value.

Hartshorne's larger point is that the pairs of meta-physical contraries are *not* related as superior to inferior, but that there are admirable and deficient manifestations of both sides. He sums this up in the principle of *the non-invidiousness of the metaphysical contraries*. If this principle is correct, and if God is conceived as the eminent embodiment of value and supremely worshipful being, then God must be conceived not in monopolar terms but as dipolar, exemplifying the admirable forms of both pairs of metaphysical contrasts. For example, rather than saying that God is in all respects active and in no respects passive, the alternative is to say that God is active in some respects and passive in other respects, each in uniquely excellent ways. This is one meaning of the expression "dipolar theism"; in light of other meanings to be given to "dipolar" in discussions of process theism, it is perhaps clearer to use Hartshorne's expression for this idea: *dual transcendence*, that is to say, God as the supreme embodiment of each pair of metaphysical contraries.

The most elegant statement of dual transcendence is in the closing pages of *Process and Reality*, a line of which we have already quoted. The complete quotation reads like a litany: It is as true to say that God is permanent and the world fluent, as that the World is permanent and God is fluent.

It is as true to say that God is one and the World many, as that the World is one and God many. It is as true to say that, in comparison with the World, God is actual eminently, as that, in comparison with God, the World is actual eminently. It is as true to say that the World is immanent in God, as that God is immanent in the World. It is as true to say that God transcends the World, as that the World transcends God. It is as true to say that God creates the World, as that the World creates God. We saw above in the discussion of divine creativity that Whitehead indulges in poetic expression and that understanding his meaning requires looking more closely at his metaphysical categories. Above all, however, what is required is a way of making principled distinctions between different aspects of God so that the doctrine of dual transcendence does not collapse into contradiction. Let us examine the different ways in which Whitehead and Hartshorne attempt to save the doctrine of dual transcendence from incoherence.

Whitehead on the Two Natures of God

In Whitehead's philosophy, every actual entity has a physical and a mental pole. For this reason, Whitehead speaks of actual entities as "dipolar" (thus, a second meaning of the word). The physical and mental poles are aspects of every real being (actual entities) but they are not real beings themselves. In other words, Whitehead is not a mind-body dualist in the manner of Descartes. It is also important to note that, for Whitehead, human consciousness is a higher form of mentality but not the only form. Thus, Whitehead does not claim that every real being is a conscious entity. As with Leibniz, Whitehead recognizes a continuum of mind-like qualities ranging from very primitive feelings to the most advanced form of self-awareness. Whereas Leibniz speaks of every real being—he calls them monads—as having apperception and appetition, Whitehead speaks of every actual entity as *prehending*, or grasping or taking account of, its environment and as striving to realize the *subjective aim* of coordinating its prehensions in some determinate fashion.

Whitehead uses the word "feeling" as a synonym for prehension to indicate the vector character of feelings—a feeling is always a feeling *of* something. Whitehead's belief in a continuum of mental qualities fits neatly with evolutionary theory where it is commonplace to conceive differing forms of organic complexity as associated with differing levels of mental capacity. For example, the frontal cortex of a human brain allows for more advanced mentality than one finds in a chimpanzee, whose brain is not as complex. Thus, as Jane Goodall points out, the psychological development of a chimpanzee and a human child is roughly parallel for a couple of years, until the human child begins to acquire language, at which point the human far surpasses its primate cousin. Whitehead is fully aware that there is an imaginative leap in applying these categories to God, but he believes the application can be done in a disciplined and systematic fashion. Whitehead conceives God as an actual entity.

In God, the physical and mental poles are called the *consequent nature* and the *primordial nature* respectively. As with the physical and mental poles of actual entities, so the two "natures" are distinguishable but inseparable aspects of deity. That is to say, neither can exist apart from the other and each requires the other. The primordial nature is God's envisagement of all possibilities; in the idiom of Leibniz, it is God's knowledge of all possible worlds. It is called "primordial" because it represents *what could be* in a sense not tethered to the actual course of events. It is logical space; deficient in actuality apart from the consequent nature says Whitehead. The consequent nature is God's prehensions of the actual processes of the world. Conversely, it is the world's influence on God. It is called "consequent" because it is consequent upon, or dependent upon, the decisions of non-divine actual entities (Whitehead calls them actual occasions).

The consequent nature is the record of all achieved fact, a perfect memory of what has been—Whitehead speaks of the "objective immortality" of the world in God. The two natures work in concert in the process of God's interaction with the creatures. The deity receives the world of actual occasions into its experience; then, comparing what has actually occurred with the realm of pure possibility, God informs the world with new ideals (new aims), customized for each actual entity, for what realistically could be achieved. Whitehead sometimes refers to this aspect of the process as the *superjective nature* of God. It is God's relevance for the world as a "lure for feeling," urging the creatures to strive for whatever perfection of which they are capable. Each of the statements in Whitehead's "litany" can be interpreted in terms of the interaction between the two natures and God's interaction with the world. God is permanent in the sense of everlastingly envisioning the realm of possibility; the world is permanent as objectively immortal in God's memory.

God is fluent in constantly acquiring new experiences of the world and the world is fluent in the rhythm of the birth and death of actual occasions. God is one in being a single actual entity; but God is many in the graded relevance of possibilities provided for each emergent occasion. The world is one in virtue of God's experience of it; the world is many because of the plurality of occasions that make it up. God is eminently actual in comparison to the world by achieving a unification of worldly occasions in the consequent nature that is beyond any of them taken singly; but the world is eminently actual in comparison to God's primordial nature, which is not concrete, although it is as infinite as the entire range of possibility. God and the world are immanent in each other in that each experience the other; yet God and the world transcend each other by being realities whose experiences are not entirely determined by the other. Finally, as we have seen, God creates the world by informing it with possibilities (technically speaking, God provides "initial aims" for every nascent occasion). The world creates God, not by bringing God into existence, but by creating something in God, namely the material for what shall become objectively immortal.

The Viability of Whitehead's God for Christian Theology

From the standpoint of Christian concerns, Whitehead's metaphysics is most distinctive in being a philosophy of creation which does not identify creative power exclusively with God. Christian thinkers, interpreting the Biblical story of creation ontologically, rejected the Greek understanding of being as self-sufficient: all being, with the notable exception of God, is seen as contingent upon the act of creation. Before there can be being, there must be the creative act of coming-into-being. Whitehead agrees insofar as the 'being' of every actuality "is constituted by its 'becoming,'" for "how an actuality becomes constitutes what that actual entity is."

Traditional theism, however, considers such 'becoming' to be the act of a transcendent creator, himself uncreated, while Whitehead regards every actuality, including God, to be at least partially self-created. Being (ens) depends upon a creative act: for Aquinas, this is the act of being; for Tillich, the power of being; for Whitehead, the inherent exercise of creativity. But for Aquinas and for Tillich, this power of creation is ultimately lodged in God, who is being-itself, while Whitehead's God is an instance of creativity, like all other actualities, and cannot be identified with "creativity-itself." For traditional theism, creativity is unified and transcendent; for process theism, it is pluralized and wholly immanent. While some theories (e.g. emanationism) have been proposed for creation as the act of a transcendent creator, this act is usually placed beyond the scope of philosophical scrutiny.

In its concrete detail immanent creativity shares this mystery of pure freedom, but the general nature of the process of becoming which renders such free creation possible can be described. If being is unity, Whitehead reasons, becoming must be unification, and unification presupposes an antecedent multiplicity to be unified. Thus creativity embodies the rhythm of the one and the many, whereby "the many become one, and are increased by one." In the world the many occasions in the past of a given actual occasion are objectified for that occasion as the many efficient causal influences it unifies in its own actuality, whereby it becomes one more actuality in the world for future occasions. In God the many occasions are unified by "the overpowering rationality of his conceptual harmonization," but this ideal unity becomes one more lure for physical realization in the actual world as the initial subjective aim of a newly emerging occasion.

In the exercise of creativity the many become one, physically in the world, conceptually in God, but in both cases the new unity contributes to a new multiplicity, and so on, ad infinitum. Thus creativity is everlasting, without beginning or end, with the world contributing to God, and God to the world. For classical theism, the most striking feature of process theism has been its insistence that God's experience grows as it is enriched by the temporal achievements of the actual world. This feature follows necessarily from Whitehead's "principle of relativity," the metaphysical generalization that every actuality causally influences every other actuality. Yet it also meets the religious need that no actualized value be excluded from the life of God.

Were creativity and God identified, God would already include all actual values as the source of their being, and not be dependent upon their actualization by others. God's involvement with temporality may be the most striking feature of process theism, but it is a derivative feature following from God's dependence upon the non-divine creativity inherent in the world.

It should be noted that this dependence is not vicious; it threatens neither God's necessary existence nor his well-being, for no matter what happens God has the conceptual resources to achieve a final beauty in his experience. He already possesses all abstract perfections, and depends upon the world solely for the enrichment of his experience in concrete content.

God is infinite in possibility and in the conceptual actualization of possibility: his physical actuality, however, is derivative from the world because all physical actualization is finite, selective, intolerant of alternatives, and ultimately somewhat arbitrary. The non-identification of God with creativity or being-it has many distinct advantages for Christian theism, some of which we may briefly enumerate:

1. In creating itself, each creature is exercising a real freedom distinct from God's. Its freedom is not compromised by being also somehow God's action, or by being already known as determinate in God's foreknowledge. Now a substance philosophy can argue that God only creates subjects which are then free to experience and act on their own, but this requires a necessary distinction between God's creative and sustaining roles, and in any case cannot apply to a process view which envisages subjects as coming into existence through their own experiences and decision. If the ultimate actualities of the world are events and not substances, these events must be either created by God or be self-created, and only the latter alternative fully preserves their freedom.
2. On this process view every actuality has ultimate significance as contributing to the experience of God. Human striving is ultimately meaningful because it enriches that cosmic, everlasting, conscious appreciation.

Its striving has not been in vain, despite the ravages of time, for otherwise God's experience would lack something it now possesses. If God's experience were complete and unchanging for all time, there seems no way in which our action could either add or detract from it and hence no way in which concrete meaning can be given to service for the sake of God's glory. Does this not merely mean that our service only affects God's reputation among creatures, and not God himself?

3. A plurality of self-creative acts introduces a measure of potential conflict and incompatibility, which is the mark of evil. God is responsible for the ideals whereby the actions of the world might be co-ordinated, but the world is responsible for all physical actualization, for its good and for its evil. Evil is not the result of the recalcitrance of some blind force of creativity, for Whitehead's creativity is actual only in its instantiations as the self-creative acts of individual creatures deciding their own destinies. Evil is not willed by God, actively or passively, for he is not merely allowing evil for the sake of fostering human freedom. Rather, God can only create by persuading the creature to create himself. Creaturely freedom is not a gift bestowed in exceptional circumstances but the precondition for creation, and that pre-condition necessarily entails the risk of freedom. Above all, the non-identification of God with creativity exempts God from the responsibility for evil.
4. If both God and the world share in a common creativity, there is a mutual solidarity between them whereby God's agency can be discerned in the activity of the world. The doctrine of a transcendent creator can easily be put to one side by a scientific pre-occupation with worldly activity, to be treated first as a deistic hypothesis which becomes dispensable with the emergence of plausible mechanisms for evolution. If the world is evolving, it was not created perfect in the first place, and God as the source of its being seems to be supporting indifferently

both its advance and its degradation. Process theism, however, can interpret the Biblical creation story cosmologically, for God's "speech" is his self-expression in terms of lures for his creatures to actualize. The ever-emergent growth of complexity and order in the world testifies to God's infinite patience and resourcefulness in supplying the world with relevant possibilities for actualization, while the dead ends, wastage, and accompanying degradation indicate creaturely willfulness and resistance. The Biblical account of creation illuminates the process of evolution once it is understood as the gradual emergence of order out of chaos through divine guidance rather than as the ontological production of being out of non-being.

5. If God and finite actualities are all alike instances of creativity such that God is also a being and not being-itself, then our knowledge of God can be metaphysically intelligible without recourse to the more desperate strategies of indirect predication. God becomes no longer an exception to the metaphysical principles but their chief exemplification. God's mystery is not thereby affronted, but discovered in its proper place, not so much at the limits of human intelligibility as in the depths of self-creative freedom.

6. If as a result of non-divine creativity God's experience is contingent upon worldly actualization, then this responsive action toward the world is also contingent. God's action necessarily exemplifies the metaphysical principles of his nature, but it is neither reducible to those principles nor deducible from them, for it is a free, creative response to the contingencies of each situation as it arises. As long as all of God's attributes and actions were regarded as necessary, nothing could be left to revelation which was not already in principle accessible to metaphysical reason, so reason had to be somehow artificially restricted to make room for revelation. Process theism no longer places that Christian thinker under this

constraint. Reason ascertains all it can about God, but in recognizing that there must be contingent aspects in God, it knows that it cannot determine what these are in concrete fact. Here we must appeal to the particularities of God's action in history, to the records of the evolutionary process for God's dealing with nature, and to the records of man's encounter with God for his dealings with man in sacred scripture. Philosophical inquiry and religious tradition complement each other in ascertaining the necessary and contingent dimensions of God, respectively.

These six points deserve further elaboration and supplementation, but that is not our task here. Before these advantages can be realized, Whitehead's concept of God must prove to be "viable." We must show how it can meet and surmount those objections which proponents of the identification of God with creativity (or being-itself) consider "fatal" to the theory of their non-identification. This is the task to which we wish to address ourselves, taking up the main objections seriatim.

Such a God is not omnipotent. If the world is constituted by a plurality of self-creative acts, God does not control its destiny. This does not mean, however, that he is limited in the exercise of the power appropriate to his nature, namely, divine persuasion. We must distinguish between two kinds of power, coercive and persuasive. Coercive influences are those we must take into account in actualization. In practical affairs we regard any measure as coercive if non-compliance threatens our lives, our well-being, our careers, our liberty or our families, yet theoretically we are still free to disregard them if we are prepared to pay the price.

Strictly speaking, then, only efficient causation is completely coercive, for no actualization can occur which does not embody its efficient causes. The coercive power of efficient causation results from the physical actualization of finite events, which create stubborn realities with which the future must cope. The causal past is coercive precisely because it is finite; it is only a limited selection of what might have been, and that limitation restricts the present in what it can become. Divine actualization, on the other hand, is conceptual rather than physical, resulting in the presentation of lures for future realization. Instead of making himself into a finite, stubborn actuality, coercively impinging upon the world, God unifies the various finite actualities of the world into a conceptual whole by means of his infinite supply of ideal possibilities. While God thus provides each occasion in the process of coming-to-be the best possibility for the unification of its efficient causal influences, that ideal is persuasive rather than coercive since one possibility does not exclude relevant alternative possibilities. Others are equally capable of realization and give measure to the occasion's freedom.

Such a God is finite. Whitehead is emphatic "that all actualization is finite" for "every occasion of actuality is in its own nature finite. There is no totality which is the harmony of all perfections. Whatever is realized in any one occasion of experience necessarily excludes the unbounded welter of contrary possibilities. There are always 'others,' which might have been and are not." Since every actuality excludes others, there is an intrinsic incompatibility among possibilities with respect to their realization, but "this notion of incompatibility has never been applied to ideals in the Divine realization. We must conceive the Divine Eros as the active entertainment of all ideals, with the urge to their finite realizations, each in its due season. Thus a process must be inherent in God's nature whereby his infinity is acquiring realization."

Whitehead here denies that God is actually infinite in the sense of being the complete actualization of all possible ideals, for such actualizations are incompatible with one another. Rather, such finite physical actualization belongs to the occasions of the world, from which God acquires his measure of finite concreteness. Yet "the conceptual entertainment of incompatibilities is possible, and so is their conceptual comparison." Thus the infinitude of all possible ideals may be present within God's conceptual entertainment, seeking their finite actualization in the world. In this way the world receives a task it can perform for God without merely reduplicating what is already present within God. Whitehead specifies that the actualization of each possibility should be in its due season, for every individual possibility is good in itself, though its incompatibilities with other actualities may produce evil. "Insistence on birth at the wrong season is the trick of evil." If only actualized with its proper fellows, every possibility would produce good and not evil, and God's unlimited appetition for the physical realization of all possibilities does not mean that he seeks indifferently the evil with the good.

While physical actualization is finite and such finitude is being temporally absorbed into God, this does not mean that God should be conceived as finite. "It belongs to the nature of physical experience that it is finite," but "conceptual experience can be infinite." To be sure, his consequent nature is finite and ever-growing as God receives into his experience the finite achievements of the world. But God's actuality is fundamentally a conceptual one, infinite, yet complete, capable of absorbing into itself an everlasting succession of physical feelings without disturbing its essentially non-temporal unity.

Whitehead's God is finite only if we apply the inappropriate standard of physical actualization, ignoring God's conceptual actualization creating the structure of possibility capable of embracing all actuality. Such "unfettered conceptual valuation, 'infinite' in Spinoza's sense of that term, is only possible once in the universe," but that is sufficient. Whitehead always affirms God's infinity, but wisely recognizes that this applies to conceptual possibility rather than to physical actuality.

Our argument is handicapped by the fact that Whitehead characteristically uses "actuality" and "actualization" as restricted only to finite, physical realization, as in the quotations above. Thus the primordial nature, taken in abstraction from the full actuality of God is "actually deficient" inasmuch as it lacks concreteness of physical prehension. On the other hand, God as primordial is "the presupposed actuality of conceptual operation, in unison of becoming with every other creative act." The question at hand is whether we can appropriately speak of both temporal and non-temporal actuality, and this depends on how we understand actuality. For Whitehead, 'decision' "constitutes the very meaning of actuality. 'Actuality' is the decision amid 'potentiality.' It represents stubborn fact which cannot be evaded."

Now the primordial envisagement of all possibility is a "created fact," conditioning all actual occasions, the outcome of a divine non-temporal decision ordering the eternal objects in terms of their relevance for actualization in the world. Apart from that decision, the eternal objects are wholly ineffective, not properly either possible or impossible. The act whereby they are rendered possible also determines what is metaphysically impossible, and by the ontological principle the reason for this determination must be found in some actuality. This actuality must necessarily be non-temporal, since the structure of possibility and impossibility conditions the world at all times.

As the determination of what is metaphysically impossible, God's primordial envisagement is "an actual efficient fact" constraining the character of physical actualization in the world, but the limits of impossibility also afford the creature with the freedom of possibility; the two go hand in hand. Since God thus non-temporally decides, it is appropriate to speak of God's infinite conceptual actualization in contrast to finite physical actualizations. From a temporal point of view, this "non-temporal act of all-inclusive valuations is ... always in concrescence and never in the past," continually being rendered concrete through the inclusion of finite achievement.

Such a God is subordinate to the metaphysical principles. Paul Tillich writes: "The being of God cannot be understood as the existence of a being alongside others or above others. If God is a being, he is subject to the categories of finitude." Langdon Gilkey adds: "Thus a philosophical use of the symbol "God" makes sense only if that symbol thematizes or has reference to the ground of ultimate coherence which the philosophy itself presupposes, if God is explicated as the source of that coherence rather than merely as a finite exemplification of it." He applies this objection explicitly to Whitehead, "whose god is subordinate to the larger process and so to the metaphysical categories explicative of that process." Yet is it true that God must be conceived either as "the ground of ultimate coherence" or as the "chief exemplification of rational principles"? What Gilkey's argument overlooks is that God was initially introduced into Whitehead's philosophy as "the ground of rationality," and this role is never abandoned.

God is metaphysically intelligible because he exemplifies the metaphysical principles, yet he also creates them. As we have already seen, God's non-temporal envisagement orders all eternal objects in terms of possibility and impossibility. Now the boundary between possibility and impossibility is determined by what is metaphysically necessary; every possibility must exemplify these metaphysical principles to be possible, while every impossibility is impossible because it cannot exemplify those principles. Thus "the ideal realization of potentialities in a primordial actual entity constitutes the metaphysical stability whereby the actual process exemplifies general principles of metaphysics." The ontological principle enjoins us to look to "the nature of God for reasons of the highest absoluteness," for his own self-actualization is the source for ultimate rationality. We tend to think of the primordial nature of God as uncreated, yet God as exemplifying creativity must be conceived as self-created. The primordial envisagement of God is his act of self-creation, which creates the metaphysical principles which both he and the world exemplify. "His conceptual actuality at once exemplifies and establishes the categoreal conditions."

Such a God is not free either to create or not to create. The very nature of creativity requires that God at least create himself, for otherwise he could not exist. Yet what usually is intended by this objection concerns the necessary existence of the world. On Whitehead's principles, there can be no temporal origin to the world, for every actual occasion depends upon the efficient causality of antecedent actual occasions. Moreover, the metaphysical principles God exemplifies necessarily require the concomitant existence of the world. For without the world, God would be deficient in physical actuality.

Consider the alternative. Were our metaphysical principles such that God's experience would be equally fulfilled whether or not the world existed, then the existence of the world would be wholly gratuitous, devoid of any ultimate significance from the divine perspective. Unless the world positively enriches the divine experience which otherwise would be impoverished, the world might just as well not have been for all the ultimate difference it makes. God's freedom within any set of metaphysical principles destroys whatever significance the world might have for God.

God's ultimate freedom, however, resides in that self-creative act whereby the metaphysical principles are established. Given the metaphysical principles which do exist, the world is necessary, but these principles could have been otherwise had God so created them. God's primordial envisagement could have so determined possibility and impossibility that his own act of concrescence would completely exhaust all creativity, permitting him to exist in solitary splendour. In that sense God could have existed without the world, for God is free to create the conditions rendering the world either necessary or impossible, though not contingent. For what God cannot do, by the nature of creativity, is create a world distinct from himself which lacks the power of self-creation. For insofar as God creates, he creates himself, and for there to be an actuality distinct from God, it must be able to create itself.

Such a God is subordinate to creativity. Creativity, together with 'many' and 'one' are the "ultimate notions" completing the Category of the Ultimate, while God is introduced under the heading, "Some Derivative Notions." "'Creativity' is the universal of universals characterizing ultimate matter of fact." "It is that ultimate notion of highest generality at the base of actuality." God is "a creature of creativity," "its primordial, non-temporal accident." Such statements seem to suggest that God is subject to a power greater than himself. Both God and the World "are in the grip of the ultimate metaphysical ground, the creative advance into novelty."

More generally, Carl G. Vaught has recently summarized four objections drawn largely from Tillich against conceiving God as a being rather than as being-itself or creativity:

a. "The concept of a being is incompatible with the concepts of intimacy and absoluteness, and hence incompatible with the concept of perfection itself.... If God were defined as a being, he would be distinguishable from the being he might possess. As a being, he would presuppose the being which he had. Being would then become the basic notion rather than God as the being who possessed it."
b. God must be regarded as self-caused, presupposing nothing other than him.
c. "Worship requires that its 'object' be infinite. But if God is to be assigned a place within the framework of beings, he is limited by contrast with them, and hence a finite being in a larger whole."

d. "An individual entity, as individualized, is deficient in the manner in which it participates in the reality of beings other than itself."

The concept of a perfect being "mistakenly presupposes that an individual entity, really distinct from other beings, can participate with perfect adequacy in the reality of beings other than itself." Creativity is clearly metaphysically ultimate for Whitehead, but that does not make it religiously ultimate.

It is metaphysically ultimate in the sense that all actuality must exemplify it, but it is nothing apart from those exemplifications. "Creativity is without a character of its own," indifferent alike to its exemplifications, whether great or small, good or evil. It is too indeterminate to be worshipped, while its exemplifications are too diverse to warrant indiscriminate devotion. Only its supreme exemplification, God, deserves worship. That which is religiously ultimate must be actual, yet creativity is actual only insofar as it is actualized in its exemplifications. Again, God must be unified to be God, an instance of creative unification, while creativity in itself is wholly indeterminate, neither one nor many.

Whitehead's principles will not permit the ascription of existence, unity, or actuality to creativity as such which would be necessary in order to make the religious ultimacy of creativity plausible. In their absence, nothing could be more religiously ultimate than God as the supreme instance of creativity.

God is a "creature of creativity," but this means precisely that he is self-created, not receiving his being from another. God presupposes creativity, because it signifies just that inherent, intrinsic act of becoming whereby each actuality, including God, constitutes itself. Much of the objection to creativity as a notion distinct from God loses its force once it is appreciated that creativity cannot be extrinsic to any actuality. Each actuality has its own creativity because it is self-created.

This plurality of self-creation, moreover, means that there cannot be one, single, all-inclusive act of creativity. Creativity is an analogical notion, inherently diverse in all its instantiations, even though each is an act of self-unification. God is "its primordial, non-temporal accident" because he is the one, infinite act of non-temporal conceptual self-unification, the accident of creativity because its character does not derive from the inherent character of creativity but from the freedom of the divine decision. That God is "in the grip of" the creative advance simply means that God is always in the act of self-creation, unifying that which he receives of the world's novelty, always in becoming, never being limited simply to his being.

God's act of creative self-unification is distinct from all finite acts of self-unification, but does this mean he is limited by contrast to them? As we have seen, that divine act, as conceptual and non-temporal, is infinite and capable of including within it the achievements of all the finite acts. Unlike physical actualization, which maintains its individuality by only partially absorbing its world into itself through deficient participation, conceptual actualization achieves its own individuality through complete participation, because the conceptual supplementation of patterned contrast permits every element to retain its own distinct individuality in the divine unification. In the world, the many become one, losing their manyness, but God prehends every actuality "into the harmony of the universal feeling, which is always immediate, always many, always and one." "Thus the consequent nature of God is composed of a multiplicity of elements with individual self-realization. It is just as much a multiplicity as it is a unity."

For the multiplicity of finite self-decisions are included within the unity of the divine self-decision, without disturbing that unity. As achievement, all is included in

God. As activity, creaturely activity is distinct from divine activity, for an all-inclusive divine activity would exclude all other activity. Either God does everything, or he is enriched by the activities of others. Whitehead adopts the second alternative as making more sense of our world.

Such a God cannot penetrate to the innermost being of man. For God's creative action cannot be identified with man's exercise of creativity, which is his innermost being. Man's decisions contribute to the life of God, but they involve acts of self-creation distinct from God's activity, which God prehends as already achieved. God cannot do the creature's decision-making for it without it losing its own freedom.

This assumption that God can only penetrate to the innermost being of man by becoming identified with his creativity is too restrictive, for there are other meanings to interpenetration. In particular, there are especially intimate ways in which God and creature may share in each other's lives in Whitehead's view. God "shares with every new creation its actual world," which means he shares the same initial spatiotemporal standpoint with which the creature initiates its becoming. God is not prehended as "out there," as simply one more item in its experience, but as "in here," as the ideal unity of all that which the occasion is seeking to unify. The initial subjective aim, which is really God present to the creature's physical actualization, is the central core of the creature prompting its own concrescence, and all that the occasion does is immediately taken up into the divine life. Such interpenetration permits all the intimacy between God and man that could possibly be desired by a mysticism of union.

At the same time, Whitehead's conceptuality keeps clear the respective roles of God and man, providing an adequate safeguard against any mysticism of identity, in accordance with the Christian tradition generally. A mysticism of identity erodes the I/Thou encounter between

God and man which this tradition, particularly in its Biblical form, has sought to affirm. Unless God and creativity are sharply distinguished, there will be a constant temptation for Christian thinkers to drift toward a mysticism of identity, thereby betraying the original genius of the tradition.

8

On Scientific Explanations of God-Experiences

Religious Faith and Experience a Biological Misunderstanding

The story was prompted by the work of molecular biologist, Dean Hamer, author of The God Gene: How Faith is hardwired into Our Genes. Hamer argues that our sense of spirituality is a biological trait hardwired into our genes by evolutionary accident, or possibly even evolutionary design. The implication of Hamer's research is that religious faith and experience are nothing more than a misinterpretation of a biological phenomenon. If spirituality has biological connections, is religious faith/experience based on genuine perceptions of a divine reality, or is religious faith/experience a biological misunderstanding caused by ignorance of our own physiology? Could belief in the divine be a myth of the mind?

Hamer's thesis developed out of a study he conducted on the topic of smoking and addiction for the National Cancer Institute. More than 1000 individuals took the standardized Temperament and Character Inventory test which includes questions that measure self-transcendence (the ability to get entirely lost in an experience, transpersonal identification, and a feeling of connectedness to a larger universe) and mysticism (an openness to things not entirely provable). Hamer used the data to conduct a spiritual experiment on the side. He theorized that if our sense of spirituality has biological connections (or causes), those who ranked higher in spirituality should share some genetic link in common that those who ranked lower did not.

As a result he "went poking around in their genes to see if he could find the DNA responsible for the differences." With over 35,000 genes and 3.2 billion chemical bases in the human genome, he limited his search for the "spiritual gene" to nine genes known to produce monoamines (brain chemicals that regulate mood and motor control). He found what he was looking for in the gene known as VMAT2. "Those with the nucleic acid cytosine in one particular spot on the gene ranked high [in spirituality]. Those with the nucleic acid adenine in the same spot ranked lower." He concluded that "a single change in a single base in the middle of the gene seemed directly related to the ability to feel self-transcendence."

While he seemed to have identified the spiritual gene, Hamer added some important disclaimers:

1. Human traits often involve the interplay of hundreds or even thousands of genes, so it is doubtful that our sense of spirituality is dictated by cytosine alone. Other genes or chemical bases are likely to be involved.
2. The presence of the nucleic acid cytosine does not directly translate into one's belief in God, or even a pursuit of spirituality. One may posses the nucleic acid and yet not believes in God, or pursues religion. They are simply more likely to do so than others.
3. There is a distinction between spirituality and religion. "Spirituality is a feeling or a state of mind; religion is the way that state gets codified into law."
4. If cytosine is related to spirituality as a contributing cause, it speaks nothing concerning the reality of God's

existence. Hamer said, "My findings are agnostic on the existence of God. If there's a God, there's a God. Just knowing what brain chemicals are involved in acknowledging that is not going to change the fact."

Science and Theology

The relationship between science and theology has a long and complicated history that goes back four or five hundred years. This discussion blends into an even longer debate over the relationship between reason and revelation. In response to science theology has undergone a profound reformulation.

The first challenge was that the success of scientific method called into question truth claims based on supernatural revelation and tradition. Science has provided the modern world its most reliable standard of knowledge. Science is the dominant paradigm of truth about the world. At the extreme we get what can be called scientism:

What cannot be known by science not only cannot be known but is not real. Along with this there was in many quarters a loss of confidence in speculative reason under the influence of philosophers like David Hume and Immanuel Kant. In the minds of many they demolished the traditional arguments for the existence of God.

This took place in the context of the Enlightenment, which urged people to think for themselves. It called into question all ancient traditions, superstitions, and any claims about reality that could not stand the test of enlightened reason. The great themes of the Enlightenment were reason, nature, and progress. If we will use our reason to understand nature and history, we can make material and moral progress as we move toward an ultimate perfection of life on earth. Among the resources of reason none was more important than science in providing the truth that would enlighten us and help us make life better. Science was based on evidence we could test.

It solved one problem after another. It worked. It was creating a picture of the world and of human beings that was so convincing to so many that it gradually weakened other ways of knowing or pushed them aside. For Christians it raised a disturbing question: If the Bible could be wrong in matters of fact, could it also be wrong about matters of faith? The second challenge was that science undermined biblical cosmology. The Bible had provided Christian Europe its basic story of the origin of the cosmos and the structure of the natural world for 1500 hundred years. Between 1500-1900 of the Christian era, this understanding was demolished. The biblical picture was that of a three-story universe with the earth in the middle, heaven above, and hell below.

This world came into being a few thousand years ago with all the species of plant and animal life reproducing after their kind. Adam and Eve were real people living in a garden that could roughly be located on a map. A series of discoveries from Copernicus to Darwin demonstrated that picture of the universe and of human origins to be in error. Copernicus showed that the earth was not in the center of the world. His suggestion that the sun was the center was also wrong, but that is another story. Next geology revealed the earth to be much older than the biblical chronology allowed.

Then came Darwin with the big bombshell. In 1859 the world was shaken by the claim that present species of life have evolved over a long period of time by natural selection to produce the forms of life that now inhabit the earth. The most disturbing feature of this theory was that human beings did not descend from Adam and Eve a few thousand years ago but evolved from earlier species that could be traced back to the first beginnings of life on earth far in the distant past. The Christian world was deeply disturbed. A few came pretty quickly to the conclusion that Darwin was right. They saw that there was no point in trying to resist.

Others were upset and simply refused to believe it. They insisted that the Bible not science gave us the true picture. In England Bishop Wilberforce reacted with sarcasm. He asked Julian Huxley, the great scientist; whether it was on his mother's side or his father's side that he was descended from apes. An upper class, aristocratic British lady upon hearing about Darwin's theory said, "Oh dear that is so dreadful. Let us hope it is not true. But if it is, let us keep quiet about it." In America Charles Hodge, the eminent Presbyterian theologian at Princeton said that Darwinism is atheism. This was all taking place from 1860-1900.

This, then, is the second impact of science. It undermined the biblical picture of the physical and biological world. The controversy raised by Darwin goes on today. Liberal Christians accept evolution and revise their view of the Bible and of the world accordingly. Fundamentalists still insist that Darwin was wrong and the Bible is right. Some want creationism taught in the public schools along with evolution. The third challenge was the fact that the scientific picture of a law-abiding world called into question the reality of miracle and the supernatural. Science pictures nature as a dynamic, causal network, self-contained and self-explanatory. There is one order of activities in which all events occurs in a law-abiding fashion.

In this view miracles are suspect. The Bible is full of miracles from the Red Sea incident to the Virgin Birth of Jesus and his Resurrection from the dead, to mention only a few. John Calvin had used miracles and the fulfillment of prophesy as evidence of the truth of Scripture. Now it was miracles themselves that were in question. Could Christians live everyday in a world that abided by the laws of nature and then go to church on Sunday and believe in miracles that violated them? The fourth challenge was that the picture of nature as a self-contained causal system called into question the need for a supernatural creator or for any reference to divine purpose. From the 17th century beginnings until the 20th century revolutions in physical science, the natural order had been described by science in mechanistic, deterministic, materialist terms.

Nature consists of bits of material stuff - matter - organized into a machine that operates in accordance with inexorable laws. The natural order is at best a neutral and at worst a meaningless process. There are causes but no reasons or purposes in nature. In nature there is no freedom, no meaning, or value. This is the most powerful and daunting challenge of all. Science seemed to imply a universe that needed no God to create it. It was a machine that required no explanation beyond itself. This machine did just what it did do, not knowing or caring what it did or having any purpose in doing it. In 1903 Bertrand Russell offered the most extreme summary of this outlook by saying that the world science presents for our belief is meaningless and void of purpose, an accidental collocation of atoms.

A lot of people, including myself, do not think that present-day science requires this world-view, but it prevailed for 300 years. Moreover, many scientists today still hold that nature is full of causes but exemplifies no purpose.

Fundamentalism: Fundamentalists hold the view that the Bible is inerrant, without error. It tells the truth about everything it mentions. It is right about nature, the universe, the origin of human beings, the reproduction of species, and so on. All of its historical claims are true. The miracle stories happened just the way the Bible says. There is to be no compromise of biblical truth. The Bible is the Word of God in a full, complete, total manner and in all respects. Hence, if the Bible teaches that Adam and Eve were literal people living a garden somewhere on earth that we could locate on earth, then that story is just true. If evolution teaches something contrary to what the right interpretation of Scripture requires, then it is wrong. True science is in harmony with the Bible.

Whatever contradicts the Bible is bad science. Some conservatives have made a variety of accommodations to science with respect to biblical cosmology, the age of the earth, and even evolution. Some even venture to distinguish between matters of science not essential to religious truth and matters of faith in which the Bible is without any error at all. As the recognition of the authority of science grows with respect to its own legitimate field of inquiry, the closer it comes to blending in with a moderate liberal approach. At some point the boundaries between science and theology and between fundamentalism and liberalism may become fuzzy.

Liberalism: What all forms of liberalism agree on is that science is not to be contested on its own terms. If the scientific evidence shows conclusively that evolution occurred in the way that present-day science says it did, then it must be accepted. We simply have to come to terms with it. The basic way of doing that is to distinguish between the realms that science and religion deal with. Here let me distinguish very broadly between two sub-types of liberal thinking that make the distinction between science and theology in somewhat different ways. They agree with the basic liberal premise is that we must distinguish between two spheres of knowledge about reality.

The first approach is deeply influenced by the philosophy of Immanuel Kant. Kant distinguished between the realm of fact that science deals with and the realm of value that morality and religion deal with. It is true that science presents us with a world of fact that is law-abiding and void of freedom and value. However, we have another faculty of understanding as moral persons who are free, who can live in accordance with duty, and make value judgments. Theology interprets the moral and religious realms. Science and religion cannot contradict each other since they deal with different spheres of human activity and deal with the world in different ways. Many theologians in the 19th and 20th centuries have taken their clues from

Kant. Karl Barth, Emil Brunner, Rudolf Bultmann, and H. Richard Niebuhr fall into this camp.

Existential theology under the joint influence of Kant and Kierkegaard takes this approach. The world, then, is one order of activities that human beings deal with in two different ways. On the one hand, we have the realm of fact, law, cause, and determinism. On the other hand, we have the realm of value, meaning, purpose, and freedom. Morality and religion are in this second sphere, and theology is the interpreter of the moral and religious experience of human beings in relation to God. Science neither contradicts nor supports religion. It has its own methods and its own subject matter. The same is true of theology. It cannot call into question the findings of science, but it can accept them whatever they are and then go on to make its own claims based on Scripture, tradition, reason, and experience. However, it does mean that much of the Bible cannot be taken literally. The Bible is not a book of science.

The creation stories Genesis have to be seen as myths that contain moral and religious truth for our lives today in a world that was produced by a long evolutionary process. Many liberals rejected the virgin birth and the literal resurrection of Jesus and many other miracle stories because these miracles are contrary to what science knows about physical and biological laws. Science tells us about facts. Religion tells us about values - to oversimplify the matter. It is important to recognize that this view holds that it does not matter to faith what science says about the nature of the world. In the 19th century and on into the early 20th the prevailing scientific cosmology was materialistic, mechanistic, and materialistic. Nature is a realm without freedom, meaning, and value. If 20th century science after relativity, quantum mechanics, indeterminacy, and the like no longer implies this particular world-view, then it does not matter much.

Faith does not look to science for its foundations, and it is not threatened by anything that science could possibly say. Hence, theology can be basically indifferent to any and all cosmologies that implied by the scientific account of nature and the world of observable objects. Faith has to do with the decisions and commitments of selves in quest of meaning and purpose as moral personalities. The two realms may converse with each other, but neither can undermine or support the other. The second type of liberal approach is very much like the first in many ways. It differs primarily in that it does not make a sharp division between science and theology or between facts and values. Instead of a dualism between the world as known by disinterested observers, on the one hand, and committed moral selves, on the other hand, this approach speaks of different dimensions of the same events or things as objective entities.

Science gives us a partial picture of the whole. It gives us one perspective on the world. The full and complete reality has many dimensions, some of which are not discerned by scientific methods. The part it deals with by its particular approach is completely true within those limits. Science abstracts from the whole and investigates nature in so far as it can be observed by the senses or measured and quantified with the aid of technology. Philosophy is needed to ask about the nature and meaning of the totality, about reality in its fullness and wholeness. Science gives us a perspective on the whole, but it does not tell us the whole truth about the whole of reality. Philosophy must do that, and theology does the same with the special task of interpreting the meaning of the Christian tradition within this framework.

Process theology under the influence of Alfred North Whitehead is the best example of this approach. It is much like the first liberal type but instead of a sharp dualism between science and theology or between facts and values, the second speaks of part and whole. Science deals with the dimension of reality that its methods allow it to examine. Philosophy deals with the whole from which science abstracts. Theology deals with the moral and religious dimensions of the whole of reality and focuses on the reality of God in relation to the world and human beings.

Religion and Science - Ecology and Ethics

The science-religion conversation as it has been conducted over the last forty years—very much under the influence of Ian Barbour in the United States and the priest-theologians John Polkinghorne and Arthur Peacocke in Britain—has tended to focus on physics in particular, not only as the source of vital data about the beginning and end of all things but also as the paradigm of rationality. Theologians have tended to be in awe of physics, and physicists in turn have sometimes developed an almost religious awe of their subject. However, environmental science has had a very different conversation with theology. Ecological thinkers have often blamed religious formulas (such as the verse of Genesis cited above) as licensing human abuse of nature; they have also been critical of science as determined to dissect nature and as providing the technology used to accelerate ecological abuse.

This criticism ignores the vital point that it is science that provides the diagnosis of our environmental state. However, the de-divinizing of nature by Christian theology that we noted above was a catalyst for Western scientific development, and science in turn has reinforced a sense that we are free to use nature as we want. It has been hard for humans to keep a sense both of God's distinctness from the world and of God's immanent presence in every aspect of that world. Here theology may need new imagery for the God-world relation; for example, Jay McDaniel offers the image of God as "heart" but also draws on Buddhist principles such as nonharming in order to derive a more sustainable environmental ethic.

Importantly, then, the science-religion conversation is not just about fine metaphysical distinctions between types of explanation of the origin of the universe; ultimately it is about the wisdom to relate appropriately to our world, and (if such is our belief) to our creator—to know how best to address our ever-growing power to influence that world, through the sheer extent of our technological life, and specifically through such advances as the new genetics. Science must inform our wisdom but cannot be its sole source.

Ways of Relating Science and Religion

A number of typologies have been suggested to classify various ways of relating science and religion. We will start with a brief review of them, since they illuminate the underlying assumptions often taken for granted which strongly shape the public as well as scholarly conversations. They can be quite useful both to specialists wishing to clarify subtle distinctions between positions and to non-specialists, including the media, educators, and clergy, by providing a basic orientation to the field.

In some cases these ways are meant as mutually exclusive, such as "conflict" versus "two worlds"; in other cases, one way might lead to and become incorporated within another, such as "dialogue" and "integration." In some cases, each way is meant as a characterization of the relation between science per se and religion per se; in other cases, they only apply to specific topics in science and in religion.

Ian Barbour's typology, called «ways of relating science and religion, was first published in 1988 expanded slightly in 1990 and in 1997, and used to restructure the material from his 1990 Gifford lectures for a wider audience in 2000. It remains the most widely used typology in the field. Barbour lists four types of relations, each with subtypes: "conflict" (scientific materialism, biblical literalism); "independence" (contrasting methods, differing languages); "dialogue" (boundary questions, methodological parallels); and "integration" (natural theology, theology of nature, systematic synthesis). His rich discussion is essential reading.

The 1980s saw other typologies, though they were less widely effective. In 1981 Arthur Peacocke published an eightfold typology. It listed both differences and similarities in realms, approaches, languages, attitudes, and objects; it also allowed for the integration of science and religion and for science to generate a metaphysics in which theology can be formulated. I later reformulated his typology as a four-dimensional model which allows for a continuum between opposite positions. In 1985, Nancey Murphy appropriated H. Richard Niebuhr's classic five-fold typology of relations between Christianity and culture and applied it to science and religion. Her distinctive claim was that theology could be a transformer not only of culture in general but even of science in particular.

In the 1990's, a variety of new topologies appeared, many responding directly to Barbour's work. John Haught's 1995 typology includes conflict, contrast, contact, and confirmation. The first three parallel those of Barbour; the fourth describes theology as providing some key philosophical assumptions underlying science. These include such "fiduciary" assumptions, that the universe is rational, coherent, ordered, whole, and grounded in love and promise. In Haught's (somewhat misleading) formulation, the term "confirmation" is not used to mean that science confirms theology. Haught then addresses nine key issues in science and religion and illustrates how each of his four approaches responds to them. In 1996, Willem B. Drees offered a nine-fold typology generated as three new realities (new scientific knowledge, new ideas in philosophy of science, and new attitudes towards nature) influence three distinct areas.

According to Drees, Barbour's typology deals with the interaction between religious cognitive claims and new scientific knowledge. In his six-fold typology, Philip Hefner includes the infusion of religious wisdom into scientific concepts, the construction of new metaphysical systems for science and the evangelical reaffirmation of traditional religious rationality.

While writing on the doctrine of creation in 1991, Anne Clifford developed a detailed typology for the relations principally between Roman Catholic theology and the natural sciences, including continuity, separation, and interaction. Ted Peters' 1998 eight-fold typology includes several refinements to Barbour's scheme. He first distinguishes between "scientific materialists", who claim that science supports atheism, and "scientific imperialists", who claim that science offers a path to God but, like scientific materialists, argue that science alone produces genuine knowledge.

He also distinguishes between Roman Catholic "ecclesiastical authoritarianism", which stretched from the nineteenth century until Vatican II and sought clerical control over secular knowledge, and twentieth century "scientific creationism", a form of Protestant fundamen-talism which sees itself as genuine science though it is based on a literal reading of Genesis. Peters' typology also includes ethical overlap, New Age spirituality and what Peters advocates, "hypothetical consonance". Mark Richardson's recent three-fold typology illuminates the striking difference in literary genre between: intellectual/rational texts (in which the laws of science reveal the mind of God); romantic/affective & aesthetic/mystical texts (here science reunites us with nature as sacred); and tradition-centered texts. Many other books and articles suggest relevant typologies of approaches to, relations between, and goals and aims for the interaction; a particularly helpful resource is the very recent textbook edited by Christopher Southgate and colleagues (1998).

The Original "Bridge" Between Science and Religion

In his ground-breaking 1966 publication, Issues in Science and Religion, Ian G. Barbour laid out a series of well-crafted arguments involving issues in epistemology (the kinds of knowledge we have), language (how it is expressed), and methodology (how it is obtained and justified). Together these arguments provided the "bridge" between science and religion which has, more than any other work, made possible the developments of the past four decades.

He has explored these arguments in detail since then, principally through his 1990 Gifford Lectures, together with their revisions in 1997and 2000. Barbour's pioneering vision continues to bear much of the now burgeoning flow of traffic. From the outset, Barbour used the term "critical realism" to stand for the specific set of arguments he developed in 1966, as have many other scholars since then.

Note that many of the writers in theology and science described here draw on philosophers of science who defend what is more commonly called "scientific realism" though typically using Barbour's term, "critical realism". Barbour viewed critical realism as an alternative to three competing interpretations of scientific theories: a) classical or "naive" realism: scientific theories provide a 'photographic' representation of the world; b) instrumentalism: scientific theories are mere calculative devices, and c) idealism: scientific theories depict reality as mental.

Instead, from a critical realist perspective, scientific theories yield partial, revisable, abstract, but referential knowledge of the world. Scientific theories are expressed linguistically through metaphors and models. Drawing on Max Black, Mary Hesse, Donald Schon, and others, Barbour defined "metaphor" as an open-ended analogy whose meaning cannot be reduced a set of literal. Scientific models, in turn, are systematically developed metaphors.

Barbour then turned to the current discussion of scientific methodology, with major breakthroughs by such philosophers of science as N. R. Hanson, Gerald Holton, Thomas Kuhn, Michael Polanyi, Steven Toulmin, and with special emphasis on the writings of Imre Lakatos. He began with the empiricism of Carl Hempel (1905-1997), whose "hypothetico-deductive" method brought together inductivist and deductivist approaches to the construction and testing of theories vis. Popperian falsificationism.

In the 1960s, this method was fundamentally recast. It was now seen to operate within both the historicist and contextualist elements which characterize the scientific community. These elements include the "theory-laddenness of data", the presence of inter-subjectivity rather than strict objectivity in scientific rationality, the structure of science through paradigms and their revolutions in the history of science, the presence of metaphysical assumptions about nature in scientific paradigms, and the role of aesthetics and values in theory choice.

Scientific theories are a human construction and their conclusions are inherently tentative and subject to revision. Nevertheless, according to Barbour, they are to be assessed by four criteria which are reasonably trans-paradigmatic: agreement with data, coherence, scope and fertility. Barbour used these criteria to articulate what he called a "critical realist" theory of truth. Like classical realism, the meaning of truth in critical realism is correspondence with reality and the key criterion of truth is agreement of theory with data. But we often have only indirect evidence for our theories; moreover, networks of theories are tested together. Thus internal coherence and scope also serve as criteria of truth, as stressed by rationalists and philosophical idealists. Even this is insufficient when competing theories are equally coherent and comprehensive; hence fruitfulness serves as a fourth criterion of truth, as pragmatists, instrumentalists and linguistic analysts stress. Thus intelligibility and explanatory power, and not just observableness or predictive success, is a guide to the real.

Turning to philosophy of religion, Barbour constructed a similar defense of critical realism. Here his sources in religious epistemology, methodology and language include the writings of John Wisdom, John Hick, Ian Ramsey and Frederick Ferré. With these arguments in place, Barbour was prepared to make his crucial, "bridging" methodological claim: the basic structure of religion is similar to that of science in some respects, though it differs at several crucial points.

Similarities: Both science and religion make cognitive claims about the world using a hypothetico-deductive method and a contextualist and historicist framework. Both communities organize observation and experience through models seen as analogical, extensible, coherent and symbolic, and these models are expressed through metaphors.

Differences

But there are important differences in the "data" of religion compared to that of science. Religious models serve non-cognitive functions which are missing in science, such as eliciting attitudes, personal involvement and transformation. Moreover, compared to science, where theories tend to dominate models, in religion models are more influential than theories. Religion lacks lower-level laws such as those found in science, and the emergence of consensus seems "an unrealizable goal."

Religion also includes elements not found in science such as story, ritual, and revelation through historical events. Barbour's argument culminates in his use of paradigm analysis to place science and religion on a continuous spectrum in which both display "subjective" as well as "objective" features, though the former are more prominent in religion and the latter in science. The subjective features include «the influence of theory on data, the resistance of comprehensive theories to falsification, and the absence of rules for choice among paradigms.

Objective features include «the presence of common data on which disputants can agree, the cumulative effect of evidence for or against a theory, and the existence of criteria which are not paradigm-dependent. It is the dynamic tension between similarities and differences, and between subjective and objective features in both science and religion, that together make Barbour's analysis so original and fruitful. Yet even while Barbour was developing this position, scientific realism was being challenged in a number of ways.

Though Thomas Kuhn (1922-1996) had focused primarily on factors internal to the scientific community, sociologists from the 1970s on explored the social construction of science. These externalist accounts of science emphasized the social history of science and the variety of political and economic influences on science. According to one school (the "strong program"), the theory-ladenness of data and the under-determination of theories by evidence heavily influence the formation and content of scientific theories and the ways they are assessed. At the same time, Marxists argued that science is a source of power over nature and thus over people, power rationalized by appeals to the myth of objectivity. Meanwhile the diversity of philosophical views on realism in science was growing, along with an increasing number of anti-realist positions.

Realists frequently argued that social and personal influences are gradually filtered out by the methods of testing used in the sciences. Moreover, the increasing success in predictive power and technological application implies that scientific knowledge is referential.

Barbour's recent assessment is that these externalist accounts provide a "valuable corrective" to the internalist view, particularly regarding the context of discovery. However, the appeal to interests is hard to document and it underestimates the constraints on theories by data and the fact that the testing of theories reduces distortions due to ideologies and interests. Finally, the charge of cultural relativism should apply to the externalist claim as well. Barbour's arguments have been developed in significant and diverse ways by a variety of scholars. In his 1979 Bampton Lectures and in his 1983 Mendenhall Lectures, Arthur Peacocke (born 1924) endorsed critical realism in both science and religion. In science, where challenges to realism from sociologists of knowledge were mounting, Peacocke draw on arguments for realism by Ernan McMullin, Hilary Putnam and Ian Hacking.

In his 1993 Gifford Lectures, Peacocke acknowledged the diversity of positions held by scientific realists but argued for a "common core" of claims: that scientific change is progressive and that the aim of science is to depict reality. Peacocke made a similar case for critical realism in theology, where the social conditioning of beliefs is generally assumed. As in science, theological concepts and models are partial, inadequate, and revisable, and, unlike those in science, they include a strong, affective function. Still Peacocke views them as the necessary and, indeed, the only ways of referring to 'God' and to God's relation with humanity, though he stresses that referring to God (e.g., the via positiva) does not mean describing God. Its grounding in a continuous community and interpretative tradition make it "reasonable" to accept theology's explication of religious experience, though metaphorical and revisable, as an inference to the best explanation.

Other scholars in theology and science have taken similar approaches. According to John Polkinghorne (born 1930), critical realism is the best explanation of the success of science, the only philosophy adequate to scientific experience, and the view most congenial to scientists themselves. In his 1994 Gifford Lectures, Polkinghorne drew on Thomas Torrance and Michael Polanyi in highlight the doubly circular character of knowledge: belief and understanding are mutually entailing, and what is known and the knowledge of it are mutually conforming. Scientific theories are shaped by the way things are, offering an ever increasing degree of verisimilitude as suggested by his motto, "epistemology models ontology".

Polkinghorne offers similar arguments for theology, too. Note that Polkinghorne is apparently restricting the term "epistemology" to the phenomena being observed and recorded whereas epistemology normally includes, and is even primarily focused on, the existing theories which account for phenomena. Thus to a critical realist the phrase "epistemology models ontology" would seem more likely to mean that the theories in science, perhaps even their specific concepts and terms, refer to reality regardless of what the phenomena might suggest.

Wentzel van Huyssteen, in his earlier writings, also viewed theology from a realist perspective, claiming that theology is scientifically committed to a realist point of view and describing the referential power of theological language about God as "reality depiction." For van Huyssteen, the hypothetical status of scientific statements becomes the eschatological dimension of theological statements. Thomas F. Torrance (born 1913), too, argues for the scientific character of theology because, like the natural sciences, it adopts a method which is determined by its object. For theology, the object is God, known to us by God's revelation in the incarnation and resurrection of the Word Thus the theoretical structures of theology disclose knowledge of God just as the theoretical structures in science, like Einstein's general relativity, provide objective knowledge of this world. According to Torrance, natural theology can find a place within positive theology, though not as a prolegomenon to it - a view which he reports he persuaded Karl Barth (1886-1968) eventually to accept.

The central role Barbour gave to metaphors, models and paradigms in both science and theology has stimulated wide discussion, too. In 1982, Sallie McFague drew directly from Barbour's work in pointing to basic similarities between models in theology and in science, but she also stressed four important differences: they provide order in theology while stimulating new discoveries in science; they more clearly carry meaning in theology than in science; and unlike in science, they are ubiquitous and hierarchical, as well as eliciting feelings and action, in theology. McFague combined this with Paul Ricoeur's notion of metaphor as "is and is not" in developing what she then termed "metaphorical theology". Using this approach she has developed new metaphors for God as Mother, Lover, and Friend, and the world as the body of God which challenge theologies patriarchal and androcentric distortions and funds her work in ecological theology.

In 1984, Mary Gerhart and Allan Russell contrasted two meanings of analogy: a) as an extension of our conceptual network from a known to an unknown and b) as a new and dynamic relation between two separate networks which distorts both and induces tension. They call the latter "metaphor", concluding that the relation between science and religion is itself a metaphor. In 1985 Janet Soskice published a thorough study of metaphor in religious and scientific language, emphasizing the distinction between metaphor and model which she found conflated in Black, Barbour, Ferré and David Tracy; Soskice, 1988). Although she vigorously defended theological realism, Soskice also stressed the social and contextual nature of scientific realism, in which theoretical terms are seen as representing reality without claiming to be representationally privileged.

Theological realism, in turn, distinguishes between referring to God and defining "God", and employs a causal theory of reference. In 1988, Hans Küng applied paradigm analysis to the history of theology and compared the results to the history of science. In contrast to the way paradigms are successively replaced in science, giving it an irreversible history, in theology contrasting paradigms, such as Thomism, Reformation theology, modernity, may well coexist in history. In science the next revolution comes at the limits of the existing paradigm.

In theology the 'primal testimony' of scripture and the events of the history of Israel and Jesus Christ are the sources of each new revolution. An important development has been the theme of "consonance" introduced in 1981 by Ernan McMullin. His concern was the search for a "coherence of world-view" to which all forms of human knowing can contribute. The consonance that characterizes such a world-view does not require or even expect direct support. Instead it would involve mutual contributions in a relation that is tentative and open to "constant slight shift".

Beginning in 1989, I combined McMullin's idea with McFague's epistemic claim about the "is and is not" structure of metaphor to include and thus to learn from both consonance and "dissonance" between scientific and theological theories. Rather than undercutting a coherent world-view, dissonance points to the dynamic character of our world view, specifying where problems arise, and shifts are required, and potentially greater coherence can be sought. Moreover, by recognizing that theories in both science and theology evolve and are eventually replaced, we can build change directly into the relation between science and theology rather than being threatened by it. Over the past decade, Ted Peters has developed this approach in terms of what he calls "hypothetical consonance". If consonance in the "strong sense" means complete harmony or accord, we might hope to find it, but we have not found it yet. What we do have are shared domains of inquiry or consonance in a "weak sense", but this is enough to encourage further exploration. He bases this on his critical realist assumption that theologians and scientists are seeking to understand the same reality.

The qualifier "hypothetical" reminds theologians to treat their assertions as fallible and subject to possible disconfirmation as well as confirmation. Willem B. Drees, though exploring the concept of consonance, has pointed out the problematic assumptions underlying realism and a correspondence theory of truth. Instead he proposes "constructing a consonance world" which includes God's otherness and the prophetic challenge of lived values. Our religious traditions invite us to wander through, and our sciences to wonder about, the reality which transcends and sustains our lives and to engage ethically with the challenge of the future.

Religion and Society

A theoretical approach that explains the existence of social institutions such as religion in terms of the needs that the institutions would meet.

Early Functionalism

At first, functionalists likened societies to higher organisms; as one would understand animal lungs and livers by what those organs do for the whole animal body, one would understand institutions by what they do for whole societies. Because the intelligence embodied in the arrangement of traditional institutions transcended any calculative ratiocination on the part of individuals in society, this kind of theory appealed to early-nineteenth-century thinkers who reacted against Enlightenment rationalism. Auguste Comte incorporated functionalism into his early-nineteenth-century amalgam of conservatism and science. Émile Durkheim had a similar insight in his concept of "organic solidarity" at the end of the century; societies held together because their dissimilar parts made unique contributions toward collective life.

In emphasizing the needs of the society, and benefits to collective life, Comte and Durkheim conceived societal or macrolevel realities that were not reducible to the wants or impulses of individuals or even groups. Their macrofunctionalism was adopted in anthropology by A. R. Radcliffe-Brown. Meanwhile, an individualist, or microfunctionalist, approach was developed by Herbert Spencer. In the tradition of Adam Smith, who saw the wider society profiting from individuals pursuing their own interests, Spencer believed individual needs to be foundational to social functions and structural change. He spoke of an evolution away from populations of similar people paralleling one another, toward societies of different kinds of persons performing different functions.

The differentiated societies were more competitive than undifferentiated ones in a struggle for survival. Because Spencer's sociology provided a rationale for disparities of power and wealth in society, it gained popularity in the gilded age and was suspect in the eyes of people concerned about impartial science. It did bring individual needs and aims into view, and that emphasis was taken up by the anthropologist Bronislaw Malinowski in a functionalism that rivaled the macro approach of Radcliffe-Brown. The sociologist Vilfredo Pareto similarly saw individual dispositions as the motor of social life; patterns in society were states of equilibrium among individual people's impulses. Religion had a prominent position in early functionalism.

According to Comte, the macrofunctionalist, it prompted simple folk to serve unseen purposes that even clever scholars could barely detect. Durkheim (1912) proposed that religion sacralized social life itself and, because the perspective of society was implicit in all cognition, religion thus served as the foundation of all knowledge. The microfunctionalist Malinowski observed that religion established, fixed, and enhanced individual attitudes that were valuable to the collective existence and survival of societies—attitudes such as reverence for tradition, harmony with the environment, and courage in the struggle with difficulties and at the prospect of death. Functionalism remained viable in anthropology, which studies small societies that can be conceived as systems, but by 1920 it seemed to have run its course in sociology. Durkheim had described a function as such an odd process that not many later sociologists wanted to make functional analyses.

According to Durkheim, a function could not be intended by people because they would use multitudinous means rather than common institutions to accomplish intended ends; rather, a function would be an effect that somehow revitalized its causes, much as punishment revitalized the collective feeling for laws. The famous German sociologist Max Weber dismissed functions as merely preliminary heuristic devices and saw the whole point of sociology to be the uncovering of typical intentions in the conduct of people.

Harvard Functionalism

Talcott Parsons (1951) revived sociological functionalism in the mid-twentieth century and, together with his students, most notably Robert K. Merton, made it a dominant paradigm in American sociology in the 1950s and 1960s. He met Weber halfway by dwelling on the attitudes, if not intentions, that somehow enhanced the workings of society. These attitudes would reflect the beliefs and values proper to the cultures of societies. Moreover, he would specify what the needs of a social system are ("functional requisites") and what institutions served which functions.

Religion would function to reconcile personality systems with social systems. In a step away from nineteenth-century analogies with animal bodies, he looked for "systems," interactions that formed patterns of relative equilibrium. According to the contemporary neofunctionalist Jeffrey C. Alexander (1985), functionalism views society as composed of elements whose interaction forms a pattern that is distinct from an environment; the elements are symbiotically interconnected without any directive or governing force. Functionalism is concerned with the degree to which ends succeed in regulating and stimulating means.

Criticisms of Functionalism

There is a serious logical problem in functionalism that social scientists have debated for decades. Functionalism seems to be a teleology, an explanatory scheme that assumes some great intelligence exists that designs features of societies to serve large purposes. The more functionalists propose unobvious functions—the more they emphasize what Robert Merton (1957) termed "latent" functions—the greater this logical problem becomes. As Pitirim Sorokin (1969:339) once put it, functionalists would say, "Birds have wings in order to fly" rather than "Birds have wings and therefore they can fly." It is difficult to explain functions apart from conscious purpose, and conscious purposes require intelligent beings with purposes. Religion often focuses on other-worldly concerns and hence has latent functions proposed for it.

Functionalism also tended to justify social arrangements as found at hand by showing some system-maintaining benefit they brought about. Many functionalists have in fact been humane thinkers who favored conscious efforts at social amelioration; so, rather than defend the conservative aspect of older functionalist thought, they have revised the approach to make it politically acceptable.

Merton proposed paying attention to system-disturbing consequences of social features—"dysfunctions," as opposed to "eufunctions." Parsons added an emphasis on social change, with increasing levels of system complexity and differentiation emerging over time. Merton, again, noted that abstracting institutions from their value-laden traditions and assessing them in terms of hardheaded system benefits can be a radical rather than conservative exercise.

Nevertheless, as Marie Augusta Neal noted (1979), functionalism fails to analyze important aspects of societies if it neglects asking in whose interest systems function and who are the victims of social arrangements, and if it neglects issues of class and power in nongovernmental and noneconomic institutions such as religion. There was also a problem of functionalism dwelling too much on the largest possible systems—whole societies. Parsons actually helped overcome this difficulty by specifying smaller systems, such as personalities and organizations, within the larger, but the more interesting functional statements about religion actually pertained to the relationships between personalities and the functioning of whole societies.

One could question whether modern life actually operates as a more or less closed pattern of interaction ("system") at all. Merton and other functionalists of the mid-twentieth century proposed that system units be specified explicitly, and that functional analyses be made of small groups and of organizations as well as of macro-level systems. Finally, there seemed to be some confusion over just what kind of question was actually a functionalist one. Were functionalists trying to explain, for example, the origins of religions, the reasons that religions persisted, or the reasons that societies that had religions survived? The question of origins was a concern largely in nineteenth-century anthropology, but late-twentieth-century sociologists took to studying the emergence of new religions in the youth culture.

The persistence of religion came to be studied in terms of some individuals in society being more religious than others, but this created problems for those who saw universal functional needs being served by religion; functionalists often defined religion broadly so that individuals would be differently religious rather than more or less so. The question of the survival of systems came to be applied to religious identity groups rather than to societies.

Applications and Potential

For all the importance placed on functionalism in general sociological textbooks and in major works of social theory, it has inspired relatively little actual research. What research there is has focused on religion. Thus studies of pre-modern societies, such as Karl-Heinz Messelken's (1977) examination of the late Roman Empire and Kai Erikson's (1966) study of the Massachusetts Bay Colony saw religion as functional for the coherence and identity, respectively, of whole societies.

Modern societies do not seem to be amenable to such analyses. For example, Richard Sykes (1969) observed that American churches typically focus on matters other than those relevant to the functioning of the wider society.

John L. Thomas (1962) noted that a minority religion, such as mid-twentieth-century American Catholicism, could not succeed in providing the function needed by its host society without losing its own internal coherence; the societal and organizational systems were mutually dysfunctional. Not only minority status but also social change creates the same dilemma, as Jean-Paul Rouleau (1990) observes in regard to Catholicism in Québec. In a few studies, the finding that religious questionnaire respondents are happier at work and more likely to endorse generous helping behavior norms are given macro-functionalist interpretations. More often surrogates for religion—political ideologies and public education, for example—are found to serve some function in lieu of religion doing so.

Sometimes different religions have been conceived as functional substitutes for one another. In between religions being societally functional and surrogates for religion being so, one finds the civil religion school of thought. Functionalist studies that have specified religious organizations as the systems having needs have tended to focus on small entities that have well-defined boundaries—a particular Quaker meeting group, a communal sect such as the Hutterites, Catholic orders of sisters.

Occasionally the system in question may be a large denomination, or some commonly encountered feature such as ritual or myth is hypothesized to be functional for any sub-societal religious system. The greater part of late-twentieth-century functionalist sociology of religion has taken a social psychological, or alternatively sociology of knowledge, approach. Involvement in society transforms individuals, born as largely biological systems, into socialized selves, persons. However, once the person manages to develop a coherent biography, further social involvements raise problems, and additionally there are always the dilemmas of suffering and death that intrude upon life.

The system having needs, especially a need for "meaning," is the socialized self in its everyday life, and external factors, ranging from the biological to the political, cause problems that can be addressed through religion. These problems, according to J. Milton Yinger (1963), become particularly critical when individuals experience social changes that place them in new, unfamiliar social lives. The functioning of religion moves from public churches, which have become marginal to societal workings anyway, and into the sphere of everyday life, in a process that Thomas Luckmann (1967 [1963]) calls "privatization." Thus many activities and experiences that have nothing to do with religion as defined in traditional institutional settings are "religious" insofar as people work out suprabiological, meaningful biographies, according to Luckmann. In a variation on this kind of thought, Volker Drehsen (1980) distinguishes personal-level functions (meaning, value integration, the ordering of emotions), interpersonal-level functions (identity security, religious construction of social reality), and transpersonal-level functions (coping with authority and contingency).

There have been a number of efforts to expand the functionalist paradigm in the study of religion. Hans Mol (1977) spoke of individual, group, and national identities that integrate lines of conduct in dialectic with processes of adaptive differentiation. For him, religion is the process of sacralizing identity; it bolsters the personal and social forces that tend toward wholeness, and thereby compensates for the numerous fragmentary facets of human existence (Mol 1982). This approach solves the logical problem of individuals not being cognizant of functional requisites; they need only be cognizant of their identities. Niklas

Luhmann (1977) developed a very similar approach, but with a more abstract and inclusive systems theory model; subsystems would define both themselves and their environmental systems through a process of selection. For Luhmann, religion manages contingency experiences brought upon personality systems by society at large; religion does this by reformulating the conditions for insecurity in religious terms, interpreting them, and making them more acceptable.

The problem of consciousness, of who is aware of system needs and responds in such a way as to occasion functions, is at the center of both the logical difficulties and the promise of functional analysis. When Mol uses the concept of identity, and when Luhmann points to the constitution of selectivity of small and environmental systems, they are locating consciousness within the functional model. This goes beyond Parsons, who saw subjectivity in the functional system but only as a recipient of functional beliefs, values, and norms. It even goes beyond the Mertoninspired analysis of inspirational religious literature conducted by Louis Schneider and Sanford Dornbusch (1958), who wondered whether a latent function could still "work" if it became too manifest, whether the inspirational writers were not blowing their cover when they promised inner peace and worldly success.

Robert Stauffer (1973) noted that different sectors of a society could be differently conscious, with elites sharing in a rationally functional religious consciousness and nonelites inoculated against such instrumental reason by preoccupations with sacralized identities and nationalisms. Frank Lechner (1985) noted conscious resistance against the rationalist functioning of the wider society, a resistance that took the form of "fundamentalist" religious movements. When taking up the study of religious consciousness, it is important to give an adequate assessment and portrayal of the subjective phenomenon of religion. If a religious experience or sub-cultural worldview largely concerns matters that have little to do with the functioning of a large system, if it works more or less on its own or is likely to be put consciously to a variety of personal purposes, as James Beckford (1989) suggests, it will hardly do to set out on a functional analysis.

This is simply to suggest that functionalism should not be a procrustean bed. Thomas O'Dea (1954) followed up an excellent exposition of Parsons's functionalist analysis of religion with an eloquent critique that argued, in effect, that a functional analysis that led to an understanding of too little of what a religion is about hardly provides an understanding at all. The problem with functionalism was that it presupposed too positivistic a model of the human, leaving too little allowance for the human as a symbolizing and myth-evolving being. To fit the human person and religious interest into a closed conceptual construct concerned with social structures and functions is to commit the logical error of including the whole in a part. There remains much promise in functionalism, however. Let us take up where O'Dea left off, with symbol, myth, and other forms in which humans manifest to one another and to themselves vague or at least non-conceptual awarenesses of life in society.

Durkheim, for example, proposed that humans externalized the authority of society in religious form. However one defines religion, it occurs in the human biography after and as a consequence of socialization. The individual is aware of society and uses that awareness to shape the contents of religious symbols; social forms are imported into the imagination. It is difficult to conceive of society not being affected by the fact that its members are often aware of it through indirection and implication, whether or not in the manner Durkheim described this occurs.

Patients with advanced cancer who used their religious faith to help cope were more likely to receive intensive life-prolonging medical care such as mechanical ventilation or cardiopulmonary resuscitation during their last week of life, according to a study in the March 18 issue of JAMA. For patients facing a life-threatening illness, religious coping, such as through prayer, meditation and religious study can offer patients a sense of meaning, comfort, control and personal growth, according to background information in the article. "Positive religious coping has been widely associated with improved psychological adjustment to stressors including serious illness," the authors write.

They add that religion may influence patients' medical decisions, but little is known about the associations between religious coping and the use of intensive life-prolonging care at the end of life. Andrea C. Phelps, M.D., of Beth Israel Deaconess Medical Center, Boston, and colleagues examined the relationship between 345 patients with advanced cancer and their use of religious coping at the start of the study and their receipt of intensive medical care during their last week of life. Positive religious coping was assessed by a questionnaire. Interviews at the beginning of the study also assessed psychosocial and religious/spiritual measures, advance care planning and end-of-life treatment preferences. Patients were followed up until death, a median (midpoint) of 122 days after the assessment at the beginning of the study.

Patients were asked about how much they rely on religion to cope with illness. A total of 272 patients (78.8 percent) reported that religion helps them cope "to a moderate extent" or more and 109 (31.6 percent) endorsed the statement that "it is the most important thing that keeps you going." Most patients (55.9 percent) endorsed engaging in times of prayer, meditation, or religious study at least daily. The researchers found that patients with a high level of positive religious coping at the start of the study had nearly three times the odds of receiving mechanical ventilation and intensive life-prolonging care in the last week of life compared with patients with a low level of religious coping.

A high level of positive religious coping was also significantly associated with preferring heroic measures (wanting physicians to do everything possible to keep the patient alive) compared with patients with a low level and was associated with less advance care planning in all forms: do-not-resuscitate order, living will and health care proxy/ durable power of attorney.

"These results suggest that relying upon religion to cope with terminal cancer may contribute to receiving aggressive medical care near death," the authors write.

"Taken together, these results highlight the need for clinicians to recognize and be sensitive to the influence of religious coping on medical decisions and goals of care at the end of life. When appropriate, clinicians might include chaplains or other trained professionals (e.g., liaison psychiatrists) to inquire about religious coping during family meetings while the patient is in an intensive care unit and end-of-life discussions occurring earlier in the disease course. Because aggressive end-of-life cancer care has been associated with poor quality of death and caregiver bereavement adjustment, intensive end-of-life care might represent a negative outcome for religious copers. These findings merit further discussion within religious communities, and consideration from those providing pastoral counsel to terminally ill patients with cancer."

Terminally ill patients who had end-of-life discussions with physicians were not more likely to experience emotional distress, received less aggressive medical care in their final week of life and had a better quality of life near death, compared to patients who did not have these discussions, according to a study in the October 8 issue of JAMA. End-of-life discussions offer patients the opportunity to define their goals and expectations for the medical care that they want to receive near death. "But these discussions also mean confronting the limitations of medical treatments and the reality that life is finite, both of which may cause psychological distress. Studies suggest that physicians and patients are ambivalent about talking about death and often avoid these conversations. To date, however, research has not examined whether these discussions are associated with patients' psychological distress or medical care near death. Without this information physicians cannot weigh the risks and benefits of end-of-life discussions," the authors write.

Alexi A. Wright, M.D., of the Dana-Farber Cancer Institute, Boston, and colleagues examined the associations between end-of-life discussions with physicians and the medical care that terminally ill patients receive near death. The study included patients with advanced cancer and their informal caregivers (n = 332 pairs). Patients were followed-up from enrollment to death, a median (midpoint) of 4.4 months later. Bereaved caregivers' psychiatric illness and quality of life was assessed a median of 6.5 months later. One hundred twenty-three of 332 (37.0 percent) patients reported having end-of-life discussions with their physicians.

The researchers found that such discussions were not associated with higher rates of major depressive disorder or more worry, but these patients received significantly fewer aggressive medical interventions near death: lower rates of ventilation (1.6 percent vs. 11.0 percent), resuscitation (0.8 percent vs. 6.7 percent), and ICU admission (4.1 percent vs. 12.4 percent).

Patients who had end-of-life discussions had earlier hospice enrollment (65.6 percent vs. 44.5 percent), and longer hospice stays were associated with better patient quality of life, while more aggressive medical care was associated with worse patient quality of life. Patients who reported engaging in these conversations were significantly more likely to accept that their illness was terminal, prefer medical treatment focused on relieving pain and discomfort over life-extending therapies, and have complete a do-not-resuscitate order.

Caregivers of patients who received any aggressive care were at higher risk for developing a major depressive disorder, experiencing regret and feeling unprepared for the patient's death, compared with caregivers of patients who did not receive aggressive care. They also had worse quality of life outcomes, including overall quality of life, self-reported health and increased role limitations. Better patient quality of life was associated with better caregiver quality of life at follow-up. "Our results suggest that end-of-life discussions may have cascading benefits for patients and their caregivers.

Despite physicians' concerns that patients may experience psychological harm due to end-of-life discussions, we found no evidence that they were significantly associated with increased emotional distress or psychiatric disorders. Instead, the worst outcomes were seen in patients who did not report having these conversations." the authors write. "Given the adverse outcomes associated with not having end-of-life discussions, there appears to be a need to increase the frequency of these conversations. By acknowledging that death is near, patients, caregivers, and physicians can focus on clarifying patients' priorities and improving pain and symptom management."

Big Bang Theory

A cosmological model to explain the origins of matter, energy, space, and time, the Big Bang theory asserts that the universe began at a certain point in the distant past—current estimates put it at roughly 13.7 billion years ago—expanding from a primordial state of tremendous heat and density. The term is also used more generally to describe the vast explosion that erupted at the beginning of space and time, bringing the universe into being.

First conceived by astronomers and physicists in the early twentieth century, the Big Bang was effectively confirmed in the middle and latter years of the century, once new telescopes and computers made it possible to peer further into the universe and process the enormous amounts of data those observations generated. The term "big bang" comes from its underlying hypothesis that the universe has not been eternal but emerged out of a sudden, almost incomprehensibly vast explosion. Scientists' understanding of the Big Bang theory emerges out of two separate fields of inquiry: theoretical physics and observational astronomy.

According to what are called the Friedmann models, a set of complex metrics named for Alexander Friedmann, an early twentieth century Soviet physicist who first developed them, the Big Bang theory fits in with two of the most important theories of twentieth century physics: the cosmological principle (which says that basic physical properties are the same throughout the universe) and Albert Einstein's General Theory of Relativity of 1915-1916, which conceives of gravity as a curvature in space and time. That convergence of ideas, say physicists, provides the theoretical underpinning of the Big Bang theory. Astronomers have made their own confirmations of the Big Bang theory. Analyzing the light coming from other galaxies, they have noted shorter and longer wavelengths proportional to the distances of the galaxies from Earth, indicating that they are moving away from the Earth and thus that space itself is expanding. The existence of cosmic microwave radiation, a remnant of hot ionized plasma of the early universe offers more proof of the Big Bang, as does the distribution of heavier and lighter elements through the universe.

Timeline of the Big Bang

The Big Bang theory hypothesizes that there were time-based stages in the origins of the universe. The first stage—or, at least, the first stage that cosmologists can theorize about given current understanding of physics—is known as the Planck era, after the German scientist of the late nineteenth and early twentieth centuries who studied the physics that explain it. The Planck era was extremely brief—

just 10-43 seconds (also known as one Planck time). During this period, all four forces of the universe—gravity, electromagnetic energy, and the weak and strong nuclear forces—were theoretically equal to one another, implying that there may have been just one unified force. The Planck era was extremely unstable, with the four forces quickly evolving into their current forms, starting with gravity and then the strong nuclear force (what binds protons and neutrons together in the nucleus of an atom), the weak nuclear force (associated with radioactive decay, it is some 100 times weaker than the strong force), and finally electromagnetic energy.

This process is known as symmetry breaking and led to a longer period in the universe's history—though, at one millionth of a second, still extremely brief in ordinary time—known as the "inflation era." Physicists, however, are not certain of the energy force that led to this inflation. At one second in age, the universe now consisted of fundamental energy and sub-atomic particles such as quarks, electrons, photons, and other less familiar particles. The next stage in the Big Bang—lasting for roughly 100,000 years and beginning about three seconds after the Planck era—consisted of the process of nucleosynthesis, as protons and neutrons came into being and began to the form the nuclei of various elements, predominantly hydrogen and helium, the two lightest elements in the periodic table and the two most common elements in the universe. Yet matter as we know it still did not exist and for those hundred thousand or so years, the universe essentially consisted of radiation in the form of light, radio waves, and X-rays.

This period, known as the "radiation era," came to a gradual end as free floating atomic nuclei bonded with free-floating electrons to produce the matter with which the universe would subsequently consist. While time was critical to the process so was temperature and density, with the various changes corresponding to a gradual cooling of the universe and the gradual dispersing of matter. It took some 200 million years for gravity to begin coalescing these free-floating atoms into the primordial gas out of which the first stars and galaxies would emerge. Over billions of years, such early stars and galaxies phased through their lifecycle, using up their nuclear fuel and collapsing in on themselves, spewing out vast new clouds of matter and energy that would eventually form new generations of stars and galaxies. The sun around which the earth and the solar system rotate is one of these later generation stars, formed roughly five billion years ago.

Fate of the Universe

The Big Bang theory concerns not just the origins of the universe but its ultimate fate. The critical question, of course, is whether the universe will continue expanding forever or eventually fall back into itself, creating, perhaps, the conditions for the next Big Bang. Gravity is the critical factor here, with three outcomes possible. The first, and most widely accepted by physicists, is that there is not the critical density, known as omega and estimated at roughly six hydrogen atoms per cubic meter, necessary to pull the universe back in on itself. In this model, referred to as the "open" model, the universe will continue to expand and cool indefinitely. If however, the density of he universe is greater than omega then the universe will eventually, after billions of years, collapse in what physicists call the "big crunch." A third and highly unlikely possibility is that omega equals precisely one; in this model, the universe gradually slows and cools to a static state. While it would seem at first glance that the fate of the universe—that is, whether matter exceeded omega or not—could be determined by the admittedly complex but not impossible task of calculating the amount of matter and dividing it by the dimensions of the universe, in fact, there is a complicating factor.

The galaxies and nebulae, or primordial dust clouds out of which stars and galaxies, do not pull on themselves or on each another as they should. That is to say, they behave as if there was more mass and, hence, gravitational pull than can be observed. For example, the Andromeda galaxy, the nearest neighbor to our own Milky Way galaxy, is rushing toward us at 200,000 miles per hour, a speed that cannot be explained by the gravitational force of the matter in the two galaxies. In fact, the two galaxies are coming together at a pace requiring some 10 times that amount of matter. Physicists offer the possibility that there is dark matter in the universe, that is, an unknown type of matter that does not emit or reflect enough electromagnetic energy to be observable by current means.

Such dark matter, according to this hypothesis, exists in haloes around galaxies and may be what composes black holes and massive clouds of neutrinos, particles formed from radioactive decay with little mass and no electric charge. Such dark matter would imply a universe that eventually collapses in on itself, except for an additional complicating factor.

Scientists hypothesize that there is also a dark energy in the universe counteracting both matter and dark matter, a kind of anti-gravitational force that is also undetectable with existing technology. While dark matter is believed to constitute 22 percent of the universe, dark energy is believe to compose 74 percent. These numbers, along with the difficulties of detecting dark matter and energy make it impossible for physicists as of the early twenty-first century to come to a definitive conclusion about the ultimate fate of the universe.

Pre-Twentieth Century Ideas of Universe's Origins

The origins of creation have, of course, preoccupied humanity since at least the beginning of civilization itself. Virtually every culture around the world has created myths to explain how the universe came into being, even if they did not necessarily comprehend the universe's magnitude and complexity. These cosmologies, or explanations for the existence of creation, generally share four basic ideas. First, there is an intelligence or creator behind creation. Second, the universe came into being at a specific point in time and that what existed before the universe came into being is irrelevant as there was no existence or time before it. A major exception to this model of a universe created at a single moment in time comes from Hindu cosmology which states that the universe exists in cycles, of roughly 4.5 billion years, or one day in the life of the Brahma, the creator, endlessly being born, dying, and being reborn.

The third component of most ancient cosmologies was that the Earth stood at the center of creation. And the final element was that, once the universe was created, it remained essentially static—nothing added, nothing taken away, all matter and energy in perpetual balance. That, too, was the model advanced by English scientist Isaac Newton in the late seventeenth and early eighteenth centuries, whose understanding of the laws of the universe dominated physics for more than 200 years. But even in Newton's own time, the idea of a perpetually balanced creation was questioned by some thinkers, who pointed out that the universe would come apart if just one object should slip out of balance. And while Newton's laws attempted to explain how the universe operated, they did not offer much insight into its origins.

Immanuel Kant, a German philosopher of the late eighteenth century, was the first major Western thinker to tackle the question that the Big Bang theory would eventually answer—had the universe always existed or did it come into existence at a specific point in time? Kant concluded that since both arguments were equally valid on the face of things and that it was impossible to determine which was fundamentally true, the question of the universe's origins, or lack thereof, was beyond human comprehension. Even as nineteenth century astronomers began to push back the envelope of what was known about the universe's scale, they did not have the means or, given their religious faith, the inclination to grapple with Kant's question.

Early Hypotheses

Early twentieth century physicists and astronomers, of course, would prove Kant wrong. In 1912, an American astronomer named Vesto Slipher noted a Doppler shift in the wavelengths of light coming from spiral nebulae, an antiquated term for galaxies, dating from before the existence of other galaxies was confirmed. The Doppler shift, named after Christian Doppler, the early nineteenth century Austrian mathematician who discovered it, says that waves alter in relation to the movement of the observer or the object causing the wave. While Slipher noted that almost all such spiral nebulae were moving away from the Earth, he failed to reach the conclusion that this meant the universe was expanding. Around the same time, Slipher was making his observations, Friedmann, the Soviet physicist, explained how Einstein's General Relativity Theory might prove that the universe was expanding.

Einstein's theory updated and revised Newton's gravitational laws, for conditions where enormous mass and energy existed. Newton concluded that gravity was a force between two masses; Einstein argued, correctly as it was proved by later experiments, that gravity was the warping of space and time caused by mass.

While Newton's model of gravity was not consistent with the Big Bang theory—since there was no mass in the primordial state of heat and density at the beginning of time—Einstein's allowed for the possibility of gravity itself coming into being, though, ironically, Einstein himself held to a static view of the universe when he came up with his General Relativity Theory.

Roughly a decade after Friedmann developed his models out of Einstein's General Relativity Theory—models that, while published, generally got overlooked by other physicists—a Belgian physicist and astronomer Georges Lemaître, independently coming up with the same theories as Friedmann, used them to reach the conclusion that had eluded Slipher—that receding nebulae meant the universe was expanding. In 1931, Lemaître also hypothesized that the universe must have begun with a single atom, an idea that came to be called the "cosmic egg" theory.

American astronomer Edwin Hubble, the first to realize that nebulae were in fact other galaxies, also confirmed that the galaxies all seemed to be moving away from us simultaneously. Extrapolating backward, Hubble believed that they all had emerged from the same high-density place, exploding outward in a kind of initial fireball. Hubble made his findings by noting shifts in the light spectrum of distant galaxies that fit in with the Doppler Effect. Despite such findings, a competing theory emerged in the years after World War II.

The "steady state" model, advocated by British astronomer Frederick Hoyle, held that new matter was created as the universe expanded. A confirmed atheist, Hoyle rejected the "cosmic egg" theory as it seemed to imply the existence of a creator. Ironically, it was Hoyle who, in the 1950s, coined the term "Big Bang," using it in a radio interview to ridicule Lemaître's ideas.

To reconcile his constant universe idea and the observed fact that galaxies were moving away from each other, Hoyle hypothesized those new galaxies came into being as older ones grew apart. While later discounted, Hoyle's work was useful in explaining how matter and energy came into existence, a key component of the Big Bang theory.

Confirmation of the Big Bang Theory

For two decades the two theories vied with each other,

though Lemaître's steadily gained more advocates. The critical confirmation of the Big Bang theory came in 1964. That year, Arno Penzias and Robert Wilson, two scientists working for Bell Laboratories, noticed that background microwave radiation, a residual form of energy from the Big Bang, permeated the universe, confirming an idea first propounded by Soviet physicist George Gamow and American physicist Ralph Alpher in the late 1940s.

With the development of ever more powerful computers to crunch the numbers in the 1980s, and the deployment of the Hubble Space telescope in the 1990s, which allowed for observations above the distortions of the Earth's atmosphere and radio waves, astronomers were able to make ever more detailed pictures of the universe and ever more precise timelines for the Big Bang.

Key to this was a worldwide study in the 1980s and 1990s of supernovas, immense outpourings of radiation caused by the collapse of massive stars, which pointed to yet another anomaly about the universe. Rather than expanding at a constant rate, it seemed to be accelerating. This led to the conclusion that there must be a dark energy in the universe working to counteract gravity. One recent hypothesis states that space actually consists of negative pressure, which grows as the universe expands thereby causing that expansion to accelerate since there is not enough matter—even with dark matter factored into the equation—to put a brake on the expansion.

According to British scientist Robert Caldwell, this accelerating expansion may lead to what he calls the "big rip," in which galaxies, stars, and even atoms are eventually torn apart by the force of dark energy, leading to the destruction of matter in the final seconds of time at the end of the universe. Much of this work on dark matter and energy remains hypothetical, of course, as it has been impossible to detect either of these two phenomena.

As the twenty-first century dawns, scientists—like the ancients long before them— are still grappling with the very moment of creation, before the radiation, inflation, and Planck eras. Many believe that unveiling that moment is connected to the development of a Grand Unified Theory, a single explanation that fits all of the known laws of the universe—including Einstein's General Relativity Theory and quantum mechanics, the study of energy and matter at the sub-atomic level—into a single equation. As British physicist Stephen Hawking notes, "At the Big Bang, the universe and time itself came into existence, so that this is the first cause. If we could understand the Big Bang, we would know why the universe is the way it is. It used to be thought that it was impossible to apply the laws of science to the beginning of the universe, and indeed that it was sacrilegious to try. But recent developments in unifying the two pillars of twentieth century science, Einstein's General Theory of Relativity and the Quantum Theory, have encouraged us to believe that it may be possible to find laws that hold even at the creation of the universe."

Cosmology and Religion

There is an ongoing battle in the United States between *Young Earth Creationists* and the scientific community over the teaching of evolutionary biology. In Kansas this dispute spilled over into cosmology. In this chapter a minor part of remarks to Glanz are quoted, regarding a misguided attempt to use General Relativity to explain the discrepancy between the 13.7 billion year age of the Universe and the Young Earth Creationists' 6000 year age for the Earth. This huge clock rate gradient defines a huge gravitational field that would create a huge gravitational blueshift in all astronomical observations, but no such effect is seen. But any discussion of cosmology and religion should remember these general principles:

- *False dichotomy between Science and Creationism*

There are *NOT* just two sides in this issue that deserve equal time. Young Earth Creationism is a belief held by a small minority [~6%] of Christians, and Christianity is followed by a minority [albeit a large one: 33%] of all people on the world. For example, Catholics outnumber Young Earth Creationists by a large factor, and the Catholic Church has no objection to either Big Bang cosmology or evolutionary biology, which they regard as the mechanisms used by God to create the Universe and the living things within it. Hindus outnumber Young Earth Creationists by a large factor, and believe in an infinitely old Universe evolving in cycles - a belief more in accord with Hoyle's Steady State Cosmology that the Big Bang, but directly contradicting the Young Earth Creationists.

And many scientists are believers who feel that God made the Universe but that evidence we find in Nature gives us the true history of the Universe: the Big Bang cosmology and biological evolution of the species. Hugh Ross is a prominent Christian believer with scientific training, who made this statement about the Kansas School Board decision on the Big Bang:

Ironically, members on both sides of the debate do agree about one thing: big bang cosmology puts their position in jeopardy. The big bang poses a problem for young-earth creationists because it makes the universe billions of years old rather than thousands. Such an assertion undercuts their system at its foundation. Big bang cosmology also presents a problem for atheistic scientists because it points directly to the existence of a transcendent Creator - a fact they dare not concede.

It is true that scientists do not know what came before or caused the Big Bang, but that is neither a necessary nor a sufficient condition for invoking the Deity.

The evangelical Protestant denominations from which most Young Earth Creationists come have much deeper and more heartfelt disputes with other Christian denominations than with science. In particular they dispute the nature of the ultimate authority: the Catholics accept the Pope as the authority, while Protestants take the Bible as their authority. But:

- *The Bible is not a Science Book*

"The Bible was written to show us how to go to heaven, not how the heavens go." - Cardinal Baronius (1598), a quote cited by Galileo.

The Bible has many self-contradictions and factual errors. Its original authors were polytheistic pagans who thought the Earth was flat and the Sun, planets and stars revolved around it. The later editing by monotheistic priests was incomplete, leaving a number of self-contradictions. Translations from the original languages have introduced further errors, but most Young Earth Creationists in the United States would take the King James Version of the Bible as being the true word of God. But the King James version makes very effective use of literary devices such as "the four corners of the Earth", an easily understandable figure of speech. But if taken literally it implies the Earth is a tetrahedron, or a flat square. Hence apologists for Biblical literalism have made detailed justifications based on the original language for the phrase that just serve to weaken the idea that the Bible, whether in the original or especially in translation, should be taken literally.

Some people claim that Biblical prophecies prove the Holy nature of the Bible. But such claims can be made about Moby Dick as well. Many people preach that current events are foretold by the Bible, but nobody has a consistent ability to predict *future events*.

If the Bible did contain an unambiguous and successful collection of prophecies there would be no question about the existence of God. In the book *Contact*, by Carl Sagan, Ellie Arroway, after traveling to Vega and back in the machine, puts a computer to work calculating the digits of pi = 3.14159... which is the ratio of the circumference to the diameter of a circle, and finds "hiding in the alternating patterns of digits, deep inside the transcendental number, was a perfect circle, its form traced out by unities in a field of noughts." That would be an unambiguous message from the Creator of the Universe, but *Contact* is science fiction, not fact.

But the authority taken by science is:

- *Science is Based on Experience*

Karl Popper, in *The Logic of Scientific Discovery*, wrote:

But I shall admit a system as an empirical or scientific theory only if it is capable of being tested by experience. These considerations suggest that not the verifiability but the falsifiability of a system is to be taken as the criterion of demarcation. In other words: I shall not require of a scientific system that it shall be capable of being singled out, once and for all, in a positive sense; but I shall require that its logical form shall be such that it can be singled out, by means of empirical tests, in a negative sense: it must be possible for an empirical scientific system to be refuted by experience.

A scientific theory must pass every test. It can be falsified but never verified, because the next datum might disagree. So Newton's Theory of Gravity was confirmed many times over two hundred years, but the excess precession of the perihelion of Mercury's orbit falsified it. By correctly fitting all of the previous 200 years of data, and also correctly explaining the motion of Mercury and the bending of light by the Sun, Einstein's General Relativity became the new and still reigning Theory of Gravity.

Are religious theories falsifiable by experience? Some are: for example, the theory of Biblical Inerrancy could be falsified by self-contradictions in the Bible - and it is! But almost all Young Earth Creationists swear by biblical inerrancy nonetheless. How is this possible? Most religious beliefs are matters of faith: a belief held in the absence of evidence or even despite contrary evidence. Such faith-based beliefs are not falsifiable by experience, and are thus not part of any scientific theory.

- *The Big Bang is not just a theory*

Popular usage equates *theory* with an untested hypothesis. But scientific theories are hypotheses that have passed many empirical tests. However, even a very well-tested theory can be falsified, as shown by Newtonian gravity. Falsifying a well-tested theory is the biggest achievement that a scientist can make, and thus many scientists are drawn to testing and retesting the best established theories. But these scientists recognize that the probability of falsifying a well-tested theory is low, and thus their work may come to naught. One can encourage the testing of well-established theories by proposing alternatives theories that explain all known facts but make different predictions for new experiments.

In the 1950's the Big Bang was not well-tested, and the Steady State model was a very useful alternative that encouraged many observations. Now the Big Bang picture is well established, but the inflationary scenario added on before events in the classic Big Bang is not well-tested. Many alternatives versions of inflation have been suggested. But do not think that these alternatives represent weaknesses of the Big Bang.

Science Matters to our Future

The years prior to World War II were marked in Germany by a campaign against "Jewish science" which included relativity. As a result Einstein, Fermi, Teller, Bethe and Szilard all left Europe. Because of Hitler's injection of religious prejudice into science, the Allies and not the Axis were first to the atomic bomb. The next big technology will probably be biotechnology, and a failure to teach modern biology could lead to our downfall. We must teach our children both the methods of science and the latest well-tested theories of biology and physics to guarantee our future.

Darwin's Impact on Science and Society

Charles Darwin, and the legacy of his work describing evolution and natural selection, is often distorted for political ends. But as Center for American Progress Senior Fellow Susan Thistlethwaite explained yesterday, the spheres of science and religion are not in conflict, and a look at Darwin's own life can help untangle the thorny cultural history of evolution. "Few people seem to remember that Darwin graduated from seminary," she said. Thistlethwaite spoke as a panelist at the Center yesterday, "Evolution, Transcendence, and the Nature of Faith," which considered Darwin's legacy for both science and religion, and the impact of evolution on public policy.

She and was joined by Arthur Caplan, the Director of the Center for Bioethics at the University of Pennsylvania, David Sloan Wilson, the co-founder of the Evolution Institute and a professor of evolutionary biology at Binghamton University, with CAP Senior Fellow Rick Weiss moderating the discussion. Sally Steenland, a senior policy adviser to CAP's Faith and Progressive Policy Initiative, noted in her opening remarks that over half of the U.S. and British populations reject Darwin's theory of evolution, which has serious consequences for education global competitiveness. Addressing the place of evolution in education, Caplan explained that religion and "Intelligent Design" do not belong in science classes. But he also said that progressives often carry the prohibition too far, implying that discussions of religion belong nowhere at all in public schools, a proposition he disagreed with.

Building on the fact that Darwin was a religious man early in life, Thistlethwaite explained that the naturalist arrived at agnosticism after watching one of his young children suffer and die. She stressed that it was this personal experience and not merely his scientific discoveries that changed his beliefs. To this, Caplan noted that the field of bioethics, which is closely allied with science, actually has its roots in religious thought. When the discipline took shape in the 1960s and 70s, "the overwhelming majority of the people who got interested in bioethical questions were from religious traditions," he said. He went on to say that theologians identified two problems with science. First, it does not generate values. "Science," he said, "does not speak a language that can tell us where to go." Second, it can be misused for horrific purposes—he noted the influence of Nazi experiments on early bioethical thinkers: "science might be perverted into social goals they would have to oppose."

"It's hard to speak religion in public," Caplan said, noting the challenges of addressing issues of public policy. Bioethics, now thought of as a secular discipline, handles these challenges to science by injecting values into the discussion, but is useful for thinking about public policy because it is able to speak in public without setting off fights. But one of the most challenging issues raised by evolutionary science is the question of what it means to be human. Several panelists noted research on the capacity of apes and other animals to show sympathy and emotional characteristics associated with humans. "Are human beings special?" asked Caplan. In response, Thistlethwaite explained that Darwin's experience with slavery and the bestiality of slaveholders, as well as his scientific research, led him to discount the unique distinctiveness of human beings. Wilson noted that, "There is more to evolution to than genetic evolution." For him, questions about the evolution of humans are not purely biological.

"When we think of managing our genes and altering our genetic destiny, we also need to think about altering our cultural evolutionary destiny." He went on to add that evolutionary theory can inform public policy by offering insight into how to manage large-scale social interactions. "The common conception of evolution is that it explains selfishness well and altruism poorly," he said. But he argued that it is possible to take lessons from evolution and tilt the playing field towards altruism. Yet scientific knowledge also allows for humans to tilt biology in their favor in radical new ways, Weiss said. "We are starting to take a greater hand in our own evolution. We are gaining the capability of changing ourselves, improving ourselves."

Caplan took up the issue, noting that parents who might choose to tweak the genomes of their children are merely trying to give them an advantage in a competitive world. Their intentions, he said, are no different from parents who send their kids to expensive private schools in an attempt to give them an educational leg up in the world. Weiss opened the discussion by reading from a satirical Onion article about "evolutionists" who flock to a Darwin-shaped wall stain in Dayton, Tennessee. The joke was readily apparent to the audience, as some anti-religious Darwin advocates plead their case with religious fervor. Thistlethwaite pointed out that despite questions that frame the issue as "Do you believe in evolution," evolution is not, in fact, a belief system.

"It's happening to you whether you like it or not," she said. Weiss closed he event by quoting Darwin's own writing on evolution, which can take on a transcendent tone: "There is grandeur in this view of life, with its several powers, having been originally breathed into a few forms or into one; and that, whilst this planet has gone cycling on according to the fixed law of gravity, from so simple a beginning endless forms most beautiful and most wonderful have been, and are being, evolved." Featured Speakers: David Sloan Wilson, Co-founder of the Evolution Institute and professor of evolutionary biology, Binghamton University Rev. Dr. Susan Brooks Thistlethwaite, Senior Fellow, Center for American Progress Arthur Caplan, Director, Center for Bioethics, University of Pennsylvania Introductory Remarks: Sally Steenland, Senior Policy Advisor, Center for American Progress Moderated by: Rick Weiss, Senior Fellow, Center for American Progress.

Science and Religion as Cultural Kindling

Everybody needs to sit back and relax. In this anniversary year of both Charles Darwin's birth and his magnum opus, we shall surely hear even more than usual about this brilliant and thinking man whose ideas changed the world forever. Let's celebrate and learn from him, whether we agree with him or not, rather than use his ideas as kindling for the 'the culture wars between science and religion.' I know: kindling and fires sell books—but let's relax and go a bit deeper. In The New Republic, Jerry Coyne, a respected professor of ecology and evolution at the University of Chicago, reviews two books that attempt to reconcile science and religion: Karl Giberson's Saving Darwin: How to be a Christian and Believe in Evolution and Kenneth Miller's Only A Theory: Evolution and the Battle for America's Soul. Coyne's own contribution to the conversation was also just published, and its title is self-explanatory: Why Evolution Is True.

It takes him a long time to say it, but Coyne's main point is that however hard Giberson or Miller or anyone else tries, they will never be able to reconcile science and religion, because science and religion are irreconcilable. Coyne does an admirable job of demonstrating this, point by (now tiresome) point. First, there's the usual collection of statistics illustrating Americans' stupidity (74% of us believe in angels, and most of us in miracles, etc.); so, clearly, we need help, and the implication is that science will provide this help if only we were more rational, for God's sake. Then, there's the God-of-the-gaps argument and why it's so weak. God-of-the-gaps goes like this: science can explain everything except blank (depending on the historical moment, fill in the blank with: how the earth moves around the sun, why we look like our parents, why the proteins in a bacterial flagellum work the way they do, why only humans can write columns like this), so God must be—or be responsible for—blank.

The problem with this, which Coyne complains both Giberson and Miller ultimately call on, is eventually science explains away the gaps, and space for God becomes smaller and smaller. There's that whole thing about how you can never (or at least so far no one has been able to) scientifically prove whether prayer works or that God exists. It's hard to jam religious experience—although many of us scientists have tried—into the controlled experiments of a scientific way of knowing. Again, Coyne's implication and really the official scientific position of many is that, therefore, spiritual experiences are at best not worth as much as scientific experiences and, at worst, not worth anything. There's the counter-claim to those who say, "Science itself is a religion, so how can scientists badmouth religion?" Coyne argues, as many have before him, that science is not a religion. What counts as evidence in the two realms of science and religion is entirely different. If an experiment or other experience cannot be repeated, it and its data are discarded by science.

And finally, there's the huge point emerging directly from Darwin's work: science, unlike religion, does not hold up humans or Earth as in any way unique or inevitable. Coyne does set off in a new and productive direction when he calls out many of those attempting the Great Reconciliation who blames the 'new atheists' for cultural discord. The line is that all these atheist scientists, Richard Dawkins and his book The God Delusion (2006) being the epitome, are inciting the masses by heaping abuse on religion and proclaiming the superiority of scientific reason. But then Coyne loses his way again by basically agreeing with Dawkins and ending his review by saying attempts at reconciliation will go on forever because reconciliation is impossible.

Here's what I'm thinking, folks: everyone's missing the point. The point is not whether Richard Dawkins and the evolutionists and the atheists are right or wrong or idiots; nor that the creationists are; nor that Miller and Giberson are. Nor that science should be battling religion or even necessarily that the two should kiss and make up. The point is to acknowledge the pink elephant, not ignore her. The point is when in the classroom and in other public forums, science teachers, scientists, politicians, clergymen, and others discuss creationism or evolution, stem cells or abortion, in vitro fertilization or genetic testing, there is a pink elephant in the room. In my university science classroom, for example, the elephant is religion.

Science can be a good and powerful force; religion can be a good and powerful force. And they, and the broad spectrum of ideas and opinions within each, can work together for more good and power than either alone. This, despite Coyne's thesis, is, if not reconciliation, at least a step toward it, and perhaps even a step beyond it toward the emergence of new possibilities.

The case of federal funding for embryonic stem-cell research is a case in point. While the positions of Presidents Bush and Obama were and are controversial, both attempted (to varying degrees) to consider the pink elephants. Both positions call for careful thinking, rethinking, and monitoring of the science and its implications for religions, life, and society.

When the pink elephant is ignored, everyone loses. My point at first appears subtle, but it makes all the difference. We don't need to embrace the pink elephant, but we must acknowledge her, bring her up to the front of the room and introduce her from all angles. I do not mean teach creationism in a science class or endorse stem-cell therapy in a church. Don't teach creationism, teach about creationism, recognize it, use it as a teaching opportunity. To not do this exacerbates the very statistics about Americans cited by Coyne; we need to do this because of those statistics.

When we do, people actually learn better, see that there are usually more than simply two sides to an argument, and aren't forced, as they currently are, to 'take sides' or reject ideas. Humans learn better when we can relate knowledge to our daily experiences and consider it from diverse perspectives. It's called education. And, yes, it's difficult. Do this and the whole conversation changes. Do this, and we'll have less yelling and less name-calling, less forced reconciliation. Provide the information in a rich, non-confrontational, engaging context. Then let people come to their own conclusions; it's called education.

Abortion and Religion

In current usage: the practice of intentionally terminating a pregnancy prior to childbirth; historically, any termination of pregnancy prior to childbirth. Abortion has occasioned a great deal of religious rhetoric and activity in the United States since the landmark case of Roe v. Wade in 1973. As such, the topic has attracted considerable attention from sociologists of religion.

There have been three general approaches to the study of abortion within the scientific study of religion. Much of the earliest work on abortion has been focused on the discourse of elites: journalists, physicians, governmental officials, judges, and lay activists. In this branch of abortion research, several different themes have merged. Because access to legal abortion has been provided by court decisions rather than acts of legislatures, both sides of the abortion controversy have invoked the language of rights.

Because rights are, by definition, basic prerogatives, the casting of abortion discourse in terms of opposing rights (a "right to choose" versus a "right to life") has rendered abortion rhetoric artificially polarized. Moreover, activist-level discourse has emphasized competing notions of women's social roles and alternative world-views concerning sexuality and sexual morality. At the activist level, the abortion controversy has come to crystalize a number of different basic values.

Finally, activist-level rhetoric on the pro-life side has become steadily less religious and more secular over time. Arguments about natural law and the meaning of specific scriptural passages have tended to give way to arguments about the humanity of the fetus and the nature of rights and obligations. This secularization of abortion rhetoric may have enhanced the possibility of ecumenical cooperation on this issue, because early abortion activists may have been divided between the Catholic "natural law" rationale for opposition to legal abortion and the evangelical tendency to invoke specific biblical passages.

Pro-life activists are less likely to fragment over theological particularism if the abortion debate is cast in the liberal democratic language of competing rights. A second research tradition on abortion has been concerned with mass-level opinion. This research has suggested that the opinions of ordinary citizens differ qualitatively from those of abortion activists. At the level of the mass public, relatively few American citizens are either unequivocally "pro-choice" or "pro-life" but tend to take varying intermediate positions on the abortion issue. Unlike other issues, this apparent ambivalence does not indicate a lack of sophistication about the issue but reflects the fact that Americans tend to value both the privacy rights of women and the value of the potential life of the fetus. In another contrast with activist-level debate, the relationship between abortion attitudes and attitudes toward women's societal roles tends to be quite weak at the mass level. Also, both religious orthodoxy and religiosity are related to pro-life attitudes, regardless of respondents' denominational affiliation.

This relationship poses an interesting agenda for future research, because the same relationship between religious observance and antiabortion attitudes pertains across diverse socialization experiences. Some denominations attempt direct religious teaching about abortion (with such observances as "Human Life Sundays" and so on), others tend to downplay the issue, and a few emphasize the right of a woman to make the final decision about abortion. Some research has suggested that religious socialization has a strong effect on denominational members (particularly Roman Catholics), but that such religious activity tends to stimulate pro-choice counter-mobilization.

The political effects of the abortion issue have varied over time. For most of the period following Roe v. Wade, the abortion issue was much more salient to those who preferred restrictive policies toward abortion. This asymmetry ended with the case of Webster v. Missouri Reproductive Services in 1989, which permitted states considerably greater latitude in regulating the delivery of abortion services (while retaining abortion as a constitutionally protected right).

This ruling was interpreted by both pro-life and pro-choice activists as a clear victory for the pro-life side, and appears to have led to the electoral mobilization of pro-choice citizens. Several studies have suggested that a number of senatorial and gubernatorial races in 1989 and 1990 were decided, in large part, by the abortion issue, with pro-choice candidates faring significantly better than might otherwise have been expected.

One similarly exists between activist-level and mass-level understandings of the abortion issue. In both cases, there has been a convergence of rationales on the pro-life side. Early in the post-Roe period, Catholics who opposed abortion tended to do so because of a respect for the human status of the fetus, while "pro-life" evangelicals tended to emphasize the effects of legal abortion on reducing the risks of nonmarital sexual activity or on increasing the incidence of pre-marital sex. By the 1980s, both groups had assimilated both rationales, with "respect for life" being a somewhat stronger predictor than sexual conservatism. Again, this reduction of religious differences in pro-life rationales has made ecumenical antiabortion activity considerably easier.

Finally, a third approach to the study of the abortion issue has focused on the causes and consequences of "direct action." In recent years, some abortion activists (especially on the "pro-life" side) have engaged in unconventional, sometimes illegal, and occasionally violent activities. These practices have included picketing, "sidewalk counseling," physically obstructing entrances to abortion clinics ("sitting in"), vandalizing the property of abortion clinics, and occasionally murdering or attempting to murder abortion providers. A number of general explanations of such activities have been offered by social scientists. Some have emphasized the role of individual psychological pathologies in accounting for unconventional protest activities. Protesters are thought to be compensating for some personal deficiency (downward economic mobility, individual feelings of inferiority, and so on).

Other analysts have focused on the effects of religious beliefs on unconventional activism, arguing that abortion violence is a natural (if not necessarily inevitable) consequence of particular religious commitments. In this style of analysis, it is often argued that people who hold an image of a vengeful, punishing God are much more likely to engage in pro-life violence than are other people. Finally, some have argued that unconventional pro-life activism is an understandable response to an inhospitable political environment.

In the aftermath of the pro-choice mobilization that followed Webster, and the election of pro-choice President Bill Clinton (with the probable consequence of preserving a pro-choice majority on the Supreme Court), conventional political activity (voting, lobbying, public education, and the like) has seemed futile to many pro-life activists. Given the very high theological and moral stakes of the abortion controversy, some have elected to take drastic action to limit the incidence of legal abortion. Indeed, several studies have suggested that fewer physicians are willing to provide abortion services since the murders of abortion doctors in 1993 and 1994.

Bibliography

Abraham J. Heschel, *God in Search of Man: A Philosophy of Judaism* reprint of 1967 edition: Noonday Press, 1997.

Ali, 'Abdullah Yusuf, *The meaning of the Holy Qur'an*, Amana: Beltsville, Maryland, 1989.

Ali, Ahmed, (trans.) *Islam: The Qur'an*, Princeton University Press, 1988.

Angelika Malinar, *The Bhagavadgita: Doctrines and Contexts*, Cambridge: Cambridge University Press, 2008

Babin, P., *The New Era in Religious Communication*, Minneapolis, MN: Fortress Press, 1991.

Barnstone, Willis (Ed.), *The Other Bible*, HarperSan Francisco, 1984.

Barrett, David V., *The New Believers: Sects, Cults and Alternative Religions*, Cassell & Co: London, 2001.

Blakney, R.B. (trans.), *The Way of Life Lao Tzu: Tao Te Ching: A New Translation*, New American Library: NY, 1955

Bavinck, J. H., *The Impact of Christianity on the Non-Christian World*, Grand Rapids: Eerdmans, 1948.

Bruce, S., *Religion in the Modern World: from Cathedrals to Cults*, Oxford: Oxford University Press, 1996.

Buddenbaum, J., *Reporting News about Religion: An Introduction for Journalists*, Ames, IA: Iowa State University Press, 1998.

Burnett, David, *World of the Spirits: A Christian Perspective on traditional and Folk Religions*, London: Monarch, 2000.

Chan, Wing-Tsit, trans. and ed. *A Source Book in Chinese Philosophy*. Princeton: Princeton University Press, 1963.

Creel, H.G., *Chinese Thought: from Confucius to Mao Tse-tung*, University of Chicago Press, 1953.

Daniel Chanan Matt, ed., *Zohar: The Book of Enlightenment*, Classics of Western Spirituality, New York: Paulist Press, 1988.

Donald S. Lopez, Jr., ed., *Buddhism in Practice*, Princeton Readings in Religions, Princeton: Princeton University Press, 1995.

Eichhoefer, Gerald W. *Enduring Issues in Philosophy*. San Diego: Greenhaven Press, Inc., 1995.

Ginsburg, F. D., L. Abu-Lughod and B. Larkin (eds), *Media Worlds: Anthropology on New Terrain*, Berkeley, CA: University of California Press, 2002.

Hiebert, Paul G., *Understanding Folk Religion: A Christian Response to Popular Beliefs and Practices*, Grand Rapids: Baker, 1999.

Hillary Rodrigues, *Introducing Hinduism*, World Religion Series, New York: Routledge, 2006.

Jacob Neusner, Judaism as Philosophy: The Method and Message of the Mishnah, Baltimore: Johns Hopkins, 1999.

Jeffrey L. Rubenstein, ed., *Rabbinic Stories*, Classics of Western Spirituality, New York: Paulist Press, 2002.

Joseph Dan, *Jewish Mysticism*, 4 vol., Northvale, NJ: Jason Aronson, 1998.

Kurtz, Lester R., *Gods in the Global Village*, Thousand Oaks, CA: Sage, 2007.

Lyden, John. *Enduring Issues in Religion*. San Diego: Greenhaven Press, Inc., 1995.

Malise Ruthven, *Islam: A Very Short Introduction*, New York: Oxford University Press, 2000.

Mark Juergensmeyer, *Global Religions: An Introduction,* New York: Oxford University Press, 2003.

Michael D. Coogan, ed., *The Illustrated Guide to World Religions,* New York: Oxford University Press, 2003.

Ninian Smart, *Dimensions of the Sacred : An Anatomy of the World's Beliefs,* Berkeley: University of California Press, 1996.

Norman Solomon, *Judaism: A Very Short Introduction* (New York: Oxford University Press, 2000.

Paul Williams, *Mahayana Buddhism: The Doctrinal Foundations,* New York: Routledge, 2008.

Peter Harvey, *An Introduction to Buddhism: Teachings, History, and Practices,* Cambridge: Cambridge University Press, 1990.

Richard Valantasis, *Religions of Late Antiquity in Practice,* Princeton: Princeton University Press, 2000.

Rinpoche, Sogyal. *The Tibetan Book of Living and Dying.* New York: Harper Collins, 1993.

Seyyed Nasr Hossein, ed., *Islamic Spirituality I: Foundations,* World Spirituality 19 (New York: Crossroad, 1987.

Tu Weiming & Mary Evelyn Tucker, eds., *Confucian Spirituality,* World Spirituality 11, New York: Herder & Herder, 2002.

Xinzhong Yao, *An Introduction to Confucianism,* Cambridge: Cambridge University Press, 2000.

Zaehner, R.C. (translation), *Hindu Scriptures,* J.M. Dent & Sons: London, 1966.

Index

S

T

U

V

Contents

PREFACE

In the following pages I have confined myself in the main to those problems of philosophy in regard to which I thought it possible to say something positive and constructive, since merely negative criticism seemed out of place. For this reason, theory of knowledge occupies a larger space than metaphysics in the present volume, and some topics much discussed by philosophers are treated very briefly, if at all.

I have derived valuable assistance from unpublished writings of G. E. Moore and J. M. Keynes: from the former, as regards the relations of sense-data to physical objects, and from the latter as regards probability and induction. I have also profited greatly by the criticisms and suggestions of Professor Gilbert Murray.

1912

CHAPTER I. APPEARANCE AND REALITY

Is there any knowledge in the world which is so certain that no reasonable man could doubt it? This question, which at first sight might not seem difficult, is really one of the most difficult that can be asked. When we have realized the obstacles in the way of a straightforward and confident answer, we shall be well launched on the study of philosophy—for philosophy is merely the attempt to answer such ultimate questions, not carelessly and dogmatically, as we do in ordinary life and even in the sciences, but critically, after exploring all that makes such questions puzzling, and after realizing all the vagueness and confusion that underlie our ordinary ideas.

In daily life, we assume as certain many things which, on a closer scrutiny, are found to be so full of apparent contradictions that only a great amount of thought enables us to know what it is that we really may believe. In the search for certainty, it is natural to begin with our present experiences, and in some sense, no doubt, knowledge is to be derived from them. But any statement as to what it is that our immediate experiences make us know is very likely to be wrong. It seems to me that I am now sitting in a chair, at a table of a certain shape, on which I see sheets of paper with writing or print. By turning my head I see out of the window buildings and clouds and the sun. I believe that the sun is about ninety-three million miles from the earth; that it is a hot globe many times bigger than the earth; that, owing to the earth's rotation, it rises every morning, and will continue to do so for an indefinite time in the future. I believe that, if any other normal person comes into my room, he will see the same chairs and tables and books and papers as I see, and that the table which I see is the same as the table which I feel pressing against my arm. All this seems to be so evident as to be hardly worth stating, except in answer to a man who doubts whether I know anything. Yet all this may be reasonably doubted, and all of it requires much careful discussion before we can be sure that we have stated it in a form that is wholly true.

To make our difficulties plain, let us concentrate attention on the table. To the eye it is oblong, brown and shiny, to the touch it is smooth and cool and hard; when I tap it, it gives out a wooden sound. Any one else who sees and feels and hears the table will agree with this description, so that it might seem as if no difficulty would arise; but as soon as we try to be more precise our troubles begin. Although I believe that the table is 'really' of the same colour all over, the parts that reflect the light look much brighter than the other parts, and some parts look white because of reflected light. I know that, if I move, the parts that reflect the light will be different, so that the apparent distribution of colours on the table will change. It follows that if several people are looking at the table at the same moment, no two of them will see exactly the same distribution of colours, because no two can see it from exactly the same point of view, and any change in the point of view makes some change in the way the light is reflected.

For most practical purposes these differences are unimportant, but to the painter they are all-important: the painter has to unlearn the habit of thinking that things seem to have the colour which common sense says they 'really' have, and to learn the habit of seeing things as they appear. Here we have already the beginning of one of the distinctions that cause most trouble in philosophy—the distinction between 'appearance' and 'reality', between what things seem to be and what they are. The painter wants to know what things seem to be, the practical man and the philosopher want to know what they are; but the philosopher's wish to know this is stronger than the practical man's, and is more troubled by knowledge as to the difficulties of answering the question.

To return to the table. It is evident from what we have found, that there is no colour which pre-eminently appears to be *the* colour of the table, or even of any one particular part of the table—it appears to be of different colours from different points of view, and there is no reason for regarding some of these as more really its colour than others. And we know that even from a given point of view the colour will seem different by artificial light, or to a colour-blind man, or to a man wearing blue spectacles, while in the dark there will be no colour at all, though to touch and hearing the table will be unchanged. This colour is not something which is inherent in the table, but something depending upon the table and the spectator and the way the light falls on the table. When, in ordinary life, we speak of *the* colour of the table, we only mean the sort of colour which it will seem to have to a normal spectator from an ordinary point of view under usual conditions of light. But the other colours which appear under other conditions have just as good a right to be considered real; and therefore, to avoid favouritism, we are compelled to deny that, in itself, the table has any one particular colour.

The same thing applies to the texture. With the naked eye one can see the grain, but otherwise the table looks smooth and even. If we looked at it through a microscope, we should see roughnesses and hills and valleys, and all sorts of differences that are imperceptible to the naked eye. Which of these is the 'real' table? We are naturally tempted to say that what we see through the microscope is more real, but that in turn would be changed by a still more powerful microscope. If, then, we cannot trust what we see with the naked eye, why should we trust what we see through a microscope? Thus, again, the confidence in our senses with which we began deserts us.

The shape of the table is no better. We are all in the habit of judging as to the 'real' shapes of things, and we do this so unreflectingly that we come to think we actually see the real shapes. But, in fact, as we all have to learn if we try to draw, a given thing looks different in shape from every different point of view. If our table is 'really' rectangular, it will look, from almost all points of view, as if it had two acute angles and two obtuse angles. If opposite sides are parallel, they will look as if they converged to a point away from the spectator; if they are of equal length, they will look as if the nearer side were longer. All these things are not commonly noticed in looking at a table, because experience has taught us to construct the 'real' shape from the apparent shape, and the 'real' shape is what interests us as practical men. But the 'real' shape is not what we see; it is something inferred from what we see. And what we see is constantly changing in shape as we move about the room; so that here again the senses seem not to give us the truth about the table itself, but only about the appearance of the table.

Similar difficulties arise when we consider the sense of touch. It is true that the table always gives us a sensation of hardness, and we feel that it resists pressure. But the sensation we obtain depends upon how hard we press the table and also upon what part of the body we press with; thus the various sensations due to various pressures or various parts of the body cannot be supposed to reveal *directly* any definite property of the table, but at most to be *signs* of some property which perhaps *causes* all the sensations, but is not actually apparent in any of them. And the same applies still more obviously to the sounds which can be elicited by rapping the table.

Thus it becomes evident that the real table, if there is one, is not the same as what we immediately experience by sight or touch or hearing. The real table, if there is one, is not *immediately* known to us at all, but must be an inference from what is immediately known. Hence, two very difficult questions at once arise; namely, (1) Is there a real table at all? (2) If so, what sort of object can it be?

It will help us in considering these questions to have a few simple terms of which the meaning is definite and clear. Let us give the name of 'sense-data' to the things that are immediately known in sensation: such things as colours, sounds, smells, hardnesses, roughnesses, and so on. We shall give the name 'sensation' to the experience of being immediately aware of these things. Thus, whenever we see a colour, we have a sensation *of* the colour, but the colour itself is a sense-datum, not a sensation. The colour is that *of* which we are immediately aware, and the awareness itself is the sensation. It is plain that if we are to know anything about the table, it must be by means of the sense-data—brown colour, oblong shape, smoothness, etc.—which we associate with the table; but, for the reasons which have been given, we cannot say that the table is the sense-data, or even that the sense-data are directly properties of the table. Thus a problem arises as to the relation of the sense-data to the real table, supposing there is such a thing.

The real table, if it exists, we will call a 'physical object'. Thus we have to consider the relation of sense-data to physical objects. The collection of all physical objects is called 'matter'. Thus our two questions may be re-stated as follows: (1) Is there any such thing as matter? (2) If so, what is its nature?

The philosopher who first brought prominently forward the reasons for regarding the immediate objects of our senses as not existing independently of us was Bishop Berkeley (1685-1753). His *Three Dialogues between Hylas and Philonous, in Opposition to Sceptics and Atheists*, undertake to prove that there is no such thing as matter at all, and that the world consists of nothing but minds and their ideas. Hylas has hitherto believed in matter, but he is no match for Philonous, who mercilessly drives him into contradictions and paradoxes, and makes his own denial of matter seem, in the end, as if it were almost common sense. The arguments employed are of very different value: some are important and sound, others are confused or quibbling. But Berkeley retains the merit of having shown that the existence of matter is capable of being denied without absurdity, and that if there are any things that exist independently of us they cannot be the immediate objects of our sensations.

There are two different questions involved when we ask whether matter exists, and it is important to keep them clear. We commonly mean by 'matter' something which is opposed to 'mind', something which we think of as occupying space and as radically incapable of any sort of thought or consciousness. It is chiefly in this sense that Berkeley denies matter; that is to say, he does not deny that the sense-data which we commonly take as signs of the existence of the table are really signs of the existence of *something* independent of us, but he does deny that this something is non-mental, that it is neither mind nor ideas entertained by some mind. He admits that there must be something which continues to exist when we go out of the room or shut our eyes, and that what we call seeing the table does really give us reason for believing in something which persists even when we are not seeing it. But he thinks that this something cannot be radically different in nature from what we see, and cannot be independent of seeing altogether, though it must be independent of *our* seeing. He is thus led to regard the 'real' table as an idea in the mind of God. Such an idea has the required permanence and independence of ourselves, without being—as matter would otherwise be—something quite unknowable, in the sense that we can only infer it, and can never be directly and immediately aware of it.

Other philosophers since Berkeley have also held that, although the table does not depend for its existence upon being seen by me, it does depend upon being seen (or otherwise apprehended in sensation) by *some* mind—not necessarily the mind of God, but more often the whole collective mind of the universe. This they hold, as Berkeley does, chiefly because they think there can be nothing real—or at any rate nothing known to be real except minds and their thoughts and feelings. We might state the argument by which they support their view in some such way as this: 'Whatever can be thought of is an idea in the mind of the person thinking of it; therefore nothing can be thought of except ideas in minds; therefore anything else is inconceivable, and what is inconceivable cannot exist.'

Such an argument, in my opinion, is fallacious; and of course those who advance it do not put it so shortly or so crudely. But whether valid or not, the argument has been very widely advanced in one form or another; and very many philosophers, perhaps a majority, have held that there is nothing real except minds and their ideas. Such philosophers are called 'idealists'. When they come to explaining matter, they either say, like Berkeley, that matter is really nothing but a collection of ideas, or they say, like Leibniz (1646-1716), that what appears as matter is really a collection of more or less rudimentary minds.

But these philosophers, though they deny matter as opposed to mind, nevertheless, in another sense, admit matter. It will be remembered that we asked two questions; namely, (1) Is there a real table at all? (2) If so, what sort of object can it be? Now both Berkeley and Leibniz admit that there is a real table, but Berkeley says it is certain ideas in the mind of God, and Leibniz says it is a colony of souls. Thus both of them answer our first question in the affirmative, and only diverge from the views of ordinary mortals in their answer to our second question. In fact, almost all philosophers seem to be agreed that there is a real table: they almost all agree that, however much our sense-data—colour, shape, smoothness, etc.—may depend upon us, yet their occurrence is a sign of something existing independently of us, something differing, perhaps, completely from our sense-data, and yet to be regarded as causing those sense-data whenever we are in a suitable relation to the real table.

Now obviously this point in which the philosophers are agreed—the view that there *is* a real table, whatever its nature may be—is vitally important, and it will be worth while to consider what reasons there are for accepting this view before we go on to the further question as to the nature of the real table. Our next chapter, therefore, will be concerned with the reasons for supposing that there is a real table at all.

Before we go farther it will be well to consider for a moment what it is that we have discovered so far. It has appeared that, if we take any common object of the sort that is supposed to be known by the senses, what the senses *immediately* tell us is not the truth about the object as it is apart from us, but only the truth about certain sense-data which, so far as we can see, depend upon the relations between us and the object. Thus what we directly see and feel is merely 'appearance', which we believe to be a sign of some 'reality' behind. But if the reality is not what appears, have we any means of knowing whether there is any reality at all? And if so, have we any means of finding out what it is like?

Such questions are bewildering, and it is difficult to know that even the strangest hypotheses may not be true. Thus our familiar table, which has roused but the slightest thoughts in us hitherto, has become a problem full of surprising possibilities. The one thing we know about it is that it is not what it seems. Beyond this modest result, so far, we have the most complete liberty of conjecture. Leibniz tells us it is a community of souls: Berkeley tells us it is an idea in the mind of God; sober science, scarcely less wonderful, tells us it is a vast collection of electric charges in violent motion.

Among these surprising possibilities, doubt suggests that perhaps there is no table at all. Philosophy, if it cannot *answer* so many questions as we could wish, has at least the power of *asking* questions which increase the interest of the world, and show the strangeness and wonder lying just below the surface even in the commonest things of daily life.

CHAPTER II. THE EXISTENCE OF MATTER

In this chapter we have to ask ourselves whether, in any sense at all, there is such a thing as matter. Is there a table which has a certain intrinsic nature, and continues to exist when I am not looking, or is the table merely a product of my imagination, a dream-table in a very prolonged dream? This question is of the greatest importance. For if we cannot be sure of the independent existence of objects, we cannot be sure of the independent existence of other people's bodies, and therefore still less of other people's minds, since we have no grounds for believing in their minds except such as are derived from observing their bodies. Thus if we cannot be sure of the independent existence of objects, we shall be left alone in a desert—it may be that the whole outer world is nothing but a dream, and that we alone exist. This is an uncomfortable possibility; but although it cannot be strictly proved to be false, there is not the slightest reason to suppose that it is true. In this chapter we have to see why this is the case.

Before we embark upon doubtful matters, let us try to find some more or less fixed point from which to start. Although we are doubting the physical existence of the table, we are not doubting the existence of the sense-data which made us think there was a table; we are not doubting that, while we look, a certain colour and shape appear to us, and while we press, a certain sensation of hardness is experienced by us. All this, which is psychological, we are not calling in question. In fact, whatever else may be doubtful, some at least of our immediate experiences seem absolutely certain.

Descartes (1596-1650), the founder of modern philosophy, invented a method which may still be used with profit—the method of systematic doubt. He determined that he would believe nothing which he did not see quite clearly and distinctly to be true. Whatever he could bring himself to doubt, he would doubt, until he saw reason for not doubting it. By applying this method he gradually became convinced that the only existence of which he could be *quite* certain was his own. He imagined a deceitful demon, who presented unreal things to his senses in a perpetual phantasmagoria; it might be very improbable that such a demon existed, but still it was possible, and therefore doubt concerning things perceived by the senses was possible.

But doubt concerning his own existence was not possible, for if he did not exist, no demon could deceive him. If he doubted, he must exist; if he had any experiences whatever, he must exist. Thus his own existence was an absolute certainty to him. 'I think, therefore I am,' he said (*Cogito, ergo sum*); and on the basis of this certainty he set to work to build up again the world of knowledge which his doubt had laid in ruins. By inventing the method of doubt, and by showing that subjective things are the most certain, Descartes performed a great service to philosophy, and one which makes him still useful to all students of the subject.

But some care is needed in using Descartes' argument. 'I think, therefore I am' says rather more than is strictly certain. It might seem as though we were quite sure of being the same person to-day as we were yesterday, and this is no doubt true in some sense. But the real Self is as hard to arrive at as the real table, and does not seem to have that absolute, convincing certainty that belongs to particular experiences. When I look at my table and see a certain brown colour, what is quite certain at once is not '*I* am seeing a brown colour', but rather, 'a brown colour is being seen'. This of course involves something (or somebody) which (or who) sees the brown colour; but it does not of itself involve that more or less permanent person whom we call 'I'. So far as immediate certainty goes, it might be that the something which sees the brown colour is quite momentary, and not the same as the something which has some different experience the next moment.

Thus it is our particular thoughts and feelings that have primitive certainty. And this applies to dreams and hallucinations as well as to normal perceptions: when we dream or see a ghost, we certainly do have the sensations we think we have, but for various reasons it is held that no physical object corresponds to these sensations. Thus the certainty of our knowledge of our own experiences does not have to be limited in any way to allow for exceptional cases. Here, therefore, we have, for what it is worth, a solid basis from which to begin our pursuit of knowledge.

The problem we have to consider is this: Granted that we are certain of our own sense-data, have we any reason for regarding them as signs of the existence of something else, which we can call the physical object? When we have enumerated all the sense-data which we should naturally regard as connected with the table, have we said all there is to say about the table, or is there still something else—something not a sense-datum, something which persists when we go out of the room? Common sense unhesitatingly answers that there is. What can be bought and sold and pushed about and have a cloth laid on it, and so on, cannot be a *mere* collection of sense-data. If the cloth completely hides the table, we shall derive no sense-data from the table, and therefore, if the table were merely sense-data, it would have ceased to exist, and the cloth would be suspended in empty air, resting, by a miracle, in the place where the table formerly was. This seems plainly absurd; but whoever wishes to become a philosopher must learn not to be frightened by absurdities.

One great reason why it is felt that we must secure a physical object in addition to the sense-data, is that we want the same object for different people. When ten people are sitting round a dinner-table, it seems preposterous to maintain that they are not seeing the same tablecloth, the same knives and forks and spoons and glasses. But the sense-data are private to each separate person; what is immediately present to the sight of one is not immediately present to the sight of another: they all see things from slightly different points of view, and therefore see them slightly differently. Thus, if there are to be public neutral objects, which can be in some sense known to many different people, there must be something over and above the private and particular sense-data which appear to various people. What reason, then, have we for believing that there are such public neutral objects?

The first answer that naturally occurs to one is that, although different people may see the table slightly differently, still they all see more or less similar things when they look at the table, and the variations in what they see follow the laws of perspective and reflection of light, so that it is easy to arrive at a permanent object underlying all the different people's sense-data. I bought my table from the former occupant of my room; I could not buy *his* sense-data, which died when he went away, but I could and did buy the confident expectation of more or less similar sense-data. Thus it is the fact that different people have similar sense-data, and that one person in a given place at different times has similar sense-data, which makes us suppose that over and above the sense-data there is a permanent public object which underlies or causes the sense-data of various people at various times.

Now in so far as the above considerations depend upon supposing that there are other people besides ourselves, they beg the very question at issue. Other people are represented to me by certain sense-data, such as the sight of them or the sound of their voices, and if I had no reason to believe that there were physical objects independent of my sense-data, I should have no reason to believe that other people exist except as part of my dream. Thus, when we are trying to show that there must be objects independent of our own sense-data, we cannot appeal to the testimony of other people, since this testimony itself consists of sense-data, and does not reveal other people's experiences unless our own sense-data are signs of things existing independently of us. We must therefore, if possible, find, in our own purely private experiences, characteristics which show, or tend to show, that there are in the world things other than ourselves and our private experiences.

In one sense it must be admitted that we can never prove the existence of things other than ourselves and our experiences. No logical absurdity results from the hypothesis that the world consists of myself and my thoughts and feelings and sensations, and that everything else is mere fancy. In dreams a very complicated world may seem to be present, and yet on waking we find it was a delusion; that is to say, we find that the sense-data in the dream do not appear to have corresponded with such physical objects as we should naturally infer from our sense-data. (It is true that, when the physical world is assumed, it is possible to find physical causes for the sense-data in dreams: a door banging, for instance, may cause us to dream of a naval engagement. But although, in this case, there is a physical cause for the sense-data, there is not a physical object corresponding to the sense-data in the way in which an actual naval battle would correspond.) There is no logical impossibility in the supposition that the whole of life is a dream, in which we ourselves create all the objects that come before us. But although this is not logically impossible, there is no reason whatever to suppose that it is true; and it is, in fact, a less simple hypothesis, viewed as a means of accounting for the facts of our own life, than the common-sense hypothesis that there really are objects independent of us, whose action on us causes our sensations.

The way in which simplicity comes in from supposing that there really are physical objects is easily seen. If the cat appears at one moment in one part of the room, and at another in another part, it is natural to suppose that it has moved from the one to the other, passing over a series of intermediate positions. But if it is merely a set of sense-data, it cannot have ever been in any place where I did not see it; thus we shall have to suppose that it did not exist at all while I was not looking, but suddenly sprang into being in a new place. If the cat exists whether I see it or not, we can understand from our own experience how it gets hungry between one meal and the next; but if it does not exist when I am not seeing it, it seems odd that appetite should grow during non-existence as fast as during existence. And if the cat consists only of sense-data, it cannot be hungry, since no hunger but my own can be a sense-datum to me. Thus the behaviour of the sense-data which represent the cat to me, though it seems quite natural when regarded as an expression of hunger, becomes utterly inexplicable when regarded as mere movements and changes of patches of colour, which are as incapable of hunger as a triangle is of playing football.

But the difficulty in the case of the cat is nothing compared to the difficulty in the case of human beings. When human beings speak—that is, when we hear certain noises which we associate with ideas, and simultaneously see certain motions of lips and expressions of face—it is very difficult to suppose that what we hear is not the expression of a thought, as we know it would be if we emitted the same sounds. Of course similar things happen in dreams, where we are mistaken as to the existence of other people. But dreams are more or less suggested by what we call waking life, and are capable of being more or less accounted for on scientific principles if we assume that there really is a physical world. Thus every principle of simplicity urges us to adopt the natural view, that there really are objects other than ourselves and our sense-data which have an existence not dependent upon our perceiving them.

Of course it is not by argument that we originally come by our belief in an independent external world. We find this belief ready in ourselves as soon as we begin to reflect: it is what may be called an *instinctive* belief. We should never have been led to question this belief but for the fact that, at any rate in the case of sight, it seems as if the sense-datum itself were instinctively believed to be the independent object, whereas argument shows that the object cannot be identical with the sense-datum. This discovery, however—which is not at all paradoxical in the case of taste and smell and sound, and only slightly so in the case of touch—leaves undiminished our instinctive belief that there *are* objects *corresponding* to our sense-data. Since this belief does not lead to any difficulties, but on the contrary tends to simplify and systematize our account of our experiences, there seems no good reason for rejecting it. We may therefore admit—though with a slight doubt derived from dreams—that the external world does really exist, and is not wholly dependent for its existence upon our continuing to perceive it.

The argument which has led us to this conclusion is doubtless less strong than we could wish, but it is typical of many philosophical arguments, and it is therefore worth while to consider briefly its general character and validity. All knowledge, we find, must be built up upon our instinctive beliefs, and if these are rejected, nothing is left. But among our instinctive beliefs some are much stronger than others, while many have, by habit and association, become entangled with other beliefs, not really instinctive, but falsely supposed to be part of what is believed instinctively.

Philosophy should show us the hierarchy of our instinctive beliefs, beginning with those we hold most strongly, and presenting each as much isolated and as free from irrelevant additions as possible. It should take care to show that, in the form in which they are finally set forth, our instinctive beliefs do not clash, but form a harmonious system. There can never be any reason for rejecting one instinctive belief except that it clashes with others; thus, if they are found to harmonize, the whole system becomes worthy of acceptance.

It is of course *possible* that all or any of our beliefs may be mistaken, and therefore all ought to be held with at least some slight element of doubt. But we cannot have *reason* to reject a belief except on the ground of some other belief. Hence, by organizing our instinctive beliefs and their consequences, by considering which among them is most possible, if necessary, to modify or abandon, we can arrive, on the basis of accepting as our sole data what we instinctively believe, at an orderly systematic organization of our knowledge, in which, though the *possibility* of error remains, its likelihood is diminished by the interrelation of the parts and by the critical scrutiny which has preceded acquiescence.

This function, at least, philosophy can perform. Most philosophers, rightly or wrongly, believe that philosophy can do much more than this—that it can give us knowledge, not otherwise attainable, concerning the universe as a whole, and concerning the nature of ultimate reality. Whether this be the case or not, the more modest function we have spoken of can certainly be performed by philosophy, and certainly suffices, for those who have once begun to doubt the adequacy of common sense, to justify the arduous and difficult labours that philosophical problems involve.

CHAPTER III. THE NATURE OF MATTER

In the preceding chapter we agreed, though without being able to find demonstrative reasons, that it is rational to believe that our sense-data—for example, those which we regard as associated with my table—are really signs of the existence of something independent of us and our perceptions. That is to say, over and above the sensations of colour, hardness, noise, and so on, which make up the appearance of the table to me, I assume that there is something else, of which these things are appearances. The colour ceases to exist if I shut my eyes, the sensation of hardness ceases to exist if I remove my arm from contact with the table, the sound ceases to exist if I cease to rap the table with my knuckles. But I do not believe that when all these things cease the table ceases. On the contrary, I believe that it is because the table exists continuously that all these sense-data will reappear when I open my eyes, replace my arm, and begin again to rap with my knuckles. The question we have to consider in this chapter is: What is the nature of this real table, which persists independently of my perception of it?

To this question physical science gives an answer, somewhat incomplete it is true, and in part still very hypothetical, but yet deserving of respect so far as it goes. Physical science, more or less unconsciously, has drifted into the view that all natural phenomena ought to be reduced to motions. Light and heat and sound are all due to wave-motions, which travel from the body emitting them to the person who sees light or feels heat or hears sound. That which has the wave-motion is either aether or 'gross matter', but in either case is what the philosopher would call matter. The only properties which science assigns to it are position in space, and the power of motion according to the laws of motion. Science does not deny that it *may* have other properties; but if so, such other properties are not useful to the man of science, and in no way assist him in explaining the phenomena.

It is sometimes said that 'light *is* a form of wave-motion', but this is misleading, for the light which we immediately see, which we know directly by means of our senses, is *not* a form of wave-motion, but something quite different—something which we all know if we are not blind, though we cannot describe it so as to convey our knowledge to a man who is blind. A wave-motion, on the contrary, could quite well be described to a blind man, since he can acquire a knowledge of space by the sense of touch; and he can experience a wave-motion by a sea voyage almost as well as we can. But this, which a blind man can understand, is not what we mean by *light*: we mean by *light* just that which a blind man can never understand, and which we can never describe to him.

Now this something, which all of us who are not blind know, is not, according to science, really to be found in the outer world: it is something caused by the action of certain waves upon the eyes and nerves and brain of the person who sees the light. When it is said that light *is* waves, what is really meant is that waves are the physical cause of our sensations of light. But light itself, the thing which seeing people experience and blind people do not, is not supposed by science to form any part of the world that is independent of us and our senses. And very similar remarks would apply to other kinds of sensations.

It is not only colours and sounds and so on that are absent from the scientific world of matter, but also *space* as we get it through sight or touch. It is essential to science that its matter should be in *a* space, but the space in which it is cannot be exactly the space we see or feel. To begin with, space as we see it is not the same as space as we get it by the sense of touch; it is only by experience in infancy that we learn how to touch things we see, or how to get a sight of things which we feel touching us. But the space of science is neutral as between touch and sight; thus it cannot be either the space of touch or the space of sight.

Again, different people see the same object as of different shapes, according to their point of view. A circular coin, for example, though we should always *judge* it to be circular, will *look* oval unless we are straight in front of it. When we judge that it *is* circular, we are judging that it has a real shape which is not its apparent shape, but belongs to it intrinsically apart from its appearance. But this real shape, which is what concerns science, must be in a real space, not the same as anybody's *apparent* space. The real space is public, the apparent space is private to the percipient. In different people's *private* spaces the same object seems to have different shapes; thus the real space, in which it has its real shape, must be different from the private spaces. The space of science, therefore, though *connected* with the spaces we see and feel, is not identical with them, and the manner of its connexion requires investigation.

We agreed provisionally that physical objects cannot be quite like our sense-data, but may be regarded as *causing* our sensations. These physical objects are in the space of science, which we may call 'physical' space. It is important to notice that, if our sensations are to be caused by physical objects, there must be a physical space containing these objects and our sense-organs and nerves and brain. We get a sensation of touch from an object when we are in contact with it; that is to say, when some part of our body occupies a place in physical space quite close to the space occupied by the object. We see an object (roughly speaking) when no opaque body is between the object and our eyes in physical space. Similarly, we only hear or smell or taste an object when we are sufficiently near to it, or when it touches the tongue, or has some suitable position in physical space relatively to our body. We cannot begin to state what different sensations we shall derive from a given object under different circumstances unless we regard the object and our body as both in one physical space, for it is mainly the relative positions of the object and our body that determine what sensations we shall derive from the object.

Now our sense-data are situated in our private spaces, either the space of sight or the space of touch or such vaguer spaces as other senses may give us. If, as science and common sense assume, there is one public all-embracing physical space in which physical objects are, the relative positions of physical objects in physical space must more or less correspond to the relative positions of sense-data in our private spaces. There is no difficulty in supposing this to be the case. If we see on a road one house nearer to us than another, our other senses will bear out the view that it is nearer; for example, it will be reached sooner if we walk along the road. Other people will agree that the house which looks nearer to us is nearer; the ordnance map will take the same view; and thus everything points to a spatial relation between the houses corresponding to the relation between the sense-data which we see when we look at the houses. Thus we may assume that there is a physical space in which physical objects have spatial relations corresponding to those which the corresponding sense-data have in our private spaces. It is this physical space which is dealt with in geometry and assumed in physics and astronomy.

Assuming that there is physical space, and that it does thus correspond to private spaces, what can we know about it? We can know *only* what is required in order to secure the correspondence. That is to say, we can know nothing of what it is like in itself, but we can know the sort of arrangement of physical objects which results from their spatial relations. We can know, for example, that the earth and moon and sun are in one straight line during an eclipse, though we cannot know what a physical straight line is in itself, as we know the look of a straight line in our visual space. Thus we come to know much more about the *relations* of distances in physical space than about the distances themselves; we may know that one distance is greater than another, or that it is along the same straight line as the other, but we cannot have that immediate acquaintance with physical distances that we have with distances in our private spaces, or with colours or sounds or other sense-data. We can know all those things about physical space which a man born blind might know through other people about the space of sight; but the kind of things which a man born blind could never know about the space of sight we also cannot know about physical space. We can know the properties of the relations required to preserve the correspondence with sense-data, but we cannot know the nature of the terms between which the relations hold.

With regard to time, our *feeling* of duration or of the lapse of time is notoriously an unsafe guide as to the time that has elapsed by the clock. Times when we are bored or suffering pain pass slowly, times when we are agreeably occupied pass quickly, and times when we are sleeping pass almost as if they did not exist. Thus, in so far as time is constituted by duration, there is the same necessity for distinguishing a public and a private time as there was in the case of space. But in so far as time consists in an *order* of before and after, there is no need to make such a distinction; the time-order which events seem to have is, so far as we can see, the same as the time-order which they do have. At any rate no reason can be given for supposing that the two orders are not the same. The same is usually true of space: if a regiment of men are marching along a road, the shape of the regiment will look different from different points of view, but the men will appear arranged in the same order from all points of view. Hence we regard the order as true also in physical space, whereas the shape is only supposed to correspond to the physical space so far as is required for the preservation of the order.

In saying that the time-order which events seem to have is the same as the time-order which they really have, it is necessary to guard against a possible misunderstanding. It must not be supposed that the various states of different physical objects have the same time-order as the sense-data which constitute the perceptions of those objects. Considered as physical objects, the thunder and lightning are simultaneous; that is to say, the lightning is simultaneous with the disturbance of the air in the place where the disturbance begins, namely, where the lightning is. But the sense-datum which we call hearing the thunder does not take place until the disturbance of the air has travelled as far as to where we are. Similarly, it takes about eight minutes for the sun's light to reach us; thus, when we see the sun we are seeing the sun of eight minutes ago. So far as our sense-data afford evidence as to the physical sun they afford evidence as to the physical sun of eight minutes ago; if the physical sun had ceased to exist within the last eight minutes, that would make no difference to the sense-data which we call 'seeing the sun'. This affords a fresh illustration of the necessity of distinguishing between sense-data and physical objects.

What we have found as regards space is much the same as what we find in relation to the correspondence of the sense-data with their physical counterparts. If one object looks blue and another red, we may reasonably presume that there is some corresponding difference between the physical objects; if two objects both look blue, we may presume a corresponding similarity. But we cannot hope to be acquainted directly with the quality in the physical object which makes it look blue or red. Science tells us that this quality is a certain sort of wave-motion, and this sounds familiar, because we think of wave-motions in the space we see. But the wave-motions must really be in physical space, with which we have no direct acquaintance; thus the real wave-motions have not that familiarity which we might have supposed them to have. And what holds for colours is closely similar to what holds for other sense-data. Thus we find that, although the *relations* of physical objects have all sorts of knowable properties, derived from their correspondence with the relations of sense-data, the physical objects themselves remain unknown in their intrinsic nature, so far at least as can be discovered by means of the senses. The question remains whether there is any other method of discovering the intrinsic nature of physical objects.

The most natural, though not ultimately the most defensible, hypothesis to adopt in the first instance, at any rate as regards visual sense-data, would be that, though physical objects cannot, for the reasons we have been considering, be *exactly* like sense-data, yet they may be more or less like. According to this view, physical objects will, for example, really have colours, and we might, by good luck, see an object as of the colour it really is. The colour which an object seems to have at any given moment will in general be very similar, though not quite the same, from many different points of view; we might thus suppose the 'real' colour to be a sort of medium colour, intermediate between the various shades which appear from the different points of view.

Such a theory is perhaps not capable of being definitely refuted, but it can be shown to be groundless. To begin with, it is plain that the colour we see depends only upon the nature of the light-waves that strike the eye, and is therefore modified by the medium intervening between us and the object, as well as by the manner in which light is reflected from the object in the direction of the eye. The intervening air alters colours unless it is perfectly clear, and any strong reflection will alter them completely. Thus the colour we see is a result of the ray as it reaches the eye, and not simply a property of the object from which the ray comes. Hence, also, provided certain waves reach the eye, we shall see a certain colour, whether the object from which the waves start has any colour or not. Thus it is quite gratuitous to suppose that physical objects have colours, and therefore there is no justification for making such a supposition. Exactly similar arguments will apply to other sense-data.

It remains to ask whether there are any general philosophical arguments enabling us to say that, if matter is real, it must be of such and such a nature. As explained above, very many philosophers, perhaps most, have held that whatever is real must be in some sense mental, or at any rate that whatever we can know anything about must be in some sense mental. Such philosophers are called 'idealists'. Idealists tell us that what appears as matter is really something mental; namely, either (as Leibniz held) more or less rudimentary minds, or (as Berkeley contended) ideas in the minds which, as we should commonly say, 'perceive' the matter. Thus idealists deny the existence of matter as something intrinsically different from mind, though they do not deny that our sense-data are signs of something which exists independently of our private sensations. In the following chapter we shall consider briefly the reasons—in my opinion fallacious—which idealists advance in favour of their theory.

CHAPTER IV. IDEALISM

The word 'idealism' is used by different philosophers in somewhat different senses. We shall understand by it the doctrine that whatever exists, or at any rate whatever can be known to exist, must be in some sense mental. This doctrine, which is very widely held among philosophers, has several forms, and is advocated on several different grounds. The doctrine is so widely held, and so interesting in itself, that even the briefest survey of philosophy must give some account of it.

Those who are unaccustomed to philosophical speculation may be inclined to dismiss such a doctrine as obviously absurd. There is no doubt that common sense regards tables and chairs and the sun and moon and material objects generally as something radically different from minds and the contents of minds, and as having an existence which might continue if minds ceased. We think of matter as having existed long before there were any minds, and it is hard to think of it as a mere product of mental activity. But whether true or false, idealism is not to be dismissed as obviously absurd.

We have seen that, even if physical objects do have an independent existence, they must differ very widely from sense-data, and can only have a *correspondence* with sense-data, in the same sort of way in which a catalogue has a correspondence with the things catalogued. Hence common sense leaves us completely in the dark as to the true intrinsic nature of physical objects, and if there were good reason to regard them as mental, we could not legitimately reject this opinion merely because it strikes us as strange. The truth about physical objects *must* be strange. It may be unattainable, but if any philosopher believes that he has attained it, the fact that what he offers as the truth is strange ought not to be made a ground of objection to his opinion.

The grounds on which idealism is advocated are generally grounds derived from the theory of knowledge, that is to say, from a discussion of the conditions which things must satisfy in order that we may be able to know them. The first serious attempt to establish idealism on such grounds was that of Bishop Berkeley. He proved first, by arguments which were largely valid, that our sense-data cannot be supposed to have an existence independent of us, but must be, in part at least, 'in' the mind, in the sense that their existence would not continue if there were no seeing or hearing or touching or smelling or tasting. So far, his contention was almost certainly valid, even if some of his arguments were not so. But he went on to argue that sense-data were the only things of whose existence our perceptions could assure us; and that to be known is to be 'in' a mind, and therefore to be mental. Hence he concluded that nothing can ever be known except what is in some mind, and that whatever is known without being in my mind must be in some other mind.

In order to understand his argument, it is necessary to understand his use of the word 'idea'. He gives the name 'idea' to anything which is *immediately* known, as, for example, sense-data are known. Thus a particular colour which we see is an idea; so is a voice which we hear, and so on. But the term is not wholly confined to sense-data. There will also be things remembered or imagined, for with such things also we have immediate acquaintance at the moment of remembering or imagining. All such immediate data he calls 'ideas'.

He then proceeds to consider common objects, such as a tree, for instance. He shows that all we know immediately when we 'perceive' the tree consists of ideas in his sense of the word, and he argues that there is not the slightest ground for supposing that there is anything real about the tree except what is perceived. Its being, he says, consists in being perceived: in the Latin of the schoolmen its '*esse*' is '*percipi*'. He fully admits that the tree must continue to exist even when we shut our eyes or when no human being is near it. But this continued existence, he says, is due to the fact that God continues to perceive it; the 'real' tree, which corresponds to what we called the physical object, consists of ideas in the mind of God, ideas more or less like those we have when we see the tree, but differing in the fact that they are permanent in God's mind so long as the tree continues to exist. All our perceptions, according to him, consist in a partial participation in God's perceptions, and it is because of this participation that different people see more or less the same tree. Thus apart from minds and their ideas there is nothing in the world, nor is it possible that anything else should ever be known, since whatever is known is necessarily an idea.

There are in this argument a good many fallacies which have been important in the history of philosophy, and which it will be as well to bring to light. In the first place, there is a confusion engendered by the use of the word 'idea'. We think of an idea as essentially something in somebody's mind, and thus when we are told that a tree consists entirely of ideas, it is natural to suppose that, if so, the tree must be entirely in minds. But the notion of being 'in' the mind is ambiguous. We speak of bearing a person in mind, not meaning that the person is in our minds, but that a thought of him is in our minds. When a man says that some business he had to arrange went clean out of his mind, he does not mean to imply that the business itself was ever in his mind, but only that a thought of the business was formerly in his mind, but afterwards ceased to be in his mind. And so when Berkeley says that the tree must be in our minds if we can know it, all that he really has a right to say is that a thought of the tree must be in our minds. To argue that the tree itself must be in our minds is like arguing that a person whom we bear in mind is himself in our minds. This confusion may seem too gross to have been really committed by any competent philosopher, but various attendant circumstances rendered it possible. In order to see how it was possible, we must go more deeply into the question as to the nature of ideas.

Before taking up the general question of the nature of ideas, we must disentangle two entirely separate questions which arise concerning sense-data and physical objects. We saw that, for various reasons of detail, Berkeley was right in treating the sense-data which constitute our perception of the tree as more or less subjective, in the sense that they depend upon us as much as upon the tree, and would not exist if the tree were not being perceived. But this is an entirely different point from the one by which Berkeley seeks to prove that whatever can be immediately known must be in a mind. For this purpose arguments of detail as to the dependence of sense-data upon us are useless. It is necessary to prove, generally, that by being known, things are shown to be mental. This is what Berkeley believes himself to have done. It is this question, and not our previous question as to the difference between sense-data and the physical object, that must now concern us.

Taking the word 'idea' in Berkeley's sense, there are two quite distinct things to be considered whenever an idea is before the mind. There is on the one hand the thing of which we are aware—say the colour of my table—and on the other hand the actual awareness itself, the mental act of apprehending the thing. The mental act is undoubtedly mental, but is there any reason to suppose that the thing apprehended is in any sense mental? Our previous arguments concerning the colour did not prove it to be mental; they only proved that its existence depends upon the relation of our sense organs to the physical object—in our case, the table. That is to say, they proved that a certain colour will exist, in a certain light, if a normal eye is placed at a certain point relatively to the table. They did not prove that the colour is in the mind of the percipient.

Berkeley's view, that obviously the colour must be in the mind, seems to depend for its plausibility upon confusing the thing apprehended with the act of apprehension. Either of these might be called an 'idea'; probably either would have been called an idea by Berkeley. The act is undoubtedly in the mind; hence, when we are thinking of the act, we readily assent to the view that ideas must be in the mind. Then, forgetting that this was only true when ideas were taken as acts of apprehension, we transfer the proposition that 'ideas are in the mind' to ideas in the other sense, i.e. to the things apprehended by our acts of apprehension. Thus, by an unconscious equivocation, we arrive at the conclusion that whatever we can apprehend must be in our minds. This seems to be the true analysis of Berkeley's argument, and the ultimate fallacy upon which it rests.

This question of the distinction between act and object in our apprehending of things is vitally important, since our whole power of acquiring knowledge is bound up with it. The faculty of being acquainted with things other than itself is the main characteristic of a mind. Acquaintance with objects essentially consists in a relation between the mind and something other than the mind; it is this that constitutes the mind's power of knowing things. If we say that the things known must be in the mind, we are either unduly limiting the mind's power of knowing, or we are uttering a mere tautology. We are uttering a mere tautology if we mean by '*in* the mind' the same as by '*before* the mind', i.e. if we mean merely being apprehended by the mind. But if we mean this, we shall have to admit that what, *in this sense*, is in the mind, may nevertheless be not mental. Thus when we realize the nature of knowledge, Berkeley's argument is seen to be wrong in substance as well as in form, and his grounds for supposing that 'ideas'—i.e. the objects apprehended—must be mental, are found to have no validity whatever. Hence his grounds in favour of idealism may be dismissed. It remains to see whether there are any other grounds.

It is often said, as though it were a self-evident truism, that we cannot know that anything exists which we do not know. It is inferred that whatever can in any way be relevant to our experience must be at least capable of being known by us; whence it follows that if matter were essentially something with which we could not become acquainted, matter would be something which we could not know to exist, and which could have for us no importance whatever. It is generally also implied, for reasons which remain obscure, that what can have no importance for us cannot be real, and that therefore matter, if it is not composed of minds or of mental ideas, is impossible and a mere chimaera.

To go into this argument fully at our present stage would be impossible, since it raises points requiring a considerable preliminary discussion; but certain reasons for rejecting the argument may be noticed at once. To begin at the end: there is no reason why what cannot have any *practical* importance for us should not be real. It is true that, if *theoretical* importance is included, everything real is of *some* importance to us, since, as persons desirous of knowing the truth about the universe, we have some interest in everything that the universe contains. But if this sort of interest is included, it is not the case that matter has no importance for us, provided it exists even if we cannot know that it exists. We can, obviously, suspect that it may exist, and wonder whether it does; hence it is connected with our desire for knowledge, and has the importance of either satisfying or thwarting this desire.

Again, it is by no means a truism, and is in fact false, that we cannot know that anything exists which we do not know. The word 'know' is here used in two different senses. (1) In its first use it is applicable to the sort of knowledge which is opposed to error, the sense in which what we know is *true*, the sense which applies to our beliefs and convictions, i.e. to what are called *judgements*. In this sense of the word we know *that* something is the case. This sort of knowledge may be described as knowledge of *truths*. (2) In the second use of the word 'know' above, the word applies to our knowledge of *things*, which we may call *acquaintance*. This is the sense in which we know sense-data. (The distinction involved is roughly that between *savoir* and *connaître* in French, or between *wissen* and *kennen* in German.)

Thus the statement which seemed like a truism becomes, when re-stated, the following: 'We can never truly judge that something with which we are not acquainted exists.' This is by no means a truism, but on the contrary a palpable falsehood. I have not the honour to be acquainted with the Emperor of China, but I truly judge that he exists. It may be said, of course, that I judge this because of other people's acquaintance with him. This, however, would be an irrelevant retort, since, if the principle were true, I could not know that any one else is acquainted with him. But further: there is no reason why I should not know of the existence of something with which nobody is acquainted. This point is important, and demands elucidation.

If I am acquainted with a thing which exists, my acquaintance gives me the knowledge that it exists. But it is not true that, conversely, whenever I can know that a thing of a certain sort exists, I or some one else must be acquainted with the thing. What happens, in cases where I have true judgement without acquaintance, is that the thing is known to me by *description*, and that, in virtue of some general principle, the existence of a thing answering to this description can be inferred from the existence of something with which I am acquainted. In order to understand this point fully, it will be well first to deal with the difference between knowledge by acquaintance and knowledge by description, and then to consider what knowledge of general principles, if any, has the same kind of certainty as our knowledge of the existence of our own experiences. These subjects will be dealt with in the following chapters.

CHAPTER V. KNOWLEDGE BY ACQUAINTANCE AND KNOWLEDGE BY DESCRIPTION

In the preceding chapter we saw that there are two sorts of knowledge: knowledge of things, and knowledge of truths. In this chapter we shall be concerned exclusively with knowledge of things, of which in turn we shall have to distinguish two kinds. Knowledge of things, when it is of the kind we call knowledge by *acquaintance,* is essentially simpler than any knowledge of truths, and logically independent of knowledge of truths, though it would be rash to assume that human beings ever, in fact, have acquaintance with things without at the same time knowing some truth about them. Knowledge of things by *description,* on the contrary, always involves, as we shall find in the course of the present chapter, some knowledge of truths as its source and ground. But first of all we must make clear what we mean by 'acquaintance' and what we mean by 'description'.

We shall say that we have *acquaintance* with anything of which we are directly aware, without the intermediary of any process of inference or any knowledge of truths. Thus in the presence of my table I am acquainted with the sense-data that make up the appearance of my table—its colour, shape, hardness, smoothness, etc.; all these are things of which I am immediately conscious when I am seeing and touching my table. The particular shade of colour that I am seeing may have many things said about it—I may say that it is brown, that it is rather dark, and so on. But such statements, though they make me know truths about the colour, do not make me know the colour itself any better than I did before so far as concerns knowledge of the colour itself, as opposed to knowledge of truths about it, I know the colour perfectly and completely when I see it, and no further knowledge of it itself is even theoretically possible. Thus the sense-data which make up the appearance of my table are things with which I have acquaintance, things immediately known to me just as they are.

My knowledge of the table as a physical object, on the contrary, is not direct knowledge. Such as it is, it is obtained through acquaintance with the sense-data that make up the appearance of the table. We have seen that it is possible, without absurdity, to doubt whether there is a table at all, whereas it is not possible to doubt the sense-data. My knowledge of the table is of the kind which we shall call 'knowledge by description'. The table is 'the physical object which causes such-and-such sense-data'. This describes the table by means of the sense-data. In order to know anything at all about the table, we must know truths connecting it with things with which we have acquaintance: we must know that 'such-and-such sense-data are caused by a physical object'. There is no state of mind in which we are directly aware of the table; all our knowledge of the table is really knowledge of truths, and the actual thing which is the table is not, strictly speaking, known to us at all. We know a description, and we know that there is just one object to which this description applies, though the object itself is not directly known to us. In such a case, we say that our knowledge of the object is knowledge by description.

All our knowledge, both knowledge of things and knowledge of truths, rests upon acquaintance as its foundation. It is therefore important to consider what kinds of things there are with which we have acquaintance.

Sense-data, as we have already seen, are among the things with which we are acquainted; in fact, they supply the most obvious and striking example of knowledge by acquaintance.

But if they were the sole example, our knowledge would be very much more restricted than it is. We should only know what is now present to our senses: we could not know anything about the past—not even that there was a past—nor could we know any truths about our sense-data, for all knowledge of truths, as we shall show, demands acquaintance with things which are of an essentially different character from sense-data, the things which are sometimes called 'abstract ideas', but which we shall call 'universals'. We have therefore to consider acquaintance with other things besides sense-data if we are to obtain any tolerably adequate analysis of our knowledge.

The first extension beyond sense-data to be considered is acquaintance by *memory*. It is obvious that we often remember what we have seen or heard or had otherwise present to our senses, and that in such cases we are still immediately aware of what we remember, in spite of the fact that it appears as past and not as present. This immediate knowledge by memory is the source of all our knowledge concerning the past: without it, there could be no knowledge of the past by inference, since we should never know that there was anything past to be inferred.

The next extension to be considered is acquaintance by *introspection*. We are not only aware of things, but we are often aware of being aware of them. When I see the sun, I am often aware of my seeing the sun; thus 'my seeing the sun' is an object with which I have acquaintance. When I desire food, I may be aware of my desire for food; thus 'my desiring food' is an object with which I am acquainted. Similarly we may be aware of our feeling pleasure or pain, and generally of the events which happen in our minds. This kind of acquaintance, which may be called self-consciousness, is the source of all our knowledge of mental things. It is obvious that it is only what goes on in our own minds that can be thus known immediately. What goes on in the minds of others is known to us through our perception of their bodies, that is, through the sense-data in us which are associated with their bodies. But for our acquaintance with the contents of our own minds, we should be unable to imagine the minds of others, and therefore we could never arrive at the knowledge that they have minds. It seems natural to suppose that self-consciousness is one of the things that distinguish men from animals: animals, we may suppose, though they have acquaintance with sense-data, never become aware of this acquaintance. I do not mean that they *doubt* whether they exist, but that they have never become conscious of the fact that they have sensations and feelings, nor therefore of the fact that they, the subjects of their sensations and feelings, exist.

We have spoken of acquaintance with the contents of our minds as *self*-consciousness, but it is not, of course, consciousness of our *self*: it is consciousness of particular thoughts and feelings. The question whether we are also acquainted with our bare selves, as opposed to particular thoughts and feelings, is a very difficult one, upon which it would be rash to speak positively. When we try to look into ourselves we always seem to come upon some particular thought or feeling, and not upon the 'I' which has the thought or feeling. Nevertheless there are some reasons for thinking that we are acquainted with the 'I', though the acquaintance is hard to disentangle from other things. To make clear what sort of reason there is, let us consider for a moment what our acquaintance with particular thoughts really involves.

When I am acquainted with 'my seeing the sun', it seems plain that I am acquainted with two different things in relation to each other. On the one hand there is the sense-datum which represents the sun to me, on the other hand there is that which sees this sense-datum. All acquaintance, such as my acquaintance with the sense-datum which represents the sun, seems obviously a relation between the person acquainted and the object with which the person is acquainted. When a case of acquaintance is one with which I can be acquainted (as I am acquainted with my acquaintance with the sense-datum representing the sun), it is plain that the person acquainted is myself. Thus, when I am acquainted with my seeing the sun, the whole fact with which I am acquainted is 'Self-acquainted-with-sense-datum'.

Further, we know the truth 'I am acquainted with this sense-datum'. It is hard to see how we could know this truth, or even understand what is meant by it, unless we were acquainted with something which we call 'I'. It does not seem necessary to suppose that we are acquainted with a more or less permanent person, the same to-day as yesterday, but it does seem as though we must be acquainted with that thing, whatever its nature, which sees the sun and has acquaintance with sense-data. Thus, in some sense it would seem we must be acquainted with our Selves as opposed to our particular experiences. But the question is difficult, and complicated arguments can be adduced on either side. Hence, although acquaintance with ourselves seems *probably* to occur, it is not wise to assert that it undoubtedly does occur.

We may therefore sum up as follows what has been said concerning acquaintance with things that exist. We have acquaintance in sensation with the data of the outer senses, and in introspection with the data of what may be called the inner sense—thoughts, feelings, desires, etc.; we have acquaintance in memory with things which have been data either of the outer senses or of the inner sense. Further, it is probable, though not certain, that we have acquaintance with Self, as that which is aware of things or has desires towards things.

In addition to our acquaintance with particular existing things, we also have acquaintance with what we shall call *universals*, that is to say, general ideas, such as *whiteness*, *diversity*, *brotherhood*, and so on. Every complete sentence must contain at least one word which stands for a universal, since all verbs have a meaning which is universal. We shall return to universals later on, in Chapter IX; for the present, it is only necessary to guard against the supposition that whatever we can be acquainted with must be something particular and existent. Awareness of universals is called *conceiving*, and a universal of which we are aware is called a *concept*.

It will be seen that among the objects with which we are acquainted are not included physical objects (as opposed to sense-data), nor other people's minds. These things are known to us by what I call 'knowledge by description', which we must now consider.

By a 'description' I mean any phrase of the form 'a so-and-so' or 'the so-and-so'. A phrase of the form 'a so-and-so' I shall call an 'ambiguous' description; a phrase of the form 'the so-and-so' (in the singular) I shall call a 'definite' description. Thus 'a man' is an ambiguous description, and 'the man with the iron mask' is a definite description. There are various problems connected with ambiguous descriptions, but I pass them by, since they do not directly concern the matter we are discussing, which is the nature of our knowledge concerning objects in cases where we know that there is an object answering to a definite description, though we are not acquainted with any such object. This is a matter which is concerned exclusively with definite descriptions. I shall therefore, in the sequel, speak simply of 'descriptions' when I mean 'definite descriptions'. Thus a description will mean any phrase of the form 'the so-and-so' in the singular.

We shall say that an object is 'known by description' when we know that it is 'the so-and-so', i.e. when we know that there is one object, and no more, having a certain property; and it will generally be implied that we do not have knowledge of the same object by acquaintance. We know that the man with the iron mask existed, and many propositions are known about him; but we do not know who he was. We know that the candidate who gets the most votes will be elected, and in this case we are very likely also acquainted (in the only sense in which one can be acquainted with some one else) with the man who is, in fact, the candidate who will get most votes; but we do not know which of the candidates he is, i.e. we do not know any proposition of the form 'A is the candidate who will get most votes' where A is one of the candidates by name. We shall say that we have 'merely descriptive knowledge' of the so-and-so when, although we know that the so-and-so exists, and although we may possibly be acquainted with the object which is, in fact, the so-and-so, yet we do not know any proposition '*a* is the so-and-so', where *a* is something with which we are acquainted.

When we say 'the so-and-so exists', we mean that there is just one object which is the so-and-so. The proposition '*a* is the so-and-so' means that *a* has the property so-and-so, and nothing else has. 'Mr. A. is the Unionist candidate for this constituency' means 'Mr. A. is a Unionist candidate for this constituency, and no one else is'. 'The Unionist candidate for this constituency exists' means 'some one is a Unionist candidate for this constituency, and no one else is'. Thus, when we are acquainted with an object which is the so-and-so, we know that the so-and-so exists; but we may know that the so-and-so exists when we are not acquainted with any object which we know to be the so-and-so, and even when we are not acquainted with any object which, in fact, is the so-and-so.

Common words, even proper names, are usually really descriptions. That is to say, the thought in the mind of a person using a proper name correctly can generally only be expressed explicitly if we replace the proper name by a description. Moreover, the description required to express the thought will vary for different people, or for the same person at different times. The only thing constant (so long as the name is rightly used) is the object to which the name applies. But so long as this remains constant, the particular description involved usually makes no difference to the truth or falsehood of the proposition in which the name appears.

Let us take some illustrations. Suppose some statement made about Bismarck. Assuming that there is such a thing as direct acquaintance with oneself, Bismarck himself might have used his name directly to designate the particular person with whom he was acquainted. In this case, if he made a judgement about himself, he himself might be a constituent of the judgement. Here the proper name has the direct use which it always wishes to have, as simply standing for a certain object, and not for a description of the object. But if a person who knew Bismarck made a judgement about him, the case is different. What this person was acquainted with were certain sense-data which he connected (rightly, we will suppose) with Bismarck's body. His body, as a physical object, and still more his mind, were only known as the body and the mind connected with these sense-data. That is, they were known by description. It is, of course, very much a matter of chance which characteristics of a man's appearance will come into a friend's mind when he thinks of him; thus the description actually in the friend's mind is accidental. The essential point is that he knows that the various descriptions all apply to the same entity, in spite of not being acquainted with the entity in question.

When we, who did not know Bismarck, make a judgement about him, the description in our minds will probably be some more or less vague mass of historical knowledge—far more, in most cases, than is required to identify him. But, for the sake of illustration, let us assume that we think of him as 'the first Chancellor of the German Empire'. Here all the words are abstract except 'German'. The word 'German' will, again, have different meanings for different people. To some it will recall travels in Germany, to some the look of Germany on the map, and so on. But if we are to obtain a description which we know to be applicable, we shall be compelled, at some point, to bring in a reference to a particular with which we are acquainted. Such reference is involved in any mention of past, present, and future (as opposed to definite dates), or of here and there, or of what others have told us. Thus it would seem that, in some way or other, a description known to be applicable to a particular must involve some reference to a particular with which we are acquainted, if our knowledge about the thing described is not to be merely what follows *logically* from the description. For example, 'the most long-lived of men' is a description involving only universals, which must apply to some man, but we can make no judgements concerning this man which involve knowledge about him beyond what the description gives. If, however, we say, 'The first Chancellor of the German Empire was an astute diplomatist', we can only be assured of the truth of our judgement in virtue of something with which we are acquainted—usually a testimony heard or read. Apart from the information we convey to others, apart from the fact about the actual Bismarck, which gives importance to our judgement, the thought we really have contains the one or more particulars involved, and otherwise consists wholly of concepts.

All names of places—London, England, Europe, the Earth, the Solar System—similarly involve, when used, descriptions which start from some one or more particulars with which we are acquainted. I suspect that even the Universe, as considered by metaphysics, involves such a connexion with particulars. In logic, on the contrary, where we are concerned not merely with what does exist, but with whatever might or could exist or be, no reference to actual particulars is involved.

It would seem that, when we make a statement about something only known by description, we often *intend* to make our statement, not in the form involving the description, but about the actual thing described. That is to say, when we say anything about Bismarck, we should like, if we could, to make the judgement which Bismarck alone can make, namely, the judgement of which he himself is a constituent. In this we are necessarily defeated, since the actual Bismarck is unknown to us. But we know that there is an object B, called Bismarck, and that B was an astute diplomatist. We can thus *describe* the proposition we should like to affirm, namely, 'B was an astute diplomatist', where B is the object which was Bismarck. If we are describing Bismarck as 'the first Chancellor of the German Empire', the proposition we should like to affirm may be described as 'the proposition asserting, concerning the actual object which was the first Chancellor of the German Empire, that this object was an astute diplomatist'. What enables us to communicate in spite of the varying descriptions we employ is that we know there is a true proposition concerning the actual Bismarck, and that however we may vary the description (so long as the description is correct) the proposition described is still the same. This proposition, which is described and is known to be true, is what interests us; but we are not acquainted with the proposition itself, and do not know it, though we know it is true.

It will be seen that there are various stages in the removal from acquaintance with particulars: there is Bismarck to people who knew him; Bismarck to those who only know of him through history; the man with the iron mask; the longest-lived of men. These are progressively further removed from acquaintance with particulars; the first comes as near to acquaintance as is possible in regard to another person; in the second, we shall still be said to know 'who Bismarck was'; in the third, we do not know who was the man with the iron mask, though we can know many propositions about him which are not logically deducible from the fact that he wore an iron mask; in the fourth, finally, we know nothing beyond what is logically deducible from the definition of the man. There is a similar hierarchy in the region of universals. Many universals, like many particulars, are only known to us by description. But here, as in the case of particulars, knowledge concerning what is known by description is ultimately reducible to knowledge concerning what is known by acquaintance.

The fundamental principle in the analysis of propositions containing descriptions is this: *Every proposition which we can understand must be composed wholly of constituents with which we are acquainted.*

We shall not at this stage attempt to answer all the objections which may be urged against this fundamental principle. For the present, we shall merely point out that, in some way or other, it must be possible to meet these objections, for it is scarcely conceivable that we can make a judgement or entertain a supposition without knowing what it is that we are judging or supposing about. We must attach *some* meaning to the words we use, if we are to speak significantly and not utter mere noise; and the meaning we attach to our words must be something with which we are acquainted. Thus when, for example, we make a statement about Julius Caesar, it is plain that Julius Caesar himself is not before our minds, since we are not acquainted with him. We have in mind some description of Julius Caesar: 'the man who was assassinated on the Ides of March', 'the founder of the Roman Empire', or, perhaps, merely 'the man whose name was *Julius Caesar*'. (In this last description, *Julius Caesar* is a noise or shape with which we are acquainted.) Thus our statement does not mean quite what it seems to mean, but means something involving, instead of Julius Caesar, some description of him which is composed wholly of particulars and universals with which we are acquainted.

The chief importance of knowledge by description is that it enables us to pass beyond the limits of our private experience. In spite of the fact that we can only know truths which are wholly composed of terms which we have experienced in acquaintance, we can yet have knowledge by description of things which we have never experienced. In view of the very narrow range of our immediate experience, this result is vital, and until it is understood, much of our knowledge must remain mysterious and therefore doubtful.

CHAPTER VI. ON INDUCTION

In almost all our previous discussions we have been concerned in the attempt to get clear as to our data in the way of knowledge of existence. What things are there in the universe whose existence is known to us owing to our being acquainted with them? So far, our answer has been that we are acquainted with our sense-data, and, probably, with ourselves. These we know to exist. And past sense-data which are remembered are known to have existed in the past. This knowledge supplies our data.

But if we are to be able to draw inferences from these data—if we are to know of the existence of matter, of other people, of the past before our individual memory begins, or of the future, we must know general principles of some kind by means of which such inferences can be drawn. It must be known to us that the existence of some one sort of thing, A, is a sign of the existence of some other sort of thing, B, either at the same time as A or at some earlier or later time, as, for example, thunder is a sign of the earlier existence of lightning. If this were not known to us, we could never extend our knowledge beyond the sphere of our private experience; and this sphere, as we have seen, is exceedingly limited. The question we have now to consider is whether such an extension is possible, and if so, how it is effected.

Let us take as an illustration a matter about which none of us, in fact, feel the slightest doubt. We are all convinced that the sun will rise to-morrow. Why? Is this belief a mere blind outcome of past experience, or can it be justified as a reasonable belief? It is not easy to find a test by which to judge whether a belief of this kind is reasonable or not, but we can at least ascertain what sort of general beliefs would suffice, if true, to justify the judgement that the sun will rise to-morrow, and the many other similar judgements upon which our actions are based.

It is obvious that if we are asked why we believe that the sun will rise to-morrow, we shall naturally answer 'Because it always has risen every day'. We have a firm belief that it will rise in the future, because it has risen in the past. If we are challenged as to why we believe that it will continue to rise as heretofore, we may appeal to the laws of motion: the earth, we shall say, is a freely rotating body, and such bodies do not cease to rotate unless something interferes from outside, and there is nothing outside to interfere with the earth between now and to-morrow. Of course it might be doubted whether we are quite certain that there is nothing outside to interfere, but this is not the interesting doubt. The interesting doubt is as to whether the laws of motion will remain in operation until to-morrow. If this doubt is raised, we find ourselves in the same position as when the doubt about the sunrise was first raised.

The *only* reason for believing that the laws of motion will remain in operation is that they have operated hitherto, so far as our knowledge of the past enables us to judge. It is true that we have a greater body of evidence from the past in favour of the laws of motion than we have in favour of the sunrise, because the sunrise is merely a particular case of fulfilment of the laws of motion, and there are countless other particular cases. But the real question is: Do *any* number of cases of a law being fulfilled in the past afford evidence that it will be fulfilled in the future? If not, it becomes plain that we have no ground whatever for expecting the sun to rise to-morrow, or for expecting the bread we shall eat at our next meal not to poison us, or for any of the other scarcely conscious expectations that control our daily lives. It is to be observed that all such expectations are only *probable*; thus we have not to seek for a proof that they *must* be fulfilled, but only for some reason in favour of the view that they are *likely* to be fulfilled.

Now in dealing with this question we must, to begin with, make an important distinction, without which we should soon become involved in hopeless confusions. Experience has shown us that, hitherto, the frequent repetition of some uniform succession or coexistence has been a *cause* of our expecting the same succession or coexistence on the next occasion. Food that has a certain appearance generally has a certain taste, and it is a severe shock to our expectations when the familiar appearance is found to be associated with an unusual taste. Things which we see become associated, by habit, with certain tactile sensations which we expect if we touch them; one of the horrors of a ghost (in many ghost-stories) is that it fails to give us any sensations of touch. Uneducated people who go abroad for the first time are so surprised as to be incredulous when they find their native language not understood.

And this kind of association is not confined to men; in animals also it is very strong. A horse which has been often driven along a certain road resists the attempt to drive him in a different direction. Domestic animals expect food when they see the person who usually feeds them. We know that all these rather crude expectations of uniformity are liable to be misleading. The man who has fed the chicken every day throughout its life at last wrings its neck instead, showing that more refined views as to the uniformity of nature would have been useful to the chicken.

But in spite of the misleadingness of such expectations, they nevertheless exist. The mere fact that something has happened a certain number of times causes animals and men to expect that it will happen again. Thus our instincts certainly cause us to believe that the sun will rise to-morrow, but we may be in no better a position than the chicken which unexpectedly has its neck wrung. We have therefore to distinguish the fact that past uniformities *cause* expectations as to the future, from the question whether there is any reasonable ground for giving weight to such expectations after the question of their validity has been raised.

The problem we have to discuss is whether there is any reason for believing in what is called 'the uniformity of nature'. The belief in the uniformity of nature is the belief that everything that has happened or will happen is an instance of some general law to which there are no exceptions. The crude expectations which we have been considering are all subject to exceptions, and therefore liable to disappoint those who entertain them. But science habitually assumes, at least as a working hypothesis, that general rules which have exceptions can be replaced by general rules which have no exceptions. 'Unsupported bodies in air fall' is a general rule to which balloons and aeroplanes are exceptions. But the laws of motion and the law of gravitation, which account for the fact that most bodies fall, also account for the fact that balloons and aeroplanes can rise; thus the laws of motion and the law of gravitation are not subject to these exceptions.

The belief that the sun will rise to-morrow might be falsified if the earth came suddenly into contact with a large body which destroyed its rotation; but the laws of motion and the law of gravitation would not be infringed by such an event. The business of science is to find uniformities, such as the laws of motion and the law of gravitation, to which, so far as our experience extends, there are no exceptions. In this search science has been remarkably successful, and it may be conceded that such uniformities have held hitherto. This brings us back to the question: Have we any reason, assuming that they have always held in the past, to suppose that they will hold in the future?

It has been argued that we have reason to know that the future will resemble the past, because what was the future has constantly become the past, and has always been found to resemble the past, so that we really have experience of the future, namely of times which were formerly future, which we may call past futures. But such an argument really begs the very question at issue. We have experience of past futures, but not of future futures, and the question is: Will future futures resemble past futures? This question is not to be answered by an argument which starts from past futures alone. We have therefore still to seek for some principle which shall enable us to know that the future will follow the same laws as the past.

The reference to the future in this question is not essential. The same question arises when we apply the laws that work in our experience to past things of which we have no experience—as, for example, in geology, or in theories as to the origin of the Solar System. The question we really have to ask is: 'When two things have been found to be often associated, and no instance is known of the one occurring without the other, does the occurrence of one of the two, in a fresh instance, give any good ground for expecting the other?' On our answer to this question must depend the validity of the whole of our expectations as to the future, the whole of the results obtained by induction, and in fact practically all the beliefs upon which our daily life is based.

It must be conceded, to begin with, that the fact that two things have been found often together and never apart does not, by itself, suffice to *prove* demonstratively that they will be found together in the next case we examine. The most we can hope is that the oftener things are found together, the more probable it becomes that they will be found together another time, and that, if they have been found together often enough, the probability will amount *almost* to certainty. It can never quite reach certainty, because we know that in spite of frequent repetitions there sometimes is a failure at the last, as in the case of the chicken whose neck is wrung. Thus probability is all we ought to seek.

It might be urged, as against the view we are advocating, that we know all natural phenomena to be subject to the reign of law, and that sometimes, on the basis of observation, we can see that only one law can possibly fit the facts of the case. Now to this view there are two answers. The first is that, even if *some* law which has no exceptions applies to our case, we can never, in practice, be sure that we have discovered that law and not one to which there are exceptions. The second is that the reign of law would seem to be itself only probable, and that our belief that it will hold in the future, or in unexamined cases in the past, is itself based upon the very principle we are examining.

The principle we are examining may be called the *principle of induction*, and its two parts may be stated as follows:

(a) When a thing of a certain sort A has been found to be associated with a thing of a certain other sort B, and has never been found dissociated from a thing of the sort B, the greater the number of cases in which A and B have been associated, the greater is the probability that they will be associated in a fresh case in which one of them is known to be present;

(b) Under the same circumstances, a sufficient number of cases of association will make the probability of a fresh association nearly a certainty, and will make it approach certainty without limit.

As just stated, the principle applies only to the verification of our expectation in a single fresh instance. But we want also to know that there is a probability in favour of the general law that things of the sort A are *always* associated with things of the sort B, provided a sufficient number of cases of association are known, and no cases of failure of association are known.

The probability of the general law is obviously less than the probability of the particular case, since if the general law is true, the particular case must also be true, whereas the particular case may be true without the general law being true. Nevertheless the probability of the general law is increased by repetitions, just as the probability of the particular case is. We may therefore repeat the two parts of our principle as regards the general law, thus:

(a) The greater the number of cases in which a thing of the sort A has been found associated with a thing of the sort B, the more probable it is (if no cases of failure of association are known) that A is always associated with B;

b) Under the same circumstances, a sufficient number of cases of the association of A with B will make it nearly certain that A is always associated with B, and will make this general law approach certainty without limit.

It should be noted that probability is always relative to certain data. In our case, the data are merely the known cases of coexistence of A and B. There may be other data, which *might* be taken into account, which would gravely alter the probability. For example, a man who had seen a great many white swans might argue, by our principle, that on the data it was *probable* that all swans were white, and this might be a perfectly sound argument. The argument is not disproved by the fact that some swans are black, because a thing may very well happen in spite of the fact that some data render it improbable. In the case of the swans, a man might know that colour is a very variable characteristic in many species of animals, and that, therefore, an induction as to colour is peculiarly liable to error. But this knowledge would be a fresh datum, by no means proving that the probability relatively to our previous data had been wrongly estimated. The fact, therefore, that things often fail to fulfil our expectations is no evidence that our expectations will not *probably* be fulfilled in a given case or a given class of cases. Thus our inductive principle is at any rate not capable of being *disproved* by an appeal to experience.

The inductive principle, however, is equally incapable of being *proved* by an appeal to experience. Experience might conceivably confirm the inductive principle as regards the cases that have been already examined; but as regards unexamined cases, it is the inductive principle alone that can justify any inference from what has been examined to what has not been examined. All arguments which, on the basis of experience, argue as to the future or the unexperienced parts of the past or present, assume the inductive principle; hence we can never use experience to prove the inductive principle without begging the question. Thus we must either accept the inductive principle on the ground of its intrinsic evidence, or forgo all justification of our expectations about the future. If the principle is unsound, we have no reason to expect the sun to rise to-morrow, to expect bread to be more nourishing than a stone, or to expect that if we throw ourselves off the roof we shall fall. When we see what looks like our best friend approaching us, we shall have no reason to suppose that his body is not inhabited by the mind of our worst enemy or of some total stranger. All our conduct is based upon associations which have worked in the past, and which we therefore regard as likely to work in the future; and this likelihood is dependent for its validity upon the inductive principle.

The general principles of science, such as the belief in the reign of law, and the belief that every event must have a cause, are as completely dependent upon the inductive principle as are the beliefs of daily life All such general principles are believed because mankind have found innumerable instances of their truth and no instances of their falsehood. But this affords no evidence for their truth in the future, unless the inductive principle is assumed.

Thus all knowledge which, on a basis of experience tells us something about what is not experienced, is based upon a belief which experience can neither confirm nor confute, yet which, at least in its more concrete applications, appears to be as firmly rooted in us as many of the facts of experience. The existence and justification of such beliefs—for the inductive principle, as we shall see, is not the only example—raises some of the most difficult and most debated problems of philosophy. We will, in the next chapter, consider briefly what may be said to account for such knowledge, and what is its scope and its degree of certainty.

CHAPTER VII. ON OUR KNOWLEDGE OF GENERAL PRINCIPLES

We saw in the preceding chapter that the principle of induction, while necessary to the validity of all arguments based on experience, is itself not capable of being proved by experience, and yet is unhesitatingly believed by every one, at least in all its concrete applications. In these characteristics the principle of induction does not stand alone. There are a number of other principles which cannot be proved or disproved by experience, but are used in arguments which start from what is experienced.

Some of these principles have even greater evidence than the principle of induction, and the knowledge of them has the same degree of certainty as the knowledge of the existence of sense-data. They constitute the means of drawing inferences from what is given in sensation; and if what we infer is to be true, it is just as necessary that our principles of inference should be true as it is that our data should be true. The principles of inference are apt to be overlooked because of their very obviousness—the assumption involved is assented to without our realizing that it is an assumption. But it is very important to realize the use of principles of inference, if a correct theory of knowledge is to be obtained; for our knowledge of them raises interesting and difficult questions.

In all our knowledge of general principles, what actually happens is that first of all we realize some particular application of the principle, and then we realize that the particularity is irrelevant, and that there is a generality which may equally truly be affirmed. This is of course familiar in such matters as teaching arithmetic: 'two and two are four' is first learnt in the case of some particular pair of couples, and then in some other particular case, and so on, until at last it becomes possible to see that it is true of any pair of couples. The same thing happens with logical principles. Suppose two men are discussing what day of the month it is. One of them says, 'At least you will admit that *if* yesterday was the 15th to-day must be the 16th.' 'Yes', says the other, 'I admit that.' 'And you know', the first continues, 'that yesterday was the 15th, because you dined with Jones, and your diary will tell you that was on the 15th.' 'Yes', says the second; 'therefore to-day *is* the 16th.'

Now such an argument is not hard to follow; and if it is granted that its premisses are true in fact, no one will deny that the conclusion must also be true. But it depends for its truth upon an instance of a general logical principle. The logical principle is as follows: 'Suppose it known that *if* this is true, then that is true. Suppose it also known that this *is* true, then it follows that that is true.' When it is the case that if this is true, that is true, we shall say that this 'implies' that, and that that 'follows from' this. Thus our principle states that if this implies that, and this is true, then that is true. In other words, 'anything implied by a true proposition is true', or 'whatever follows from a true proposition is true'.

This principle is really involved—at least, concrete instances of it are involved—in all demonstrations. Whenever one thing which we believe is used to prove something else, which we consequently believe, this principle is relevant. If any one asks: 'Why should I accept the results of valid arguments based on true premisses?' we can only answer by appealing to our principle. In fact, the truth of the principle is impossible to doubt, and its obviousness is so great that at first sight it seems almost trivial. Such principles, however, are not trivial to the philosopher, for they show that we may have indubitable knowledge which is in no way derived from objects of sense.

The above principle is merely one of a certain number of self-evident logical principles. Some at least of these principles must be granted before any argument or proof becomes possible. When some of them have been granted, others can be proved, though these others, so long as they are simple, are just as obvious as the principles taken for granted. For no very good reason, three of these principles have been singled out by tradition under the name of 'Laws of Thought'.

They are as follows:

(1) *The law of identity*: 'Whatever is, is.'

(2) *The law of contradiction*: 'Nothing can both be and not be.'

(3) *The law of excluded middle*: 'Everything must either be or not be.'

These three laws are samples of self-evident logical principles, but are not really more fundamental or more self-evident than various other similar principles: for instance, the one we considered just now, which states that what follows from a true premiss is true. The name 'laws of thought' is also misleading, for what is important is not the fact that we think in accordance with these laws, but the fact that things behave in accordance with them; in other words, the fact that when we think in accordance with them we think *truly*. But this is a large question, to which we must return at a later stage.

In addition to the logical principles which enable us to prove from a given premiss that something is *certainly* true, there are other logical principles which enable us to prove, from a given premiss, that there is a greater or less probability that something is true. An example of such principles—perhaps the most important example is the inductive principle, which we considered in the preceding chapter.

One of the great historic controversies in philosophy is the controversy between the two schools called respectively 'empiricists' and 'rationalists'. The empiricists—who are best represented by the British philosophers, Locke, Berkeley, and Hume—maintained that all our knowledge is derived from experience; the rationalists—who are represented by the Continental philosophers of the seventeenth century, especially Descartes and Leibniz—maintained that, in addition to what we know by experience, there are certain 'innate ideas' and 'innate principles', which we know independently of experience. It has now become possible to decide with some confidence as to the truth or falsehood of these opposing schools. It must be admitted, for the reasons already stated, that logical principles are known to us, and cannot be themselves proved by experience, since all proof presupposes them. In this, therefore, which was the most important point of the controversy, the rationalists were in the right.

On the other hand, even that part of our knowledge which is *logically* independent of experience (in the sense that experience cannot prove it) is yet elicited and caused by experience. It is on occasion of particular experiences that we become aware of the general laws which their connexions exemplify. It would certainly be absurd to suppose that there are innate principles in the sense that babies are born with a knowledge of everything which men know and which cannot be deduced from what is experienced. For this reason, the word 'innate' would not now be employed to describe our knowledge of logical principles. The phrase '*a priori*' is less objectionable, and is more usual in modern writers. Thus, while admitting that all knowledge is elicited and caused by experience, we shall nevertheless hold that some knowledge is *a priori*, in the sense that the experience which makes us think of it does not suffice to prove it, but merely so directs our attention that we see its truth without requiring any proof from experience.

There is another point of great importance, in which the empiricists were in the right as against the rationalists. Nothing can be known to *exist* except by the help of experience. That is to say, if we wish to prove that something of which we have no direct experience exists, we must have among our premisses the existence of one or more things of which we have direct experience. Our belief that the Emperor of China exists, for example, rests upon testimony, and testimony consists, in the last analysis, of sense-data seen or heard in reading or being spoken to. Rationalists believed that, from general consideration as to what must be, they could deduce the existence of this or that in the actual world. In this belief they seem to have been mistaken. All the knowledge that we can acquire *a priori* concerning existence seems to be hypothetical: it tells us that if one thing exists, another must exist, or, more generally, that if one proposition is true, another must be true. This is exemplified by the principles we have already dealt with, such as '*if* this is true, and this implies that, then that is true', or '*if* this and that have been repeatedly found connected, they will probably be connected in the next instance in which one of them is found'. Thus the scope and power of *a priori* principles is strictly limited. All knowledge that something exists must be in part dependent on experience. When anything is known immediately, its existence is known by experience alone; when anything is proved to exist, without being known immediately, both experience and *a priori* principles must be required in the proof. Knowledge is called *empirical* when it rests wholly or partly upon experience. Thus all knowledge which asserts existence is empirical, and the only *a priori* knowledge concerning existence is hypothetical, giving connexions among things that exist or may exist, but not giving actual existence.

A priori knowledge is not all of the logical kind we have been hitherto considering. Perhaps the most important example of non-logical *a priori* knowledge is knowledge as to ethical value. I am not speaking of judgements as to what is useful or as to what is virtuous, for such judgements do require empirical premisses; I am speaking of judgements as to the intrinsic desirability of things. If something is useful, it must be useful because it secures some end; the end must, if we have gone far enough, be valuable on its own account, and not merely because it is useful for some further end. Thus all judgements as to what is useful depend upon judgements as to what has value on its own account.

We judge, for example, that happiness is more desirable than misery, knowledge than ignorance, goodwill than hatred, and so on. Such judgements must, in part at least, be immediate and *a priori*. Like our previous *a priori* judgements, they may be elicited by experience, and indeed they must be; for it seems not possible to judge whether anything is intrinsically valuable unless we have experienced something of the same kind. But it is fairly obvious that they cannot be proved by experience; for the fact that a thing exists or does not exist cannot prove either that it is good that it should exist or that it is bad. The pursuit of this subject belongs to ethics, where the impossibility of deducing what ought to be from what is has to be established. In the present connexion, it is only important to realize that knowledge as to what is intrinsically of value is *a priori* in the same sense in which logic is *a priori*, namely in the sense that the truth of such knowledge can be neither proved nor disproved by experience.

All pure mathematics is *a priori*, like logic. This was strenuously denied by the empirical philosophers, who maintained that experience was as much the source of our knowledge of arithmetic as of our knowledge of geography. They maintained that by the repeated experience of seeing two things and two other things, and finding that altogether they made four things, we were led by induction to the conclusion that two things and two other things would *always* make four things altogether. If, however, this were the source of our knowledge that two and two are four, we should proceed differently, in persuading ourselves of its truth, from the way in which we do actually proceed. In fact, a certain number of instances are needed to make us think of two abstractly, rather than of two coins or two books or two people, or two of any other specified kind. But as soon as we are able to divest our thoughts of irrelevant particularity, we become able to see the general principle that two and two are four; any one instance is seen to be *typical*, and the examination of other instances becomes unnecessary.(1)

(1) Cf. A. N. Whitehead, *Introduction to Mathematics* (Home University Library).

The same thing is exemplified in geometry. If we want to prove some property of *all* triangles, we draw some one triangle and reason about it; but we can avoid making use of any property which it does not share with all other triangles, and thus, from our particular case, we obtain a general result. We do not, in fact, feel our certainty that two and two are four increased by fresh instances, because, as soon as we have seen the truth of this proposition, our certainty becomes so great as to be incapable of growing greater. Moreover, we feel some quality of necessity about the proposition 'two and two are four', which is absent from even the best attested empirical generalizations. Such generalizations always remain mere facts: we feel that there might be a world in which they were false, though in the actual world they happen to be true. In any possible world, on the contrary, we feel that two and two would be four: this is not a mere fact, but a necessity to which everything actual and possible must conform.

The case may be made clearer by considering a genuinely-empirical generalization, such as 'All men are mortal.' It is plain that we believe this proposition, in the first place, because there is no known instance of men living beyond a certain age, and in the second place because there seem to be physiological grounds for thinking that an organism such as a man's body must sooner or later wear out. Neglecting the second ground, and considering merely our experience of men's mortality, it is plain that we should not be content with one quite clearly understood instance of a man dying, whereas, in the case of 'two and two are four', one instance does suffice, when carefully considered, to persuade us that the same must happen in any other instance. Also we can be forced to admit, on reflection, that there may be some doubt, however slight, as to whether *all* men are mortal. This may be made plain by the attempt to imagine two different worlds, in one of which there are men who are not mortal, while in the other two and two make five. When Swift invites us to consider the race of Struldbugs who never die, we are able to acquiesce in imagination. But a world where two and two make five seems quite on a different level. We feel that such a world, if there were one, would upset the whole fabric of our knowledge and reduce us to utter doubt.

The fact is that, in simple mathematical judgements such as 'two and two are four', and also in many judgements of logic, we can know the general proposition without inferring it from instances, although some instance is usually necessary to make clear to us what the general proposition means. This is why there is real utility in the process of *deduction*, which goes from the general to the general, or from the general to the particular, as well as in the process of *induction*, which goes from the particular to the particular, or from the particular to the general. It is an old debate among philosophers whether deduction ever gives *new* knowledge. We can now see that in certain cases, at least, it does do so. If we already know that two and two always make four, and we know that Brown and Jones are two, and so are Robinson and Smith, we can deduce that Brown and Jones and Robinson and Smith are four. This is new knowledge, not contained in our premisses, because the general proposition, 'two and two are four', never told us there were such people as Brown and Jones and Robinson and Smith, and the particular premisses do not tell us that there were four of them, whereas the particular proposition deduced does tell us both these things.

But the newness of the knowledge is much less certain if we take the stock instance of deduction that is always given in books on logic, namely, 'All men are mortal; Socrates is a man, therefore Socrates is mortal.' In this case, what we really know beyond reasonable doubt is that certain men, A, B, C, were mortal, since, in fact, they have died. If Socrates is one of these men, it is foolish to go the roundabout way through 'all men are mortal' to arrive at the conclusion that *probably* Socrates is mortal. If Socrates is not one of the men on whom our induction is based, we shall still do better to argue straight from our A, B, C, to Socrates, than to go round by the general proposition, 'all men are mortal'. For the probability that Socrates is mortal is greater, on our data, than the probability that all men are mortal. (This is obvious, because if all men are mortal, so is Socrates; but if Socrates is mortal, it does not follow that all men are mortal.) Hence we shall reach the conclusion that Socrates is mortal with a greater approach to certainty if we make our argument purely inductive than if we go by way of 'all men are mortal' and then use deduction.

This illustrates the difference between general propositions known *a priori* such as 'two and two are four', and empirical generalizations such as 'all men are mortal'. In regard to the former, deduction is the right mode of argument, whereas in regard to the latter, induction is always theoretically preferable, and warrants a greater confidence in the truth of our conclusion, because all empirical generalizations are more uncertain than the instances of them.

We have now seen that there are propositions known *a priori*, and that among them are the propositions of logic and pure mathematics, as well as the fundamental propositions of ethics. The question which must next occupy us is this: How is it possible that there should be such knowledge? And more particularly, how can there be knowledge of general propositions in cases where we have not examined all the instances, and indeed never can examine them all, because their number is infinite? These questions, which were first brought prominently forward by the German philosopher Kant (1724-1804), are very difficult, and historically very important.

CHAPTER VIII. HOW *A PRIORI* KNOWLEDGE IS POSSIBLE

Immanuel Kant is generally regarded as the greatest of the modern philosophers. Though he lived through the Seven Years War and the French Revolution, he never interrupted his teaching of philosophy at Königsberg in East Prussia. His most distinctive contribution was the invention of what he called the 'critical' philosophy, which, assuming as a datum that there is knowledge of various kinds, inquired how such knowledge comes to be possible, and deduced, from the answer to this inquiry, many metaphysical results as to the nature of the world. Whether these results were valid may well be doubted. But Kant undoubtedly deserves credit for two things: first, for having perceived that we have *a priori* knowledge which is not purely 'analytic', i.e. such that the opposite would be self-contradictory, and secondly, for having made evident the philosophical importance of the theory of knowledge.

Before the time of Kant, it was generally held that whatever knowledge was *a priori* must be 'analytic'. What this word means will be best illustrated by examples. If I say, 'A bald man is a man', 'A plane figure is a figure', 'A bad poet is a poet', I make a purely analytic judgement: the subject spoken about is given as having at least two properties, of which one is singled out to be asserted of it. Such propositions as the above are trivial, and would never be enunciated in real life except by an orator preparing the way for a piece of sophistry. They are called 'analytic' because the predicate is obtained by merely analysing the subject. Before the time of Kant it was thought that all judgements of which we could be certain *a priori* were of this kind: that in all of them there was a predicate which was only part of the subject of which it was asserted. If this were so, we should be involved in a definite contradiction if we attempted to deny anything that could be known *a priori*. 'A bald man is not bald' would assert and deny baldness of the same man, and would therefore contradict itself. Thus according to the philosophers before Kant, the law of contradiction, which asserts that nothing can at the same time have and not have a certain property, sufficed to establish the truth of all *a priori* knowledge.

Hume (1711-76), who preceded Kant, accepting the usual view as to what makes knowledge *a priori*, discovered that, in many cases which had previously been supposed analytic, and notably in the case of cause and effect, the connexion was really synthetic. Before Hume, rationalists at least had supposed that the effect could be logically deduced from the cause, if only we had sufficient knowledge. Hume argued—correctly, as would now be generally admitted—that this could not be done. Hence he inferred the far more doubtful proposition that nothing could be known *a priori* about the connexion of cause and effect. Kant, who had been educated in the rationalist tradition, was much perturbed by Hume's scepticism, and endeavoured to find an answer to it. He perceived that not only the connexion of cause and effect, but all the propositions of arithmetic and geometry, are 'synthetic', i.e. not analytic: in all these propositions, no analysis of the subject will reveal the predicate. His stock instance was the proposition 7 + 5 = 12. He pointed out, quite truly, that 7 and 5 have to be put together to give 12: the idea of 12 is not contained in them, nor even in the idea of adding them together. Thus he was led to the conclusion that all pure mathematics, though *a priori*, is synthetic; and this conclusion raised a new problem of which he endeavoured to find the solution.

The question which Kant put at the beginning of his philosophy, namely 'How is pure mathematics possible?' is an interesting and difficult one, to which every philosophy which is not purely sceptical must find some answer. The answer of the pure empiricists, that our mathematical knowledge is derived by induction from particular instances, we have already seen to be inadequate, for two reasons: first, that the validity of the inductive principle itself cannot be proved by induction; secondly, that the general propositions of mathematics, such as 'two and two always make four', can obviously be known with certainty by consideration of a single instance, and gain nothing by enumeration of other cases in which they have been found to be true. Thus our knowledge of the general propositions of mathematics (and the same applies to logic) must be accounted for otherwise than our (merely probable) knowledge of empirical generalizations such as 'all men are mortal'.

The problem arises through the fact that such knowledge is general, whereas all experience is particular. It seems strange that we should apparently be able to know some truths in advance about particular things of which we have as yet no experience; but it cannot easily be doubted that logic and arithmetic will apply to such things. We do not know who will be the inhabitants of London a hundred years hence; but we know that any two of them and any other two of them will make four of them. This apparent power of anticipating facts about things of which we have no experience is certainly surprising. Kant's solution of the problem, though not valid in my opinion, is interesting. It is, however, very difficult, and is differently understood by different philosophers. We can, therefore, only give the merest outline of it, and even that will be thought misleading by many exponents of Kant's system.

What Kant maintained was that in all our experience there are two elements to be distinguished, the one due to the object (i.e. to what we have called the 'physical object'), the other due to our own nature. We saw, in discussing matter and sense-data, that the physical object is different from the associated sense-data, and that the sense-data are to be regarded as resulting from an interaction between the physical object and ourselves. So far, we are in agreement with Kant. But what is distinctive of Kant is the way in which he apportions the shares of ourselves and the physical object respectively. He considers that the crude material given in sensation—the colour, hardness, etc.—is due to the object, and that what we supply is the arrangement in space and time, and all the relations between sense-data which result from comparison or from considering one as the cause of the other or in any other way. His chief reason in favour of this view is that we seem to have *a priori* knowledge as to space and time and causality and comparison, but not as to the actual crude material of sensation. We can be sure, he says, that anything we shall ever experience must show the characteristics affirmed of it in our *a priori* knowledge, because these characteristics are due to our own nature, and therefore nothing can ever come into our experience without acquiring these characteristics.

The physical object, which he calls the 'thing in itself',(1) he regards as essentially unknowable; what can be known is the object as we have it in experience, which he calls the 'phenomenon'. The phenomenon, being a joint product of us and the thing in itself, is sure to have those characteristics which are due to us, and is therefore sure to conform to our *a priori* knowledge. Hence this knowledge, though true of all actual and possible experience, must not be supposed to apply outside experience. Thus in spite of the existence of *a priori* knowledge, we cannot know anything about the thing in itself or about what is not an actual or possible object of experience. In this way he tries to reconcile and harmonize the contentions of the rationalists with the arguments of the empiricists.

(1) Kant's 'thing in itself' is identical in *definition* with the physical object, namely, it is the cause of sensations. In the properties deduced from the definition it is not identical, since Kant held (in spite of some inconsistency as regards cause) that we can know that none of the categories are applicable to the 'thing in itself'.

Apart from minor grounds on which Kant's philosophy may be criticized, there is one main objection which seems fatal to any attempt to deal with the problem of *a priori* knowledge by his method. The thing to be accounted for is our certainty that the facts must always conform to logic and arithmetic. To say that logic and arithmetic are contributed by us does not account for this. Our nature is as much a fact of the existing world as anything, and there can be no certainty that it will remain constant. It might happen, if Kant is right, that to-morrow our nature would so change as to make two and two become five. This possibility seems never to have occurred to him, yet it is one which utterly destroys the certainty and universality which he is anxious to vindicate for arithmetical propositions. It is true that this possibility, formally, is inconsistent with the Kantian view that time itself is a form imposed by the subject upon phenomena, so that our real Self is not in time and has no to-morrow. But he will still have to suppose that the time-order of phenomena is determined by characteristics of what is behind phenomena, and this suffices for the substance of our argument.

Reflection, moreover, seems to make it clear that, if there is any truth in our arithmetical beliefs, they must apply to things equally whether we think of them or not. Two physical objects and two other physical objects must make four physical objects, even if physical objects cannot be experienced. To assert this is certainly within the scope of what we mean when we state that two and two are four. Its truth is just as indubitable as the truth of the assertion that two phenomena and two other phenomena make four phenomena. Thus Kant's solution unduly limits the scope of *a priori* propositions, in addition to failing in the attempt at explaining their certainty.

Apart from the special doctrines advocated by Kant, it is very common among philosophers to regard what is *a priori* as in some sense mental, as concerned rather with the way we must think than with any fact of the outer world. We noted in the preceding chapter the three principles commonly called 'laws of thought'. The view which led to their being so named is a natural one, but there are strong reasons for thinking that it is erroneous. Let us take as an illustration the law of contradiction. This is commonly stated in the form 'Nothing can both be and not be', which is intended to express the fact that nothing can at once have and not have a given quality. Thus, for example, if a tree is a beech it cannot also be not a beech; if my table is rectangular it cannot also be not rectangular, and so on.

Now what makes it natural to call this principle a law of *thought* is that it is by thought rather than by outward observation that we persuade ourselves of its necessary truth. When we have seen that a tree is a beech, we do not need to look again in order to ascertain whether it is also not a beech; thought alone makes us know that this is impossible. But the conclusion that the law of contradiction is a law of *thought* is nevertheless erroneous. What we believe, when we believe the law of contradiction, is not that the mind is so made that it must believe the law of contradiction. *This* belief is a subsequent result of psychological reflection, which presupposes the belief in the law of contradiction. The belief in the law of contradiction is a belief about things, not only about thoughts. It is not, e.g., the belief that if we *think* a certain tree is a beech, we cannot at the same time *think* that it is not a beech; it is the belief that if the tree *is* a beech, it cannot at the same time *be* not a beech. Thus the law of contradiction is about things, and not merely about thoughts; and although belief in the law of contradiction is a thought, the law of contradiction itself is not a thought, but a fact concerning the things in the world. If this, which we believe when we believe the law of contradiction, were not true of the things in the world, the fact that we were compelled to *think* it true would not save the law of contradiction from being false; and this shows that the law is not a law of *thought*.

A similar argument applies to any other *a priori* judgement. When we judge that two and two are four, we are not making a judgement about our thoughts, but about all actual or possible couples. The fact that our minds are so constituted as to believe that two and two are four, though it is true, is emphatically not what we assert when we assert that two and two are four. And no fact about the constitution of our minds could make it *true* that two and two are four. Thus our *a priori* knowledge, if it is not erroneous, is not merely knowledge about the constitution of our minds, but is applicable to whatever the world may contain, both what is mental and what is non-mental.

The fact seems to be that all our *a priori* knowledge is concerned with entities which do not, properly speaking, *exist*, either in the mental or in the physical world. These entities are such as can be named by parts of speech which are not substantives; they are such entities as qualities and relations. Suppose, for instance, that I am in my room. I exist, and my room exists; but does 'in' exist? Yet obviously the word 'in' has a meaning; it denotes a relation which holds between me and my room. This relation is something, although we cannot say that it exists *in the same sense* in which I and my room exist. The relation 'in' is something which we can think about and understand, for, if we could not understand it, we could not understand the sentence 'I am in my room'. Many philosophers, following Kant, have maintained that relations are the work of the mind, that things in themselves have no relations, but that the mind brings them together in one act of thought and thus produces the relations which it judges them to have.

This view, however, seems open to objections similar to those which we urged before against Kant. It seems plain that it is not thought which produces the truth of the proposition 'I am in my room'. It may be true that an earwig is in my room, even if neither I nor the earwig nor any one else is aware of this truth; for this truth concerns only the earwig and the room, and does not depend upon anything else. Thus relations, as we shall see more fully in the next chapter, must be placed in a world which is neither mental nor physical. This world is of great importance to philosophy, and in particular to the problems of *a priori* knowledge. In the next chapter we shall proceed to develop its nature and its bearing upon the questions with which we have been dealing.

CHAPTER IX. THE WORLD OF UNIVERSALS

At the end of the preceding chapter we saw that such entities as relations appear to have a being which is in some way different from that of physical objects, and also different from that of minds and from that of sense-data. In the present chapter we have to consider what is the nature of this kind of being, and also what objects there are that have this kind of being. We will begin with the latter question.

The problem with which we are now concerned is a very old one, since it was brought into philosophy by Plato. Plato's 'theory of ideas' is an attempt to solve this very problem, and in my opinion it is one of the most successful attempts hitherto made. The theory to be advocated in what follows is largely Plato's, with merely such modifications as time has shown to be necessary.

The way the problem arose for Plato was more or less as follows. Let us consider, say, such a notion as *justice*. If we ask ourselves what justice is, it is natural to proceed by considering this, that, and the other just act, with a view to discovering what they have in common. They must all, in some sense, partake of a common nature, which will be found in whatever is just and in nothing else. This common nature, in virtue of which they are all just, will be justice itself, the pure essence the admixture of which with facts of ordinary life produces the multiplicity of just acts. Similarly with any other word which may be applicable to common facts, such as 'whiteness' for example. The word will be applicable to a number of particular things because they all participate in a common nature or essence. This pure essence is what Plato calls an 'idea' or 'form'. (It must not be supposed that 'ideas', in his sense, exist in minds, though they may be apprehended by minds.) The 'idea' *justice* is not identical with anything that is just: it is something other than particular things, which particular things partake of. Not being particular, it cannot itself exist in the world of sense. Moreover it is not fleeting or changeable like the things of sense: it is eternally itself, immutable and indestructible.

Thus Plato is led to a supra-sensible world, more real than the common world of sense, the unchangeable world of ideas, which alone gives to the world of sense whatever pale reflection of reality may belong to it. The truly real world, for Plato, is the world of ideas; for whatever we may attempt to say about things in the world of sense, we can only succeed in saying that they participate in such and such ideas, which, therefore, constitute all their character. Hence it is easy to pass on into a mysticism. We may hope, in a mystic illumination, to see the ideas as we see objects of sense; and we may imagine that the ideas exist in heaven. These mystical developments are very natural, but the basis of the theory is in logic, and it is as based in logic that we have to consider it.

The word 'idea' has acquired, in the course of time, many associations which are quite misleading when applied to Plato's 'ideas'. We shall therefore use the word 'universal' instead of the word 'idea', to describe what Plato meant. The essence of the sort of entity that Plato meant is that it is opposed to the particular things that are given in sensation. We speak of whatever is given in sensation, or is of the same nature as things given in sensation, as a *particular*; by opposition to this, a *universal* will be anything which may be shared by many particulars, and has those characteristics which, as we saw, distinguish justice and whiteness from just acts and white things.

When we examine common words, we find that, broadly speaking, proper names stand for particulars, while other substantives, adjectives, prepositions, and verbs stand for universals. Pronouns stand for particulars, but are ambiguous: it is only by the context or the circumstances that we know what particulars they stand for. The word 'now' stands for a particular, namely the present moment; but like pronouns, it stands for an ambiguous particular, because the present is always changing.

It will be seen that no sentence can be made up without at least one word which denotes a universal. The nearest approach would be some such statement as 'I like this'. But even here the word 'like' denotes a universal, for I may like other things, and other people may like things. Thus all truths involve universals, and all knowledge of truths involves acquaintance with universals.

Seeing that nearly all the words to be found in the dictionary stand for universals, it is strange that hardly anybody except students of philosophy ever realizes that there are such entities as universals. We do not naturally dwell upon those words in a sentence which do not stand for particulars; and if we are forced to dwell upon a word which stands for a universal, we naturally think of it as standing for some one of the particulars that come under the universal. When, for example, we hear the sentence, 'Charles I's head was cut off', we may naturally enough think of Charles I, of Charles I's head, and of the operation of cutting off *his* head, which are all particulars; but we do not naturally dwell upon what is meant by the word 'head' or the word 'cut', which is a universal: We feel such words to be incomplete and insubstantial; they seem to demand a context before anything can be done with them. Hence we succeed in avoiding all notice of universals as such, until the study of philosophy forces them upon our attention.

Even among philosophers, we may say, broadly, that only those universals which are named by adjectives or substantives have been much or often recognized, while those named by verbs and prepositions have been usually overlooked. This omission has had a very great effect upon philosophy; it is hardly too much to say that most metaphysics, since Spinoza, has been largely determined by it. The way this has occurred is, in outline, as follows: Speaking generally, adjectives and common nouns express qualities or properties of single things, whereas prepositions and verbs tend to express relations between two or more things. Thus the neglect of prepositions and verbs led to the belief that every proposition can be regarded as attributing a property to a single thing, rather than as expressing a relation between two or more things. Hence it was supposed that, ultimately, there can be no such entities as relations between things. Hence either there can be only one thing in the universe, or, if there are many things, they cannot possibly interact in any way, since any interaction would be a relation, and relations are impossible.

The first of these views, advocated by Spinoza and held in our own day by Bradley and many other philosophers, is called *monism*; the second, advocated by Leibniz but not very common nowadays, is called *monadism*, because each of the isolated things is called a *monad*. Both these opposing philosophies, interesting as they are, result, in my opinion, from an undue attention to one sort of universals, namely the sort represented by adjectives and substantives rather than by verbs and prepositions.

As a matter of fact, if any one were anxious to deny altogether that there are such things as universals, we should find that we cannot strictly prove that there are such entities as *qualities*, i.e. the universals represented by adjectives and substantives, whereas we can prove that there must be *relations*, i.e. the sort of universals generally represented by verbs and prepositions. Let us take in illustration the universal *whiteness*. If we believe that there is such a universal, we shall say that things are white because they have the quality of whiteness. This view, however, was strenuously denied by Berkeley and Hume, who have been followed in this by later empiricists. The form which their denial took was to deny that there are such things as 'abstract ideas '. When we want to think of whiteness, they said, we form an image of some particular white thing, and reason concerning this particular, taking care not to deduce anything concerning it which we cannot see to be equally true of any other white thing. As an account of our actual mental processes, this is no doubt largely true. In geometry, for example, when we wish to prove something about all triangles, we draw a particular triangle and reason about it, taking care not to use any characteristic which it does not share with other triangles. The beginner, in order to avoid error, often finds it useful to draw several triangles, as unlike each other as possible, in order to make sure that his reasoning is equally applicable to all of them. But a difficulty emerges as soon as we ask ourselves how we know that a thing is white or a triangle. If we wish to avoid the universals *whiteness* and *triangularity*, we shall choose some particular patch of white or some particular triangle, and say that anything is white or a triangle if it has the right sort of resemblance to our chosen particular. But then the resemblance required will have to be a universal. Since there are many white things, the resemblance must hold between many pairs of particular white things; and this is the characteristic of a universal. It will be useless to say that there is a different resemblance for each pair, for then we shall have to say that these resemblances resemble each other, and thus at last we shall be forced to admit resemblance as a universal. The relation of resemblance, therefore, must be a true universal. And having been forced to admit this universal, we find that it is no longer worth while to invent difficult and unplausible theories to avoid the admission of such universals as whiteness and triangularity.

Berkeley and Hume failed to perceive this refutation of their rejection of 'abstract ideas', because, like their adversaries, they only thought of *qualities*, and altogether ignored *relations* as universals. We have therefore here another respect in which the rationalists appear to have been in the right as against the empiricists, although, owing to the neglect or denial of relations, the deductions made by rationalists were, if anything, more apt to be mistaken than those made by empiricists.

Having now seen that there must be such entities as universals, the next point to be proved is that their being is not merely mental. By this is meant that whatever being belongs to them is independent of their being thought of or in any way apprehended by minds. We have already touched on this subject at the end of the preceding chapter, but we must now consider more fully what sort of being it is that belongs to universals.

Consider such a proposition as 'Edinburgh is north of London'. Here we have a relation between two places, and it seems plain that the relation subsists independently of our knowledge of it. When we come to know that Edinburgh is north of London, we come to know something which has to do only with Edinburgh and London: we do not cause the truth of the proposition by coming to know it, on the contrary we merely apprehend a fact which was there before we knew it. The part of the earth's surface where Edinburgh stands would be north of the part where London stands, even if there were no human being to know about north and south, and even if there were no minds at all in the universe. This is, of course, denied by many philosophers, either for Berkeley's reasons or for Kant's. But we have already considered these reasons, and decided that they are inadequate. We may therefore now assume it to be true that nothing mental is presupposed in the fact that Edinburgh is north of London. But this fact involves the relation 'north of', which is a universal; and it would be impossible for the whole fact to involve nothing mental if the relation 'north of', which is a constituent part of the fact, did involve anything mental. Hence we must admit that the relation, like the terms it relates, is not dependent upon thought, but belongs to the independent world which thought apprehends but does not create.

This conclusion, however, is met by the difficulty that the relation 'north of' does not seem to *exist* in the same sense in which Edinburgh and London exist. If we ask 'Where and when does this relation exist?' the answer must be 'Nowhere and nowhen'. There is no place or time where we can find the relation 'north of'. It does not exist in Edinburgh any more than in London, for it relates the two and is neutral as between them. Nor can we say that it exists at any particular time. Now everything that can be apprehended by the senses or by introspection exists at some particular time. Hence the relation 'north of' is radically different from such things. It is neither in space nor in time, neither material nor mental; yet it is something.

It is largely the very peculiar kind of being that belongs to universals which has led many people to suppose that they are really mental. We can think *of* a universal, and our thinking then exists in a perfectly ordinary sense, like any other mental act. Suppose, for example, that we are thinking of whiteness. Then *in one sense* it may be said that whiteness is 'in our mind'. We have here the same ambiguity as we noted in discussing Berkeley in Chapter IV. In the strict sense, it is not whiteness that is in our mind, but the act of thinking of whiteness. The connected ambiguity in the word 'idea', which we noted at the same time, also causes confusion here. In one sense of this word, namely the sense in which it denotes the *object* of an act of thought, whiteness is an 'idea'. Hence, if the ambiguity is not guarded against, we may come to think that whiteness is an 'idea' in the other sense, i.e. an act of thought; and thus we come to think that whiteness is mental. But in so thinking, we rob it of its essential quality of universality. One man's act of thought is necessarily a different thing from another man's; one man's act of thought at one time is necessarily a different thing from the same man's act of thought at another time. Hence, if whiteness were the thought as opposed to its object, no two different men could think of it, and no one man could think of it twice. That which many different thoughts of whiteness have in common is their *object*, and this object is different from all of them. Thus universals are not thoughts, though when known they are the objects of thoughts.

We shall find it convenient only to speak of things *existing* when they are in time, that is to say, when we can point to some time at which they exist (not excluding the possibility of their existing at all times). Thus thoughts and feelings, minds and physical objects exist. But universals do not exist in this sense; we shall say that they *subsist* or *have being*, where 'being' is opposed to 'existence' as being timeless. The world of universals, therefore, may also be described as the world of being. The world of being is unchangeable, rigid, exact, delightful to the mathematician, the logician, the builder of metaphysical systems, and all who love perfection more than life. The world of existence is fleeting, vague, without sharp boundaries, without any clear plan or arrangement, but it contains all thoughts and feelings, all the data of sense, and all physical objects, everything that can do either good or harm, everything that makes any difference to the value of life and the world. According to our temperaments, we shall prefer the contemplation of the one or of the other. The one we do not prefer will probably seem to us a pale shadow of the one we prefer, and hardly worthy to be regarded as in any sense real. But the truth is that both have the same claim on our impartial attention, both are real, and both are important to the metaphysician. Indeed no sooner have we distinguished the two worlds than it becomes necessary to consider their relations.

But first of all we must examine our knowledge of universals. This consideration will occupy us in the following chapter, where we shall find that it solves the problem of *a priori* knowledge, from which we were first led to consider universals.

CHAPTER X. ON OUR KNOWLEDGE OF UNIVERSALS

In regard to one man's knowledge at a given time, universals, like particulars, may be divided into those known by acquaintance, those known only by description, and those not known either by acquaintance or by description.

Let us consider first the knowledge of universals by acquaintance. It is obvious, to begin with, that we are acquainted with such universals as white, red, black, sweet, sour, loud, hard, etc., i.e. with qualities which are exemplified in sense-data. When we see a white patch, we are acquainted, in the first instance, with the particular patch; but by seeing many white patches, we easily learn to abstract the whiteness which they all have in common, and in learning to do this we are learning to be acquainted with whiteness. A similar process will make us acquainted with any other universal of the same sort. Universals of this sort may be called 'sensible qualities'. They can be apprehended with less effort of abstraction than any others, and they seem less removed from particulars than other universals are.

We come next to relations. The easiest relations to apprehend are those which hold between the different parts of a single complex sense-datum. For example, I can see at a glance the whole of the page on which I am writing; thus the whole page is included in one sense-datum. But I perceive that some parts of the page are to the left of other parts, and some parts are above other parts. The process of abstraction in this case seems to proceed somewhat as follows: I see successively a number of sense-data in which one part is to the left of another; I perceive, as in the case of different white patches, that all these sense-data have something in common, and by abstraction I find that what they have in common is a certain relation between their parts, namely the relation which I call 'being to the left of'. In this way I become acquainted with the universal relation.

In like manner I become aware of the relation of before and after in time. Suppose I hear a chime of bells: when the last bell of the chime sounds, I can retain the whole chime before my mind, and I can perceive that the earlier bells came before the later ones. Also in memory I perceive that what I am remembering came before the present time. From either of these sources I can abstract the universal relation of before and after, just as I abstracted the universal relation 'being to the left of'. Thus time-relations, like space-relations, are among those with which we are acquainted.

Another relation with which we become acquainted in much the same way is resemblance. If I see simultaneously two shades of green, I can see that they resemble each other; if I also see a shade of red: at the same time, I can see that the two greens have more resemblance to each other than either has to the red. In this way I become acquainted with the universal *resemblance* or *similarity*.

Between universals, as between particulars, there are relations of which we may be immediately aware. We have just seen that we can perceive that the resemblance between two shades of green is greater than the resemblance between a shade of red and a shade of green. Here we are dealing with a relation, namely 'greater than', between two relations. Our knowledge of such relations, though it requires more power of abstraction than is required for perceiving the qualities of sense-data, appears to be equally immediate, and (at least in some cases) equally indubitable. Thus there is immediate knowledge concerning universals as well as concerning sense-data.

Returning now to the problem of *a priori* knowledge, which we left unsolved when we began the consideration of universals, we find ourselves in a position to deal with it in a much more satisfactory manner than was possible before. Let us revert to the proposition 'two and two are four'. It is fairly obvious, in view of what has been said, that this proposition states a relation between the universal 'two' and the universal 'four'. This suggests a proposition which we shall now endeavour to establish: namely, *All* a priori *knowledge deals exclusively with the relations of universals.* This proposition is of great importance, and goes a long way towards solving our previous difficulties concerning *a priori* knowledge.

The only case in which it might seem, at first sight, as if our proposition were untrue, is the case in which an *a priori* proposition states that *all* of one class of particulars belong to some other class, or (what comes to the same thing) that *all* particulars having some one property also have some other. In this case it might seem as though we were dealing with the particulars that have the property rather than with the property. The proposition 'two and two are four' is really a case in point, for this may be stated in the form 'any two and any other two are four', or 'any collection formed of two twos is a collection of four'. If we can show that such statements as this really deal only with universals, our proposition may be regarded as proved.

One way of discovering what a proposition deals with is to ask ourselves what words we must understand—in other words, what objects we must be acquainted with—in order to see what the proposition means. As soon as we see what the proposition means, even if we do not yet know whether it is true or false, it is evident that we must have acquaintance with whatever is really dealt with by the proposition. By applying this test, it appears that many propositions which might seem to be concerned with particulars are really concerned only with universals. In the special case of 'two and two are four', even when we interpret it as meaning 'any collection formed of two twos is a collection of four', it is plain that we can understand the proposition, i.e. we can see what it is that it asserts, as soon as we know what is meant by 'collection' and 'two' and 'four'. It is quite unnecessary to know all the couples in the world: if it were necessary, obviously we could never understand the proposition, since the couples are infinitely numerous and therefore cannot all be known to us. Thus although our general statement *implies* statements about particular couples, *as soon as we know that there are such particular couples*, yet it does not itself assert or imply that there are such particular couples, and thus fails to make any statement whatever about any actual particular couple. The statement made is about 'couple', the universal, and not about this or that couple.

Thus the statement 'two and two are four' deals exclusively with universals, and therefore may be known by anybody who is acquainted with the universals concerned and can perceive the relation between them which the statement asserts. It must be taken as a fact, discovered by reflecting upon our knowledge, that we have the power of sometimes perceiving such relations between universals, and therefore of sometimes knowing general *a priori* propositions such as those of arithmetic and logic. The thing that seemed mysterious, when we formerly considered such knowledge, was that it seemed to anticipate and control experience. This, however, we can now see to have been an error. *No* fact concerning anything capable of being experienced can be known independently of experience. We know *a priori* that two things and two other things together make four things, but we do *not* know *a priori* that if Brown and Jones are two, and Robinson and Smith are two, then Brown and Jones and Robinson and Smith are four. The reason is that this proposition cannot be understood at all unless we know that there are such people as Brown and Jones and Robinson and Smith, and this we can only know by experience. Hence, although our general proposition is *a priori*, all its applications to actual particulars involve experience and therefore contain an empirical element. In this way what seemed mysterious in our *a priori* knowledge is seen to have been based upon an error.

It will serve to make the point clearer if we contrast our genuine *a priori* judgement with an empirical generalization, such as 'all men are mortals'. Here as before, we can *understand* what the proposition means as soon as we understand the universals involved, namely *man* and *mortal*. It is obviously unnecessary to have an individual acquaintance with the whole human race in order to understand what our proposition means. Thus the difference between an *a priori* general proposition and an empirical generalization does not come in the *meaning* of the proposition; it comes in the nature of the *evidence* for it. In the empirical case, the evidence consists in the particular instances. We believe that all men are mortal because we know that there are innumerable instances of men dying, and no instances of their living beyond a certain age. We do not believe it because we see a connexion between the universal *man* and the universal *mortal*. It is true that if physiology can prove, assuming the general laws that govern living bodies, that no living organism can last for ever, that gives a connexion between *man* and *mortality* which would enable us to assert our proposition without appealing to the special evidence of *men* dying. But that only means that our generalization has been subsumed under a wider generalization, for which the evidence is still of the same kind, though more extensive. The progress of science is constantly producing such subsumptions, and therefore giving a constantly wider inductive basis for scientific generalizations. But although this gives a greater *degree* of certainty, it does not give a different *kind*: the ultimate ground remains inductive, i.e. derived from instances, and not an *a priori* connexion of universals such as we have in logic and arithmetic.

Two opposite points are to be observed concerning *a priori* general propositions. The first is that, if many particular instances are known, our general proposition may be arrived at in the first instance by induction, and the connexion of universals may be only subsequently perceived. For example, it is known that if we draw perpendiculars to the sides of a triangle from the opposite angles, all three perpendiculars meet in a point. It would be quite possible to be first led to this proposition by actually drawing perpendiculars in many cases, and finding that they always met in a point; this experience might lead us to look for the general proof and find it. Such cases are common in the experience of every mathematician.

The other point is more interesting, and of more philosophical importance. It is, that we may sometimes know a general proposition in cases where we do not know a single instance of it. Take such a case as the following: We know that any two numbers can be multiplied together, and will give a third called their *product*. We know that all pairs of integers the product of which is less than 100 have been actually multiplied together, and the value of the product recorded in the multiplication table. But we also know that the number of integers is infinite, and that only a finite number of pairs of integers ever have been or ever will be thought of by human beings. Hence it follows that there are pairs of integers which never have been and never will be thought of by human beings, and that all of them deal with integers the product of which is over 100. Hence we arrive at the proposition: 'All products of two integers, which never have been and never will be thought of by any human being, are over 100.' Here is a general proposition of which the truth is undeniable, and yet, from the very nature of the case, we can never give an instance; because any two numbers we may think of are excluded by the terms of the proposition.

This possibility, of knowledge of general propositions of which no instance can be given, is often denied, because it is not perceived that the knowledge of such propositions only requires a knowledge of the relations of universals, and does not require any knowledge of instances of the universals in question. Yet the knowledge of such general propositions is quite vital to a great deal of what is generally admitted to be known. For example, we saw, in our early chapters, that knowledge of physical objects, as opposed to sense-data, is only obtained by an inference, and that they are not things with which we are acquainted. Hence we can never know any proposition of the form 'this is a physical object', where 'this' is something immediately known. It follows that all our knowledge concerning physical objects is such that no actual instance can be given. We can give instances of the associated sense-data, but we cannot give instances of the actual physical objects. Hence our knowledge as to physical objects depends throughout upon this possibility of general knowledge where no instance can be given. And the same applies to our knowledge of other people's minds, or of any other class of things of which no instance is known to us by acquaintance.

We may now take a survey of the sources of our knowledge, as they have appeared in the course of our analysis. We have first to distinguish knowledge of things and knowledge of truths. In each there are two kinds, one immediate and one derivative. Our immediate knowledge of things, which we called *acquaintance*, consists of two sorts, according as the things known are particulars or universals. Among particulars, we have acquaintance with sense-data and (probably) with ourselves. Among universals, there seems to be no principle by which we can decide which can be known by acquaintance, but it is clear that among those that can be so known are sensible qualities, relations of space and time, similarity, and certain abstract logical universals. Our derivative knowledge of things, which we call knowledge by *description*, always involves both acquaintance with something and knowledge of truths. Our immediate knowledge of *truths* may be called *intuitive* knowledge, and the truths so known may be called *self-evident* truths. Among such truths are included those which merely state what is given in sense, and also certain abstract logical and arithmetical principles, and (though with less certainty) some ethical propositions. Our *derivative* knowledge of truths consists of everything that we can deduce from self-evident truths by the use of self-evident principles of deduction.

If the above account is correct, all our knowledge of truths depends upon our intuitive knowledge. It therefore becomes important to consider the nature and scope of intuitive knowledge, in much the same way as, at an earlier stage, we considered the nature and scope of knowledge by acquaintance. But knowledge of truths raises a further problem, which does not arise in regard to knowledge of things, namely the problem of *error*. Some of our beliefs turn out to be erroneous, and therefore it becomes necessary to consider how, if at all, we can distinguish knowledge from error. This problem does not arise with regard to knowledge by acquaintance, for, whatever may be the object of acquaintance, even in dreams and hallucinations, there is no error involved so long as we do not go beyond the immediate object: error can only arise when we regard the immediate object, i.e. the sense-datum, as the mark of some physical object. Thus the problems connected with knowledge of truths are more difficult than those connected with knowledge of things. As the first of the problems connected with knowledge of truths, let us examine the nature and scope of our intuitive judgements.

CHAPTER XI. ON INTUITIVE KNOWLEDGE

There is a common impression that everything that we believe ought to be capable of proof, or at least of being shown to be highly probable. It is felt by many that a belief for which no reason can be given is an unreasonable belief. In the main, this view is just. Almost all our common beliefs are either inferred, or capable of being inferred, from other beliefs which may be regarded as giving the reason for them. As a rule, the reason has been forgotten, or has even never been consciously present to our minds. Few of us ever ask ourselves, for example, what reason there is to suppose the food we are just going to eat will not turn out to be poison. Yet we feel, when challenged, that a perfectly good reason could be found, even if we are not ready with it at the moment. And in this belief we are usually justified.

But let us imagine some insistent Socrates, who, whatever reason we give him, continues to demand a reason for the reason. We must sooner or later, and probably before very long, be driven to a point where we cannot find any further reason, and where it becomes almost certain that no further reason is even theoretically discoverable. Starting with the common beliefs of daily life, we can be driven back from point to point, until we come to some general principle, or some instance of a general principle, which seems luminously evident, and is not itself capable of being deduced from anything more evident. In most questions of daily life, such as whether our food is likely to be nourishing and not poisonous, we shall be driven back to the inductive principle, which we discussed in Chapter VI. But beyond that, there seems to be no further regress. The principle itself is constantly used in our reasoning, sometimes consciously, sometimes unconsciously; but there is no reasoning which, starting from some simpler self-evident principle, leads us to the principle of induction as its conclusion. And the same holds for other logical principles. Their truth is evident to us, and we employ them in constructing demonstrations; but they themselves, or at least some of them, are incapable of demonstration.

Self-evidence, however, is not confined to those among general principles which are incapable of proof. When a certain number of logical principles have been admitted, the rest can be deduced from them; but the propositions deduced are often just as self-evident as those that were assumed without proof. All arithmetic, moreover, can be deduced from the general principles of logic, yet the simple propositions of arithmetic, such as 'two and two are four', are just as self-evident as the principles of logic.

It would seem, also, though this is more disputable, that there are some self-evident ethical principles, such as 'we ought to pursue what is good'.

It should be observed that, in all cases of general principles, particular instances, dealing with familiar things, are more evident than the general principle. For example, the law of contradiction states that nothing can both have a certain property and not have it. This is evident as soon as it is understood, but it is not so evident as that a particular rose which we see cannot be both red and not red. (It is of course possible that parts of the rose may be red and parts not red, or that the rose may be of a shade of pink which we hardly know whether to call red or not; but in the former case it is plain that the rose as a whole is not red, while in the latter case the answer is theoretically definite as soon as we have decided on a precise definition of 'red'.) It is usually through particular instances that we come to be able to see the general principle.

Only those who are practised in dealing with abstractions can readily grasp a general principle without the help of instances.

In addition to general principles, the other kind of self-evident truths are those immediately derived from sensation. We will call such truths 'truths of perception', and the judgements expressing them we will call 'judgements of perception'. But here a certain amount of care is required in getting at the precise nature of the truths that are self-evident. The actual sense-data are neither true nor false. A particular patch of colour which I see, for example, simply exists: it is not the sort of thing that is true or false. It is true that there is such a patch, true that it has a certain shape and degree of brightness, true that it is surrounded by certain other colours. But the patch itself, like everything else in the world of sense, is of a radically different kind from the things that are true or false, and therefore cannot properly be said to be *true*. Thus whatever self-evident truths may be obtained from our senses must be different from the sense-data from which they are obtained.

It would seem that there are two kinds of self-evident truths of perception, though perhaps in the last analysis the two kinds may coalesce. First, there is the kind which simply asserts the *existence* of the sense-datum, without in any way analysing it. We see a patch of red, and we judge 'there is such-and-such a patch of red', or more strictly 'there is that'; this is one kind of intuitive judgement of perception. The other kind arises when the object of sense is complex, and we subject it to some degree of analysis. If, for instance, we see a *round* patch of red, we may judge 'that patch of red is round'. This is again a judgement of perception, but it differs from our previous kind. In our present kind we have a single sense-datum which has both colour and shape: the colour is red and the shape is round. Our judgement analyses the datum into colour and shape, and then recombines them by stating that the red colour is round in shape. Another example of this kind of judgement is 'this is to the right of that', where 'this' and 'that' are seen simultaneously. In this kind of judgement the sense-datum contains constituents which have some relation to each other, and the judgement asserts that these constituents have this relation.

Another class of intuitive judgements, analogous to those of sense and yet quite distinct from them, are judgements of *memory*. There is some danger of confusion as to the nature of memory, owing to the fact that memory of an object is apt to be accompanied by an image of the object, and yet the image cannot be what constitutes memory. This is easily seen by merely noticing that the image is in the present, whereas what is remembered is known to be in the past. Moreover, we are certainly able to some extent to compare our image with the object remembered, so that we often know, within somewhat wide limits, how far our image is accurate; but this would be impossible, unless the object, as opposed to the image, were in some way before the mind. Thus the essence of memory is not constituted by the image, but by having immediately before the mind an object which is recognized as past. But for the fact of memory in this sense, we should not know that there ever was a past at all, nor should we be able to understand the word 'past', any more than a man born blind can understand the word 'light'. Thus there must be intuitive judgements of memory, and it is upon them, ultimately, that all our knowledge of the past depends.

The case of memory, however, raises a difficulty, for it is notoriously fallacious, and thus throws doubt on the trustworthiness of intuitive judgements in general. This difficulty is no light one. But let us first narrow its scope as far as possible. Broadly speaking, memory is trustworthy in proportion to the vividness of the experience and to its nearness in time. If the house next door was struck by lightning half a minute ago, my memory of what I saw and heard will be so reliable that it would be preposterous to doubt whether there had been a flash at all. And the same applies to less vivid experiences, so long as they are recent. I am absolutely certain that half a minute ago I was sitting in the same chair in which I am sitting now. Going backward over the day, I find things of which I am quite certain, other things of which I am almost certain, other things of which I can become certain by thought and by calling up attendant circumstances, and some things of which I am by no means certain. I am quite certain that I ate my breakfast this morning, but if I were as indifferent to my breakfast as a philosopher should be, I should be doubtful. As to the conversation at breakfast, I can recall some of it easily, some with an effort, some only with a large element of doubt, and some not at all. Thus there is a continual gradation in the degree of self-evidence of what I remember, and a corresponding gradation in the trustworthiness of my memory.

Thus the first answer to the difficulty of fallacious memory is to say that memory has degrees of self-evidence, and that these correspond to the degrees of its trustworthiness, reaching a limit of perfect self-evidence and perfect trustworthiness in our memory of events which are recent and vivid.

It would seem, however, that there are cases of very firm belief in a memory which is wholly false. It is probable that, in these cases, what is really remembered, in the sense of being immediately before the mind, is something other than what is falsely believed in, though something generally associated with it. George IV is said to have at last believed that he was at the battle of Waterloo, because he had so often said that he was. In this case, what was immediately remembered was his repeated assertion; the belief in what he was asserting (if it existed) would be produced by association with the remembered assertion, and would therefore not be a genuine case of memory. It would seem that cases of fallacious memory can probably all be dealt with in this way, i.e. they can be shown to be not cases of memory in the strict sense at all.

One important point about self-evidence is made clear by the case of memory, and that is, that self-evidence has degrees: it is not a quality which is simply present or absent, but a quality which may be more or less present, in gradations ranging from absolute certainty down to an almost imperceptible faintness. Truths of perception and some of the principles of logic have the very highest degree of self-evidence; truths of immediate memory have an almost equally high degree. The inductive principle has less self-evidence than some of the other principles of logic, such as 'what follows from a true premiss must be true'. Memories have a diminishing self-evidence as they become remoter and fainter; the truths of logic and mathematics have (broadly speaking) less self-evidence as they become more complicated. Judgements of intrinsic ethical or aesthetic value are apt to have some self-evidence, but not much.

Degrees of self-evidence are important in the theory of knowledge, since, if propositions may (as seems likely) have some degree of self-evidence without being true, it will not be necessary to abandon all connexion between self-evidence and truth, but merely to say that, where there is a conflict, the more self-evident proposition is to be retained and the less self-evident rejected.

It seems, however, highly probable that two different notions are combined in 'self-evidence' as above explained; that one of them, which corresponds to the highest degree of self-evidence, is really an infallible guarantee of truth, while the other, which corresponds to all the other degrees, does not give an infallible guarantee, but only a greater or less presumption. This, however, is only a suggestion, which we cannot as yet develop further. After we have dealt with the nature of truth, we shall return to the subject of self-evidence, in connexion with the distinction between knowledge and error.

CHAPTER XII. TRUTH AND FALSEHOOD

Our knowledge of truths, unlike our knowledge of things, has an opposite, namely *error*. So far as things are concerned, we may know them or not know them, but there is no positive state of mind which can be described as erroneous knowledge of things, so long, at any rate, as we confine ourselves to knowledge by acquaintance. Whatever we are acquainted with must be something; we may draw wrong inferences from our acquaintance, but the acquaintance itself cannot be deceptive. Thus there is no dualism as regards acquaintance. But as regards knowledge of truths, there is a dualism. We may believe what is false as well as what is true. We know that on very many subjects different people hold different and incompatible opinions: hence some beliefs must be erroneous. Since erroneous beliefs are often held just as strongly as true beliefs, it becomes a difficult question how they are to be distinguished from true beliefs. How are we to know, in a given case, that our belief is not erroneous? This is a question of the very greatest difficulty, to which no completely satisfactory answer is possible. There is, however, a preliminary question which is rather less difficult, and that is: What do we *mean* by truth and falsehood? It is this preliminary question which is to be considered in this chapter. In this chapter we are not asking how we can know whether a belief is true or false: we are asking what is meant by the question whether a belief is true or false. It is to be hoped that a clear answer to this question may help us to obtain an answer to the question what beliefs are true, but for the present we ask only 'What is truth?' and 'What is falsehood?' not 'What beliefs are true?' and 'What beliefs are false?' It is very important to keep these different questions entirely separate, since any confusion between them is sure to produce an answer which is not really applicable to either.

There are three points to observe in the attempt to discover the nature of truth, three requisites which any theory must fulfil.

(1) Our theory of truth must be such as to admit of its opposite, falsehood. A good many philosophers have failed adequately to satisfy this condition: they have constructed theories according to which all our thinking ought to have been true, and have then had the greatest difficulty in finding a place for falsehood. In this respect our theory of belief must differ from our theory of acquaintance, since in the case of acquaintance it was not necessary to take account of any opposite.

(2) It seems fairly evident that if there were no beliefs there could be no falsehood, and no truth either, in the sense in which truth is correlative to falsehood. If we imagine a world of mere matter, there would be no room for falsehood in such a world, and although it would contain what may be called 'facts', it would not contain any truths, in the sense in which truths are things of the same kind as falsehoods. In fact, truth and falsehood are properties of beliefs and statements: hence a world of mere matter, since it would contain no beliefs or statements, would also contain no truth or falsehood.

(3) But, as against what we have just said, it is to be observed that the truth or falsehood of a belief always depends upon something which lies outside the belief itself. If I believe that Charles I died on the scaffold, I believe truly, not because of any intrinsic quality of my belief, which could be discovered by merely examining the belief, but because of an historical event which happened two and a half centuries ago. If I believe that Charles I died in his bed, I believe falsely: no degree of

vividness in my belief, or of care in arriving at it, prevents it from being false, again because of what happened long ago, and not because of any intrinsic property of my belief. Hence, although truth and falsehood are properties of beliefs, they are properties dependent upon the relations of the beliefs to other things, not upon any internal quality of the beliefs.

The third of the above requisites leads us to adopt the view—which has on the whole been commonest among philosophers—that truth consists in some form of correspondence between belief and fact. It is, however, by no means an easy matter to discover a form of correspondence to which there are no irrefutable objections. By this partly—and partly by the feeling that, if truth consists in a correspondence of thought with something outside thought, thought can never know when truth has been attained—many philosophers have been led to try to find some definition of truth which shall not consist in relation to something wholly outside belief. The most important attempt at a definition of this sort is the theory that truth consists in *coherence*. It is said that the mark of falsehood is failure to cohere in the body of our beliefs, and that it is the essence of a truth to form part of the completely rounded system which is The Truth.

There is, however, a great difficulty in this view, or rather two great difficulties. The first is that there is no reason to suppose that only *one* coherent body of beliefs is possible. It may be that, with sufficient imagination, a novelist might invent a past for the world that would perfectly fit on to what we know, and yet be quite different from the real past. In more scientific matters, it is certain that there are often two or more hypotheses which account for all the known facts on some subject, and although, in such cases, men of science endeavour to find facts which will rule out all the hypotheses except one, there is no reason why they should always succeed.

In philosophy, again, it seems not uncommon for two rival hypotheses to be both able to account for all the facts. Thus, for example, it is possible that life is one long dream, and that the outer world has only that degree of reality that the objects of dreams have; but although such a view does not seem inconsistent with known facts, there is no reason to prefer it to the common-sense view, according to which other people and things do really exist. Thus coherence as the definition of truth fails because there is no proof that there can be only one coherent system.

The other objection to this definition of truth is that it assumes the meaning of 'coherence' known, whereas, in fact, 'coherence' presupposes the truth of the laws of logic. Two propositions are coherent when both may be true, and are incoherent when one at least must be false. Now in order to know whether two propositions can both be true, we must know such truths as the law of contradiction. For example, the two propositions, 'this tree is a beech' and 'this tree is not a beech', are not coherent, because of the law of contradiction. But if the law of contradiction itself were subjected to the test of coherence, we should find that, if we choose to suppose it false, nothing will any longer be incoherent with anything else. Thus the laws of logic supply the skeleton or framework within which the test of coherence applies, and they themselves cannot be established by this test.

For the above two reasons, coherence cannot be accepted as giving the *meaning* of truth, though it is often a most important *test* of truth after a certain amount of truth has become known.

Hence we are driven back to *correspondence with fact* as constituting the nature of truth. It remains to define precisely what we mean by 'fact', and what is the nature of the correspondence which must subsist between belief and fact, in order that belief may be true.

In accordance with our three requisites, we have to seek a theory of truth which (1) allows truth to have an opposite, namely falsehood, (2) makes truth a property of beliefs, but (3) makes it a property wholly dependent upon the relation of the beliefs to outside things.

The necessity of allowing for falsehood makes it impossible to regard belief as a relation of the mind to a single object, which could be said to be what is believed. If belief were so regarded, we should find that, like acquaintance, it would not admit of the opposition of truth and falsehood, but would have to be always true. This may be made clear by examples. Othello believes falsely that Desdemona loves Cassio. We cannot say that this belief consists in a relation to a single object, 'Desdemona's love for Cassio', for if there were such an object, the belief would be true. There is in fact no such object, and therefore Othello cannot have any relation to such an object. Hence his belief cannot possibly consist in a relation to this object.

It might be said that his belief is a relation to a different object, namely 'that Desdemona loves Cassio'; but it is almost as difficult to suppose that there is such an object as this, when Desdemona does not love Cassio, as it was to suppose that there is 'Desdemona's love for Cassio'. Hence it will be better to seek for a theory of belief which does not make it consist in a relation of the mind to a single object.

It is common to think of relations as though they always held between two terms, but in fact this is not always the case. Some relations demand three terms, some four, and so on. Take, for instance, the relation 'between'. So long as only two terms come in, the relation 'between' is impossible: three terms are the smallest number that render it possible. York is between London and Edinburgh; but if London and Edinburgh were the only places in the world, there could be nothing which was between one place and another. Similarly *jealousy* requires three people: there can be no such relation that does not involve three at least. Such a proposition as 'A wishes B to promote C's marriage with D' involves a relation of four terms; that is to say, A and B and C and D all come in, and the relation involved cannot be expressed otherwise than in a form involving all four. Instances might be multiplied indefinitely, but enough has been said to show that there are relations which require more than two terms before they can occur.

The relation involved in *judging* or *believing* must, if falsehood is to be duly allowed for, be taken to be a relation between several terms, not between two. When Othello believes that Desdemona loves Cassio, he must not have before his mind a single object, 'Desdemona's love for Cassio', or 'that Desdemona loves Cassio ', for that would require that there should be objective falsehoods, which subsist independently of any minds; and this, though not logically refutable, is a theory to be avoided if possible. Thus it is easier to account for falsehood if we take judgement to be a relation in which the mind and the various objects concerned all occur severally; that is to say, Desdemona and loving and Cassio must all be terms in the relation which subsists when Othello believes that Desdemona loves Cassio. This relation, therefore, is a relation of four terms, since Othello also is one of the terms of the relation. When we say that it is a relation of four terms, we do not mean that Othello has a certain relation to Desdemona, and has the same relation to loving and also to Cassio. This may be true of some other relation than believing; but believing, plainly, is not a relation which Othello has to *each* of the three terms concerned, but to *all* of them together: there is only one example of the relation of believing involved, but this one example knits together four terms. Thus the actual occurrence, at the moment when Othello is entertaining his belief, is that the relation called 'believing' is knitting together into one complex whole the four terms Othello, Desdemona, loving, and

Cassio. What is called belief or judgement is nothing but this relation of believing or judging, which relates a mind to several things other than itself. An *act* of belief or of judgement is the occurrence between certain terms at some particular time, of the relation of believing or judging.

We are now in a position to understand what it is that distinguishes a true judgement from a false one. For this purpose we will adopt certain definitions. In every act of judgement there is a mind which judges, and there are terms concerning which it judges. We will call the mind the *subject* in the judgement, and the remaining terms the *objects*. Thus, when Othello judges that Desdemona loves Cassio, Othello is the subject, while the objects are Desdemona and loving and Cassio. The subject and the objects together are called the *constituents* of the judgement. It will be observed that the relation of judging has what is called a 'sense' or 'direction'. We may say, metaphorically, that it puts its objects in a certain *order*, which we may indicate by means of the order of the words in the sentence. (In an inflected language, the same thing will be indicated by inflections, e.g. by the difference between nominative and accusative.) Othello's judgement that Cassio loves Desdemona differs from his judgement that Desdemona loves Cassio, in spite of the fact that it consists of the same constituents, because the relation of judging places the constituents in a different order in the two cases. Similarly, if Cassio judges that Desdemona loves Othello, the constituents of the judgement are still the same, but their order is different. This property of having a 'sense' or 'direction' is one which the relation of judging shares with all other relations. The 'sense' of relations is the ultimate source of order and series and a host of mathematical concepts; but we need not concern ourselves further with this aspect.

We spoke of the relation called 'judging' or 'believing' as knitting together into one complex whole the subject and the objects. In this respect, judging is exactly like every other relation. Whenever a relation holds between two or more terms, it unites the terms into a complex whole. If Othello loves Desdemona, there is such a complex whole as 'Othello's love for Desdemona'. The terms united by the relation may be themselves complex, or may be simple, but the whole which results from their being united must be complex. Wherever there is a relation which relates certain terms, there is a complex object formed of the union of those terms; and conversely, wherever there is a complex object, there is a relation which relates its constituents. When an act of believing occurs, there is a complex, in which 'believing' is the uniting relation, and subject and objects are arranged in a certain order by the 'sense' of the relation of believing. Among the objects, as we saw in considering 'Othello believes that Desdemona loves Cassio', one must be a relation—in this instance, the relation 'loving'. But this relation, as it occurs in the act of believing, is not the relation which creates the unity of the complex whole consisting of the subject and the objects. The relation 'loving', as it occurs in the act of believing, is one of the objects—it is a brick in the structure, not the cement. The cement is the relation 'believing'. When the belief is *true*, there is another complex unity, in which the relation which was one of the objects of the belief relates the other objects. Thus, e.g., if Othello believes *truly* that Desdemona loves Cassio, then there is a complex unity, 'Desdemona's love for Cassio', which is composed exclusively of the *objects* of the belief, in the same order as they had in the belief, with the relation which was one of the objects occurring now as the cement that binds together the other objects of the belief. On the other hand, when a belief is *false*, there is no such complex unity composed only of the objects of the belief. If Othello believes *falsely* that Desdemona loves Cassio, then there is no such complex unity as 'Desdemona's love for Cassio'.

Thus a belief is *true* when it *corresponds* to a certain associated complex, and *false* when it does not. Assuming, for the sake of definiteness, that the objects of the belief are two terms and a relation, the terms being put in a certain order by the 'sense' of the believing, then if the two terms in that order are united by the relation into a complex, the belief is true; if not, it is false. This constitutes the definition of truth and falsehood that we were in search of. Judging or believing is a certain complex unity of which a mind is a constituent; if the remaining constituents, taken in the order which they have in the belief, form a complex unity, then the belief is true; if not, it is false.

Thus although truth and falsehood are properties of beliefs, yet they are in a sense extrinsic properties, for the condition of the truth of a belief is something not involving beliefs, or (in general) any mind at all, but only the *objects* of the belief. A mind, which believes, believes truly when there is a *corresponding* complex not involving the mind, but only its objects. This correspondence ensures truth, and its absence entails falsehood. Hence we account simultaneously for the two facts that beliefs (a) depend on minds for their *existence*, (b) do not depend on minds for their *truth*.

We may restate our theory as follows: If we take such a belief as 'Othello believes that Desdemona loves Cassio', we will call Desdemona and Cassio the *object-terms*, and loving the *object-relation*. If there is a complex unity 'Desdemona's love for Cassio', consisting of the object-terms related by the object-relation in the same order as they have in the belief, then this complex unity is called the *fact corresponding to the belief*. Thus a belief is true when there is a corresponding fact, and is false when there is no corresponding fact.

It will be seen that minds do not *create* truth or falsehood. They create beliefs, but when once the beliefs are created, the mind cannot make them true or false, except in the special case where they concern future things which are within the power of the person believing, such as catching trains. What makes a belief true is a *fact*, and this fact does not (except in exceptional cases) in any way involve the mind of the person who has the belief.

Having now decided what we *mean* by truth and falsehood, we have next to consider what ways there are of knowing whether this or that belief is true or false. This consideration will occupy the next chapter.

CHAPTER XIII. KNOWLEDGE, ERROR, AND PROBABLE OPINION

The question as to what we mean by truth and falsehood, which we considered in the preceding chapter, is of much less interest than the question as to how we can know what is true and what is false. This question will occupy us in the present chapter. There can be no doubt that *some* of our beliefs are erroneous; thus we are led to inquire what certainty we can ever have that such and such a belief is not erroneous. In other words, can we ever *know* anything at all, or do we merely sometimes by good luck believe what is true? Before we can attack this question, we must, however, first decide what we mean by 'knowing', and this question is not so easy as might be supposed.

At first sight we might imagine that knowledge could be defined as 'true belief'. When what we believe is true, it might be supposed that we had achieved a knowledge of what we believe. But this would not accord with the way in which the word is commonly used. To take a very trivial instance: If a man believes that the late Prime Minister's last name began with a B, he believes what is true, since the late Prime Minister was Sir Henry Campbell Bannerman. But if he believes that Mr. Balfour was the late Prime Minister, he will still believe that the late Prime Minister's last name began with a B, yet this belief, though true, would not be thought to constitute knowledge. If a newspaper, by an intelligent anticipation, announces the result of a battle before any telegram giving the result has been received, it may by good fortune announce what afterwards turns out to be the right result, and it may produce belief in some of its less experienced readers. But in spite of the truth of their belief, they cannot be said to have knowledge. Thus it is clear that a true belief is not knowledge when it is deduced from a false belief.

In like manner, a true belief cannot be called knowledge when it is deduced by a fallacious process of reasoning, even if the premisses from which it is deduced are true. If I know that all Greeks are men and that Socrates was a man, and I infer that Socrates was a Greek, I cannot be said to *know* that Socrates was a Greek, because, although my premisses and my conclusion are true, the conclusion does not follow from the premisses.

But are we to say that nothing is knowledge except what is validly deduced from true premisses? Obviously we cannot say this. Such a definition is at once too wide and too narrow. In the first place, it is too wide, because it is not enough that our premisses should be *true*, they must also be *known*. The man who believes that Mr. Balfour was the late Prime Minister may proceed to draw valid deductions from the true premiss that the late Prime Minister's name began with a B, but he cannot be said to *know* the conclusions reached by these deductions. Thus we shall have to amend our definition by saying that knowledge is what is validly deduced from *known* premisses. This, however, is a circular definition: it assumes that we already know what is meant by 'known premisses'. It can, therefore, at best define one sort of knowledge, the sort we call derivative, as opposed to intuitive knowledge. We may say: '*Derivative* knowledge is what is validly deduced from premisses known intuitively'. In this statement there is no formal defect, but it leaves the definition of *intuitive* knowledge still to seek.

Leaving on one side, for the moment, the question of intuitive knowledge, let us consider the above suggested definition of derivative knowledge. The chief objection to it is that it unduly limits knowledge. It constantly happens that people entertain a true belief, which has grown up in them because of some piece of intuitive knowledge from which it is capable of being validly inferred, but from which it has not, as a matter of fact, been inferred by any logical process.

Take, for example, the beliefs produced by reading. If the newspapers announce the death of the King, we are fairly well justified in believing that the King is dead, since this is the sort of announcement which would not be made if it were false. And we are quite amply justified in believing that the newspaper asserts that the King is dead. But here the intuitive knowledge upon which our belief is based is knowledge of the existence of sense-data derived from looking at the print which gives the news. This knowledge scarcely rises into consciousness, except in a person who cannot read easily. A child may be aware of the shapes of the letters, and pass gradually and painfully to a realization of their meaning. But anybody accustomed to reading passes at once to what the letters mean, and is not aware, except on reflection, that he has derived this knowledge from the sense-data called seeing the printed letters. Thus although a valid inference from the-letters to their meaning is possible, and *could* be performed by the reader, it is not in fact performed, since he does not in fact perform any operation which can be called logical inference. Yet it would be absurd to say that the reader does not *know* that the newspaper announces the King's death.

We must, therefore, admit as derivative knowledge whatever is the result of intuitive knowledge even if by mere association, provided there *is* a valid logical connexion, and the person in question could become aware of this connexion by reflection. There are in fact many ways, besides logical inference, by which we pass from one belief to another: the passage from the print to its meaning illustrates these ways. These ways may be called 'psychological inference'. We shall, then, admit such psychological inference as a means of obtaining derivative knowledge, provided there is a discoverable logical inference which runs parallel to the psychological inference. This renders our definition of derivative knowledge less precise than we could wish, since the word 'discoverable' is vague: it does not tell us how much reflection may be needed in order to make the discovery. But in fact 'knowledge' is not a precise conception: it merges into 'probable opinion', as we shall see more fully in the course of the present chapter. A very precise definition, therefore, should not be sought, since any such definition must be more or less misleading.

The chief difficulty in regard to knowledge, however, does not arise over derivative knowledge, but over intuitive knowledge. So long as we are dealing with derivative knowledge, we have the test of intuitive knowledge to fall back upon. But in regard to intuitive beliefs, it is by no means easy to discover any criterion by which to distinguish some as true and others as erroneous. In this question it is scarcely possible to reach any very precise result: all our knowledge of truths is infected with some degree of doubt, and a theory which ignored this fact would be plainly wrong. Something may be done, however, to mitigate the difficulties of the question.

Our theory of truth, to begin with, supplies the possibility of distinguishing certain truths as *self-evident* in a sense which ensures infallibility. When a belief is true, we said, there is a corresponding fact, in which the several objects of the belief form a single complex. The belief is said to constitute *knowledge* of this fact, provided it fulfils those further somewhat vague conditions which we have been considering in the present chapter. But in regard to any fact, besides the knowledge constituted by belief, we may also have the kind of knowledge constituted by *perception* (taking this word in its widest possible sense). For example, if you know the hour of the sunset, you can at that hour know the fact that the sun is setting: this is knowledge of the fact by way of knowledge of *truths*; but you can also, if the weather is fine, look to the west and actually see the setting sun: you then know the same fact by the way of knowledge of *things*.

Thus in regard to any complex fact, there are, theoretically, two ways in which it may be known: (1) by means of a judgement, in which its several parts are judged to be related as they are in fact related; (2) by means of *acquaintance* with the complex fact itself, which may (in a large sense) be called perception, though it is by no means confined to objects of the senses. Now it will be observed that the second way of knowing a complex fact, the way of acquaintance, is only possible when there really is such a fact, while the first way, like all judgement, is liable to error. The second way gives us the complex whole, and is therefore only possible when its parts do actually have that relation which makes them combine to form such a complex. The first way, on the contrary, gives us the parts and the relation severally, and demands only the reality of the parts and the relation: the relation may not relate those parts in that way, and yet the judgement may occur.

It will be remembered that at the end of Chapter XI we suggested that there might be two kinds of self-evidence, one giving an absolute guarantee of truth, the other only a partial guarantee. These two kinds can now be distinguished.

We may say that a truth is self-evident, in the first and most absolute sense, when we have acquaintance with the fact which corresponds to the truth. When Othello believes that Desdemona loves Cassio, the corresponding fact, if his belief were true, would be 'Desdemona's love for Cassio'. This would be a fact with which no one could have acquaintance except Desdemona; hence in the sense of self-evidence that we are considering, the truth that Desdemona loves Cassio (if it were a truth) could only be self-evident to Desdemona. All mental facts, and all facts concerning sense-data, have this same privacy: there is only one person to whom they can be self-evident in our present sense, since there is only one person who can be acquainted with the mental things or the sense-data concerned. Thus no fact about any particular existing thing can be self-evident to more than one person. On the other hand, facts about universals do not have this privacy. Many minds may be acquainted with the same universals; hence a relation between universals may be known by acquaintance to many different people. In all cases where we know by acquaintance a complex fact consisting of certain terms in a certain relation, we say that the truth that these terms are so related has the first or absolute kind of self-evidence, and in these cases the judgement that the terms are so related *must* be true. Thus this sort of self-evidence is an absolute guarantee of truth.

But although this sort of self-evidence is an absolute guarantee of truth, it does not enable us to be *absolutely* certain, in the case of any given judgement, that the judgement in question is true. Suppose we first perceive the sun shining, which is a complex fact, and thence proceed to make the judgement 'the sun is shining'. In passing from the perception to the judgement, it is necessary to analyse the given complex fact: we have to separate out 'the sun' and 'shining' as constituents of the fact. In this process it is possible to commit an error; hence even where a *fact* has the first or absolute kind of self-evidence, a judgement believed to correspond to the fact is not absolutely infallible, because it may not really correspond to the fact. But if it does correspond (in the sense explained in the preceding chapter), then it *must* be true.

The second sort of self-evidence will be that which belongs to judgements in the first instance, and is not derived from direct perception of a fact as a single complex whole. This second kind of self-evidence will have degrees, from the very highest degree down to a bare inclination in favour of the belief. Take, for example, the case of a horse trotting away from us along a hard road. At first our certainty that we hear the hoofs is complete; gradually, if we listen intently, there comes a moment when we think perhaps it was imagination or the blind upstairs or our own heartbeats; at last we become doubtful whether there was any noise at all; then we *think* we no longer hear anything, and at last we *know* we no longer hear anything. In this process, there is a continual gradation of self-evidence, from the highest degree to the least, not in the sense-data themselves, but in the judgements based on them.

Or again: Suppose we are comparing two shades of colour, one blue and one green. We can be quite sure they are different shades of colour; but if the green colour is gradually altered to be more and more like the blue, becoming first a blue-green, then a greeny-blue, then blue, there will come a moment when we are doubtful whether we can see any difference, and then a moment when we know that we cannot see any difference. The same thing happens in tuning a musical instrument, or in any other case where there is a continuous gradation. Thus self-evidence of this sort is a matter of degree; and it seems plain that the higher degrees are more to be trusted than the lower degrees.

In derivative knowledge our ultimate premisses must have some degree of self-evidence, and so must their connexion with the conclusions deduced from them. Take for example a piece of reasoning in geometry. It is not enough that the axioms from which we start should be self-evident: it is necessary also that, at each step in the reasoning, the connexion of premiss and conclusion should be self-evident. In difficult reasoning, this connexion has often only a very small degree of self-evidence; hence errors of reasoning are not improbable where the difficulty is great.

From what has been said it is evident that, both as regards intuitive knowledge and as regards derivative knowledge, if we assume that intuitive knowledge is trustworthy in proportion to the degree of its self-evidence, there will be a gradation in trustworthiness, from the existence of noteworthy sense-data and the simpler truths of logic and arithmetic, which may be taken as quite certain, down to judgements which seem only just more probable than their opposites. What we firmly believe, if it is true, is called *knowledge*, provided it is either intuitive or inferred (logically or psychologically) from intuitive knowledge from which it follows logically. What we firmly believe, if it is not true, is called *error*. What we firmly believe, if it is neither knowledge nor error, and also what we believe hesitatingly, because it is, or is derived from, something which has not the highest degree of self-evidence, may be called *probable opinion*. Thus the greater part of what would commonly pass as knowledge is more or less probable opinion.

In regard to probable opinion, we can derive great assistance from *coherence*, which we rejected as the *definition* of truth, but may often use as a *criterion*. A body of individually probable opinions, if they are mutually coherent, become more probable than any one of them would be individually. It is in this way that many scientific hypotheses acquire their probability. They fit into a coherent system of probable opinions, and thus become more probable than they would be in isolation. The same thing applies to general philosophical hypotheses. Often in a single case such hypotheses may seem highly doubtful, while yet, when we consider the order and coherence which they introduce into a mass of probable opinion, they become pretty nearly certain. This applies, in particular, to such matters as the distinction between dreams and waking life. If our dreams, night after night, were as coherent one with another as our days, we should hardly know whether to believe the dreams or the waking life. As it is, the test of coherence condemns the dreams and confirms the waking life. But this test, though it increases probability where it is successful, never gives absolute certainty, unless there is certainty already at some point in the coherent system. Thus the mere organization of probable opinion will never, by itself, transform it into indubitable knowledge.

CHAPTER XIV. THE LIMITS OF PHILOSOPHICAL KNOWLEDGE

In all that we have said hitherto concerning philosophy, we have scarcely touched on many matters that occupy a great space in the writings of most philosophers. Most philosophers—or, at any rate, very many—profess to be able to prove, by *a priori* metaphysical reasoning, such things as the fundamental dogmas of religion, the essential rationality of the universe, the illusoriness of matter, the unreality of all evil, and so on. There can be no doubt that the hope of finding reason to believe such theses as these has been the chief inspiration of many life-long students of philosophy. This hope, I believe, is vain. It would seem that knowledge concerning the universe as a whole is not to be obtained by metaphysics, and that the proposed proofs that, in virtue of the laws of logic such and such things *must* exist and such and such others cannot, are not capable of surviving a critical scrutiny. In this chapter we shall briefly consider the kind of way in which such reasoning is attempted, with a view to discovering whether we can hope that it may be valid.

The great representative, in modern times, of the kind of view which we wish to examine, was Hegel (1770-1831). Hegel's philosophy is very difficult, and commentators differ as to the true interpretation of it. According to the interpretation I shall adopt, which is that of many, if not most, of the commentators and has the merit of giving an interesting and important type of philosophy, his main thesis is that everything short of the Whole is obviously fragmentary, and obviously incapable of existing without the complement supplied by the rest of the world. Just as a comparative anatomist, from a single bone, sees what kind of animal the whole must have been, so the metaphysician, according to Hegel, sees, from any one piece of reality, what the whole of reality must be—at least in its large outlines. Every apparently separate piece of reality has, as it were, hooks which grapple it to the next piece; the next piece, in turn, has fresh hooks, and so on, until the whole universe is reconstructed. This essential incompleteness appears, according to Hegel, equally in the world of thought and in the world of things. In the world of thought, if we take any idea which is abstract or incomplete, we find, on examination, that if we forget its incompleteness, we become involved in contradictions; these contradictions turn the idea in question into its opposite, or antithesis; and in order to escape, we have to find a new, less incomplete idea, which is the synthesis of our original idea and its antithesis. This new idea, though less incomplete than the idea we started with, will be found, nevertheless, to be still not wholly complete, but to pass into its antithesis, with which it must be combined in a new synthesis. In this way Hegel advances until he reaches the 'Absolute Idea', which, according to him, has no incompleteness, no opposite, and no need of further development. The Absolute Idea, therefore, is adequate to describe Absolute Reality; but all lower ideas only describe reality as it appears to a partial view, not as it is to one who simultaneously surveys the Whole. Thus Hegel reaches the conclusion that Absolute Reality forms one single harmonious system, not in space or time, not in any degree evil, wholly rational, and wholly spiritual. Any appearance to the contrary, in the world we know, can be proved logically—so he believes—to be entirely due to our fragmentary piecemeal view of the universe. If we saw the universe whole, as we may suppose God sees it, space and time and matter and evil and all striving and struggling would disappear, and we should see instead an eternal perfect unchanging spiritual unity.

In this conception, there is undeniably something sublime, something to which we could wish to yield assent. Nevertheless, when the arguments in support of it are carefully examined, they appear to involve much confusion and many unwarrantable assumptions. The fundamental tenet upon which the system is built up is that what is incomplete must be not self-subsistent, but must need the support of other things before it can exist. It is held that whatever has relations to things outside itself must contain some reference to those outside things in its own nature, and could not, therefore, be what it is if those outside things did not exist. A man's nature, for example, is constituted by his memories and the rest of his knowledge, by his loves and hatreds, and so on; thus, but for the objects which he knows or loves or hates, he could not be what he is. He is essentially and obviously a fragment: taken as the sum-total of reality he would be self-contradictory.

This whole point of view, however, turns upon the notion of the 'nature' of a thing, which seems to mean 'all the truths about the thing'. It is of course the case that a truth which connects one thing with another thing could not subsist if the other thing did not subsist. But a truth about a thing is not part of the thing itself, although it must, according to the above usage, be part of the 'nature' of the thing. If we mean by a thing's 'nature' all the truths about the thing, then plainly we cannot know a thing's 'nature' unless we know all the thing's relations to all the other things in the universe. But if the word 'nature' is used in this sense, we shall have to hold that the thing may be known when its 'nature' is not known, or at any rate is not known completely. There is a confusion, when this use of the word 'nature' is employed, between knowledge of things and knowledge of truths. We may have knowledge of a thing by acquaintance even if we know very few propositions about it—theoretically we need not know any propositions about it. Thus, acquaintance with a thing does not involve knowledge of its 'nature' in the above sense. And although acquaintance with a thing is involved in our knowing any one proposition about a thing, knowledge of its 'nature', in the above sense, is not involved. Hence, (1) acquaintance with a thing does not logically involve a knowledge of its relations, and (2) a knowledge of some of its relations does not involve a knowledge of all of its relations nor a knowledge of its 'nature' in the above sense. I may be acquainted, for example, with my toothache, and this knowledge may be as complete as knowledge by acquaintance ever can be, without knowing all that the dentist (who is not acquainted with it) can tell me about its cause, and without therefore knowing its 'nature' in the above sense. Thus the fact that a thing has relations does not prove that its relations are logically necessary. That is to say, from the mere fact that it is the thing it is we cannot deduce that it must have the various relations which in fact it has. This only *seems* to follow because we know it already.

It follows that we cannot prove that the universe as a whole forms a single harmonious system such as Hegel believes that it forms. And if we cannot prove this, we also cannot prove the unreality of space and time and matter and evil, for this is deduced by Hegel from the fragmentary and relational character of these things. Thus we are left to the piecemeal investigation of the world, and are unable to know the characters of those parts of the universe that are remote from our experience. This result, disappointing as it is to those whose hopes have been raised by the systems of philosophers, is in harmony with the inductive and scientific temper of our age, and is borne out by the whole examination of human knowledge which has occupied our previous chapters.

Most of the great ambitious attempts of metaphysicians have proceeded by the attempt to prove that such and such apparent features of the actual world were self-contradictory, and therefore could not be real. The whole tendency of modern thought, however, is more and more in the direction of showing that the supposed contradictions were illusory, and that very little can be proved *a priori* from considerations of what *must* be. A good illustration of this is afforded by space and time. Space and time appear to be infinite in extent, and infinitely divisible. If we travel along a straight line in either direction, it is difficult to believe that we shall finally reach a last point, beyond which there is nothing, not even empty space. Similarly, if in imagination we travel backwards or forwards in time, it is difficult to believe that we shall reach a first or last time, with not even empty time beyond it. Thus space and time appear to be infinite in extent.

Again, if we take any two points on a line, it seems evident that there must be other points between them however small the distance between them may be: every distance can be halved, and the halves can be halved again, and so on *ad infinitum*. In time, similarly, however little time may elapse between two moments, it seems evident that there will be other moments between them. Thus space and time appear to be infinitely divisible. But as against these apparent facts—infinite extent and infinite divisibility—philosophers have advanced arguments tending to show that there could be no infinite collections of things, and that therefore the number of points in space, or of instants in time, must be finite. Thus a contradiction emerged between the apparent nature of space and time and the supposed impossibility of infinite collections.

Kant, who first emphasized this contradiction, deduced the impossibility of space and time, which he declared to be merely subjective; and since his time very many philosophers have believed that space and time are mere appearance, not characteristic of the world as it really is. Now, however, owing to the labours of the mathematicians, notably Georg Cantor, it has appeared that the impossibility of infinite collections was a mistake. They are not in fact self-contradictory, but only contradictory of certain rather obstinate mental prejudices. Hence the reasons for regarding space and time as unreal have become inoperative, and one of the great sources of metaphysical constructions is dried up.

The mathematicians, however, have not been content with showing that space as it is commonly supposed to be is possible; they have shown also that many other forms of space are equally possible, so far as logic can show. Some of Euclid's axioms, which appear to common sense to be necessary, and were formerly supposed to be necessary by philosophers, are now known to derive their appearance of necessity from our mere familiarity with actual space, and not from any *a priori* logical foundation. By imagining worlds in which these axioms are false, the mathematicians have used logic to loosen the prejudices of common sense, and to show the possibility of spaces differing—some more, some less—from that in which we live. And some of these spaces differ so little from Euclidean space, where distances such as we can measure are concerned, that it is impossible to discover by observation whether our actual space is strictly Euclidean or of one of these other kinds. Thus the position is completely reversed. Formerly it appeared that experience left only one kind of space to logic, and logic showed this one kind to be impossible. Now, logic presents many kinds of space as possible apart from experience, and experience only partially decides between them. Thus, while our knowledge of what is has become less than it was formerly supposed to be, our knowledge of what may be is enormously increased. Instead of being shut in within narrow walls, of which every nook and cranny could be explored, we find ourselves in an open world of free possibilities, where much remains unknown because there is so much to know.

What has happened in the case of space and time has happened, to some extent, in other directions as well. The attempt to prescribe to the universe by means of *a priori* principles has broken down; logic, instead of being, as formerly, the bar to possibilities, has become the great liberator of the imagination, presenting innumerable alternatives which are closed to unreflective common sense, and leaving to experience the task of deciding, where decision is possible, between the many worlds which logic offers for our choice. Thus knowledge as to what exists becomes limited to what we can learn from experience—not to what we can actually experience, for, as we have seen, there is much knowledge by description concerning things of which we have no direct experience. But in all cases of knowledge by description, we need some connexion of universals, enabling us, from such and such a datum, to infer an object of a certain sort as implied by our datum. Thus in regard to physical objects, for example, the principle that sense-data are signs of physical objects is itself a connexion of universals; and it is only in virtue of this principle that experience enables us to acquire knowledge concerning physical objects. The same applies to the law of causality, or, to descend to what is less general, to such principles as the law of gravitation.

Principles such as the law of gravitation are proved, or rather are rendered highly probable, by a combination of experience with some wholly *a priori* principle, such as the principle of induction. Thus our intuitive knowledge, which is the source of all our other knowledge of truths, is of two sorts: pure empirical knowledge, which tells us of the existence and some of the properties of particular things with which we are acquainted, and pure *a priori* knowledge, which gives us connexions between universals, and enables us to draw inferences from the particular facts given in empirical knowledge. Our derivative knowledge always depends upon some pure *a priori* knowledge and usually also depends upon some pure empirical knowledge.

Philosophical knowledge, if what has been said above is true, does not differ essentially from scientific knowledge; there is no special source of wisdom which is open to philosophy but not to science, and the results obtained by philosophy are not radically different from those obtained from science. The essential characteristic of philosophy, which makes it a study distinct from science, is criticism. It examines critically the principles employed in science and in daily life; it searches out any inconsistencies there may be in these principles, and it only accepts them when, as the result of a critical inquiry, no reason for rejecting them has appeared. If, as many philosophers have believed, the principles underlying the sciences were capable, when disengaged from irrelevant detail, of giving us knowledge concerning the universe as a whole, such knowledge would have the same claim on our belief as scientific knowledge has; but our inquiry has not revealed any such knowledge, and therefore, as regards the special doctrines of the bolder metaphysicians, has had a mainly negative result. But as regards what would be commonly accepted as knowledge, our result is in the main positive: we have seldom found reason to reject such knowledge as the result of our criticism, and we have seen no reason to suppose man incapable of the kind of knowledge which he is generally believed to possess.

When, however, we speak of philosophy as a *criticism* of knowledge, it is necessary to impose a certain limitation. If we adopt the attitude of the complete sceptic, placing ourselves wholly outside all knowledge, and asking, from this outside position, to be compelled to return within the circle of knowledge, we are demanding what is impossible, and our scepticism can never be refuted. For all refutation must begin with some piece of knowledge which the disputants share; from blank doubt, no argument can begin. Hence the criticism of knowledge which philosophy employs must not be of this destructive kind, if any result is to be achieved. Against this absolute scepticism, no *logical* argument can be advanced. But it is not difficult to see that scepticism of this kind is unreasonable. Descartes' 'methodical doubt', with which modern philosophy began, is not of this kind, but is rather the kind of criticism which we are asserting to be the essence of philosophy. His 'methodical doubt' consisted in doubting whatever seemed doubtful; in pausing, with each apparent piece of knowledge, to ask himself whether, on reflection, he could feel certain that he really knew it. This is the kind of criticism which constitutes philosophy. Some knowledge, such as knowledge of the existence of our sense-data, appears quite indubitable, however calmly and thoroughly we reflect upon it. In regard to such knowledge, philosophical criticism does not require that we should abstain from belief. But there are beliefs—such, for example, as the belief that physical objects exactly resemble our sense-data—which are entertained until we begin to reflect, but are found to melt away when subjected to a close inquiry. Such beliefs philosophy will bid us reject, unless some new line of argument is found to support them. But to reject the beliefs which do not appear open to any objections, however closely we examine them, is not reasonable, and is not what philosophy advocates.

The criticism aimed at, in a word, is not that which, without reason, determines to reject, but that which considers each piece of apparent knowledge on its merits, and retains whatever still appears to be knowledge when this consideration is completed. That some risk of error remains must be admitted, since human beings are fallible. Philosophy may claim justly that it diminishes the risk of error, and that in some cases it renders the risk so small as to be practically negligible. To do more than this is not possible in a world where mistakes must occur; and more than this no prudent advocate of philosophy would claim to have performed.

CHAPTER XV. THE VALUE OF PHILOSOPHY

Having now come to the end of our brief and very incomplete review of the problems of philosophy, it will be well to consider, in conclusion, what is the value of philosophy and why it ought to be studied. It is the more necessary to consider this question, in view of the fact that many men, under the influence of science or of practical affairs, are inclined to doubt whether philosophy is anything better than innocent but useless trifling, hair-splitting distinctions, and controversies on matters concerning which knowledge is impossible.

This view of philosophy appears to result, partly from a wrong conception of the ends of life, partly from a wrong conception of the kind of goods which philosophy strives to achieve. Physical science, through the medium of inventions, is useful to innumerable people who are wholly ignorant of it; thus the study of physical science is to be recommended, not only, or primarily, because of the effect on the student, but rather because of the effect on mankind in general. Thus utility does not belong to philosophy. If the study of philosophy has any value at all for others than students of philosophy, it must be only indirectly, through its effects upon the lives of those who study it. It is in these effects, therefore, if anywhere, that the value of philosophy must be primarily sought.

But further, if we are not to fail in our endeavour to determine the value of philosophy, we must first free our minds from the prejudices of what are wrongly called 'practical' men. The 'practical' man, as this word is often used, is one who recognizes only material needs, who realizes that men must have food for the body, but is oblivious of the necessity of providing food for the mind. If all men were well off, if poverty and disease had been reduced to their lowest possible point, there would still remain much to be done to produce a valuable society; and even in the existing world the goods of the mind are at least as important as the goods of the body. It is exclusively among the goods of the mind that the value of philosophy is to be found; and only those who are not indifferent to these goods can be persuaded that the study of philosophy is not a waste of time.

Philosophy, like all other studies, aims primarily at knowledge. The knowledge it aims at is the kind of knowledge which gives unity and system to the body of the sciences, and the kind which results from a critical examination of the grounds of our convictions, prejudices, and beliefs. But it cannot be maintained that philosophy has had any very great measure of success in its attempts to provide definite answers to its questions. If you ask a mathematician, a mineralogist, a historian, or any other man of learning, what definite body of truths has been ascertained by his science, his answer will last as long as you are willing to listen. But if you put the same question to a philosopher, he will, if he is candid, have to confess that his study has not achieved positive results such as have been achieved by other sciences. It is true that this is partly accounted for by the fact that, as soon as definite knowledge concerning any subject becomes possible, this subject ceases to be called philosophy, and becomes a separate science. The whole study of the heavens, which now belongs to astronomy, was once included in philosophy; Newton's great work was called 'the mathematical principles of natural philosophy'. Similarly, the study of the human mind, which was a part of philosophy, has now been separated from philosophy and has become the science of psychology. Thus, to a great extent, the uncertainty of philosophy is more apparent than real: those questions which are already capable of definite answers are placed in the sciences, while those only to which, at present, no definite answer can be given, remain to form the residue which is called philosophy.

This is, however, only a part of the truth concerning the uncertainty of philosophy. There are many questions—and among them those that are of the profoundest interest to our spiritual life—which, so far as we can see, must remain insoluble to the human intellect unless its powers become of quite a different order from what they are now. Has the universe any unity of plan or purpose, or is it a fortuitous concourse of atoms? Is consciousness a permanent part of the universe, giving hope of indefinite growth in wisdom, or is it a transitory accident on a small planet on which life must ultimately become impossible? Are good and evil of importance to the universe or only to man? Such questions are asked by philosophy, and variously answered by various philosophers. But it would seem that, whether answers be otherwise discoverable or not, the answers suggested by philosophy are none of them demonstrably true. Yet, however slight may be the hope of discovering an answer, it is part of the business of philosophy to continue the consideration of such questions, to make us aware of their importance, to examine all the approaches to them, and to keep alive that speculative interest in the universe which is apt to be killed by confining ourselves to definitely ascertainable knowledge.

Many philosophers, it is true, have held that philosophy could establish the truth of certain answers to such fundamental questions. They have supposed that what is of most importance in religious beliefs could be proved by strict demonstration to be true. In order to judge of such attempts, it is necessary to take a survey of human knowledge, and to form an opinion as to its methods and its limitations. On such a subject it would be unwise to pronounce dogmatically; but if the investigations of our previous chapters have not led us astray, we shall be compelled to renounce the hope of finding philosophical proofs of religious beliefs. We cannot, therefore, include as part of the value of philosophy any definite set of answers to such questions. Hence, once more, the value of philosophy must not depend upon any supposed body of definitely ascertainable knowledge to be acquired by those who study it.

The value of philosophy is, in fact, to be sought largely in its very uncertainty. The man who has no tincture of philosophy goes through life imprisoned in the prejudices derived from common sense, from the habitual beliefs of his age or his nation, and from convictions which have grown up in his mind without the co-operation or consent of his deliberate reason. To such a man the world tends to become definite, finite, obvious; common objects rouse no questions, and unfamiliar possibilities are contemptuously rejected. As soon as we begin to philosophize, on the contrary, we find, as we saw in our opening chapters, that even the most everyday things lead to problems to which only very incomplete answers can be given. Philosophy, though unable to tell us with certainty what is the true answer to the doubts which it raises, is able to suggest many possibilities which enlarge our thoughts and free them from the tyranny of custom. Thus, while diminishing our feeling of certainty as to what things are, it greatly increases our knowledge as to what they may be; it removes the somewhat arrogant dogmatism of those who have never travelled into the region of liberating doubt, and it keeps alive our sense of wonder by showing familiar things in an unfamiliar aspect.

Apart from its utility in showing unsuspected possibilities, philosophy has a value—perhaps its chief value—through the greatness of the objects which it contemplates, and the freedom from narrow and personal aims resulting from this contemplation. The life of the instinctive man is shut up within the circle of his private interests: family and friends may be included, but the outer world is not regarded except as it may help or hinder what comes within the circle of instinctive wishes. In such a life there is something feverish and confined, in comparison with which the philosophic life is calm and free. The private world of instinctive interests is a small one, set in the midst of a great and powerful world which must, sooner or later, lay our private world in ruins. Unless we can so enlarge our interests as to include the whole outer world, we remain like a garrison in a beleagured fortress, knowing that the enemy prevents escape and that ultimate surrender is inevitable. In such a life there is no peace, but a constant strife between the insistence of desire and the powerlessness of will. In one way or another, if our life is to be great and free, we must escape this prison and this strife.

One way of escape is by philosophic contemplation. Philosophic contemplation does not, in its widest survey, divide the universe into two hostile camps—friends and foes, helpful and hostile, good and bad—it views the whole impartially. Philosophic contemplation, when it is unalloyed, does not aim at proving that the rest of the universe is akin to man. All acquisition of knowledge is an enlargement of the Self, but this enlargement is best attained when it is not directly sought. It is obtained when the desire for knowledge is alone operative, by a study which does not wish in advance that its objects should have this or that character, but adapts the Self to the characters which it finds in its objects. This enlargement of Self is not obtained when, taking the Self as it is, we try to show that the world is so similar to this Self that knowledge of it is possible without any admission of what seems alien. The desire to prove this is a form of self-assertion and, like all self-assertion, it is an obstacle to the growth of Self which it desires, and of which the Self knows that it is capable. Self-assertion, in philosophic speculation as elsewhere, views the world as a means to its own ends; thus it makes the world of less account than Self, and the Self sets bounds to the greatness of its goods. In contemplation, on the contrary, we start from the not-Self, and through its greatness the boundaries of Self are enlarged; through the infinity of the universe the mind which contemplates it achieves some share in infinity.

For this reason greatness of soul is not fostered by those philosophies which assimilate the universe to Man. Knowledge is a form of union of Self and not-Self; like all union, it is impaired by dominion, and therefore by any attempt to force the universe into conformity with what we find in ourselves. There is a widespread philosophical tendency towards the view which tells us that Man is the measure of all things, that truth is man-made, that space and time and the world of universals are properties of the mind, and that, if there be anything not created by the mind, it is unknowable and of no account for us. This view, if our previous discussions were correct, is untrue; but in addition to being untrue, it has the effect of robbing philosophic contemplation of all that gives it value, since it fetters contemplation to Self. What it calls knowledge is not a union with the not-Self, but a set of prejudices, habits, and desires, making an impenetrable veil between us and the world beyond. The man who finds pleasure in such a theory of knowledge is like the man who never leaves the domestic circle for fear his word might not be law.

The true philosophic contemplation, on the contrary, finds its satisfaction in every enlargement of the not-Self, in everything that magnifies the objects contemplated, and thereby the subject contemplating. Everything, in contemplation, that is personal or private, everything that depends upon habit, self-interest, or desire, distorts the object, and hence impairs the union which the intellect seeks. By thus making a barrier between subject and object, such personal and private things become a prison to the intellect. The free intellect will see as God might see, without a *here* and *now*, without hopes and fears, without the trammels of customary beliefs and traditional prejudices, calmly, dispassionately, in the sole and exclusive desire of knowledge—knowledge as impersonal, as purely contemplative, as it is possible for man to attain. Hence also the free intellect will value more the abstract and universal knowledge into which the accidents of private history do not enter, than the knowledge brought by the senses, and dependent, as such knowledge must be, upon an exclusive and personal point of view and a body whose sense-organs distort as much as they reveal.

The mind which has become accustomed to the freedom and impartiality of philosophic contemplation will preserve something of the same freedom and impartiality in the world of action and emotion. It will view its purposes and desires as parts of the whole, with the absence of insistence that results from seeing them as infinitesimal fragments in a world of which all the rest is unaffected by any one man's deeds. The impartiality which, in contemplation, is the unalloyed desire for truth, is the very same quality of mind which, in action, is justice, and in emotion is that universal love which can be given to all, and not only to those who are judged useful or admirable. Thus contemplation enlarges not only the objects of our thoughts, but also the objects of our actions and our affections: it makes us citizens of the universe, not only of one walled city at war with all the rest. In this citizenship of the universe consists man's true freedom, and his liberation from the thraldom of narrow hopes and fears.

Thus, to sum up our discussion of the value of philosophy; Philosophy is to be studied, not for the sake of any definite answers to its questions, since no definite answers can, as a rule, be known to be true, but rather for the sake of the questions themselves; because these questions enlarge our conception of what is possible, enrich our intellectual imagination and diminish the dogmatic assurance which closes the mind against speculation; but above all because, through the greatness of the universe which philosophy contemplates, the mind also is rendered great, and becomes capable of that union with the universe which constitutes its highest good.

BIBLIOGRAPHICAL NOTE

The student who wishes to acquire an elementary knowledge of philosophy will find it both easier and more profitable to read some of the works of the great philosophers than to attempt to derive an all-round view from handbooks. The following are specially recommended:

Plato: *Republic*, especially Books VI and VII.

Descartes: *Meditations*.

Spinoza: *Ethics*.

Leibniz: *The Monadology*.

Berkeley: *Three Dialogues between Hylas and Philonous*.

Hume: *Enquiry concerning Human Understanding*.

Kant: *Prolegomena to any Future Metaphysic*.